Motivation and Personality

THIRD EDITION

Abraham H. Maslow

Late, Brandeis University

⌗ HarperCollins*Publishers*

Sponsoring Editor: Leslie Carr
Project Coordination: R. David Newcomer Associates
Copy Editor: Judith Hibbard
Proofreader: Joseph Pascale
Cover Design: ARCON
Compositor: Auto-Graphics, Inc.
Printer and Binder: R. R. Donnelley & Sons Company

Library of Congress Cataloging-in-Publication Data

Maslow, Abraham Harold.
  Motivation and personality.

  Bibliography: p.
  Includes index.
  1. Motivation (Psychology) 2. Self-actualization (Psychology) I. Title.
BF503.M375 1987   153.8   86-27051
ISBN 0-06-041987-3

95 10 9

CONTENTS

two

PSYCHOPATHOLOGY AND NORMALITY 73

three

SELF-ACTUALIZATION 123

afterword
_____

PREFACE TO THE THIRD EDITION

Motivation and Personality is an original record of the work in progress of one of the most creative psychologists of this century. It has become a primary reference for anyone interested in Abraham H. Maslow's theories, as clearly evidenced by growing attention from authors in many major professional journals in psychology, education, business, and social studies, among other fields. Although the first edition of this book was published in 1954 and the second in 1970, its influence has continued to grow over the years. From 1971 to 1976, *Motivation and Personality* was cited as a reference 489 times, an average of over 97 references a year. From 1976 to 1980, more than 20 years after publication of the first edition, citations rose to 791, an average of over 198 citations a year.

This third edition of *Motivation and Personality* has been revised to highlight Maslow's creative thinking and emphasize his far-reaching concepts. Within the text itself, we have reordered the chapters, added new headings and subheadings in one chapter, and deleted a few sections of dated material. Chapter 13 is a new addition to this book. It is the text of a lecture Maslow gave in 1958 at Michigan State University. In the hope of enhancing the reader's sense of the historical and intellectual context of the book, several other features have been added to this edition: a brief biography of Maslow, an afterword on the extensive effect of Maslow's vision in contemporary lives, chapter introductions, a citation study, and a complete bibliography of his work.

This edition has four major sections: 1. Motivation Theory, 2. Psychopathology and Normality, 3. Self-Actualization, and 4. Methodologies for a Human Science.

Chapter 1, "Preface to Motivation Theory," provides a humanistic critique of traditional behaviorist theories of motivation. Maslow systematically lists the limitations of traditional motivation theory. He emphasizes the need to consider the whole person, the effects of culture, environment, multiple motivation, non-motivated behavior, healthy motivation. In short, Maslow lays out the major foundations for a truly human theory of motivation.

Chapter 2, "A Theory of Human Motivation," is a classic presentation of Maslow's hierarchy of needs. Maslow provides a brilliant and elegant integration of behaviorist, Freudian, and humanistic psychology. The need hierarchy has become a widely used paradigm in business, advertising, and other applications of psychology.

Maslow argues that all human needs can be arrranged in a hierarchy, beginning with physical needs—for air, food, and water. Next come four levels of psychological needs—for safety, love, esteem, and self-actualization. Maslow argues that our higher needs are as real and as integral a part of human nature as our need for food. He avoids the oversimplifications of both behaviorist and Freudian positions.

In Chapter 3, "Gratification of Basic Needs," Maslow explores some of the implications of his need hierarchy. He discusses need gratification, its consequences, and its relation to learning, character formation, psychological health, pathology, and a variety of other phenomena.

Maslow reexamines the classic psychological theory of instinct in Chapter 4, "Instinct Theory Reexamined." This theory applies the biological concept of instinct to human behavior. Instinctivists look for the roots of all behavior in inherited instincts, as opposed to the behaviorists who have tended to explain all behavior in terms of learning.

In this chapter, Maslow summarizes the major problems of the instinctivist approach. He argues that any careful look at human behavior will show a mixture of the effects of heredity and environment. Maslow writes that human needs do have an instinctive component, but generally one that is weak. Normal, healthy human beings are not dominated by their instinctive needs, nor are they deeply frustrated if some of their instinctive needs are unfulfilled.

Freud held that the demands of our egos and our culture are inevitably at odds with our deepest, essentially selfish instincts. Maslow disagrees. He argues that we are essentially good and cooperative, that we can be fulfilled by our culture rather than frustrated by it.

In Chapter 5, "The Hierarchy of Needs," Maslow discusses the differences between needs that are higher and those that are lower in the need hierarchy. He argues that higher needs are later evolutionary developments and also that they develop later in each individual. Higher needs are less demanding and can be postponed longer. Satisfaction of higher needs produces more happiness and leads to greater individual growth. It also requires a better external environment.

Next, Maslow explores some of the implications of his hierarchy. Maslow's need hierarchy is one way of doing justice to the richness and complexity of higher human functioning and at the same time placing human behavior on a single continuum with the motivation and behavior of all organisms. Maslow also outlines the model's implications for philosophy, values, psychotherapy, culture, and theology.

In Chapter 6, "Unmotivated Behavior," Maslow expands traditional psychological concerns to include expressive and artistic behavior. Behavioral psychologists of his day tended to ignore everything but learned, motivated behavior. Maslow points out that not all behavior is motivated or purposive. Expressive behaviors, including singing, dancing, and play, are relatively spontaneous, unpurposeful, and enjoyable in their own right. They are also worthy of the attention of psychology.

Maslow discusses two kinds of need frustration in Chapter 7, "Origins of Pathology." Threatening frustration produces pathology. Nonthreatening frustration does not. Maslow argues that not all frustration is threatening, and, in fact, deprivation may have positive as well as negative effects. Maslow also discusses threatening and nonthreatening conflict, arguing here too that some kinds of conflict can have positive consequences.

In Chapter 8, "Is Destructiveness Instinctive?," Maslow argues that destructiveness is not innate. He reviews evidence from studies of animals, children, and cross-cultural behavior indicating that in a healthy, supportive environment there is virtually no destructive behavior. He argues that for destructiveness, as for any behavior, we must consider three factors: the individual's character structure, cultural pressures, and the immediate situation.

Maslow begins Chapter 9, "Psychotherapy as Good Human Relationships," by relating psychotherapy to traditional concepts of experimental psychology, such as threat, act completion, and need-gratification.

By acknowledging the central theoretical role of need-gratification, Maslow argues that we can understand how different therapeutic systems are all effective and how relatively untrained psychotherapists can also be effective. He points out that our basic needs can be satisfied only interpersonally. These include satisfaction of the needs in Maslow's need hierarchy—needs for safety, belongingness, love, and self-esteem.

Maslow argues that good human relations are essentially therapeutic and, conversely, that good therapy is built on a good human relationship between therapist and patient. For Maslow, a good society is one in which good human relations are fostered and encouraged. A good society is also a psychologically healthy society. Maslow stresses that there will always be a role for professional psychotherapists, especially for those people who no longer even seek basic need gratification and could not accept such gratification if offered. For such individuals, professional therapy is needed to make consciously available their unconscious thoughts, desires, frustrations, and inhibitions.

In Chapter 10, "Approaches to Normality and Health," Maslow discusses the major definitions of psychological normality—in statistical, conventional, and cultural terms and in terms of being well-adjusted and without dysfunction. He suggests a more positive definition in terms of positive psychological health. Maslow relates psychological health to the process of self-actualization and to the gratification of the other inherent needs of his need hierarchy. He also discusses how psychological health is best supported by an environment that freely allows each individual a wide range of choices.

In Chapter 11, "Self-actualizing People: A Study of Psychological Health," Maslow describes his ground-breaking investigation of self-actualization. He outlines the methods he used in selecting and testing his subjects. Most of the chapter is devoted to detailed descriptions of the qualities and attributes common among Maslow's self-actualizing subjects. These include: accurate perception, spontaneity, detachment, independence, peak experience, sense of humor, and creativeness.

Maslow also indicates that his subjects were far from perfect human beings and discusses their failings. In addition he discusses the role of values in self-actualization and the resolving of conflicting dichotomies among self-actualizing people, dichotomies such as heart versus head, selfishness versus unselfishness, duty versus pleasure.

The importance of studying love, especially love in healthy people, is emphasized in Chapter 12, "Love in Self-actualizing People." He discusses the interrelationship of sex and love. He also discusses how love can lead us to transcend our egos and to affirm the independence and dignity of our beloved. Maslow also discusses the intrinsically rewarding and altruistic nature of love.

In Chapter 13, "Creativity in Self-actualizing People," Maslow compares the creativity of artists, poets, and others in "creative professions" with self-actualizing creativeness, which springs more directly from the personality. This second kind of creativity manifests as a tendency to do anything originally and creatively, whether teaching, cooking, sports, or the like.

Creative self-actualizing people tend to see the world with clear, fresh eyes and to be more spontaneous and expressive than most. Because they accept themselves, more of themselves is available for creative purposes. Maslow also calls this "primary creativity," the original insight and inspiration that form the basis of great art, music, and so forth. Maslow points out that while only a few of the gifted and well trained can achieve artistically creative success, primary self-actualizing creativeness is a fundamental aspect of our basic humanness.

In Chapter 14, "Questions for a New Psychology," Maslow outlines a series of questions that emerge from his new approach to psychology. These include new approaches to the traditional psychological topics of learning, perception, emotions, motivation, intelligence, cognition, clinical psychology, animal psychology, social psychology, and personality theory.

Maslow gives us a psychological interpretation of science in Chapter 15, "A Psychological Approach to Science": Scientists are people. Their behavior as scientists follows psychological principles. This includes the role in science of values and of human fears, hopes, and dreams. Maslow also emphasizes that science is not the only way to discover truth. He recommends that, to the traditional scientific outlook, we add the approaches of the poets, philosophers, dreamers, and others. The healthy, happy, well-rounded person is likely to be a better, more creative scientist.

In Chapter 16, "Means Centering Versus Problem Centering," Maslow argues that many of the problems of science, especially of psychology, are due to excessive means centering. Means centering refers to a focus on the instruments, apparatus, and techniques of scientific research. This often leads to methodolog-ically sound research that is trivial. Means centering tends to create scientific orthodoxies, to stifle originality, and to limit the questions that science can study.

In Chapter 17, "Stereotyping Versus True Cognition," Maslow differentiates two types of thinking and argues that much of what passes for thinking is second-rate categorizing. He emphasizes the importance of first attending to a new ex-perience, seeing it clearly and in detail, rather than immediately categorizing new experiences. For Maslow, stereotyping is one example of blind categorizing; habits are another example. While some stability is useful and necessary, too much categorizing leads to rigidity and lack of awareness of the present. It also leads to ineffective problem sloving. New problems are either unrecognized or handled with inappropriate techniques, old solutions that do not fit.

In Chapter 18, "A Holistic Approach to Psychology," Maslow argues that complex human behavior is not reducible to simpler parts. Even in studying spe-cific personality aspects, Maslow insists we remember that we are studying a part of a whole rather than a discrete entity. Maslow introduces the concept of "per-sonality syndrome," a structured, organized complex of apparently diverse parts, and discusses in detail various implications of this approach.

We sincerely hope you will enjoy this book as much as we have enjoyed editing it. Abraham Maslow has inspired us as a man and as a thinker. If his vision of psychology and human potential touches you and leads you to contem-plate the issues he raises, this book has been a success.

Robert Frager

ACKNOWLEDGMENTS

The editors wish to thank Bertha Maslow for her support and George Middendorf whose initial vision and encouragement led to this edition.

Ruth Cox wishes to thank Cynthia McReynolds, Jim Fadiman, Bob Frager, and the 1984 class of graduate students of the California Institute of Transpersonal Psychology for their comments on earlier drafts. Thanks are also due to Miles Vich for his perspective and to Milton Chen and Paul Cox for their editorial advice.

PREFACE TO THE SECOND EDITION[1]

I have tried in this revision to incorporate the main lessons of the last sixteen years. These lessons have been considerable. I consider it a real and extensive revision—even though I had to do only a moderate amount of rewriting—because the main thrust of the book has been modified in important ways which I shall detail below.

When this book appeared in 1954 it was essentially an effort to build *upon* the classical psychologies available rather than to repudiate them or to establish another rival psychology. It attempted to enlarge our conception of the human personality by reaching into the "higher" levels of human nature. (The title I had first planned to use for the book was *Higher Ceilings for Human Nature*.) If I had had to condense the thesis of this book into a single sentence, I would have said that, in *addition* to what the psychologies of the time had to say about human nature, man also had a higher nature and that this was instinctoid,[2] i.e., part of his essence. And if I could have had a second sentence, I would have stressed the profoundly holistic nature of human nature in contradiction to the analytic–dissecting–atomistic–Newtonian approach of the behaviorisms and of Freudian psychoanalysis.

Or to say it another way, I certainly accepted and built upon the available

---

[1]Reprinted exactly as it appeared in the second edition; therefore, chapter numbers may not correspond to the organization of this edition. Reference citations have been omitted.

[2]Maslow created the term *instinctoid* to convey two meanings: that the higher aspects of human nature are as innate, natural, and psychologically built in as "instincts"; that these higher qualities operate in ways similar to, but not identical with, instincts. To improve readability, we have changed the term *instinctoid* to *instinctlike* within the actual text.

data of experimental psychology and psychoanalysis. I accepted also the empirical and experimental spirit of the one, and the unmasking and depth-probing of the other, while yet rejecting the *images* of man which they generated. That is, this book represented a different philosophy of human nature, a new image of man.

However, what I took then to be an argument within the family of psychologists has in my opinion turned out since then to be rather a local manifestation of a new *Zeitgeist,* a new general comprehensive philosophy of life. This new "humanistic" *Weltanschauung* seems to be a new and far more hopeful and encouraging way of conceiving any and every area of human knowledge: e.g., economics, sociology, biology, and every profession: e.g., law, politics, medicine, and all of the social institutions: e.g., the family, education, religion, etc. I have acted upon this personal conviction in revising this book, writing into the psychology presented herein, the belief that it is an aspect of a much broader world view and of a comprehensive life-philosophy, which is already partly worked out, at least to the point of plausibility, and must, therefore, be taken seriously.

I must say a word about the irritating fact that this veritable revolution (a new image of man, of society, of nature, of science, of ultimate values, of philosophy, etc., etc.) is still almost completely overlooked by much of the intellectual community, especially that portion of it that controls the channels of communication to the educated public and to youth. (For this reason I have taken to calling it the Unnoticed Revolution.)

Many members of this community propound an outlook characterized by a profound despair and cynicism which sometimes degenerates into corrosive malice and cruelty. In effect they deny the possibility of improving human nature and society, or of discovering intrinsic human values, or of being life-loving in general.

Doubting the realness of honesty, of kindness, of generosity, of affection, they go beyond a reasonable skepticism or a withholding of judgment into an active hostility when confronted by people whom they sneer at as fools, "Boy Scouts," squares, innocents, do-gooders, or Pollyannas. This active debunking, hating and rending goes beyond contempt; it sometimes looks like an outraged counterattack against what they consider to be an insulting effort to fool them, to take them in, to pull their legs. The psychoanalyst would, I think, see in it a dynamics of rage and revenge for past disappointments and disillusionments.

This subculture of despair, this "more corrosive than thou" attitude, this counter-morality in which predation and hopelessness are real and good will is not, is flatly contradicted by the humanistic psychologies, and by the kind of preliminary data presented in this book and in many of the writings listed in the Bibliography. While it is still necessary to be very cautious about affirming the preconditions for "goodness" in human nature (see Chapters 7, 9, 11, 16), it is already possible to reject firmly the despairing belief that human nature is ultimately and basically depraved and evil. Such a belief is no longer a matter of taste merely. It can now be maintained only by a determined blindness and ignorance, by a refusal to consider the facts. It must therefore be considered to be a personal projection rather than a reasoned philosophical or scientific position.

The humanistic and holistic conceptions of science presented in the first two chapters and in Appendix B have been powerfully corroborated by many developments of the past decade, but especially by Michael Polanyi's great book *Personal Knowledge.* My own book, *The Psychology of Science,* carries forward very similar theses. These books are in blunt contradiction to the classical, conventional philosophy of science still too widely prevalent, and they offer a far better substitute for scientific work with persons.

The book is holistic throughout, but a more intensive and perhaps more difficult treatment is contained in Appendix B. Holism is obviously true—after all, the cosmos is one and interrelated; any society is one and interrelated; any person is one and interrelated, etc.—and yet the holistic outlook has a hard time being implemented and being used as it should be, as a way of looking at the world. Recently I have become more and more inclined to think that the atomistic way of thinking is a form of mild psychopathology, or is at least one aspect of the syndrome of cognitive immaturity. The holistic way of thinking and seeing seems to come quite naturally and automatically to healthier, self-actualizing people, and seems to be extraordinarily difficult for less evolved, less mature, less healthy people. To date this is only an impression, of course, and I do not want to push it too hard. Yet I feel justified in presenting it here as a hypothesis to be checked, something which should be relatively easy to do.

The motivation theory presented in Chapters 3 through 7, and to some extent throughout the book, has had an interesting history. First presented in 1942 to a psychoanalytic society, it was an effort to integrate into a single theoretical structure the partial truths I saw in Freud, Adler, Jung, D. M. Levy, Fromm, Horney, and Goldstein. I had learned from my own scattered experiences in therapy that each of these writers was correct at various times and for various persons. My question was essentially the clinical one: which earlier deprivations produce neurosis? Which psychological medicines cure neurosis? Which prophylaxis prevents neurosis? In which order are the psychological medicines demanded? Which are most powerful? Which most basic?

It is fair to say that this theory has been quite successful in a clinical, social and personological way, but not in a laboratory and experimental way. It has fitted very well with the personal experience of most people, and has often given them a structured theory that has helped them to make better sense of their inner lives. It seems for most people to have a direct, personal, subjective plausibility. And yet it still lacks experimental verification and support. I have not yet been able to think of a good way to put it to the test in the laboratory.

Part of the answer to this puzzle came from Douglas McGregor, who applied this theory of motivation to the industrial situation. Not only did he find it useful in ordering his data and his observations, but also these data served retroactively as a source of validation and verification for the theory. It is from *this* area, rather than from the laboratory, that empirical support is now coming. (The Bibliography contains a sampling of such reports.)

The lesson I had learned from this and from subsequent validation from other areas of life was this: when we talk about the needs of human beings, we talk about the essence of their lives. How *could* I have thought that this essence could be put to the test in some animal laboratory or some test tube situation? Obviously it needs a life situation of the total human being in his social environment. This is where confirmatiuon or disconfirmation will come from.

Chapter 4 betrays its clincial-therapeutic origins by its stress on neurosis producers rather than on motivations which do not make trouble for the psychotherapist, e.g., inertia and laziness, sensory pleasures, and the need for sensory stimulations and for activity, the sheer zest for life, or the lack of it, the proneness to hope or to hopelessness, the tendency to regress more or less easily under fear, anxiety, scarcity, etc., not to mention the highest human values which are also motivators: beauty, truth, excellence, completion, justice, order, consistency, harmony, etc.

These necessary complements to Chapters 3 and 4 are discussed in Chapters 3, 4, and 5 of my *Toward a Psychology of Being,* in the chapter on Lower Grumbles, Higher Grumbles and Metagrumbles in my *Eupsychian Management,* and in A Theory of Metamotivation: the Biological Rooting of the Value-Life.

Human life will never be understood unless its highest aspirations are taken into account. Growth, self-actualization, the striving toward health, the quest for identity and autonomy, the yearning for excellence (and other ways of phrasing the striving "upward") must by now be accepted beyond question as a widespread and perhaps universal human tendency.

And yet there are also other regressive, fearful, self-diminishing tendencies as well, and it is very easy to forget them in our intoxication with "personal growth," especially for inexperienced youngsters. I consider that a necessary prophylactic against such illusions is a thorough knowledge of psychopathology and of depth psychology. We must appreciate that many people choose the worse rather than the better, that growth is often a painful process and may for this reason be shunned, that we are afraid of our own best possibilities in addition to loving them and that we are all of us profoundly ambivalent about truth, beauty, virtue, loving them and fearing them too. Freud is still required reading for the humanistic psychologist (his facts, not his metaphysics). I should like also to recommend an extraordinarily sensitive book by Hoggart which will certainly help us to understand compassionately the pull toward the vulgar, the trivial, the cheap and the fake in the less educated people he writes about.

Chapter 4, and Chapter 6 on "The Instinctoid Nature of Basic Needs," constitute for me the foundation of a system of intrinsic human values, human goods that validate themselves, that are intrinsically good and desirable and that need no further justification. This is a hierarchy of values which are to be found in the very essence of human nature itself. These are not only wanted and desired by all human beings, but also needed in the sense that they are necessary to avoid illness and psychopathology. To say the same thing in another vocabulary, these basic needs and the metaneeds are also the intrinsic reinforcers, the unconditioned stimuli which can be used as a basis upon which can be erected all sorts of instrumental learnings and conditionings. That is to say that in order to get these intrinsic goods, animals and men are willing to learn practically anything that will achieve for them these ultimate goods.

I want to be sure to mention here, even though I do not have the space for expanding upon the idea, that it is legitimate and fruitful to regard instinctoid basic needs and the metaneeds as *rights* as well as needs. This follows immediately upon granting that human beings have a right to be human in the same sense that cats have a right to be cats. In order to be fully human, these need and metaneed gratifications are necessary, and may therefore be considered to be natural rights.

The hierarchy of needs and metaneeds has been helpful to me in another way. I find that it serves as a kind of smorgasbord table from which people can choose in accordance with their own tastes and appetites. That is to say, that in any judging of the motivations for a person's behavior, the character of the judge also has to be taken into account. He *chooses* the motivations to which he will attribute the behavior, for instance, in accord with his generalized optimism or pessimism. I find the latter choice to be made far more frequently today, so frequently that I find it useful to name the phenomenon "downlevelling of the motivations." Briefly put, this is the tendency to prefer, for explanatory purposes, the lower needs to the middle needs, and the middle needs to the higher. A purely materialistic motivation is preferred to a social or metamotivated one, or to a mixture of all three. It is a kind of paranoid-like suspicion, a form of devaluation of human nature, which I see often but which, to my knowledge, has not been sufficiently described. I think that any complete theory of motivation must include this additional variable.

And of course I am sure that the historian of ideas would find it very easy to find many examples, in different cultures and in different times, of either a general trend to downlevelling or uplevelling of human motivations. At the moment of writing, the trend in our culture is very clearly toward widespread downlevelling. The lower needs are being heavily overused for explanatory purposes and the higher and metaneeds are being badly underused. In my opinion this tendency rests far more on preconception than on empirical fact. I find the higher needs and metaneeds to be far more determinative than my subjects themselves suspect, and certainly far, far more than contemporary intellectuals dare admit. Obviously, this is an empirical and scientific question, and just as obviously it is far too important a matter to be left to cliques and in-groups.

I had added to Chapter 5 on gratification theory a section on the pathology of gratification. Certainly this is something that we were not prepared for fifteen or twenty years ago, that pathological consequences might ensue after having attained what one had been *trying* to attain, and which was supposed to bring happiness. We have learned with Oscar Wilde to beware of what we wish—for the tragedy may come about that our wishes may be granted. This seems to be possible at *any* of the motivational levels, whether the material, or the interpersonal, or the transcendent.

We can learn from this unexpected finding that the gratification of the basic needs does not in itself automatically bring about a system of values in which to believe and to which one may commit himself. Rather, we have learned that one of the possible consequences of basic need gratifications may be boredom, aimlessness, anomie and the like. Apparently we function best when we are striving for something that we lack, when we wish for something that we do not have, and when we organize our powers in the service of striving toward the gratification of that wish. The state of gratification turns out to be not necessarily a state of guaranteed happiness or contentment. It is a moot state, one that raises problems as well as solving problems.

This discovery implies that for many people the *only* definition of the meaningful life that they can think of is "to be lacking something essential and to be striving for it." But we know that self-actualizing people, even though all their basic needs have already been gratified, find life to be even *more* richly meaningful because they can live, so to speak, in the realm of Being. The ordinary, widespread philosophy of a meaningful life is, therefore, a mistaken one, or at least an immature one.

Just as important for me has been the growing realization of what I have been calling Grumble Theory. In brief, what I have observed is that need gratifications lead to only temporary happiness which in turn tends to be succeeded by another and (hopefully) higher discontent. It looks as if the human hope for eternal happiness can never be fulfilled. Certainly happiness does come and is obtainable and is real. But it looks as if we must accept its intrinsic transience, especially if we focus on its more intense forms. Peak experiences do not last, and *cannot* last. Intense happiness is episodic, not continuous.

But this amounts to a revision of the theory of happiness that has ruled us for three thousand years and that has determined our concepts of heaven, of the Garden of Eden, of the good life, the good society, the good person. Our love stories have traditionally ended "And they lived happily ever after." And so also have our theories of social improvement and social revolution. So also, for instance, have we been over-sold—and consequently disillusioned—by the very real though limited improvements in our society. We were over-sold on the benefits of labor unionism, of women's suffrage, of the direct election of Senators, of the graded income tax, and of many other improvements that we have built into, e.g., the amendments to the Constitution. Each one of them was supposed to bring a millenium, eternal happiness, the final solution of all problems. The result has tended to be disillusionment after the fact. But disillusionment means that there had been illusions. And this seems to be the clear point to make, that we may reasonably expect improvements to take place. But we can no longer reasonably expect perfection to come to pass, or permanent happiness to be achieved.

I must call attention also to what has been overlooked almost universally even though now it seems very obvious, namely that the blessings we have already achieved come to be taken for granted, to be forgotten, to drop out of consciousness, and finally, even, not to be valued any more—at least until they are taken away from us. For instance, it is characteristic of the American culture as I write this preface in January, 1970, that the undoubted advancements and improvements that have been struggled for and achieved through 150 years are being flicked aside by many thoughtless and shallow people as being all a fake, as being of no value whatsoever, as being unworthy of fighting for or protecting, or valuing, just because the society is not yet perfect.

The present struggle for women's "liberation" will serve as a single example (I could have chosen dozens of others) to illustrate this complex but important point, and to show how many people tend to think in a dichotomous and splitting way rather than in a hierarchical and integrative way. In general it may be said that today, in our culture, the young girl's dream, a dream beyond which she cannot see, is most often of a man who falls in love with her, who gives her a home, and who gives her a baby. In her fantasies she then lives happily ever after. But the fact of the matter is that no matter how much one longs for a home or for a baby, or for a lover, that sooner or later one can become sated with these blessings, will take them for granted, and will start to feel restless and discontented as if something were lacking, as if something more had to be attained. The frequent mistake then is to turn upon the home and the baby and the husband as something of a fake, or perhaps even a trap or an enslavement, and then to long for the higher needs and higher gratifications in an either/or way, e.g., for professional work, for freedom to travel, for personal autonomy, and the like. The main point of Grumble Theory, and of Hierarchical–Integrative Theory of Needs, is that it is immature and unwise to think of these as mutually exclusive alternatives. It is best to think of the discontented woman as profoundly wishing to hang on to everything that she has and then—like the labor unionists—asking for *more!* That is to say that she generally would like to keep all her blessings and have additional ones as well. But even here it is as if we have not yet learned this eternal lesson, that whatever she yearns for, a career or whatever, when it is achieved the whole process will repeat itself. After the period of happiness, excitement, and fulfillment comes the inevitable taking it all for granted, and becoming restless and discontented again for *more!*

I offer for thought the real possibility that if we become fully aware of these human traits, if we can give up the dream of permanent and uninterrupted happiness, if we can accept the fact that we will be only transiently ecstatic and then inevitably discontented and grumbling for more, that then we may be able to teach the general population what self-actualizing people do automatically, i.e., to be able to count their blessings, to be grateful for them, and to avoid the traps of making either/or choices. It is possible for a woman to have all the specifically female fulfillments (being loved, having the home, having the baby) and *then,* without giving up any of the satisfactions already achieved, go on beyond femaleness to the full humanness that she shares with males, for example, the full development of her intelligence, of any talents that she may have, of her own particular idiosyncratic genius, of her own individual fulfillment.

The main thrust of Chapter 6, "The Instinctoid Nature of Basic Needs," has shifted considerably. The great advances of the last decade or so in the science of genetics has forced us to assign somewhat more determining power to the genes than we did fifteen years ago. Most important of these discoveries for the psychologists has been, I think, the various things that can happen to the X and Y chromosomes: doubling, tripling, loss, etc.

Chapter 9, "Is Destructiveness Instinctoid?," has also been considerably changed by these new discoveries.

Perhaps these developments in genetics may help to make my position more clear and communicable than it aparently has been. Currently, debate on the role of heredity and environment is almost as simplistic as it has been for the last fifty years. If still alternates between a simplistic theory of instincts on the one hand, total instincts of the sorts found in animals, and on the other hand, a complete rejection of the whole instinctual point of view in favor of a total environmentalism. Both positions are easily refuted, and in my opinion are so untenable as to be called stupid. In contrast with these two polarized positions the theory set forth in Chapter 6 and throughout the remainder of the book gives a third position, namely that there are *very weak* instinct-remnants left in the human species, nothing that could be called full instincts in the animal sense. These instinct-remnants and instinctoid tendencies are so weak that culture and learning easily overwhelm them and must be considered to be far more powerful. In fact, the techniques of psychoanalysis and other uncovering therapies, let alone the "quest for identity,"may all be conceived as the very difficult and delicate task of discovering through the overlay of learning, habit, and culture, what our instinct-remnants and instinctoid tendencies, our weakly indicated essential nature may be. In a word, man has a biological essence, but this is very weakly and subtly determined, and needs special hunting techniques to discover it; we must discover, individually and subjectively, our animality, our specieshood.

What this amounts to is the conclusion that human nature is extremely malleable in the sense that it is easy for culture and environment to kill off altogether or to diminish genetic potential, although it cannot create or even increase this potential. So far as society is concerned, this seems to me to be an extremely strong argument in favor of absolute equality of opportunity for every baby born into the world. It is also an especially powerful argument in favor of the good society, since human potentials are so easily lost or destroyed by the bad environment. This is quite apart from the contention already put forward that the sheer fact of membership in the human species constitutes *ipso facto* a right to become fully human, i.e., to actualize all the human potentials possible. *Being* a human being—in the sense of being born to the human species—must be defined also in terms of *becoming* a human being. In this sense a baby is only potentially a human being, and must grow into humanness in the society and the culture, the family.

Ultimately this point of view will force us to take far more seriously than we do the fact of individual differences, as well as species membership. We will have to learn to think of them in this new way as being, 1) very plastic, superficial, easily changed, easily stamped out, but producing thereby all sorts of subtle pathologies. This leads to the delicate task, 2) of trying to uncover the temperament, the constitution, the hidden *bent* of each individual so that he can grow unhampered in his own individual style. This attitude will require far greater attention than has been given by the psychologists to the subtle psychological and physiological costs and sufferings of denying one's true bent, sufferings that are not necessarily conscious or easily seen from the outside. This, in turn, means much more careful attention to the operational meaning of "good growth" at every age level.

Finally, I must point out that we shall have to prepare ourselves in principle for the shaking consequences of giving up the alibi of social injustice. The more we continue to reduce social injustice, the more we shall find this replaced by "biological injustice," by the fact that babies are born into the world with different genetic potentials. If we get to the point of giving full opportunity to every baby's good potentials, then this means accepting poor potentials as well. Whom shall we blame when a baby is born with a bad heart, or weak kidneys, or with neurological defects? If only nature is there to blame, what will this mean for the self-esteem of the individual "unfairly" treated by nature itself?

In this chapter, and also in other papers, I have introduced the concept of "subjective biology." I have found this to be a very helpful tool in bridging the gap between the subjective and the objective, the phenomenological and the behavioral. I hope this discovery, that one can and must study one's own biology introspectively and subjectively, will be of help to others, especially to biologists.

Chapter 9 on Destructiveness has been extensively reworked. I have subsumed it under the more inclusive category of the psychology of evil, hoping to demonstrate by this careful treatment of one aspect of evil, that the whole problem is empirically and scientifically workable. Bringing it under the jurisdiction of empirical science means for me that we can confidently look forward to steadily increased understanding which always has meant being able to do something about it.

Aggression, we have learned, is both genetically and culturally determined. Also I consider extremely important the distinction between healthy and unhealthy aggression.

Just as aggression cannot be blamed entirely on *either* society *or* inner human nature, so also is it already clear that evil in general is neither a social product alone or a psychological product alone. This may sound too obvious to be mentioned, but there are today many people who not only believe in these untenable theories but who act upon them as well.

I have introduced in Chapter 10, "The Expressive Component of Behavior," the concept of Apollonian controls, i.e., desirable controls which do not endanger gratification but rather enhance it. I consider this concept to be profoundly important both for pure psychological theory and for applied psychology. It has enabled me to differentiate between (sick) impulsivity and (healthy) spontaneity, a distinction very badly needed today, especially by young people, and by many others who tend to think of *any* controls as necessarily repressive and evil. I hope this insight will be as helpful to others as it has been to me.

I have not taken the time to bring this conceptual tool to bear upon the old problems of freedom, ethics, politics, happiness, and the like, but I think its relevance and power will be obvious to any serious thinker in these fields. The psychoanalyst will notice that this solution overlaps to some extent with Freud's integration of pleasure principle and reality principle. To think through the similarities and differences will, I think, be a profitable exercise for the theorist of psychodynamics.

In Chapter 11 on self-actualization I have removed one source of confusion by confining the concept very definitely to older people. By the criteria I used, self-actualization does not occur in young people. In our culture at least, youngsters have not yet achieved identity, or autonomy, nor have they had time enough to experience an enduring, loyal, post-romantic love relationship, nor have they generally found their calling, the altar upon which to offer themselves. Nor have they worked out their *own* system of values; nor have they had experience enough (responsibility for others, tragedy, failure, achievement, success) to shed perfectionistic illusions and become realistic; nor have they generally made their peace with death; nor have they learned how to be patient; nor have they learned enough about evil in themselves and others to be compassionate; nor have they had time to become post-ambivalent about parents and elders, power and authority; nor have they generally become knowledgeable and educated enough to open the possibility of becoming wise; nor have they generally acquired enough courage to be unpopular, to be unashamed about being openly virtuous, etc.

In any case, it is better psychological strategy to separate the concept of mature, fully-human, self-actualizing people in whom the human potentialities have been realized and actualized from the concept of health at *any* age level. This translates itself, I have found, into "good-growth-toward-self-actualization," a quite meaningful and researchable concept. I have done enough exploration with college age youngsters to have satisfied myself that it *is* possible to differentiate "healthy" from "unhealthy." It is my impression that healthy young men and women tend to be still growing, likeable, and even lovable, free of malice, secretly kind and altruistic (but very shy about it), privately affectionate of those of their elders who deserve it. Young people are unsure of themselves, not yet formed, uneasy because of their minority position with their peers (their private opinions and tastes are more square, straight, metamotivated, i.e., virtuous, than average). They are secretly uneasy about the cruelty, meanness, and mob spirit so often found in young people, etc.

Of course I do not know that this syndrome inevitably grows into the self-actualization I have described for older people. Only longitudinal studies can determine this.

I have described my self-actualizing subjects as transcending nationalism. I could have added that they also transcend class and caste. This is true in my experience even though I would expect a priori that affluence and social dignity are apt to make self-actualization more probable.

Another question which I did not anticipate in my first report has been this: Are these people capable of living only with "good" people and in a good world only? My retrospective impression, which of course remains to be checked, is that self-actualizing people are essentially *flexible,* and can adapt themselves realistically to any people, any environment. I think they are ready to handle good people *as* good people, while also being able to handle bad people *as* bad people.

Another addition to the description of self-actualizing people emerged from my study of "grumbles" and the widespread tendency to undervalue one's already achieved need-gratifications, or even to devalue them and throw them away. Self-actualizing persons are relatively exempted from this profound source of human unhappiness. In a word, they are capable of "gratitude." The blessedness of their blessings remains conscious. Miracles remain miracles even though occurring again and again. The awareness of undeserved good luck, of gratuitous grace, guarantees for them that life remains precious and never grows stale.

My study of self-actualizing persons has worked out very well—to my great relief, I must confess. It was, after all, a great gamble, doggedly pursuing an intuitive conviction and, in the process, defying some of the basic canons of scientific method and of philosophical criticism. These were, after all, rules which I myself had believed and accepted, and I was very much aware that I was skating on thin ice. Accordingly, my explorations proceeded against a background of anxiety, conflict, and self-doubt.

Enough verifications and supports have accumulated in the last few decades (see Bibliography) so that this kind of basic alarm is no longer necessary. And yet I am very much aware that these basic methodological and theoretical problems still confront us. The work that *has* been done is a bare beginning. We are now ready for far more objective, consensual and impersonal team methods of selecting self-actualizing (healthy, fully-human, autonomous) individuals for study. Cross-cultural work is clearly indicated. Follow-ups, from the cradle to the grave, will furnish the only truly satisfactory validation, at least in my opinion. Sampling the total population is clearly necessary in addition to selecting, as I did, the equivalent of Olympic gold medal winners. Nor do I think we can ever understand irreducible human evil until we explore more fully than I did the "incurable" sins and the shortcomings of the best human beings we can find.

Such studies I am convinced will change our philosophy of science, of ethics and values, of religion, of work, management and interpersonal relations, of society, and who knows what else. In addition, I think that great social and educational changes could occur almost immediately if, for instance, we could teach our young people to give up their unreal perfectionism, their demands for perfect human beings, a perfect society, perfect teachers, perfect parents, perfect politicians, perfect marriages, perfect friends, perfect organizations, etc., none of which exist and simply can not exist—that is, except for transient moments of peak-experience, of perfect fusion, etc. Such expectations we already know, even with our inadequate knowledge, are illusions and, therefore, must inevitably and inexorably breed disillusionment along with attendant disgust, rage, depression and revenge. The demand for "Nirvana *Now!*" is itself a major source of evil, I am finding. If you demand a perfect leader or a perfect society, you thereby give up choosing between better and worse. If the imperfect is defined as evil, then everything becomes evil, since everything is imperfect.

I believe also, on the positive side, that this great frontier of research is our most likely source of knowledge of the values intrinsic to human nature. Here lies the value system, the religion-surrogate, the idealism-satisfier, the normative philosophy of life that all human beings seem to need, to yearn for, and without which they become nasty and mean, vulgar and trivial.

Psychological health not only feels good subjectively but is also correct, true, real. In this sense, it is "better" than sickness and superior to it. Not only is it correct and true, but it is more perspicuous, seeing more truths as well as higher truths. That is, the lack of health not only feels awful but is a form of blindness, a cognitive pathology as well as moral and emotional loss. Furthermore, it is a form of crippling, of loss of capacities, of lesser ability to do and to achieve.

Healthy persons exist even though not in great numbers. Health with all its values—truth, goodness, beauty, etc.—having been demonstrated to be possible is, therefore, in principle an attainable reality. For those who prefer seeing to being blind, feeling good to feeling bad, wholeness to being crippled, it can be recommended that they seek psychological health. One remembers the little girl who, when asked why goodness was better than evil, answered, "Because it's *nicer.*" I think we can do better than that: the same line of thinking can demonstrate that living in a "good society" (brotherly, synergic, trusting, Theory Y) is "better" than living in a jungle society (Theory X, authoritarian, adversary, Hobbesian) *both* because of biological, medical and Darwinian survival values, and growth values, both subjective and objective. The same is true of a good marriage, a good friendship, good parents. Not only are these desired (preferred, chosen), but they are also, in specific senses, "desirable." I realize that this can make considerable trouble for professional philosophers, but I am confident that they will manage.

The demonstration that wonderful people *can* and do exist—even though in very short supply, and having feet of clay—is enough to give us courage, hope, strength to fight on, faith in ourselves and in our own possibilities for growth. Also, hope for human nature, however sober, should help us toward brotherliness and compassion.

I have decided to omit the last chapter of the first edition of this book, "Toward a Positive Psychology"; what was 98 percent true in 1954 is only two-thirds true today. A positive psychology is at least available today though not very widely. The humanistic psychologies, the new transcendent psychologies, the existential, the Rogerian, the experiential, the holistic, the value-seeking psychologies, are all thriving and available, at least in the United States, though unfortunately not yet in most departments of psychology, so that the interested student must seek them out or just stumble across them. For the reader who would like to taste for himself, I think a good sampling of the people, the ideas and the data is most easily available in the various books of readings by Moustakas, Severin, Bugental, and Sutich and Vich. For addresses of the appropriate schools, journals, societies, I would recommend the Eupsychian Network, an appendix in my book, *Toward a Psychology of Being*.

For uneasy graduate students I would still recommend this last chapter in the first edition, which is probably available in most university libraries. Also recommended is my *Psychology of Science* for the same reasons. For those who are willing to take these questions seriously enough to work hard at them, the great book in the field is Polanyi's *Personal Knowledge*.

This revised edition is an example of the increasingly firm rejection of traditionally value-free science—or rather of the futile effort to have a value-free science. It is more frankly normative than it was, more confidently affirming science to be a value-instigated search by value-seeking scientists who can, I claim, uncover intrinsic and ultimate and species-wide values in the structure of human nature itself.

To some this will seem like an assault upon the science that they love and revere, and which I do too. I accept that their fear is sometimes well founded. There are many, especially in the social sciences, who see total political commitment (by definition in the absence of full information) as the only conceivable alternative to value-free science and mutually exclusive with it. Embracing the one means for them necessarily rejecting the other.

That this dichotomizing is sophomoric is proven at once by the simple fact that it is best to get correct information even when you are fighting an enemy, even when you are avowedly a politician.

But quite beyond this self-defeating foolishness, and addressing ourselves to this very serious question at the highest levels of which we are capable, I believe it can be shown that normative zeal (to do good, to help mankind, to better the world) is quite compatible with scientific objectivity and indeed even makes conceivable a better, a more powerful science with a far wider jurisdiction than it now has when it tries to be value-neutral (leaving values to be arbitrarily affirmed by non-scientists on non-factual grounds). This is achieved simply by enlarging our conception of objectivity to include not only "spectator-knowledge" (laissez-faire, uninvolved knowledge, knowledge about, knowledge from the outside) but also experential knowledge and what I may call love-knowledge or Taoistic knowledge.

The simple model of Taoistic objectivity comes from the phenomenology of disinterested love and admiration for the Being of the other (B-love). For instance, loving one's baby, or friend, or profession, or even one's "problem" or field in science, can be so complete and accepting that it becomes non-interfering, non-intrusive, i.e., liking it just as it is and as it will become with no impulse to change it or improve it. It takes great love to be able to leave something alone, to let it be and to become. One can love one's child that purely, letting him become what is in him to become. But—and this is the point of my argument— one can love the truth *in the same way*. One can love it enough to trust also its *becoming*. It is possible to love one's baby even before it is born, and to wait with bated breath and with great happiness to see what kind of person it will be, and now to love that future person.

A priori plans for the child, ambitions for it, prepared roles, even hopes that it will become this or that—all these are non-Taoistic. They represent demands upon the child that it become what the parent has already decided it *should* become. Such a baby is born into an invisible straitjacket.

Similarly, it is possible to love the truth yet to come, to trust it, to be happy and to marvel as its nature reveals itself. One can believe that the uncontaminated, unmanipulated, unforced, undemanded truth will be more beautiful more pure, more *truly* true than that same truth would have been had we forced it to conform to a priori expectations or hopes or plans or current political needs. Truth also can be born into an "invisible straitjacket."

Normative zeal *can* be wrongly understood and *can* distort the truth-to-come by a priori demands, and I am afraid that some scientists do just this, in effect giving up science for politics. But this is not at all a necessity for the more Taoistic scientist who can love the truth-yet-to-be-born enough to assume that it will be for the best and, for this reason, will let-it-be, precisely for the sake of his normative zeal.

I too believe this: that the purer the truth, and the less contaminated it is by doctrinaires whose minds are made up in advance, the better it will be for the future of mankind. I trust that the world will be more benefited by the truth of the future than by the political convictions which I hold today. I trust what will be known more than I trust my present knowledge.

This is a humanistic-scientific version of "Not my will but Thine be done." My fears and hopes for mankind, my eagerness to do good, my desire for peace and brotherhood, my normative zeal—all these I feel are best served if I remain modestly open to the truth, objective and disinterested in the Taoistic sense of refusing to pre-judge the truth or to tamper with it, and if I continue to trust that the more I know the better helper I can become.

At many points in this book, and in many publications since, I have assumed that the actualization of a person's real potentialities is conditioned upon the presence of basic-need satisfying parents and other people, upon all those factors now called "ecological," upon the "health" of the culture, or the lack of it, upon the world situation, etc. Growth toward self-actualization and full-humanness is made possible by a complex hierarchy of "good preconditions." These physical, chemical, biological, interpersonal, cultural conditions matter for the individual finally to the extent that they do or do not supply him with the basic human necessities and "rights" which permit him to become strong enough, and person enough, to take over his own fate.

As one studies these preconditions, one becomes saddened by the ease with which human potentiality can be destroyed or repressed, so that a fully-human person can seem like a miracle, so improbable a happening as to be awe-inspiring. And simultaneously one is heartened by the fact that self-actualizing persons do in fact exist, that they are therefore possible, that the gauntlet of dangers can be run, that the finish line can be crossed.

The investigator here is almost certain to be caught in a cross-fire of accusations both interpersonal and intrapsychic, about being either "optimistic" or "pessimistic," depending on where he is focusing at the moment. So also will he be accused from one side of being hereditarian, from the other of being environmentalist. Political groups will certainly try to plaster him with one or another label, depending on the headlines of the moment.

The scientist of course will resist these all-or-none tendencies to dichotomize and rubricize, and will continue to think in terms of degree, and to be holistically aware of many, many determinants acting simultaneously. He will try as hard as he can to be receptive to the data, differentiating them as clearly as he can from his wishes, hopes, and fears. It is now quite clear that these problems—what is the good person and what is the good society—fall well within the jurisdiction of empirical science, and that we may confidently hope to advance knowledge in these areas.

This book focuses much more on the first problem—the fully-human person, than on the second problem—what kind of society makes him possible. I have written a good deal on the subject since 1954 when this book first appeared, but have refrained from trying to incorporate these findings into this revised edition. Instead I will refer the reader to some of my writings on the subject and also urge as strongly as I can the necessity of becoming acquainted with the rich research literature on normative social psychology (called variously Organizational Development, Organization Theory, Management Theory, etc.). The implications of these theories, case reports and researches seem to me to be profound, offering as they do a real alternative, for instance, to the various versions of Marxian theory, of democratic and authoritarian theories, and of other available social philosophies. I am again and again astonished that so few psychologists are even aware of the work of, for instance, Argyris, Bennis, Likert, and McGregor, to mention only a few of the well-known workers in the field. In any case, anyone who wishes to take seriously the theory of self-actualization must also take seriously this new kind of social psychology. if I were to choose a single journal to recommend to the person who wishes to keep in touch with the current developments in this area, it would be the *Journal of Applied Behavioral Sciences*, in spite of its totally misleading title.

Finally, I wish to say a word about this book as a transition to humanistic psychology, or what has come to be called Third Force. Immature though it yet is from a scientific point of view, humanistic psychology has already opened the doors to study of all those psychological phenomena which can be called transcendent or transpersonal, data which were closed off in principle by the inherent philosophical limitations of behaviorism and Freudianism. Among such phenomena I include not only higher and more positive states of consciousness and of personality, i.e., transcending materialism, the skin-bounded ego, atomistic-splitting-divisive-adversary attitudes, etc., but also a conception of values (eternal verities) as part of a much enlarged self. Already a new *Journal of Transpersonal Psychology* has begun publishing on these subjects.

It is possible already to start *thinking* about the transhuman, a psychology and a philosophy which transcends the human species itself. This is yet to come.

A. H. M.

W. P. Laughlin Charitable Foundation

foreword

THE INFLUENCE OF ABRAHAM MASLOW

By Robert Frager

One cannot choose wisely for a life unless he dares to listen to himself, his own self, at each moment in life.

ABRAHAM H. MASLOW
The Farther Reaches of Human Nature, 1971

INTRODUCTION

Abraham H. Maslow was a man who dared to listen deeply to himself and to his unwavering belief in the positive potential of the human species. He has been called a pioneer, a visionary, a philosopher of science, and an optimist. He was one of the foremost spokespersons of the humanistic or "Third Force" psychologies, and *Movitation and Emotion,* originally published in 1954, contains his significant questions and early explorations into human psychology. The ideas elaborated in *Motivation and Personality* formed the foundation of Maslow's lifework. This book has had a tremendous influence in creating a positive and whole view of human nature. It continues to be a unique, penetrating, and influential resource, as indicated by current trends in psychology, education, business, and culture. In many fields there is a growing emphasis on self-actualization, values, choice, and a more holistic view of the individual.

MASLOW'S INFLUENCE

Esquire magazine's 50th anniversary issue featured articles on the most important American figures of the mid-twentieth century. The editors chose Maslow as the

most influential psychologist and also as one of the most important contributors
to our modern view of human nature. George Leonard wrote:

> He wrote with none of the dark grandeur of a Freud or the learned grace of
> an Erik Erikson or the elegant precision of a B. F. Skinner. He was not a
> brilliant speaker; in his early years he was so shy he could hardly bring himself
> to mount the podium. . . . The branch of Psychology he founded has not
> achieved a dominant position in the colleges and universities. He died in 1970,
> but a full-scale biography remains to be written.

> And yet, Abraham Maslow has done more to change our view of human nature
> and human possibilties than has any other American psychologist of the past
> fifty years. His influence, both direct and indirect, continues to grow, especially
> in the fields of health, education, and management theory, and in the personal
> and social lives of millions of Americans. (Leonard, 1983, p. 326)

When Maslow began his career, there were only two major forces in psychology: the experimental, behaviorist approach and the clinical, psychoanalytic
approach. These models were not sufficient for Maslow. "On the whole . . . I
think it fair to say that human history is a record of the ways in which human
nature has been sold short. The highest possibilities of human nature have practically always been underestimated" (1971, p. 7).

In his intellectual career Maslow sought to balance this underestimation with
ground-breaking investigations of the highest possibilities for human growth and
development. He was instrumental in the emergence of two major new forces in
psychology: the humanistic and the transpersonal. Both explore the full, rich complexity of human nature without restricting human behavior to a mechanistic or
pathological model.

Maslow's greartest strength was in his ability to ask significant questions.
He posed questions for psychology that are central to the lives of all of us: What
is it to be a good human being? Of what are human beings capable? What makes
for happy, creative, fulfilled human beings? How can we determine that a person
has fully actualized his or her potentialities unless we know what those potentialities are? How can we truly transcend the immaturity and insecurity of childhood, and under what circumstances can we do so? How can we develop a complete model of human nature, honoring our extraordinary potentional, without
losing sight of our nonrational, nonaccomplishing side? What motivates psychologically healthy individuals?

> Is the self-actualizing person the truest representation of what human nature
> really *is* beneath the surface? This is one of those very large questions to
> which only fools and visionaries dare offer definitive answers. What Maslow
> offered in self-actualization was not just a psycholoical fact but a full-blown
> vision of human nature. Where others dwelt on eroticism or power or self-
> integration or stimulus and response, Maslow's was a vision of gnostic truth
> and pagan joy. (Lowry, 1973, p. 50)

The creative questions that Maslow asked continue to inspire important insights into human nature and encourage farther exploration.

Maslow's life was dedicated to the study of people that he considered to be psychologically healthy: "indeed, self-actualizing people, those who have come to a high level of maturation, health and self-fulfillment, have so much to teach us that sometimes they seem almost like a different breed of human beings" (Maslow, 1968, p. 71).

He discovered that human functioning is different for people who operate in a state of positive health rather than a state of deficiency. Maslow called this new approach "Being-psychology." He found that self-actualizing people were motivated by "Being-values." These are values that are naturally developed by healthy human beings and are not imposed by religion or culture. He maintained that "we have come to the point in biological history where we are now responsible for our own evolution. We have become self-evolvers. Evolution means selecting and therefore choosing and deciding, and this means valuing" (1971, p. 11). the values that self-actualizers appreciate include truth, creativity, beauty, goodness, wholeness, aliveness, uniqueness, justice, simplicity, and self-sufficiency.

Maslow's study of human nature led him to many conclusions, including these central ideas:

1. Human beings have an innate tendency to move toward higher levels of health, creativity, and self-fulfillment.
2. Neurosis may be regarded as a blockage of the tendency toward self-actualization.
3. The evolution of a synergistic society is a natural and essential process. This is a society in which *all* individuals may reach a high level of self-development, without restricting each others' freedom.
4. Business efficiency and personal growth are not incompatible. In fact, the process of self-actualization leads each individual to the highest levels of efficiency.

In 1968 Maslow commented that the revolution inside psychology that he spearheaded had become solidly established. "Furthermore, it is beginning to be *used,* especially in education, industry, religion, organization and management, therapy and self improvement . . ." (p. iii) Indeed, his work is an integral part of the dominant intellectual trends of this century. In his book on Maslow and modern psychology, Colin Wilson wrote:

> The first half of the 20th century saw a reaction against the age of romanticism. Biology was dominated by a rigid Darwinism, philosophy by various forms of positivism and rationalism, science by determinism. This latter could be summarized as the notion that if we could build a giant computer, and feed all our present scientific knowledge into it, the computer could take over the future of scientific discovery.
>
> The early psychologists had restricted themselves to trying to explain our feelings and responses in terms of brain mechanisms; that is, to construing a mechanical picture of the mind. Freud's picture was altogether more "rich and strange," but it was deeply pessimistic—what Aldous Huxley called the "basement with basement" view of the mind. . . . Maslow was the first person to create a truly comprehensive psychology, stretching, so to speak, from the

basement to the attic. He accepted Freud's clinical method without accepting his philosophy. . . . The "transcendent" urges—aesthetic, creative, religious—are as basic and permanent a part of human nature as dominance or sexuality. If they are less obviously "universal," this is only because fewer human beings reach the point at which they take over.

Maslow's achievement is enormous. Like all original thinkers, he has opened up a new way of *seeing* the universe. (Wilson, 1972, pp. 181–184)

Throughout his life, Maslow was an intellectual pioneer. He was constantly breaking new ground, then moving on to still newer areas. He presented personal hunches, intuitions, and affirmations along with scholarly studies. He often left to others the careful analysis and testing of his theories. The questions that Maslow posed are invitingly unfinished.

A SHORT BIOGRAPHY

Abraham H. Maslow was born on April 1, 1908, in Brooklyn, New York. His parents were Russian-Jewish immigrants. His father was a barrel maker by trade who moved to the United States from Russia as a young man. After he became settled, he wrote to a female cousin in Russia, asking her to come to the United States and marry him. She did.

Maslow was the first of their seven children. He was an extraordinarily shy, neurotic young man, depressed, terribly unhappy, lonely, and self-rejecting.

With my childhood, it's a wonder I'm not psychotic. I was the little Jewish boy in the non-Jewish neighborhood. It was a little like being the first Negro enrolled in the all-white school. I was isolated and unhappy. I grew up in libraries and among books, without friends.

Both my mother and father were uneducated. My father wanted me to be a lawyer. . . .

I tried law school for two weeks. Then I came home to my poor father one night . . . and told him I couldn't be a lawyer.

"Well, son," he said, "what do you want?" I told him I wanted to study—to study everything. He was uneducated and couldn't understand my passion for learning, but he was a nice man. (Maslow, in Hall, 1968, p. 37)

Maslow's love of learning, combined with his tremendous raw intelligence, made him a brilliant student. (Years later his IQ was scored at 195, the second highest measured at that time.) Maslow explored the rich cultural life of New York and fell in love with classical music and the theater. He went to two concerts a week at Carnegie Hall, and even sold peanuts to get into the theater.

Maslow also fell deeply in love with his cousin Bertha. At 19 he finally got up enough nerve to kiss her. He was amazed and delighted that she did not reject him. Bertha's acceptance and love was a tremendous boost to Maslow's shaky self-esteem. They were married a year later.

In 1928, Maslow transferred to the University of Wisconsin where he majored in psychology. There he received solid training in experimental research from some of the country's finest experimental psychologists. Harry Harlow, the famous primate researcher, became Maslow's major professor. Harlow was first in a series of distinguished scholars who were drawn to this brilliant, shy young man, and who taught him, inspired him, fed him, and helped him get jobs.

Maslow's first postdoctoral position was as a research associate for the distinguished behaviorist Edward Thorndike. Maslow was impressed with the potentials of behaviorism, typified by John B. Watson's optimistic belief that scientific psychology could be used to train anybody to be anything—"doctor, lawyer, or Indian chief." Maslow eventually realized the limitations of the strict behaviorist approach to life.

> It was the beautiful program of Watson that brought me into psychology. But its fatal flaw is that it's good for the lab and in the lab, but you put it on and take it off like a lab coat. . . . It does not generate an image of man, a philosophy of life, a conception of human nature. It's not a guide to living, to values, to choices. It's a way of collecting facts upon facts about behavior, what you can see and touch and hear through the senses.
>
> But behavior in the human being is sometimes a defense, a way of concealing motives and thoughts, as language can be a way of hiding your thoughts and preventing communication.
>
> If you treat your children at home in the same way you treat your animals in the lab, your wife will scratch your eyes out. My wife ferociously warned me against experimenting on her babies. (Maslow, in Lowry, 1979, Vol. II, pp. 1059–1060)

Maslow also believed that Freudian theory provided a major contribution to human understanding, especially in illuminating the central role of sexuality in human behavior. At Columbia University he caused a controversy by interviewing college women about their sexual lives. This was in 1936, when research on sexuality was unheard of. Maslow may have inspired Kinsey's work, which began two years later. Maslow found that sexual activity was related to "dominance," a trait he had studied in Harlow's primate lab.

Maslow accepted a professorship in psychology at Brooklyn College and taught there for 14 years. He inspired his students with his own love of learning and with his enthusiasm for psychology. Many Brooklyn College students were from immigrant families, and felt ill at ease in a totally new, academic environment. Maslow was one of the few professors who cared. The students deeply appreciated his loving concern for them. Maslow was one of the most popular teachers there; he was known as "the Frank Sinatra of Brooklyn College."

New York City was one of the world's greatest intellectual centers at this time, home to many of the finest European scholars who fled from Nazi persecution. Maslow's mentors at The New School for Social Research in New York included Alfred Adler, Erich Fromm, Karen Horney, and Margaret Mead. Two other great scholars became not only teachers but also Maslow's close friends: Ruth Benedict, the anthropologist, and Max Wertheimer, the founder of Gestalt psychology.

Maslow was deeply inspired by Benedict and Wertheimer. Not only were they brilliant, creative, highly productive scholars, but they were also warm, caring, mature human beings. He began keeping a notebook on them, trying to analyze what made them such marvelous human beings as well as brilliant scholars. Maslow contrasted Benedict and Wertheimer with Hitler—examples of the best and worst of humanity.

> My investigations on self-actualization were not planned to be research and did not start out as research. They started out as the effort of a young intellectual trying to understand two of his teachers whom he loved, adored, and admired; and who were very, very wonderful people. It was a kind of high-IQ devotion. I could not be content simply to adore, but sought to understand why these two people were so different from the run-of-the-mill people in the world. These two people were Ruth Benedict and Max Wertheimer. They were my teachers after I came with a Ph.D. from the West to New York City, and they were most remarkable human beings. It was as if they were not quite people, but something more than people. My own investigation began as a prescientific activity. I made descriptions and notes on Max Wertheimer and I made notes on Ruth Benedict. When I tried to understand them, think about them, and write about them in my journal and my notes, I realized in one wonderful moment that their two patterns could be generalized. I was talking about a kind of person, not about two noncomparable individuals. There was wonderful excitement in that. I tried to see whether this pattern could be found elsewhere, and I did find it elsewhere, in one person after another. (Maslow, 1971, p. 41)

At the beginning of World War II, Maslow was moved to tears by a patriotic parade. He decided to give up his career in experimental research in order to try to understand psychologically the causes of hatred, prejudice, and war.

> As I watched, the tears ran down my face. I felt we didn't understand—not Hitler, nor the Germans, nor Stalin, nor the Communists. We didn't understand any of them. I felt that if we could understand, then we could make progress. . . .
>
> I was too old to go into the army. It was at that moment that I realized that the rest of my life must be devoted to discovering a psychology for the peace table. . . .
>
> I wanted to prove that human beings are capable of something grander than war and prejudice and hatred.
>
> I wanted to make science consider all the problems that nonscientists have been handling—religion, poetry, values, philosophy, art.
>
> I went about it by trying to understand great people, the best specimens of mankind I could find. (Maslow, in Hall, 1968, pp. 54–55)

In 1951, Maslow finally left Brooklyn College to move to the newly established Brandeis University. He became the first chairman of the psychology department and was deeply committed to the university's growth and development. Maslow remained at Brandeis until 1969, a year before his death. During this period he refined his ideas, always moving toward a fully comprehensive theory of human nature. In 1962 he helped found the Association for Humanistic Psychology with a group of eminent colleagues, including Rollo May and Carl Rogers. In continuing to explore the farther reaches of human potential, Maslow also inspired the founding of the *Journal of Transpersonal Psychology*. He wrote of these two psychologies:

> I must confess that I have come to think of this humanist trend in psychology as a revolution in the truest, oldest sense of the word, the sense in which Galileo, Darwin, Einstein, Freud, and Marx made revolutions, i.e., new ways of perceiving and thinking, new images of man and of society, new conceptions of ethics and of values, new directions in which to move.

> This Third Psychology is now one facet of a . . . new philosophy of life, a new conception of man, the beginning of a new century of work. . . .

> I should say also that I consider Humanistic, Third Force Psychology to be transitional, a preparation for a still "higher" Fourth Psychology, transpersonal, transhuman, centered in the cosmos rather than in human needs and interest. (Maslow, 1968, pp. iii–iv)

Maslow also became interested in the world of business. In the summer of 1962 he became a visiting fellow to Non-Linear Systems, an innovative, high-tech California corporation. Maslow discovered that his theories were relevant to business management and that there were many self-actualizing people in industry.

He found that many successful businessmen were employing the same positive approach to human nature he was advocating in psychology. He was pleased to discover that managers who treated their subordinates with trust and respect created a more supportive, more productive, and more creative work situation. Maslow's abstract theories were actually being tested and confirmed in the marketplace.

> Have been asked over and over again what got me to go to Non-Linear systems. . . . One thing was the slow realization that my theories, especially of motivation, were being used and put to the test in the industrial lab rather than in the experimental lab. I've felt guilty because I couldn't figure out how to test motivation theory and SA [self-actualization] theory in the lab. They relieved me of this guilt and freed me forever from the lab. How could it be otherwise. Non-Linear is one big lab and one big experiment.

> I gave up my simple notion that management psychology was simply the application of pure psychology. Pure psychology could learn more from real-life work-research than vice versa. Life psychology had better be tested in life-labs. The chemistry lab and the test-tube experiment are lousy models for human life research. (Maslow, in Lowry, 1979, Vol. I, p. 191)

Maslow experienced still another new world that summer in California. He and Bertha were driving along the California coast for a vacation. They made much slower progress than they had planned, and it got dark as they were driving through Big Sur. They pulled over into what seemd to be a motel. They found a group of people in an old lodge, all reading Maslow's new book, *Toward a Psychology of Being*.

The Maslows had pulled off into Esalen Institute. The world's first growth center was just about to open. Michael Murphy, Esalen's cofounder, had just read Maslow's new book and enthusiastically bought copies for the Esalen staff. Maslow and Murphy soon became friends, and Maslow's ideas became a major influence on Esalen and on the whole human potential movement.

Maslow was too much of an intellectual to beocme a convert to the almost total emphasis on feeling and experiencing in the human potential scene. He gave his first Esalen workshop two years after Esalen began. The Institute had been gaining a national reputation as *the* avant-garde center for encounter groups and other intense, emotionally charged workshops. Maslow's weekend was, in complete contrast, purely intellectual. Because they were interested in his ideas, several of the Esalen staff members sat in on his talks and discussions.

In the middle of Maslow's first evening talk, Fritz Perls, the founder of Gestalt therapy and enfant terrible of Esalen, got bored with the lack of emotional action. He began crawling toward an attractive woman across the room, chanting "You are my mother; I want my mother; you are my mother." This effectively broke up the evening session. Maslow left the room upset and offended. Characteristically, he shut himself in his cabin that night and thought through some of the differences between his own approach and the experiential emphasis prevalent at Esalen. That night he completed the outline of a classic article contrasting Appolonian control with Dionysian abandon.

In spite of the revolutionary and controversial nature of Maslow's work, in 1967 he was elected president of the American Psychological Association. His colleagues acknowledged Maslow's influence even while they objected to his innovations in theory and methodology.

In 1968 Maslow was given a grant that enabled him to devote his last years to writing. He left Brandeis and went to California, where he died of a heart attack in 1970.

The following is from his last diary entry, dated May 7, 1970.

Somebody asked me the question . . . How did a timid youngster get transformed into a (seemingly) "courageous" leader and spokesman? How come I was willing to talk up, to take unpopular positions, while most others didn't? My immediate tendency was to say: "Intelligence—just realistic seeing of the facts," but I held that answer back because—alone—it's wrong. "Good will, compassion *and* intelligence," I finally answered. I think I added that I'd simply *learned* a lot from my self-actualizing subjects and from their way of life and from their metamotivations, which have now become *mine*. So I respond emotionally to the injustice, the meanness, the lies, the untruths, the hatred and violence, the simplistic answers. . . . So I feel cheap and guilty and unmanly when I *don't* talk up. So then, in a sense, *I have to.*

What the kids *and* the intellectuals—and everybody else too—need is an ethos, a scientific value system and way of life and humanistic politics, *with* the theory, the facts, etc., all set forth soberly. . . . So *again* I must say to myself: to work! (Lowry, 1979, Vol. II, p. 1309)

REFERENCES

Hall, M. H. (1968). A conversation with Abraham H. Maslow. *Psychology Today, 35*–37, 54–57.

International Study Project. (1972). *Abraham H. Maslow: A memorial volume*. Monterey, CA: Brooks/Cole.

Leonard, G. (1983, December). Abraham Maslow and the new self. *Esquire*, pp. 326–336.

Lowry, R. (1973). *A. H. Maslow: An intellectual portrait*. Monterey, CA: Brooks/Cole.

Lowry, R. (Ed.). (1979). *The journals of Abraham Maslow* (2 vols.). Monterey, CA: Brooks/Cole.

Maslow, A. (1968). *Toward a psychology of being* (2nd ed.). New York: Van Nostrand.

Maslow, A. (1971). *The farther reaches of human nature*. New York: Viking Press.

Wilson, C. (1972). *New pathways in psychology: Maslow and the post-Freudian revolution*. New York: Mentor.

one

MOTIVATION THEORY

chapter *1*

Preface to
Motivation Theory

In this chapter are presented 17 propositions about motivation that must be incorporated into any sound motivation theory. Some of these propositions are so true as to be platitudinous. These I feel need reemphasis. Others may be found less acceptable and more debatable.

HOLISTIC APPROACH

Our first proposition states that the individual is an integrated, organized whole. That it is an experimental reality as well as a theoretical one must be realized before sound experimentation and sound motivation theory are possible. In motivation theory this proposition means many specific things. For instance, it means the whole individual is motivated rather than just a part. In good theory there is no such entity as a need of the stomach or mouth, or a genital need. There is only a need of the individual. It is John Smith who wants food, not John Smith's stomach. Furthermore satisfaction comes to the whole individual and not just to a part of him. Food satisfies John Smith's hunger and not his stomach's hunger.

Dealing with hunger as a function merely of the gastrointestinal tract has made experimenters neglect the fact that when individuals are hungry they change not only in their gastrointestinal functions, but in many, perhaps even in most other functions of which they are capable. Perceptions change (food is perceived more readily than at other times). Memories change (a good meal is more apt to be remembered at this time than at other times). Emotions change (there is more tension and nervousness than at other times). The content of thinking changes (a person is more apt to think of getting food than of solving an algebraic problem).

And this list can be extended to almost every other faculty, capacity, or function, both physiological and psychic. In other words, when people are hungry, they are hungry all over; they are different as individuals from what they are at other times.

A PARADIGM FOR MOTIVATIONAL STATES

The choice of hunger as a paradigm for all other motivation states is both theoretically and practically unwise and unsound. It can be seen upon closer analysis that the hunger drive is more a special case of motivation than a general one. It is more isolated (using this word as used by the Gestalt and Goldsteinian psychologists) than other motivations; it is less common than other motivations; and finally, it is different from other motivations in that it has a known somatic base, which is unusual for motivational states. What are the more common immediate motivations? We can find these easily enough by introspecting during the course of an average day. The desires that flit through consciousness are most often desires for clothes, automobiles, friendliness, company, praise, prestige, and the like. Customarily these have been phrased as secondary or cultural drives and have been regarded as of a different order from the truly "respectable" or primary drives, namely, the physiological needs. In actuality these are far more important for us and they are far more common. It would therefore be well to make one of them the paradigm, rather than the hunger drive.

The common assumption has been that all drives will follow the example set by the physiological drives. It is fair to predict now that this will never be. Most drives are not isolable, nor can they be localized somatically, nor can they be considered as if they were the only things happening in the organism at the time. The typical drive or need or desire is not and probably never will be related to a specific, isolated, localized somatic base. The typical desire is much more obviously a need of the whole person. It would be far better to take as a model for research such a drive, let us say, as the desire for money rather than the sheer hunger drive, or even better, rather than any partial goal, a more fundamental one, like the desire for love. Considering all the evidence now in hand, it is probably true that we could never understand fully the need for love no matter how much we might know about the hunger drive. Indeed a stronger statement is possible, namely, that from a full knowledge of the need for love we can learn more about general human motivation (including the hunger drive) than we could from a thorough study of the hunger drive.

It is well in this connection to recall the critical analysis of the concept of simplicity that has been made so often by the Gestalt psychologists. The hunger drive, which seems simple when compared with the drive of love, is actually not so simple in the long run (Goldstein, 1939). The appearance of simplicity can be obtained by selecting isolated cases, activities that are relatively independent of the wholeness of the organism. An important activity can easily be shown to have dynamic relationships with almost everything else of importance in the person. Why then take an activity that is not at all average in this sense, an activity that is selected out for special attention only because it is easier to deal with by our customary (but not necessarily correct) experimental technique of isolation, reduction, or of independence from other activities? If we are faced with the choice of dealing with either (1) experimentally simple problems that are however trivial or invalid or (2) experimental problems that are fearfully difficult but important, we should certainly not hesitate to choose the latter.

MEANS AND ENDS

If we examine carefully the average desires that we have in daily life, we find that they have at least one important characteristic, that they are usually means to an end rather than ends in themselves. We want money so that we can have an automobile. In turn we want an automobile because the neighbors have one and we do not wish to feel inferior to them, so we can retain our own self-respect and so we can be loved and respected by others. Usually when a conscious desire is analyzed we find that we can go behind it, so to speak, to other, more fundamental aims of the individual. In other words, we have here a situation that parallels very much the role of symptoms in psychopathology. The symptoms are important, not so much in themselves, but for what they ultimately mean, that is, for what their ultimate goals or effects may be. The study of symptoms in themselves is quite unimportant, but the study of the dynamic meaning of symptoms is important because it is fruitful—for instance, making possible psychotherapy. The particular desires that pass through our consciousness dozens of times a day are not in themselves so important as what they stand for, where they lead, what they ultimately mean upon deeper analysis.

It is characteristic of this deeper analysis that it will always lead ultimately to certain goals or needs behind which we cannot go, that is, to certain need satisfactions that seem to be ends in themselves and seem not to need any further justification or demonstration. These needs have the particular quality in the average person of not being seen directly very often but of being more often a kind of conceptual derivation from the multiplicity of specific conscious desires. In other words, then, the study of motivation must be in part the study of the ultimate human goals or desires or needs.

UNCONSCIOUS MOTIVATION

These facts imply another necessity for sound motivation theory. Since these goals are not often seen directly in consciousness, we are at once forced into the necessity of dealing with the whole problem of unconscious motivation. Careful study of the conscious motivational life alone will often leave out much that is as important as or even more important than what can be seen in consciousness. Psychoanalysis has often demonstrated that the relationship between a conscious desire and the ultimate unconscious aim that underlies it need not be at all direct. Indeed the relationship may actually be a negative one, as in reaction formations. We may then assert that sound motivation theory cannot possibly afford to neglect the unconscious life.

COMMONALITY OF HUMAN DESIRES

There is now sufficient anthropological evidence to indicate that the fundamental or ultimate desires of all human beings do not differ nearly as much as do their conscious everyday desires. The main reason for this is that two different cultures may provide two completely different ways of satisfying a particular desire, let us say, for self-esteem. In one society, one obtains self-esteem by being a good hunter; in another society by being a great healer or a bold warrior, or a very unemotional person and so on. It may then be that, if we think of ultimates, the one individual's desire to be a good hunter has the same dynamics and the same fundamental aim as the desire of the other individual to be a good healer. We may then assert that it would be more useful to combine these two seemingly disparate conscious desires into the same category than to put them into different categories on purely behavioral grounds. Apparently ends in themselves are far more universal than the roads taken to achieve those ends, for these roads are determined locally in the specific culture. Human beings are more alike than one would think at first.

MULTIPLE MOTIVATIONS

A conscious desire or a motivated behavior may serve as a kind of channel through which other purposes may express themselves. There are several ways of showing this. For instance, it is well known that sexual behavior and conscious sexual desires may be tremendously complex in their underlying, unconscious purposes. In one individual sexual desire may actually mean the desire to assure himself of his masculinity. It may in other individuals represent fundamentally a desire to impress, or a desire for closeness, friendliness, for safety, for love, or for any combination of these. Consciously the sexual desire in all these individuals may have the same content, and probably all of them would make the mistake of thinking that they seek only sexual gratification. But we now know that this is not correct, that it is useful in understanding these individuals to deal with what the sexual desire and behavior represent fundamentally rather than what the individual consciously thinks they represent. (This holds true for either preparatory or consummatory behavior.)

Another line of evidence supporting this same point is the finding that a single psychopathological symptom may represent at one and the same time several different, even opposing desires. A hysterically paralyzed arm may represent the fulfillment of simultaneous wishes for revenge, for pity, for love, and for respect. To take either the conscious wish in the first example or the overt symptom in the second in a purely behavioral fashion means that we arbitrarily throw out the possibility of a total understanding of the behavior and of the motivational state of the individual. Let us emphasize that it is unusual, *not* usual, for an act or a conscious wish to have but one motivation.

MOTIVATING STATES

In a certain sense almost any organismic state of affairs whatsoever is in itself also a motivating state. Current conceptions of motivation seem to proceed on the assumption that a motivational state is a special, peculiar state, sharply marked off from the other happenings in the organism. Sound motivational theory should, on the contrary, assume that motivation is constant, never ending, fluctuating, and complex, and that it is an almost universal characteristic of practically every organismic state of affairs.

Consider, for instance, what we mean when we say that a person feels rejected. A static psychology would be content to put a period to this statement. But a dynamic psychology would imply very many more things by this statement with full empirical justification. Such a feeling has repercussions throughout the whole organism both in its somatic and psychic aspects. Furthermore, such a state of affairs automatically and of necessity leads to many other happenings, such as compulsive desires to win back affection, defensive efforts of various kinds, piling up of hostility, and so on. It is clear then that we will explain the state of affairs implied in the statement "This person feels rejected" only if we add many, many more statements about what happens to the person as a result of feeling rejected. In other words, the feeling of rejection is itself a motivating state.

SATISFACTIONS GENERATE NEW MOTIVATIONS

The human being is a wanting animal and rarely reaches a state of complete satisfaction except for a short time. As one desire is satisfied, another pops up to take its place. When this is satisfied, still another comes into the foreground, and so on. It is a characteristic of human beings throughout their whole lives that they are practically always desiring something. We are faced then with the necessity for studying the relationships of all the motivations to each other and we are concomitantly faced with the necessity of giving up the motivational units in isolation if we are to achieve the broad understanding that we seek. The appearance of the drive or desire, the actions that it arouses, and the satisfaction that comes from attaining the goal object, all taken together, give us only an artificial, isolated, single instance taken out of the total complex of the motivational unit. This appearance practically always depends on the state of satisfaction or dissatisfaction of all other motivations that the total organism may have, that is on the fact that such and such other prepotent desires have attained states of relative satisfaction. Wanting anything in itself implies already existing satisfactions of other wants. We should never have the desire to compose music or create mathematical systems, or to adorn our homes, or to be well dressed if our stomachs were empty most of the time, or if we were continually dying of thirst, or if we were continually threatened by an always-impending catastrophe, or if everyone hated us. There are two important facts here: first, that the human being is never satisfied except in a relative or one-step-along-the-path fashion, and second, that wants seem to arrange themselves in some sort of hierarchy of prepotency.

IMPOSSIBILITY OF LISTING DRIVES

We should give up the attempt once and for all to make atomistic lists of drives or needs. For several different reasons such lists are theoretically unsound. First of all, they imply an equality of the various drives that are listed, an equality of potency and probability of appearance. This is incorrect because the probability of any one desire emerging into consciousness depends on the state of satisfaction or dissatisfaction of other prepotent desires. There are great differences in probability of appearance of the various particular drives.

Second, such a listing implies an isolatedness of each of these drives from each of the others. Of course they are not isolated in any such fashion.

Third, such a listing of drives, since it is usually made on a behavioral basis, neglects completely all that we know about the dynamic nature of drives, for example, that their conscious and unconscious aspects may be different and that a particular desire may actually be a channel through which several other desires express themselves.

Such listings are foolish because drives do not arrange themselves in an arithmetical sum of isolated, discrete members. They arrange themselves rather in a hierarchy of specificity. What is meant by this is that the number of drives one chooses to list depends entirely on the degree of specificity with which one chooses to analyze them. The true picture is not one of a great many sticks lying side by side, but rather of a nest of boxes in which 1 box contains 3 others, and in which each of these 3 contains 10 others, and in which each of these 10 contains 50 others, and so on. Or another analogy might be that of a description of a histological section under various degrees of magnification. Thus we can speak of a need for gratification or equilibrium, or more specifically of a need to eat, or still more specifically of a need to fill the stomach, or still more specifically of a desire for proteins, or still more specifically of a desire for a particular protein, and so on. Too many of the listings that we now have available have indiscriminately combined needs at various levels of magnification. With such a confusion it is understandable that some lists should contain three or four needs and others contain hundreds of needs. If we wished, we could have such a list of drives contain anywhere from one to a million drives, depending entirely on the specificity of analysis. Furthermore, it should be recognized that if we attempt to discuss the fundamental desires they should be clearly understood as sets of desires, as fundamental categories or *collections* of desires. In other words, such an enumeration of fundamental goals would be an abstract classification rather than a cataloguing list (Angyal, 1965).

Furthermore, all the lists of drives that have ever been published seem to imply mutual exclusiveness among the various drives. But there is not mutual exclusiveness. There is usually such an overlapping that it is almost impossible to separate quite clearly and sharply any one drive from any other. It should also be pointed out in any critique of drive theory that the very concept of drive itself probably emerges from a preoccupation with the physiological needs. It is very easy in dealing with these needs to separate the instigation, the motivated behavior, and the goal object. But it is not easy to distinguish the drive from the goal object when we talk of a desire for love. Here the drive, the desire, the goal object, the activity seem all to be the same thing.

CLASSIFYING MOTIVATION ACCORDING TO FUNDAMENTAL GOALS

The weight of evidence now available seems to indicate that the only sound and fundamental basis on which any classification of motivational life may be constructed is that of the fundamental goals or needs, rather than any listing of drives in the ordinary sense of instigation (the "pulls" rather than the "pushes"). It is only the fundamental goals that remain constant through all the flux that a dynamic approach forces upon psychological theorizing.

Certainly motivated behavior is not a good basis for classification, since we have seen that it may express many things. The specific goal object is not a good basis for classification for the same reason. A human being having a desire for food, behaving in the proper fashion to get it, and then chewing and eating it may actually be seeking safety rather than food. An individual going through the whole process of sexual desire, courting behavior, and consummatory love making may actually be seeking self-esteem rather than sexual gratification. The drive as it appears introspectively in consciousness, the motivated behavior, and even the explicitly apparent goal objects or effects sought for are none of them a sound foundation on which to base a dynamic classification of the motivational life of the human being. If only by the process of logical exclusion alone we are finally left with the largely unconscious fundamental goals or needs as the only sound foundations for classification in motivation theory.

INADEQUACY OF ANIMAL DATA

Academic psychologists have relied largely on animal experimentation in working in the field of motivation. It is a truism to say that a white rat is not a human being, but unfortunately it is necessary to say it again, since too often the results of animal experiments are considered the basic data on which we must base our theorizing of human nature. Animal data certainly can be of great use, but only when they are used cautiously and wisely.

There are certain further considerations that are pertinent to the contention that motivation theory must be anthropocentric rather than animalcentric. First let us discuss the concept of instinct, which we can define rigidly as a motivational unit in which the drive, motivated behavior, and the goal object or the goal effect are all appreciably determined by heredity. As we go up the phyletic scale there is a steady trend toward disappearance of the instincts so defined. For instance, in the white rat it is fair to say that, by our definition, there are found the hunger instinct, the sex instinct, and the maternal instinct. In the monkey the sexual instinct has definitely disappeared, the hunger instinct has clearly been modified in various ways, and only the maternal instinct is undoubtedly present. In the human being, by our definition, they have all three disappeared, leaving in their place conglomerations of hereditary reflexes, hereditary drives, autogenous learning, and cultural learning in the motivated behavior and in the choice of goal objects (see Chapter 4). Thus if we examine the sexual life of the human being we find that sheer drive itself is given by heredity but that the choice of object and the choice of behavior must be acquired or learned in the course of the life history.

As we go up the phyletic scale appetites become more and more important and hungers less and less important. That is to say there is much less variability, for instance, in the choice of food in the white rat than there is in the monkey, and there is less variability in the monkey than there is in the human being (Maslow, 1935).

Finally as we go up the phyletic scale and as the instincts drop away there is more and more dependence on the culture as an adaptive tool. If then we have to use animal data let us realize these facts and, for instance, let us prefer the monkey to the white rat as a subject for motivation experiments if only for the simple reason that we human beings are much more like monkeys than we are like white rats, as Harlow (1952) and many other primatologists (Howells and Vine, 1940) have amply demonstrated. Reliance on animal data has contributed to an arbitrary exclusion of the concept of purpose or goal from motivation theory (Young, 1941). Because we cannot ask rats for their purpose, is it necessary to point out that we *can* ask human beings for their purpose? Instead of rejecting purpose or goal as a concept because we cannot ask rats about it, it would seem much more sensible to reject rats because we cannot ask them about their purpose.

ENVIRONMENT

So far we have spoken only of the nature of the organism itself. It is now necessary to say at least a word about the situation or environment in which the organism finds itself. We must certainly grant at once that human motivation rarely actualizes itself in behavior except in relation to the situation and to other people. Any theory of motivation must of course take account of this fact by including the role of cultural determination in both the environment and the organism itself.

Once this is granted it remains to caution against too great a preoccupation with the exterior, the culture, the environment, or the situation. Our central object of study here is, after all, the organism or the character structure. It is easy to go to the extreme in situation theory of making the organism just one additional object in the field, equivalent with perhaps a barrier or some object that it tries to obtain. We must remember that individuals partly *create* their barriers and their objects of value, that they must be defined partially in terms set by the particular organism in the situation. We know of no way of defining or describing a field universally in such a way that this description can be independent of the particular organism functioning within it. It certainly must be pointed out that a child who is trying to attain a certain object of value to him or her, but who is restrained by a barrier of some sort, determines not only that the object is of value, but also that the barrier is a barrier. Psychologically there is no such thing as a barrier; there is only a barrier for a particular person who is trying to get something that he or she wants.

A theory that stresses constant fundamental needs finds them to be relatively constant and more independent of the particular situation in which the organism finds itself. For not only does the need organize its action possibilities, so to speak, in the most efficient way feasible and with a great deal of variation, but it also organizes and even creates the external reality. Another way of saying this is that the only satisfactory way of understanding how a geographical environment becomes a psychological environment is to understand that the principle of organization of the psychological environment is the current goal of the organism in that particular environment.

Sound motivation theory must then take account of the situation, but must never become pure situation theory, that is, unless we are explicitly willing to give up our search for an understanding of the nature of the constancy of the organism in favor of understanding the world it lives in. Let us stress that we are now concerned, not with behavior theory, but with motivation theory. Behavior is determined by several classes of determinants, of which motivation is one and environmental forces are another. The study of motivation does not negate or deny the study of situational determinants, but rather supplements it. They both have their places in a larger structure.

INTEGRATED ACTION

Any motivation theory must take account not only of the fact that the organism behaves ordinarily as an integrated whole, but also of the fact that sometimes it does not. There are specific isolated conditionings and habits to account for, segmental responses of various kinds, and a host of phenomena of dissocation and lack of integration that we know about. The organism furthermore can even react in a nonunitary fashion in daily life as when we do many things at the same time.

Apparently the organism is most unified in its integration when it is successfully facing either a great joy or creative moment or else a major problem or a threat or emergency. But when the threat is overwhelming or when the organism is too weak or helpless to manage it, it tends to disintegrate. On the whole, when life is easy and successful the organism can simultaneously do many things and turn in many directions.

It is our belief that a fair share of the phenomena that seem to be specific and isolated actually are not. Often it is possible to demonstrate with deeper analysis that they take a meaningful place in the whole structure (e.g., conversion hysterical symptoms). This apparent lack of integration may sometimes be simply a reflection of our own ignorance, but we also know enough now to be sure that isolated, segmental, or unintegrated responses are possible under certain circumstances. Furthermore it is now becoming more and more clear that such phenomena are not necessarily to be regarded as weak or bad or pathological. Rather they are often to be regarded as evidence of one of the most important capacities of the organism, that is, to deal with unimportant or with familiar or with easily conquered problems in a partial, specific, or segmental fashion so that the main capacities of the organism are still left free for the more important or more challenging problems that it faces (Goldstein, 1939).

UNMOTIVATED BEHAVIORS

Not all behaviors or reactions are motivated, at least not in the ordinary sense of seeking need gratifications, that is seeking for what is lacked or needed. The phenomena of maturation, of expression, and of growth or self-actualization are all instances of exceptions to the rule of universal motivation, and had much better be considered expression rather than coping. They will be discussed at length later, especially in Chapter 6.

In addition, Norman Maier (1949) has forcibly called our attention to a distinction often implied by the Freudians. Most neurotic symptoms or trends amount to basic-need-gratification-bent impulses that have somehow got stymied or misdirected or confused with other needs or fixated on the wrong means. Other symptoms, however, are no longer gratification-bent but are simply protective or defensive. They have no goal but to prevent further hurt or threat or frustration. The difference is like that between the fighter who still hopes to win and the one who has no hope of winning, trying only to lose as painlessly as possible.

Since giving up and hopelessness are very definitely of considerable relevance to prognosis in therapy, to expectations of learning, even probably to longevity, this differentiation must be handled by any definitive motivation theory.

POSSIBILITY OF ATTAINMENT

Dewey (1939) and Thorndike (1940) have stressed one important aspect of motivation that has been completely neglected by most psychologists, namely, possibility. On the whole we yearn consciously for that which might conceivably be actually attained.

As their income increases people find themselves actively wishing for and striving for things that they never dreamed of a few years before. The average Americans yearn for automobiles, refrigerators, and television sets because these are real possibilities; they do not yearn for yachts or planes because these are in fact not within the reach of the average Americans. It is quite probable that they do not long for them *unconsciously* either.

Attention to this factor of possibility of attainment is crucial for understanding the differences in motivations among various classes and castes within a given population and among different countries and cultures.

REALITY AND THE UNCONSCIOUS

Related to this problem is that of the influence of reality on unconscious impulses. For Freud, an id impulse is a discrete entity having no intrinsic relatedness to anything else in the world, not even other id impulses.

> We can come nearer to the id with images, and call it a chaos, a cauldron of seething excitement. . . . These instincts fill it with energy, but it has no organization and no unified will, only an impulsion to obtain satisfaction for the instinctual needs, in accordance with the pleasure principle. The laws of logic—above all, the law of contradiction—do not hold for processes in the id. Contradictory impulses exist side by side without neutralizing each other or drawing apart; at most they combine in compromise formations under the overpowering economic pressure towards discharging their energy. There is nothing in the id which can be compared to negation, and we are astonished

to find in it an exception to the philosophers' assertion that space and time are necessary forms of our mental acts. . . .

Naturally, the id knows no values, no good and evil, no morality. The economic, or, if you prefer, the quantitative factor, which is so closely bound up with the pleasure-principle, dominates all its processes. Instinctual cathexes seeking discharge—that, in our view, is all that the id contains. (Freud, 1933, pp. 103–105)

To the extent that these impulses are controlled, modified, or held back from discharge by reality conditions, they become part of the ego rather than the id.

One can hardly go wrong in regarding the ego as that part of the id which has been modified by its proximity to the external world and the influence that the latter has had on it, and which serves the purpose of receiving stimuli and protecting the organism from them, like the cortical layer with which a particle of living substance surrounds itself. This relation to the external world is decisive for the ego. The ego has taken over the task of representing the external world for the id and so of saving it; for the id, blindly striving to gratify its instincts in complete disregard of the superior strength of the outside forces, could not otherwise escape annihilation. In the fulfillment of this function, the ego has to observe the external world and preserve a true picture of it in the memory traces left by its perceptions, and, by means of the reality-test, it has to eliminate any element in this picture of the external world which is a contribution from internal sources of excitation. On behalf of the id, the ego controls the path of access to motility, but it interpolates between desire and action, the procrastinating factor of thought, during which it makes use of the residues of experience stored up in memory. In this way it dethrones the pleasure-principle, which exerts undisputed sway over the processes in the id, and substitutes for it the reality-principle, which promises greater security and greater success. (Freud, 1933, p. 106)

It is, however, John Dewey's contention that all impulses in the adult—or at least the characteristic impulse—are integrated with and affected by reality. In a word, this is the equivalent of maintaining that there are no id impulses, or, reading between the lines, if there are, that they are intrinsically pathological rather than intrinsically healthy.

This contradiction is noted here, even though no empirical solution can be offered, because it is a crucial, head-on difference.

As it appears to us, the question is not whether there exist id impulses of the sort Freud describes. Any psychoanalyst will testify to the occurrence of fantasy impulses that exist without regard to reality, common sense, logic, or even personal advantage. The question is whether they are evidences of sickness or of regression or revelation of the inmost core of the healthy human being? At what point in the life history does the infantile fantasy begin to be modified by perception of reality? Is it the same for all, neurotic and healthy alike? Can the efficiently functioning human being maintain completely free of such influence any hidden corner of his impulse life? Or if it does turn out that such impulses, completely intraorganismic in origin, *do* exist in all of us, then we must ask:

When do they appear? Under what conditions? Are they necessarily the trouble-makers that Freud assumed them to be? *Must* they be in opposition to reality?

MOTIVATION OF HIGHEST HUMAN CAPACITIES

Most of what we know of human motivation comes not from psychologists but from psychotherapists treating patients. These patients are a great source of error as well as of useful data, for they obviously constitute a poor sample of the population. The motivational life of neurotic sufferers should, even in principle, be rejected as a paradigm for healthy motivation. Health is not simply the absence of disease or even the opposite of it. Any theory of motivation that is worthy of attention must deal with the highest capacities of the healthy and strong person as well as with the defensive maneuvers of crippled spirits. The most important concerns of the greatest and finest people in human history must all be encompassed and explained.

This understanding we shall never get from sick people alone. We must turn our attention to healthy men and women as well. Motivation theorists must become more positive in their orientation.

chapter 2

A Theory of Human Motivation

This chapter is an attempt to formulate a positive theory of motivation that will satisfy the theoretical demands listed in the previous chapter and at the same time conform to the known facts, clinical and observational as well as experimental. It derives most directly, however, from clinical experience. This theory is in the functionalist tradition of James and Dewey, and is fused with the holism of Wertheimer, Goldstein, and Gestalt psychology and with the dynamism of Freud, Fromm, Horney, Reich, Jung, and Adler. This integration or synthesis may be called a holistic-dynamic theory.

THE BASIC NEED HIERARCHY

The Physiological Needs

The needs that are usually taken as the starting point for motivation theory are the so-called physiological drives. Two lines of research make it necessary to revise our customary notions about these needs: first, the development of the concept of homeostasis and second, the finding that appetites (preferential choices among foods) are a fairly efficient indication of actual needs or lacks in the body.

Homeostasis refers to the body's automatic efforts to maintain a constant, normal state of the blood stream. Cannon (1932) described this process for (1) the water content of the blood, (2) salt content, (3) sugar content, (4) protein content, (5) fat content, (6) calcium content, (7) oxygen content, (8) constant hydrogen-ion level (acid-base balance), and (9) constant temperature of the blood. Obviously this list could be extended to include other minerals, the hormones, vitamins, and so on.

Young (1941, 1948) summarized the work on appetite in its relation to body needs. If the body lacks some chemical, the individual will tend (in an imperfect way) to develop a specific appetite or partial hunger for that missing food element.

Thus it seems impossible as well as useless to make any list of fundamental physiological needs, for they can come to almost any number one might wish, depending on the degree of specificity of description. We cannot identify all physiological needs as homeostatic. That sexual desire, sleepiness, sheer activity and exercise, and maternal behavior in animals are homeostatic has not yet been demonstrated. Furthermore, this list would not include the various sensory pleasures (tastes, smells, tickling, stroking), which are probably physiological and which may become the goals of motivated behavior. Nor do we know what to make of the fact that the organism has simultaneously a tendency to inertia, laziness, and least effort and *also* a need for activity, stimulation, and excitement.

In the previous chapter it was pointed out that these physiological drives or needs are to be considered unusual rather than typical because they are isolable and because they are localizable somatically. That is to say, they are relatively independent of each other, of other motivations, and of the organism as a whole, and, in many cases, it is possible to demonstrate a localized, underlying somatic base for the drive. This is true less generally than has been thought (exceptions are fatigue, sleepiness, maternal responses) but it is still true in the classic instances of hunger, sex, and thirst.

It should be pointed out again that any of the physiological needs and the consummatory behavior involved with them serve as channels for all sorts of other needs as well. That is to say, the person who thinks he or she is hungry may actually be seeking more for comfort, or dependence, than for vitamins or proteins. Conversely, it is possible to satisfy the hunger need in part by other activities such as drinking water or smoking cigarettes. In other words, relatively isolable as these physiological needs are, they are not completely so.

Undoubtedly these physiological needs are the most prepotent of all needs. What this means specifically is that in the human being who is missing everything in life in an extreme fashion, it is most likely that the major motivation would be the physiological needs rather than any others. A person who is lacking food, safety, love, and esteem would most probably hunger for food more strongly than for anything else.

If all the needs are unsatisfied, and the organism is then dominated by the physiological needs, all other needs may become simply nonexistent or be pushed into the background. It is then fair to characterize the whole organism by saying simply that it is hungry, for consciousness is almost completely preempted by hunger. All capacities are put into the service of hunger satisfaction, and the organization of these capacities is almost entirely determined by the one purpose of satisfying hunger. The receptors and effectors, the intelligence, memory, habits, all may now be defined simply as hunger-gratifying tools. Capacities that are not useful for this purpose lie dormant, or are pushed into the background. The urge to write poetry, the desire to acquire an automobile, the interest in American history, the desire for a new pair of shoes are, in the extreme case, forgotten or become of secondary importance. For the human who is extremely and dangerously hungry, no other interests exist but food. He or she dreams food, remembers food, thinks about food, emotes only about food, perceives only food, and wants only food. The more subtle determinants that ordinarily fuse with the physiological drives in organizing even feeding, drinking, or sexual behavior, may now be so completely overwhelmed as to allow us to speak at this time (but *only* at this time) of pure hunger drive and behavior, with the one unqualified aim of relief.

Another peculiar characteristic of the human organism when it is dominated by a certain need is that the whole philosophy of the future tends also to change. For our chronically and extremely hungry person, Utopia can be defined simply as a place where there is plenty of food. He or she tends to think that, if only guaranteed food for the rest of life, he or she will be perfectly happy and will never want anything more. Life itself tends to be defined in terms of eating. Anything else will be defined as unimportant. Freedom, love, community feeling, respect, philosophy, may all be waved aside as fripperies that are useless, since they fail to fill the stomach. Such a person may fairly be said to live by bread alone.

It cannot possibly be denied that such things are true, but their *generality* can be denied. Emergency conditions are, almost by definition, rare in the normally functioning peaceful society. That this truism can be forgotten is attributable mainly to two reasons. First, rats have few motivations other than physiological ones, and since so much of the research on motivation has been made with these animals, it is easy to carry the rat picture over to the human being. Second, it is too often not realized that culture itself is an adaptive tool, one of whose main functions is to make the physiological emergencies come less and less often. In the United States, chronic extreme hunger of the emergency type is rare, rather than common. Average American citizens are experiencing appetite rather than hunger when they say, "I am hungry." They are apt to experience sheer life-and-death hunger only by accident and then only a few times through their entire lives.

Obviously a good way to obscure the higher motivations, and to get a lopsided view of human capacities and human nature, is to make the organism extremely and chronically hungry or thirsty. Anyone who attempts to make an emergency picture into a typical one and who will measure all of humanity's goals and desires by behavior during extreme physiological deprivation is certainly being blind to many things. It is quite true that humans live by bread alone—when there is no bread. But what happens to their desires when there *is* plenty of bread and when their bellies are chronically filled?

Dynamics of the Need Hierarchy

At once other (and higher) needs emerge and these, rather than physiological hungers, dominate the organism. And when these in turn are satisfied, again new (and still higher) needs emerge, and so on. This is what we mean by saying that the basic human needs are organized into a hierarchy of relative prepotency. One main implication of this phrasing is that gratification becomes as important a concept as deprivation in motivation theory, for it releases the organism from the domination of a relatively more physiological need, permitting thereby the emergence of other more social goals. The physiological needs, along with their partial goals, when chronically gratified cease to exist as active determinants or organizers of behavior. They now exist only in a potential fashion in the sense that they may emerge again to dominate the organism if they are thwarted. But a want that is satisfied is no longer a want. The organism is dominated and its behavior organized only by unsatisfied needs. If hunger is satisfied, it becomes unimportant in the current dynamics of the individual.

This statement is somewhat qualified by a hypothesis to be discussed more fully later, namely, that it is precisely those individuals in whom a certain need has always been satisfied who are best equipped to tolerate deprivation of that need in the future and that, furthermore, those who have been deprived in the past will react differently to current satisfactions from the one who has never been deprived.

The Safety Needs

If the physiological needs are relatively well gratified, there then emerges a new set of needs, which we may categorize roughly as the safety needs (security; stability; dependency; protection; freedom from fear, anxiety, and chaos; need for structure, order, law, and limits; strength in the protector; and so on). All that has been said of the physiological needs is equally true, although in less degree, of these desires. The organism may equally well be wholly dominated by them. They may serve as the almost exclusive organizers of behavior, recruiting all the capacities of the organism in their service, and we may then fairly describe the whole organism as a safety-seeking mechanism. Again we may say of the receptors, the effectors, the intellect, and the other capacities that they are primarily safety-seeking tools. Again, as in the hungry human, we find that the dominating goal is a strong determinant not only of their current world outlook and philosophy but also of their philosophy of the future and of values. Practically everything looks less important than safety and protection (even sometimes the physiological needs, which, being satisfied, are now underestimated). A person in this state, if it is extreme enough and chronic enough, may be characterized as living almost for safety alone.

However, the healthy and fortunate adults in our culture are largely satisfied in their safety needs. The peaceful, smoothly running, stable, good society ordinarily makes its members feel safe enough from wild animals, extremes of temperature, criminal assault, murder, chaos, tyranny, and so on. Therefore, in a very real sense, they no longer have any safety needs as active motivators. Just as a sated person no longer feels hungry, a safe one no longer feels endangered. If we wish to see these needs directly and clearly we must turn to neurotic or near-neurotic individuals, and to the economic and social underdogs, or else to social chaos, revolution, or breakdown of authority. In between these extremes, we can perceive the expressions of safety needs only in such phenomena as, for instance, the common preference for a job with tenure and protection, the desire for a saving account, and for insurance of various kinds (medical, dental, unemployment, disability, old age).

Other, broader aspects of the attempt to seek safety and stability in the world are seen in the very common preference for familiar rather than unfamiliar things (Maslow, 1937), or for the known rather than the unknown. The tendency to have some religion or world philosophy that organizes the universe and the people in it into some sort of satisfactorily coherent, meaningful whole is also in part motivated by safety seeking. Here too we may list science and philosophy in general as partially motivated by the safety needs (we shall see later that there are also other motivations to scientific, philosophical, or religious endeavor).

Otherwise the need for safety is seen as an active and dominant mobilizer of the organism's resources only in real emergencies, such as war, disease, natural catastrophes, crime waves, societal disorganization, neurosis, brain injury, breakdown of authority, or chronically bad situations. Some neurotic adults in our society are, in many ways, like unsafe children in their desire for safety. Their reactions are often to unknown psychological dangers in a world that is perceived to be hostile, overwhelming, and threatening. Such people behave as if a great catastrophe were almost always impending—they are usually responding as if to an emergency. Their safety needs often find specific expression in a search for a protector, or a stronger person or system, on whom they may depend. It is as if their childish attitudes of fear and threat reaction to a dangerous world have gone underground and, untouched by the growing-up and learning processes, remain ready even now to be called out by any stimulus that would make a child feel endangered. Horney (1937), in particular, has written well about "basic anxiety."

The neurosis in which the search for safety takes its clearest form is in the compulsive-obsessive neurosis.[1] Compulsive-obsessives try frantically to order and stabilize the world so that no unmanageable, unexpected, or unfamiliar dangers will ever appear. They hedge themselves about with all sorts of ceremonials, rules, and formulas so that every possible contingency may be provided for and so that no new contingencies may appear. They manage to maintain their equilibrium by avoiding everything unfamiliar and strange and by ordering their restricted world in such a neat, disciplined, orderly fashion that everything in the world can be counted on. They try to arrange the world so that anything unexpected (dangers) cannot possibly occur. If, through no fault of their own, something unexpected does occur, they go into a panic reaction as if this unexpected occurrence constituted a grave danger. What we can see only as a none-too-strong preference in the healthy person (e.g., preference for the familiar) becomes a life-and-death necessity in abnormal cases. The healthy taste for the novel and unknown is missing or at a minimum in the average neurotic.

The safety needs can become very urgent on the social scene whenever there are real threats to law, to order, to the authority of society. The threat of chaos or of nihilism can be expected in most human beings to produce a regression from any higher needs to the more prepotent safety needs. A common, almost an expectable reaction, is the easier acceptance of dictatorship or of military rule. This tends to be true for all human beings, including healthy ones, since they too

---

[1]Not all neurotic individuals feel unsafe. Neurosis may have at its core a thwarting of the affection and esteem needs in a person who is generally safe.

will tend to respond to danger with realistic regression to the safety need level and will prepare to defend themselves. But it seems to be most true of people who are living near the safety line. They are particularly disturbed by threats to authority, to legality, and to the representatives of the law.

The Belongingness and Love Needs

If both the physiological and the safety needs are fairly well gratified, there will emerge the love and affection and belongingness needs, and the whole cycle already described will repeat itself with this new center. The love needs involve giving and receiving affection. When they are unsatisfied, a person will feel keenly the absence of friends, mate, or children. Such a person will hunger for relations with people in general—for a place in the group or family—and will strive with great intensity to achieve this goal. Attaining such a place will matter more than anything else in the world and he or she may even forget that once, when hunger was foremost, love seemed unreal, unnecessary, and unimportant. Now the pangs of loneliness, ostracism, rejection, friendlessness, and rootlessness are preeminent.

We have very little scientific information about the belongingness need, although this is a common theme in novels, autobiographies, poems, and plays and also in the newer sociological literature. From these we know in a general way the destructive effects on children of moving too often; of disorientation; of the general overmobility that is forced by industrialization; of being without roots, or of despising one's roots, one's origins, one's group; of being torn from one's home and family, friends, and neighbors; of being a transient or a newcomer rather than a native. We still underplay the deep importance of the neighborhood, of one's territory, of one's clan, of one's own "kind," one's class, one's gang, one's familiar working colleagues. And we have largely forgotten our deep animal tendencies to herd, to flock, to join, to belong.[2]

I believe that the tremendous and rapid increase in training groups (T-groups), personal growth groups, and intentional communities may in part be motivated by this unsatisfied hunger for contact, intimacy, and belongingness. Such social phenomena may arise to overcome the widespread feelings of alienation, strangeness, and loneliness that have been worsened by increasing mobility, the breakdown of traditional groupings, the scattering of families, the generation gap, and steady urbanization. My strong impression is also that *some* proportion of youth rebellion groups—I don't know how many or how much—is motivated by the profound hunger for group feelings, for contact, for real togetherness in the face of a common enemy, *any* enemy that can serve to form an amity group simply by posing an external threat. The same kind of thing has been observed in groups of soldiers who were pushed into an unwonted brotherliness and intimacy by their common external danger, and who may stick together throughout a lifetime as a consequence. Any good society must satisfy this need, one way or another, if it is to survive and be healthy.

---

[2]Ardrey's *Territorial Imperative* (1966) will help to make all of this conscious. Its very rashness was good for me because it stressed as crucial what I had been only casual about and forced me to think seriously about the matter. Perhaps it will do the same for other readers.

In our society the thwarting of these needs is the most commonly found core in cases of maladjustment and more severe pathology. Love and affection, as well as their possible expression in sexuality, are generally looked upon with ambivalence and are customarily hedged about with many restrictions and inhibitions. Practically all theorists of psychopathology have stressed thwarting of the love needs as basic in the picture of maladjustment. Many clinical studies have therefore been made of this need, and we know more about it perhaps than any of the other needs except the physiological ones. Suttie (1935) has written an excellent analysis of our "taboo on tenderness."

One thing that must be stressed at this point is that love is not synonymous with sex. Sex may be studied as a purely physiological need, although ordinarily human sexual behavior is multidetermined. That is to say, it is determined not only by sexual but also by other needs, chief among which are the love and affection needs. Also not to be overlooked is the fact that the love needs involve both giving *and* receiving love.

The Esteem Needs

All people in our society (with a few pathological exceptions) have a need or desire for a stable, firmly based, usually high evaluation of themselves, for self-respect or self-esteem, and for the esteem of others. These needs may therefore be classified into two subsidiary sets. These are, first, the desire for strength, achievement, adequacy, mastery and competence, confidence in the face of the world, and independence and freedom.[3] Second, we have what we may call the desire for reputation or prestige (defining it as respect or esteem from other people), status, fame and glory, dominance, recognition, attention, importance, dignity, or appreciation. These needs have been relatively stressed by Alfred Adler and his followers, and have been relatively neglected by Freud. More and more today, however, there is appearing widespread appreciation of their central importance among psychoanalysts as well as among clinical psychologists.

Satisfaction of the self-esteem need leads to feelings of self-confidence, worth, strength, capability, and adequacy, of being useful and necessary in the world. But thwarting of these needs produces feelings of inferiority, of weakness, and of helplessness. These feelings in turn give rise to either basic discouragement or else compensatory or neurotic trends.

From the theologians' discussion of pride and *hubris,* from the Frommian theories about the self-perception of untruth to one's own nature, from the Rogerian work with self, from essayists like Ayn Rand (1943), and from other sources as well, we have been learning more and more of the dangers of basing self-esteem on the opinions of others rather than on real capacity, competence,

[3]Whether or not this particular desire is universal we do not know. The crucial question, especially important today, is: Will men who are enslaved and dominated inevitably feel dissatisfied and rebellious? We may assume on the basis of commonly known clinical data that people who have known true freedom (not paid for by giving up safety and security but rather built on the basis of adequate safety and security) will not willingly or easily allow their freedom to be taken away from them. But we do not know for sure that this is true for people born into slavery. See discussion of this problem in Fromm (1941).

and adequacy to the task. The most stable and therefore most healthy self-esteem is based on *deserved* respect from others rather than on external fame or celebrity and unwarranted adulation. Even here it is helpful to distinguish the actual competence and achievement that is based on sheer will power, determination, and responsibility from that which comes naturally and easily out of one's own true inner nature, one's constitution, one's biological fate or destiny, or, as Horney puts it, out of one's Real Self rather than out of the idealized pseudo-self (1950).

The Self-actualization Need

Even if all these needs are satisfied, we may still often (if not always) expect that a new discontent and restlessness will soon develop, unless the individual is doing what *he* or *she,* individually, is fitted for. Musicians must make music, artists must paint, poets must write if they are to be ultimately at peace with themselves. What humans *can* be, they *must* be. They must be true to their own nature. This need we may call self-actualization. (See Chapters 11, 12, and 13 for a fuller description.)

This term, first coined by Kurt Goldstein (1939), is being used in this book in a much more specific and limited fashion. It refers to people's desire for self-fulfillment, namely, the tendency for them to become actualized in what they are potentially. This tendency might be phrased as the desire to become more and more what one idiosyncratically is, to become everything that one is capable of becoming.

The specific form that these needs will take of course vary greatly from person to person. In one individual they may take the form of the desire to be an excellent parent, in another they may be expressed athletically, and in still another they may be expressed in painting pictures or in inventing things.[4] At this level, individual differences are greatest. However, the comon feature of the needs for self-actualization is that their emergence usually rests upon some prior satisfaction of the physiological, safety, love, and esteem needs.

Preconditions of the Basic Needs

There are certain conditions that are immediate prerequisites for the basic need satisfactions. Such conditions as freedom to speak, freedom to do what one wishes so long as no harm is done to others, freedom to express oneself, freedom to investigate and seek for information, freedom to defend oneself, justice, fairness, honesty, and orderliness in the group are examples of such preconditions for basic need satisfactions. These conditions are not ends in themselves but they are *almost* so since they are so closely related to the basic needs, which are apparently the only ends in themselves. Danger to these freedoms is reacted to with emergency

---

[4]Clearly, creative behavior is like any other behavior in having multiple determinants. It may be seen in innately creative people whether they are satisfied or not, happy or unhappy, hungry or sated. Also it is clear that creative activity may be compensatory, ameliorative, or purely economic. In any case, here too we must distinguish, in a dynamic fashion, the overt behavior itself from its various motivations or purposes.

response as if there were direct danger to the basic needs themselves. These conditions are defended because without them the basic satisfactions are quite impossible, or at least severely endangered.

If we remember that the cognitive capacities (perceptual, intellectual, learning) are a set of adjustive tools, which have among other functions that of satisfaction of our basic needs, then it is clear that any danger to them, any deprivation or blocking of their free use, must also be indirectly threatening to the basic needs themselves. Such a statement is a partial solution of the general problems of curiosity, the search for knowledge, truth, and wisdom, and the ever-persistent urge to solve the cosmic mysteries. Secrecy, censorship, dishonesty, and blocking of communication threaten *all* the basic needs.

THE BASIC COGNITIVE NEEDS

The Desires to Know and to Understand

The main reason we know little about the cognitive impulses, their dynamics, or their pathology is that they are not important in the clinic, and certainly not in the clinic dominated by the medical-therapeutic tradition of getting rid of disease. The florid, exciting, and mysterious symptoms found in the classical neuroses are lacking here. Cognitive psychopathology is pale, subtle, and easily overlooked or defined as normal. It does not cry for help. As a consequence we find nothing on the subject in the writings of the great inventors of psychotherapy and psychodynamics, Freud, Adler, Jung, and others.

Schilder is the only major psychoanalyst I know in whose writings curiosity and understanding are seen dynamically.[5] So far, we have mentioned the cognitive needs only in passing. Acquiring knowledge and systematizing the universe have been considered as, in part, techniques for the achievement of basic safety in the world, or for the intelligent person, expressions of self-actualization. Also freedom of inquiry and expression have been discussed as preconditions of satisfaction of the basic needs. Useful though these formulations may be, they do not constitute definitive answers to the questions as to the motivational role of curiosity, learning, philosophizing, experimenting, and so on. They are at best no more than partial answers.

Above and beyond these negative determinants for acquiring knowledge (anxiety, fear), there are some reasonable grounds for postulating positive per se impulses to satisfy curiosity, to know, to explain, and to understand (Maslow, 1968).

1. Something like human curiosity can easily be observed in the higher animals. The monkey will pick things apart, will poke its finger into

[5]"However, human beings have a genuine interest in the world, in action, and in experimentation. They derive a deep satisfaction when they venture into the world. They do not experience reality as a threat to existence. Organisms, and especially human organisms, have a genuine feeling of safety and security in this world. Threats come merely from specific situations and deprivations. Even then, discomfort and danger are experienced as passing points, which finally leads to a security and safety in touch with the world" (Schilder, 1942).

holes, will explore in all sorts of situations where it is improbable that hunger, fear, sex, comfort status, and so on are involved. Harlow's experiments (1950) have amply demonstrated this in an acceptably experimental way.

2. The history of humanity supplies us with a satisfactory number of instances in which people looked for facts and created explanations in the face of the greatest danger, even to life itself. There have been innumerable humbler Galileos.

3. Studies of psychologically healthy people indicate that they are, as a defining characteristic, attracted to the mysterious, to the unknown, to the chaotic, unorganized, and unexplained. This seems to be a per se attractiveness; these areas are in themselves and of their own right interesting. The contrasting reaction to the well known is one of boredom.

4. It may be found valid to extrapolate from the psychopathological. The compulsive-obsessive neurotic shows (at the clinical level of observation) a compulsive and anxious clinging to the familiar and a dread of the unfamiliar, the anarchic, the unexpected, the undomesticated. On the other hand, there are some phenomena that may turn out to nullify this possibility. Among these are forced unconventionality, a chronic rebellion against any authority whatsoever, and the desire to shock and to startle, all of which may be found in certain neurotic individuals, as well as in those in the process of deacculturation.

5. Probably there are true psychopathological effects when the cognitive needs are frustrated (Maslow, 1967, 1968c). The following clinical impressions are also pertinent: I have seen a few cases in which it seemed clear that the pathology (boredom, loss of zest in life, self-dislike, general depression of the bodily functions, steady deterioration of the intellectual life and of tastes, and so on)[6] were produced in intelligent people leading stupid lives in stupid jobs. I had at least one case in which the appropriate cognitive therapy (resuming parttime studies, getting a position that was more intellectually demanding, insight) removed the symptoms. I have seen *many* women, intelligent, prosperous, and unoccupied, slowly develop these same symptoms of intellectual inanition. Those who followed the recommendation to immerse themselves in something worthy of them showed improvement or cure often enough to impress me with the reality of the cognitive needs. In those countries in which access to the news, to information, and to the facts were cut off, and in those where official theories were profoundly contradicted by obvious facts, at least some people responded with generalized cynicism, mistrust of *all* values, suspicion even of the obvious, a profound disruption of ordinary interpersonal relationships, hopelessness, loss of morale, and so on. Others seem to have responded in the more passive direction with dullness, submission, loss of capacity, coarctation, and loss of initiative.

6. The needs to know and to understand are seen in late infancy and childhood, perhaps even more strongly than in adulthood. Furthermore this seems to be a spontaneous product of maturation rather than of learning,

---

[6]This syndrome is very similar to what Ribot (1896) and later Myerson (1925) called *anhedonia* but which they ascribed to other sources.

however defined. Children do not have to be taught to be curious. But they *may* be taught, as by institutionalization, *not* to be curious.

7. Finally, the gratification of the cognitive impulses is subjectively satisfying and yields end-experience. Though this aspect of insight and understanding has been neglected in favor of achieved results, learning, and so on, it nevertheless remains true that insight is usually a bright, happy, emotional spot in any person's life, perhaps even a high spot in the life span. The overcoming of obstacles, the occurrence of pathology upon thwarting, the widespread occurrence (cross-species, cross-cultural), the never-dying (though weak) insistent pressure, the necessity of gratification of this need as a prerequisite for the fullest development of human potentialities, the spontaneous appearance in the early history of the individual, all these point to a basic cognitive need.

This postulation, however, is not enough. Even after we know, we are impelled to know more and more minutely and microscopically on the one hand, and on the other, more and more extensively in the direction of a world philosophy, theology, and so on. This process has been phrased by some as the search for meaning. We shall then postulate a desire to understand, to systematize, to organize, to analyze, to look for relations and meanings, to construct a system of values.

Once these desires are accepted for discussion, we see that they too form themselves into a small hierachy in which the desire to know is prepotent over the desire to understand. All the characteristics of a hierarchy of prepotency that we have described above seem to hold for this one as well.

We must guard ourselves against the too-easy tendency to separate these desires from the basic needs we have discussed above, that is, to make a sharp dichotomy between cognitive and conative needs. The desire to know and to understand are themselves conative (i.e., having a striving character) and are as much personality needs as the basic needs we have already discussed. Furthermore, as we have seen, the two hierarchies are interrelated rather than sharply separated and, as we shall see below, they are synergic rather than antagonistic. For further development of the ideas in this section, see Maslow, *Toward a Psychology of Being* (1968c).

The Aesthetic Needs

We know even less about these than about the others, and yet the testimony of history, of the humanities, and of aestheticians forbids us to bypass this area. Attempts to study this phenomenon on a clinical-personological basis with selected individuals have at least shown that in *some* individuals there is a truly basic aesthetic need. They get sick (in special ways) from ugliness, and are cured by beautiful surroundings; they *crave* actively, and their cravings can be satisfied *only* by beauty (Maslow, 1967). It is seen almost universally in healthy children. Some evidence of such an impulse is found in every culture and in every age as far back as the cave dwellers.

Much overlapping with conative and cognitive needs makes it impossible to separate them sharply. The needs for order, for symmetry, for closure, for completion of the act, for system, and for structure may be indiscriminately assigned to cognitive, conative, aesthetic, or even to neurotic needs.

CHARACTERISTICS OF THE BASIC NEEDS

Exceptions in the Hierarchy of Needs

We have spoken so far as if this hierarchy were a fixed order, but actually it is not nearly so rigid as we may have implied. It is true that most of the people with whom we have worked have seemed to have these basic needs in about the order that has been indicated. However, there have been a number of exceptions.

1. There are some people in whom, for instance, self-esteem seems to be more important than love. This most common reversal in the hierarchy is usually due to the development of the notion that the person who is most likely to be loved is a strong or powerful person, one who inspires respect or fear and who is self-confident or aggressive. Therefore such people who lack love and seek it may try hard to put on a front of aggressive, confident behavior. But essentially they seek high self-esteem and its behavior expressions more as a means to an end than for its own sake; they seek self-assertion for the sake of love rather than for self-esteem itself.

2. There are other apparently innately creative people in whom the drive to creativeness seems to be more important than any other counterdeterminant. Their creativeness might appear not as self-actualization released by basic satisfaction, but in spite of lack of basic satisfaction.

3. In certain people the level of aspiration may be permanently deadened or lowered. That is to say, the less prepotent goals may simply be lost and may disappear forever, so people who have experienced life at a very low level (e.g., chronic unemployment) may continue to be satisfied for the rest of their lives if only they can get enough food.

4. The so-called psychopathic personality is another example of permanent loss of the love needs. One understanding of this personality dysfunction is that there are people who have been starved for love in the earliest months of their lives and have simply lost forever the desire and the ability to give and to receive affection (as animals lose sucking or pecking reflexes that are not exercised soon enough after birth).

5. Another cause of reversal of the hierarchy is that when a need has been satisfied for a long time, this need may be underevaluated. People who have never experienced chronic hunger are apt to underestimate its effects and to look upon food as a rather unimportant thing. If they are dominated by a higher need, this higher need will seem to be the most important of all. It then becomes possible, and indeed does actually happen, that they may, for the sake of this higher need, put themselves into the position of being deprived of a more basic need. We may expect that after a long-time deprivation of the more basic need there will be a tendency to reevaluate both needs so that the more prepotent need will actually become consciously prepotent for the individual who may have

given it up lightly. Thus a person who has given up a job rather than lose self-respect, and who then starves for six months or so, may be willing to take the job back even at the price of losing self-respect.

6. Another partial explanation of *apparent* reversals is seen in the fact that we have been talking about the hierarchy of prepotency in terms of consciously felt wants or desires rather than of behavior. Looking at behavior itself may give us the wrong impression. What we have claimed is that the person will *want* the more basic of two needs when deprived in both. There is no necessary implication here that he or she will act on these desires. Let us stress again that there are many determinants of behavior other than the needs and desires.

7. Perhaps more important than all these exceptions are the ones that involve ideals, high social standards, high values, and the like. With such values people become martyrs; they will give up everything for the sake of a particular ideal or value. These people may be understood, at least in part, by reference to one basic concept (or hypothesis), which may be called increased frustration tolerance through early gratification. People who have been satisfied in their basic needs throughout their lives, particularly in their earlier years, seem to develop exceptional power to withstand present or future thwarting of these needs simply because they have strong, healthy character structure as a result of basic satisfaction. They are the strong people who can easily weather disagreement or opposition, who can swim against the stream of public opinion, and who can stand up for the truth at great personal cost. It is just the ones who have loved and been well loved and who have had many deep friendships who can hold out against hatred, rejection, or persecution.

We say all this in spite of the fact that a certain amount of sheer habituation is also involved in any full discussion of frustration tolerance. For instance, it is likely that those persons who have been accustomed to relative starvation for a long time are partially enabled thereby to withstand food deprivation. What sort of balance must be made between these two tendencies, of habituation on the one hand and of past satisfaction breeding present frustration tolerance on the other hand, remains to be worked out by further research. Meanwhile we may assume that both are operative, side by side, since they do not contradict each other. In respect to this phenomenon of increased frustration tolerance, it seems probable that the most important gratifications come in the first few years of life. That is to say, people who have been made secure and strong in the earliest years tend to remain secure and strong thereafter in the face of whatever threatens.

Degrees of Satisfaction

So far, our theoretical discussion may have given the impression that these five sets of needs—physiological, safety, belongingness, esteem, and self-actualization—are somehow in such terms as the following: If one need is satisfied, then another emerges. This statement might give the false impression that a need must be satisfied 100 percent before the next need emerges. In actual fact, most members of our society who are normal are partially satisfied in all their basic needs and partially unsatisfied in all their basic needs at the same time. A more realistic description of the hierarchy would be in terms of decreasing percentages of satisfaction as we go up the hierarchy of prepotency. For instance, to assign arbitrary figures for the sake of illustration, it is as if the average citizen is satisfied perhaps 85 percent in physiological needs, 70 percent in safety needs, 50 percent in love needs, 40 percent in self-esteem needs, and 10 percent in self-actualization needs.

As for the concept of emergence of a new need after satisfaction of the prepotent need, this emergence is not a sudden, saltatory phenomenon, but rather a gradual emergence by slow degrees from nothingness. For instance, if prepotent need A is satisfied only 10 percent, then need B may not be visible at all. However, as this need A becomes satisfied 25 percent need B may emerge 5 percent, as need A becomes satisfied 75 percent need B may emerge 50 percent, and so on.

Unconscious Needs

These needs are neither necessarily conscious nor unconscious. On the whole, however, in the average person, they are more often unconscious than conscious. It is not necessary at this point to overhaul the tremendous mass of evidence that indicates the crucial importance of unconscious motivation. What we have called the basic needs are often largely unconscious although they may, with suitable techniques and with sophisticated people, become conscious.

Cultural Specificity

This classification of basic needs makes some attempts to take account of the relative unity behind the superficial differences in specific desires from one culture to another. Certainly in any particular culture an individual's conscious motivational content will usually be extremely different from the conscious motivational content of an individual in another society. However, it is the common experience of anthropologists that people, even in different societies, are much more alike than we would think from our first contact with them, and that as we know them better we seem to find more and more of this commonness. We then recognize the most startling differences to be superficial rather than basic (e.g., differences in style of hairdress or clothes, tastes in food). Our classification of basic needs is in part an attempt to account for this unity behind the apparent diversity from culture to culture. No claim is made yet that it is ultimate or universal for all cultures. The claim is made only that it is relatively *more* ultimate, *more* universal, *more* basic than the superficial conscious desires, and makes a closer approach to common human characteristics. Basic needs are more common among humanity than are superficial desires or behaviors.

Multiple Motivations of Behavior

These needs must be understood *not* to be exclusive or single determiners of certain kinds of behavior. An example may be found in any behavior that seems to be physiologically motivated, such as eating, sexual play, or the like. The clinical psychologists have long since found that any behavior may be a channel through which flow various impulses. Or to say it in another way, most behavior is overdetermined or multimotivated. Within the sphere of motivational determinants any behavior tends to be determined by several or *all* of the basic needs simultaneously rather than by only one of them. The latter would be more an exception than the former. Eating may be partially for the sake of filling the stomach, and partially for the sake of comfort and amelioration of other needs. One may make love not only for pure sexual release, but also to convince oneself of one's sexuality, to feel powerful, or to win affection. As an illustration, it would be possible (theoretically if not practically) to analyze a single act of an individual and see in it the expression of physiological needs, safety needs, love needs, esteem needs, and self-actualization. This contrasts sharply with the more naive brand of trait psychology in which one trait or one motive accounts for a certain kind of act—for example, an aggressive act is traced solely to a trait of aggressiveness.

Unmotivated Behavior

There is a basic difference between expressive behavior and coping behavior (functional striving, purposive goal seeking). An expressive behavior does not try to do anything; it is simply a reflection of the personality. A stupid man behaves stupidly, not because he wants to, or tries to, or is motivated to, but simply because he *is* what he is. The same is true when I speak in a bass voice rather than tenor or soprano. The random movements of a healthy child, the smile on the face of a happy woman even when she is alone, the springiness of the healthy woman's walk, and the erectness of her carriage are other examples of expressive, nonfunctional behavior. Also the *style* in which a person carries out almost all behavior, motivated as well as unmotivated, is most often expressive (Allport and Vernon, 1933; Wolff, 1943).

We may then ask, is *all* behavior expressive or reflective of the character structure? The answer is No. Rote, habitual, automatized, or conventional behavior may or may not be expressive. The same is true for most stimulus-bound behaviors.

It is finally necessary to stress that expressiveness of behavior and goal-directedness of behavior are not mutually exclusive categories. Average behavior is usually both. (See Chapter 6 for a fuller discussion.)

Animal and Human Centering

This theory starts with the human being rather than any lower and presumably simpler animal. Too many of the findings that have been made in animals have been proved to be true for animals but not for the human being. There is no reason whatsoever why we should start with animals in order to study human motivation. The logic or rather illogic behind this general fallacy of pseudosimplicity has been exposed often enough by philosophers and logicians as well as by scientists in each of the various fields. It is no more necessary to study animals before one can study humans than it is to study mathematics *before* one can study geology or psychology or biology.

Motivation and Pathology

The conscious motivational content of everyday life has, according to the fore-going, been conceived to be relatively important or unimportant accordingly as it is more or less closely related to the basic goals. A desire for ice cream might actually be an indirect expression of a desire for love. If it is, this desire for ice cream becomes extremely important motivation. If, however, the ice cream is simply something to cool the mouth with, or a casual appetitive reaction, the desire is relatively unimportant. Everyday conscious desires are to be regarded as symptoms, as *surface indicators of more basic needs*. If we were to take these superficial desires at their face value we would find ourselves in a state of complete confusion that could never be resolved, since we would be dealing seriously with symptoms rather than with what lay behind the symptoms.

Thwarting of unimportant desires produces no psychopathological results; thwarting of basically important needs does produce such results. Any theory of psychopathogenesis must then be based on a sound theory of motivation. A conflict or a frustration is not necessarily pathogenic. It becomes so only when it threatens or thwarts the basic needs or partial needs that are closely related to the basic needs.

Role of Gratification

It has been pointed out above several times that our needs usually emerge only when more prepotent needs have been gratified. Thus gratification has an important role in motivation theory. Apart from this, however, needs cease to play an active determining or organizing role as soon as they are gratified.

What this means is that, for example, a basically satisfied person no longer has the needs for esteem, love, safety, and so on. The only sense in which he or she might be said to have them is in the almost metaphysical sense that a sated person has hunger or a filled bottle has emptiness. If we are interested in what *actually* motivates us, and not in what has, will, or might motivate us, then a satisfied need is not a motivator. It must be considered for all practical purposes simply not to exist, to have disappeared. This point should be emphasized because it has been either overlooked or contradicted in every theory of motivation we know. The perfectly healthy, normal, fortunate person has no sex needs or hunger needs, or needs for safety, or for love, or for prestige, or self-esteem, except in stray moments of quickly passing threat. If we were to say otherwise, we should also have to affirm that every person had all the pathological reflexes (e.g., Babinski), because if the nervous system were damaged, these would appear.

It is such considerations as these that suggest the bold postulation that a person who is thwarted in any of the basic needs may fairly be envisaged simply as sick or at least less than fully human. This is a fair parallel to our designation as sick of the person who lacks vitamins or minerals. Who will say that a lack of love is less important than a lack of vitamins? Since we know the pathogenic effects of love starvation, who is to say that we are invoking value questions in an unscientific or illegitimate way, any more than the physician does who diagnoses and treats pellagra or scurvy?

If we were permitted this usage, we should then say simply that healthy people are primarily motivated by their needs to develop and actualize their fullest potentialities and capacities. If a person has any other basic needs in any active chronic sense, he or she is simply unhealthy, as surely sick as if he or she had suddenly developed a strong salt hunger or calcium hunger. If we were to use the word *sick* in this way, we should then also have to face squarely the relations of people to their society. One clear implication of our definition would be that (1) since a person is to be called sick who is basically thwarted, and (2) since such basic thwarting is made possible ultimately only by forces outside the individual, then (3) sickness in the individual must come ultimately from a sickness in the society. The good or healthy society would then be defined as one that permitted people's highest purposes to emerge by satisfying all their basic needs.

If these statements seem unusual or paradoxical, the reader may be assured that this is only one among many such paradoxes that will appear as we revise our ways of looking at deeper motivations. When we ask what humans want of life, we deal with their very essence.

Functional Autonomy

Higher *basic* needs may become, after long gratification, independent both of their more powerful prerequisites and of their own proper satisfactions.[7] For instance, an adult who was love-satisfied in early years becomes *more* independent than average with regard to safety, belongingness, and love gratification. It is the strong, healthy, autonomous person who is most capable of withstanding loss of love and popularity. But this strength and health have been ordinarily produced in our society by early chronic gratifications of safety, love, belongingness, and esteem needs. Which is to say that these aspects of the person have become functionally autonomous, that is independent of the very gratifications that created them. We prefer to think of the character structure as the most important single instance of functional autonomy in psychology.

---

[7]Gordon Allport (1960, 1961) has expounded and generalized the principle that means to an end may become ultimate satisfactions themselves, connected only historically to their origins. They may *come* to be wanted for their own sake. This reminder of the tremendous importance of learning and change on the motivational life superimposes upon everything that has gone before an enormous additional complexity. There is no contradiction between these two sets of psychological principles; they complement each other. Whether or not any needs so acquired may be considered true *basic* needs by the criteria so far used is a question for further research.

chapter *3*

Gratification of Basic Needs

This chapter explores some of the many theoretical consequences of the approach to human motivation set forth in the last chapter, and should serve as a positive or healthy balance to one-sided stress on frustration and pathology.

We have seen that the chief principle of organization in human motivational life is the arrangement of basic needs in a hierarchy of less or greater priority or potency. The chief dynamic principle animating this organization is the emergence in the healthy person of less potent needs upon gratification of the more potent ones. The physiological needs, when unsatisfied, dominate the organism, pressing all capacities into their service and organizing these capacities so that they may be most efficient in this service. Relative gratification submerges them and allows the next higher set of needs in the hierarchy to emerge, dominate, and organize the personality, so that instead of being, for example, hunger obsessed, it now becomes safety obsessed. The principle is the same for the other sets of needs in the hierarchy (i.e., love, esteem, and self-actualization).

It is also probably true that higher needs may occasionally emerge, not after gratification, but rather after forced or voluntary deprivation, renunciation, or suppression of lower basic needs and gratifications (asceticism, sublimation, strengthening effects of rejection, discipline, persecution, isolation, etc.). Such phenomena do not contradict the theses of this book, since it is not claimed that gratification is the only source of strength or of other psychological desiderata.

Gratification theory is obviously a special, limited, or partial theory, not capable of independent existence or validity. It may achieve such validity only when structured with, at least, (1) frustration theory, (2) learning theory, (3) theory of neurosis, (4) theory of psychological health, (5) theory of values, and

(6) theory of discipline, will, responsibility, and so on. This chapter attempts to trace only one thread through the complex web of psychological determinants of behavior, the subjective life, and the character structure. Meanwhile, in lieu of a more rounded picture, it is freely granted that there are determinants other than basic need gratification, that basic need gratification may be necessary but it is certainly not sufficient, that gratification and deprivation each have both desirable and undesirable consequences, and that basic need gratification differs from neurotic need gratification in important respects.

CONSEQUENCES OF SATISFYING A BASIC NEED

The most basic consequence of satiation of any need is that this need is submerged and a new and higher need emerges.[1] Other consequences are epiphenomena of this fundamental fact. Examples of these secondary consequences are as follows.

1. Independence of and a certain disdain for the old satisfiers and goal objects, with a new dependence on satisfiers and goal objects that hitherto had been overlooked, not wanted, or only casually wanted. This exchange of old satisfiers for new ones involves many tertiary consequences. Thus there are changes in interests. That is, certain phenomena become interesting for the first time and old phenomena become boring, or even repulsive. This is the same as saying that there are changes in human values. In general, there tend to be: (1) overestimation of the satisfiers of the most powerful of the ungratified needs, (2) underestimation of the satisfiers of the less powerful of the ungratified needs (and of the strength of these needs), and (3) underestimation and even devaluation of the satisfiers of the needs already gratified (and of the strength of these needs). This shift in values involves, as a dependent phenomenon, reconstruction in philosophy of the future, of the Utopia, of the heaven and hell, of the good life, and of the unconscious wish-fulfillment state of the individual in a crudely predictable direction. In a word, we tend to take for granted the blessings we already have, especially if we don't have to work or struggle for them. The food, the security, the love, the admiration, the freedom that have always been there, that have never been lacking or yearned for, tend not only to be unnoticed but also even to be devalued or mocked or destroyed. This phenomenon of failing to count one's blessings is, of course, not realistic and can therefore be considered to be a form of pathology. In most instances it is cured very easily, simply by experiencing the appropriate deprivation or lack (e.g., pain, hunger, poverty, loneliness, rejection, or injustice). This relatively neglected phenomenon of postgratification forgetting and devaluation is of very great potential importance and power. Further elaborations can be found in the chapter "On Low Grumbles, High Grumbles, and Metagrumbles," in *Eupsychian Management: A Journal* (Maslow, 1965b). In no other way can we make sense of the puzzling way in which affluence (economic and psychological) can make possible *either* growth to loftier levels of human nature *or* the various forms of value pathology

---

[1] All these statements apply to basic needs only.

just hinted at, and spelled out in the newspaper headlines of recent years. Long ago, Adler (1939, 1964; Ansbacher and Ansbacher, 1956) in many of his writings talked of the "pampered style of life," and perhaps we should use this term to differentiate pathogenic gratifications from healthy, necessary ones.

2. With this change in values go changes in the cognitive capacities. Attention, perception, learning, remembering, forgetting, thinking, all are changed in a crudely predictable direction because of the new interests and values of the organism.

3. These new interests, satisfiers, and needs, are not only new, but in certain senses are also higher (see Chapter 5). When the safety needs are gratified, the organism is released to seek for love, independence, respect, self-respect, and so on. The easiest technique for releasing the organism from the bondage of the lower, more material, more selfish needs is to gratify them. (Needless to say, there are other techniques as well.)

4. Gratification of any need whatsoever, so long as this be a true gratification (i.e., of a basic rather than of a neurotic or pseudoneed), helps to determine character formation (see below). Furthermore, any true need gratification tends toward the improvement, strengthening, and healthy development of the individual. That is, gratification of any basic need insofar as we can speak of it in isolation, is a move in the healthy direction, away from the neurotic direction. It is in this sense undoubtedly that Kurt Goldstein spoke of *any* specific need gratification as being in the long run a step toward self-actualization.

5. Specific need gratifications and satiations have in addition to these general results certain specific ad hoc results as well. For instance, other factors being equal, a satisfaction of the safety needs brings specifically a subjective feeling of safety more restful sleep, loss of feeling of danger, and greater boldness and courage.

LEARNING AND GRATIFICATION

A first consequence of exploring the effects of need gratification must be a growing dissatisfaction with the overexpanded role attributed to purely associative learning by its proponents.

In general, gratification phenomena (e.g., any loss of appetite after satiation, the change in quantity and type of defensiveness after safety need gratification, etc.) demonstrate (1) *disappearance* with increased exercise (or repetition, use, or practice) and (2) *disappearance* with increased reward (or satisfaction, praise, or reinforcement). Furthermore, not only do gratification phenomena such as those listed at the end of this chapter flout the laws of association in spite of the fact that they are acquired changes in adaptation, but examination shows also that arbitrary association is not involved except in a secondary fashion. Any definition of learning must therefore be insufficient if it stresses simply changes in the connection between stimuli and responses.

The impact of need gratification is almost entirely limited to intrinsically appropriate satisfiers. In the long run, there can be no casual and arbitrary choice, except for nonbasic needs. For the love-hungry, there is only one genuine, long-run satisfier: honest and satisfying affection. For the sex-starved, food-starved, or water-starved person, only sex, food, or water will ultimately serve. Here, no fortuitous collocation or accidental or arbitrary juxtaposition will do. Nor will signals or warnings or associates of the satisfiers do (G. Murphy, 1947); only the satisfiers themselves gratify needs.

The essence of this critique of associative, behavioristic learning theory is that it takes entirely for granted the ends (purposes, goals) of the organism. It deals entirely with the manipulation of *means* to unstated ends. In contrast, the theory of basic needs presented here is a theory of the ends and ultimate values of the organism. These ends are intrinsically, and in themselves, valuable to the organism. It will therefore do anything necessary to achieve these goals, even to learning arbitrary, irrelevant, trivial or silly procedures that an experimenter may set up as the only way to get to these goals. These tricks are of course expendable, and are discarded (extinguished) when they no longer buy intrinsic satisfactions (or intrinsic reinforcements).

It seems quite clear then that the behavioral and subjective changes listed in Chapter 5 cannot possibly be explained by the laws of associative learning alone. Indeed, it is more likely that they play only a secondary role. If a parent kisses a child often, the drive itself disappears and the child learns *not* to crave kisses (Levy, 1944). Most contemporary writers on personality, traits, attitudes, and tastes speak of them as habit aggregations, acquired according to the laws of associative learning, but it now seems advisable to reconsider and correct this usage.

Not even in the more defensible sense of acquisition of insight and understanding (Gestalt learning) can character traits be considered to be wholly learned. This broader, Gestalt approach to learning, partly because of its coolness to the findings of psychoanalysis, is yet too limited in its rationalistic stress on the cognition of intrinsic structure in the outside world. We need a stronger tie to the conative and affective process *within* the person than is afforded either by associative learning or Gestalt learning. (But see also the writings of Kurt Lewin (1935), which undoubtedly help to solve this problem.)

Without attempting any detailed discussion at this time, we tentatively suggest what can be described as character learning, or intrinsic learning, which takes as its centering point changes in the character structure rather than in behavior. Among its main components are (1) the educative effects of unique (nonrepetitive) and of profound personal experiences, (2) the *affective* changes produced by repetitive experience, (3) the conative changes produced by gratification–frustration experiences, (4) the broad attitudinal, expectational, or even philosophical changes produced by certain types of early experience (Levy, 1938), and (5) the determination by constitution of the variation in selective assimilation of any experience by the organism.

Such considerations point to a closer rapprochement between the concepts of learning and character formation, until ultimately, as this writer believes, it may become fruitful for psychologists to define typical paradigmatic learning as *change in personal development, in character structure,* that is as movement toward self-actualization and beyond (Maslow, 1969a, b, c).

GRATIFICATION AND CHARACTER FORMATION

Certain a priori considerations strongly connect need gratification with the development of some, perhaps even many, character traits. Such doctrine would be no more than the logical opposite of an already well-established relationship between frustration and psychopathology.

If it is easy to accept basic need frustration as one determinant of hostility, it is quite as easy to accept the opposite of frustration (i.e., basic need gratification) as an a priori determinant of the opposite of hostility (i.e., friendliness). One is as strongly implied by psychoanalytic findings as the other. And even though explicit theoretical formulation is still lacking, psychotherapeutic *practice* accepts our hypothesis in its stress on implicit reassurance, support, permissiveness, approval, acceptance, that is to say, the ultimate gratification of the deep-lying needs of the patient for safety, love, protection, respect, worth, and so on. Especially is this true with children, in whom love hunger, independence hunger, safety hunger, and so on are often, without further ado, treated directly with replacement or gratification therapy by feeding them respectively love, independence, or safety.

It is a pity that there is so small a body of experimental material. What there is, however, is very impressive, for example, the experiments of Levy (1934a, b, 1937, 1938, 1944, 1951). The general pattern of these experiments was to take a group of animals at birth (e.g., puppies) and submit them to either satiation of a need or partial frustration of it, for example, the suckling need.

Experiments of this type were made with pecking in chicks, suckling in human babies, activity in various species of animals. In all cases, it was discovered that a need that was fully gratified ran its typical course and then, depending on its nature, either disappeared altogether (e.g., suckling) or else maintained a certain low optimum level for the rest of the life span (e.g., activity). Those animals in which the need was frustrated developed various semipathological phenomena, of which the most relevant for us were persistence of the need past its normal time of disappearance and greatly increased activity of the need.

The full relevance of childhood gratification to adult character formation is suggested especially by Levy's work with love (1943, 1944). It seems quite clear that many traits characteristic of the healthy adult are positive consequences of childhood gratification of the love needs, for example, ability to allow independence to the loved one, the ability to withstand lack of love, the ability to love without giving up autonomy, and so on.

To phrase this opposition in theory as clearly and flatly as possible, what it amounts to is that a mother loving her child well produces in the child (by her rewards, reinforcements, repetition, exercise, etc.) a *reduction* of the strength of love need through later life, a lowered probability of, for example, kissing, a lesser amount of clinging to her, and so on. The best way to teach a child to go seeking in all directions for affection and to have a constant craving for it is partially to *deny* the child love (Levy, 1944). This is another illustration of the functional autonomy principle (see page 31) that forced Allport to be skeptical about contemporary learning theory.

All teachers of psychology meet this theory of character traits as learned whenever they speak of basic need gratification with children or of free choice experimentation. "If you pick up the child when she wakes from her dream, won't she learn to cry whenever she wants to be picked up (since you reward the crying)?" "If you allow the child to eat what he chooses, won't he be spoiled?" "If you pay attention to the child's antics, won't she learn to be silly in order to attract your attention?" "If you give the child his way, won't he want his way always?" These questions can*not* be answered by learning theories alone; we must *also* invoke gratification theory and the theory of functional autonomy to round out the picture.

Another type of data supporting the relationship between need gratification and character formation is available in the directly observable clinical effects of gratification. Such data are available to every person working directly with people, and can be confidently expected in almost every therapeutic contact.

The easiest way to convince ourselves of this is to examine the direct and immediate effects of gratification of the basic needs, beginning with the most potent. So far as the physiological needs are concerned, we in our culture do not regard as character traits food satiation or water satiation, although under other cultural conditions we might. Even at this physiological level, however, we get some borderline cases for our thesis. Certainly, if we may speak of the needs for rest and sleep, we may therefore also speak of their frustration and its effects (sleepiness, fatigue, lack of energy, loginess, perhaps even laziness, lethargy, etc.), and gratification (alertness, vigor, zest, etc.). Here are immediate consequences of simple need gratification, which, if they are not accepted character traits, are at least of definite interest to the student of personality. And while we are not accustomed yet to thinking so, the same can be said for the sex need, that is, the category of sex obsession and the contrasting one of sex gratification for which we have as yet no respectable vocabulary.

At any rate, when we speak of the safety needs we are on much firmer ground. Apprehensiveness, fear, dread and anxiety, tension, nervousness, and jitteriness are all consequences of safety-need frustration. The same type of clinical observation clearly shows corresponding effects of safety need gratification (for which as usual we lack adequate vocabulary), such as lack of anxiety, lack of nervousness, relaxedness, confidence in the future, assurance, security, and so on. Whatever words we use, there is a character difference between the individual who feels safe and the one who lives life as if a spy in enemy territory.

So it is for the other basic emotional needs for belongingness, for love, for respect, and for self-esteem. Gratification of these needs permits the appearance of such characterisitcs as affectionateness, self-respect, self-confidence, or security.

One step removed from these immediate characterological consequences of need gratification are such general traits as kindliness, generosity, unselfishness, bigness (as opposed to pettiness), equanimity, serenity, happiness, contentment, and the like. These seem to be consequences of the consequences, by-products of general need gratification, that is, of generally improving psychological life condition, of surplus, plenty, affluence.

It is obvious that learning, in both its restricted and broader forms, also plays a role of importance in the genesis of these and other character traits. Whether it is a more powerful determiner the data available today do not permit us to say, and this would ordinarily be brushed aside as a fruitless question. And yet the consequences of greater stress on one or the other are so contrasting that we must at least be aware of the problem. Whether character education can take place in the classroom, whether books, lectures, catechisms, and exhortations are the best tools to use, whether sermons and Sunday schools can produce good human beings, or rather, whether the good life produces the good person, whether love, warmth, friendship, respect, and good treatment of the child are more consequential for later character structure—these are the alternatives presented by adherence to one or the other theory of character formation and of education.

GRATIFICATION AND HEALTH

Let us say that person A has lived for several weeks in a dangerous jungle, managing to stay alive by finding occasional food and water. Person B not only stays alive but also has a rifle and a hidden cave with a closable entrance. Person C has all of these and has two more people along with him as well. Person D has the food, the gun, the allies, the cave, and in addition, has a best-loved friend. Finally, Person E, in the same jungle, has all of these, and in addition is the well-respected leader of a band. For the sake of brevity we may call these people, respectively, the merely surviving, the safe, the belonging, the loved, and the respected.

But this is not only a series of increasing basic need gratifications; it is as well *a series of increasing degrees of psychological health*.[2] It is clear that, other things being equal, a person who is safe and belongs and is loved will be healthier (by *any* reasonable definition) than one who is safe and belongs, but who is rejected and unloved. And if, in addition, the person wins respect and admiration and because of this develops self-respect, then he or she is still *more* healthy, self-actualizing, or fully human.

It would seem that degree of basic need gratification is positively correlated with degree of psychological health. Can we go further and affirm the limit of such a correlation, namely, that complete gratification of basic needs and ideal health are the same? Gratification theory would at least *suggest* such a possibility (but see Maslow, 1969b). Although of course the answer to such a question awaits future research, even the bare statement of such a hypothesis directs our gaze to neglected facts and bids us ask again old and unanswered questions.

For instance, we must of course grant that there are other paths to health as well. And yet it is fair to ask, as we choose life paths for our children, what are the relative frequencies of gratification health and frustration health? That is, just how often health is achieved through ascetism, through renunciation of basic

---

[2]It is pointed out further on that this same continuum of increasing degree of need gratification may also be used as the basis for a possible classification of personalities. Taken as steps or levels of maturing or personal growth toward self-actualization, through the individual's life span, it supplies a schema for a developmental theory roughly approximating and paralleling Freud's and Erikson's developmental system (Erikson, 1959; Freud, 1920).

needs, through discipline, and through tempering in the fire of frustration, tragedy, and unhappiness?

This theory also confronts us with the prickly problem of selfishness: Are all needs ipso facto selfish and ego-centered? It is true that self-actualization, the ultimate need, is defined by Goldstein and in this book in a highly individualistic way, and yet empirical study of very healthy people shows them to be at the same time extremely individual and healthily selfish and extremely compassionate and altruistic, as will be seen in Chapter 11.

When we posit the concept of gratification health (or happiness health), we implicitly align ourselves thereby with those writers—Goldstein, Jung, Adler, Angyal, Horney, Fromm, May, Buhler, Rogers, and, increasingly, others—who postulate some positive growth tendency in the organism that, from within, drives it to fuller development.

For if we assume that the healthy organism is, paradigmatically, basic need-gratified and therefore released for self-actualization, then we have thereby also assumed that this organism develops from within by intrinsic growth tendencies, in the Bergsonian sense, rather than from without, in the behavioristic sense of environmental determinism. The neurotic organism is one that lacks basic need satisfactions that can come only from other people. It is therefore more dependent on other people and is less autonomous and self-determined—more shaped by the nature of the environment and less shaped by its own intrinsic nature. Such relative independence of environment as is found in the healthy person does not, of course, mean lack of commerce with it; it means only that in these contacts the person's *ends* and his or her own nature are the primary determinants, and that the environment is primarily a means to the person's self-actualizing ends. This is truly psychological freedom (Riesman, 1950).

GRATIFICATION AND PATHOLOGY

Life in recent years has certainly taught us something about the pathology of *material* (lower need) affluence, of such outcomes as boredom, selfishness, feelings of eliteness, and of "deserved" superiority, of fixation at a low level of immaturity, of the destruction of community feeling. Clearly, living the material or lower need life is not in itself satisfying for any length of time.

But now we are being confronted by a new possibility of pathology of psychological affluence; that is, of suffering from the consequences (apparently) of being loved and cared for devotedly, of being adored, admired, applauded, and listened to self-effacedly, of being given the center of the stage, of having loyal servants, of having every here-and-now wish granted, even of being the objects of self-sacrifice and self-abnegation.

It is true that we just don't know much about these new phenomena, certainly not in any developed scientific sense. All we have are strong suspicions, widespread clinical impressions, the slowly hardening opinion of child psychologists and educators that merely and only basic need gratification is not enough, but that some experience with firmness, toughness, frustration, discipline, and limits is also needed by the child. Or to say it another way, basic need gratification had better be defined more carefully because it so easily slips over into unbridled indulgence, self-abnegation, total permissiveness, overprotection, and toadyism. Love and respect for the child must at the very least be integrated with love and respect for oneself as a parent and for adulthood in general. Children are certainly persons, but they are not experienced persons. They must be counted on to be unwise about many things, and positively stupid about some.

Gratification-produced pathology may also turn out to be in part what could be called metapathology, an absence of values, of meaningfulness, and of fulfillment in life. It is believed by many humanists and existential psychologists—not yet with sufficient data to be sure, however—that gratification of all the basic needs does not *automatically* solve the problem of identity, of a value system, of a calling in life, of the meaning of life. For some people at least, especially young people, these are separate and additional life tasks beyond the gratification of the basic needs.

Finally, we mention again the little-understood facts that human beings seem almost never to be permanently satisfied or content and—deeply connected with this—that people tend to get used to their blessings, to forget them, to take them for granted, even to cease to value them. For many people—we don't know how many—even the highest pleasures may grow stale and may lose their newness (Wilson, 1969), and it may be *necessary* to experience loss of their blessings in order to be able to appreciate them again.

IMPLICATIONS OF GRATIFICATION THEORY

What follows is a brief listing of a few of the more important hypotheses that are suggested by gratification theory. Others are listed in the next section.

Psychotherapy

It could probably be maintained that basic need gratification is primary in the dynamics of actual cure or improvement. Certainly it must be granted that, at minimum, it is *one* such factor and an especially important one because so far neglected. This thesis will be discussed more fully in Chapter 9.

Attitudes, Interest, Tastes, and Values

Several examples were given of the ways in which interests are determined by the gratification and frustration of needs (also see Maier, 1949). It would be possible to go *much* further with this, ultimately involving necessarily a discussion of morality, values, and ethics, insofar as these are more than etiquette, manners, folkways, and other local social habits. The current fashion is to treat attitudes, tastes, interests, and indeed values of *any* kind as if they had no determinant other than local cultural associative learning, that is, as if they were determined wholly by arbitrary environmental forces. But we have seen that it is necessary to invoke also intrinsic requiredness and the effects of gratification of organismic needs.

Classification of Personality

If we think of gratification of the hierarchy of basic emotional needs as a straight-line continuum, we are furnished with a helpful (even though imperfect) tool for classifying types of personality. If most people have similar organismic needs, each person can be compared with any other in the degree to which these needs are satisfied. This is a holistic or organismic principle because it classifies whole persons on a single continuum rather than parts or aspects of persons on a multiplicity of unrelated continua.

Boredom and Interest

What, after all, is boredom but overgratification? And yet here too we may find unsolved and unperceived problems. Why does repeated contact with painting A, friend A, music A produce boredom, while the same number of contacts with painting B, friend B, music B produces enhanced interest and heightened pleasure?

Happiness, Joy, Contentment, Elation, and Ecstasy

What role does need gratification play in the production of the positive emotions? Students of emotion have too long confined their studies to the affective effects of frustration.

Social Effects

In the next section are listed various ways in which gratification seems to have good social effects. That is, it is put forward as a thesis for further investigation that satisfying a person's basic needs (all things being equal, putting aside certain puzzling exceptions, and for the moment neglecting the desirable effects of deprivation and of discipline) improves the individual not only in character structure but as a citizen on the national and international scene as well as in face-to-face relationships. The possible implications for political, economic, educational, historical, and sociological theory are both tremendous and obvious (Aronoff, 1967; Davies, 1963; Myerson, 1925; Wootton, 1967).

Frustration Level

In a certain sense, paradoxical though it may seem, need gratification is a determinant of need frustration. This is true because higher needs will not even appear in consciousness until lower, prepotent needs are gratified. And in a sense, until they exist consciously they cannot produce feelings of frustration. The merely surviving person will not worry much over the higher things of life, the study of geometry, the right to vote, civic pride, respect; he or she is primarily concerned with more basic goods. It takes a certain amount of gratification of lower needs to elevate an individual to the point of enough civilization to feel frustration about the larger personal, social and intellectual issues.

As a consequence, we may grant that even though most people are doomed to wish for what they do not have, it is nevertheless useful to work for greater satisfaction for all. Thus we learn simultaneously not to expect miracles from any single social reform (e.g., women's suffrage, free education, secret ballot, labor unions, good housing, direct primaries), and yet not to underrate the reality of slow advance.

If a person must feel frustrated or worried, it is better for society that he or she worry about ending war rather than about being cold or hungry. Clearly raising the frustration level (if we may speak of higher and lower frustrations) has not only personal but also social consequences. Approximately the same may be said of the level of guilt and shame.

Fun, Aimlessness, and Random Behavior

Long remarked upon by philosophers, artists, and poets, this whole area of behavior has been strangely neglected by the scientific psychologists. Possibly this is because of the widely accepted dogma that all behavior is motivated. Without wishing at this moment to argue this (in the writer's opinion) mistake, there can yet be no question about the observation that, immediately after satiation, the organism allows itself to give up pressure, tension, urgency, and necessity, to loaf, laze, and relax, to putter, to be passive, to enjoy the sun, to ornament, decorate, polish the pots and pans, to play and have fun, to observe what is of no importance, to be casual and aimless, to learn incidentally rather than with purpose; in a word, to be (relatively) unmotivated. Need gratification permits the emergence of unmotivated behavior (see Chapter 6 for fuller discussion).

Autonomy of Higher Needs

Although it is generally true that we move to higher need levels after gratification of the lower needs, it yet remains an observable phenomenon that once having attained these higher need levels and the values and tastes that go with them they may become autonomous, no longer depending on lower need gratifications. Such persons may even despise and spurn the lower need gratifications that made possible their "higher life," in about the same spirit that third-generation wealth becomes ashamed of first-generation wealth, or as the educated children of immigrants may be ashamed of their cruder parents.

INFLUENCE OF GRATIFICATION

The following is a partial list of phenomena that are determined in large part by the gratification of basic needs.

A. Conative-Affective
   1. Feelings of physical sating and glut, regarding food, sex, sleep, and so on, and, as *by-products,* well-being, health, energy, euphoria, physical contentment

2. Feelings of safety, peace, security, protection, lack of danger and threat
3. Feelings of belongingness, of being one of a group, of identification with group goals and triumphs, of acceptance or having a place, at-homeness
4. Feelings of loving and being loved, of being loveworthy, of love identification
5. Feelings of self-reliance, self-respect, self-esteem, confidence, trust in oneself; feeling of ability, achievement, competence, success, ego strength, respectworthiness, prestige, leadership, independence
6. Feelings of self-actualization, self-fulfillment, self-realization, of more and more complete development and fruition of one's resources and potentialities and consequent feeling of growth, maturity, health, and autonomy
7. Satisfied curiosity, feeling of learning and of knowing more and more
8. Satisfied understanding, more and more philosophical satisfaction; movement toward larger and larger, more and more inclusive and unitary philosophy or religion; increased perception of connections and relations; awe; value commitment
9. Satisfied beauty need, thrill, sensuous shock, delight, ecstasy, sense of symmetry, rightness, suitability, or perfection
10. Emergence of higher needs
11. Temporary or long-run dependence on and independence of various satisfiers; increasing independence of and disdain for lower needs and lower satisfiers
12. Aversion and appetite feelings
13. Boredom and interest
14. Improvement in values; refinement in taste; better choosing
15. Greater possibility of and greater intensity of pleasant excitement, happiness, joy, delight, contentment, calm, serenity, exultation; richer and more positive emotional life
16. More frequent occurrence of ecstasy, peak experiences, orgasmic emotion, exaltation, and mystic experience
17. Changes in aspiration level
18. Changes in frustration level
19. Movement toward metamotivation and being-values (Maslow, 1964a)

B. Cognitive
1. Keener, more efficient, more realistic cognition of all types; better reality testing
2. Improved intuitive powers; more successful hunches
3. Mystic experience with illuminations and insights
4. More reality-object-and-problem centering; less projection and ego centering; more transpersonal and transhuman cognitions
5. Improvement in world view and in philosophy (in sense of becoming more true, more realistic, less destructive of self and others, more comprehensive, more integrated and holistic, etc.)
6. More creativeness, more art, poetry, music, wisdom, science
7. Less rigid robotlike conventionality; less stereotyping, less compulsive categorizing (see Chapter 17); better perception of individual uniqueness through screen of human-made categories and rubrics; less dichotomizing

8. Many of the more basic, deeper attitudes (democratic, basic respect for all human beings, affection for others, love and respect for people of different ages, genders, and races)
9. Less preference and need for the familiar, especially for important things; less fear of the novel and unfamiliar
10. More possibility of incidental or latent learning
11. Less need for the simple; more pleasure in the complex

C. Character Traits
1. More calmness, equanimity, serenity, peace of mind (opposite of tension, nervousness, unhappiness, feeling miserable)
2. Kindness, kindliness, sympathy, unselfishness (opposite of cruelty)
3. Healthy generosity
4. Bigness (opposite of pettiness, meanness, smallness)
5. Self-reliance, self-respect, self-esteem, confidence, trust in oneself
6. Feelings of safety, peacefulness, lack of danger
7. Friendliness (opposite of character-based hostility)
8. Greater frustration tolerance
9. Tolerance of, interest in, and approval of individual differences and therefore loss of prejudice and generalized hostility (but not loss of judgment); greater feeling of human kinship, comradeship, brotherly love, respect for others
10. More courage; less fear
11. Psychological health and all its by-products; movement away from neurosis, psychopathic personality, and perhaps psychosis
12. More profoundly democratic (fearless and realistic respect for others who are worthy of it)
13. Relaxation; less tension
14. More honesty, genuineness, and straightforwardness; less cant, less phoniness
15. Stronger will; more enjoyment of responsibility

D. Interpersonal
1. Better citizen, neighbor, parent, friend, lover
2. Political, economic, religious, educational growth and openness
3. Respect for children, employees, minorities and other groups with less power
4. More democratic, less authoritarian
5. Less unwarranted hostility and more friendliness, more interest in others, easier identification with others
6. Better judge of people, better chooser; as, for example, in choosing friends, sweethearts, leaders
7. Nicer person, more attractive; more beautiful
8. Better psychotherapist

E. Miscellaneous
1. Changed picture of heaven, hell, Utopia, good life, success and failure, etc.
2. Move toward higher values; toward higher "spiritual life"

3. Changes in all expressive behavior (e.g., smile, laugh, facial expression, demeanor, walk, handwriting); movement toward more expressive behavior and less coping behavior
4. Energy changes, lassitude, sleep, quiet, rest, alertness
5. Hopefulness, interest in future (opposite of loss of morale, apathy, anhedonia)
6. Changes in dream life, fantasy life, early memories (Allport, 1959)
7. Changes in (character-based) morality, ethics, values
8. Move away from win-lose, adversary, zero-sum game way of life

chapter *4*

Instinct Theory Reexamined

THE IMPORTANCE OF REEXAMINATION

The theories of basic needs sketched out in previous chapters suggest and even call for a reconsideration of instinct theory, if only because of the necessity for differentiating between more and less basic, more and less healthy, more and less natural.

There are also a considerable number of other theoretical, clinical, and experimental considerations pointing in this same direction, that is, the desirability of reevaluating instinct theory and perhaps even of resurrecting it in some form or other. These all support a certain skepticism with regard to the current, almost exclusive stress by psychologists, sociologists, and anthropologists on the plasticity, flexibility, and adaptability of human beings and on their ability to learn. Human beings seem to be far more autonomous and self-governed than current psychological theory allows for.

Contemporary researchers suggest strongly that the organism is more trustworthy, more self-protecting, self-directing, and self-governing than it is usually given credit for (Cannon, 1932; Goldstein, 1939; Levy, 1951; Rogers, 1954; and others). In addition, we may add that various developments have shown the theoretical necessity for the postulation of some sort of positive growth or self-actualization tendency within the organism, which is different from its conserving, equilibrating, or homeostatic tendency as well as from the tendency to respond to impulses from the outside world. This kind of tendency to growth or self-actualization, in one or another vague form, has been postulated by thinkers as diverse as Aristotle and Bergson, and by many other philosophers. Among psychiatrists, psychoanalysts, and psychologists it has been found necessary by Gold-stein, Bühler, Jung, Horney, Fromm, Rogers, and many others.

Perhaps, however, the most important influence in favor of reexamining instinct theory is the experience of the psychotherapists, especially the psychoanalysts. In this area, the logic of facts, however unclearly seen, has been unmistakable; inexorably, the therapist has been forced to differentiate more basic from less basic wishes (or needs, or impulses). It is as simple as this: The frustration of some needs produces pathology, the frustration of other needs does not. The gratification of these needs produces health, of others not. These needs are inconceivably stubborn and recalcitrant. They resist all blandishments, substitutions, bribes, and alternatives; nothing will do for them but their proper and intrinsic gratifications. Consciously or unconsciously they are craved and sought forever. They behave always like stubborn, irreducible, final, unanalyzable facts that must be taken as given or as starting points not to be questioned. It should be an overwhelmingly impressive point that almost every school of psychiatry, psychoanalysis, clinical psychology, social work, or child therapy has *had* to postulate some doctrine of instinctlike needs no matter how much they disagreed on every other point.

Inevitably, such experiences remind us of species characteristics, of constitution, and of heredity rather than of superficial and easily manipulated habits. Wherever a choice has had to be made between the horns of this dilemma, the therapist has almost always chosen the instinct rather than the conditioned response or the habit as the basic building block. This is of course unfortunate, for, as we shall see, there are other intermediate and more valid alternatives from among which we may now make a more satisfying choice; there are more than two horns to the dilemma.

But it does seem clear that, from the point of view of the demands of general dynamic theory, the instinct theory, as presented especially by McDougall and Freud, had certain virtues that were not sufficiently appreciated at the time, perhaps because its mistakes were so much more evident. Instinct theory accepted the fact that humans are self-movers; that their own nature as well as their environment helps to decide behavior; that their own nature supplies them with a ready-made framework of ends, goals, or values; that most often, under good conditions, what they want is what they need (what is good for them) in order to avoid sickness; that all people form a single biological species; that behavior is senseless unless one understands its motivations and its goals; and that, on the whole, organisms left to their own resources often display a kind of biological efficiency, or wisdom, that needs explaining.

CRITIQUE OF TRADITIONAL INSTINCT THEORY

It will be our contention here that many of the mistakes of the instinct theorists, while profound and deserving of rejection, were by no means intrinsic or inevitable and that, furthermore, a fair number of these mistakes were shared by both the instinctivists and their critics.

Reductionism

Most anti-instinctivists, such as Bernard, Watson, Kuo, and others, in the 1920s and 1930s criticized instinct theory on the ground that instincts could not be described in specific stimulus-response terms. What this boils down to is the accusation that instincts do not conform to simple behavioristic theory. This is true; they do not indeed. Such a criticism, however, is not taken seriously today by dynamic and humanistic psychologists, who uniformly consider that it is impossible to define *any* important human whole quality or whole activity in stimulus-response terms alone.

Such an attempt can breed little more than confusion. We can take as a single typical instance the confounding of reflex with the classical lower animal instinct. The former is a pure motor act; the latter is this and a great deal more: predetermined impulse, expressive behavior, coping behavior, goal object, and affect.

All-or-Nothing Approach

There is no reason why we should be forced to choose between the full instinct, complete in all its parts, and the noninstinct. Why may there not be instinct remnants, instinctlike aspects of impulse alone or of behavior alone, difference of degree, partial instincts?

Too many writers used the word *instinct* indiscriminately to cover need, aim, ability, behavior, perception, expression, value, and emotional concomitants, singly or in combination. The result was a hodgepodge of loose usage in which almost every known human reaction was characterized as instinctive by one or another writer, as Marmor (1942) and Bernard (1924) have pointed out.

Our main hypothesis is that human *urges* or *basic needs* alone may be innately given to at least some appreciable degree. The pertinent behavior or ability, cognition or affection need not also be innate, but may be (by our hypothesis) learned or expressive. (Of course, many human *abilities* or *capacities* are strongly determined or made possible by hereditary, e.g., color vision, but they are of no concern to us at this point.) This is to say that the hereditary component of basic needs may be seen as simple conative lack, tied to no intrinsic goal-achieving behavior, as blind, directionless demands, like Freud's id impulses. (We shall see below that the satisfiers of these basic needs seem also to be intrinsic in a definable way.) What has to be learned is goal-bent (coping) behavior.

It was a mistake of both the instinctivists and their opponents to think in black-and-white dichotomous terms instead of in terms of degree. How can it be said that a complex set of reactions is either *all* determined by heredity or *not at all* determined by heredity? There is no structure, however simple, let alone any whole reaction, that has genic determinants alone. At the other extreme it is also obvious that nothing is completely free of the influence of heredity, for humans are a biological species.

One confusing consequence of this dichotomy is the tendency to define any activity as noninstinctive if *any* learning can be demonstrated or, contrariwise, to define an activity as instinctive if *any* hereditary influence at all can be demonstrated. Since for most, perhaps all, urges, abilities, or emotions it is easy to demonstrate both kinds of determination, such arguments must be forever insoluble.

Overpowering Forces

The paradigm for instinct theorists was the animal instinct. This led to various mistakes, such as failing to look for instincts unique to the human species. The one most misleading lesson, however, that was learned from the lower animals was the axiom that instincts were powerful, strong, unmodifiable, uncontrollable, and unsuppressible. However this may be for salmon, or frogs, or lemmings, it is not true for humans.

If, as we feel, basic needs have an appreciable hereditary base, we may very well have blundered when we looked for instincts with only the naked eye and considered an entity instinctive only when it was obviously and unmistakably independent of and more powerful than all environmental forces. Why should there not be needs that, though instinctlike, are yet easily repressed, suppressed, or otherwise controlled and that are easily masked or modified or even suppressed by habits, suggestions, by cultural pressures, by guilt, and so on (as, for instance, seems to be true for the love need)? That is to say, why not *weak* instincts?

It may be that the motive power behind the culturalists' attack on instinct theory comes largely from this mistaken identification of instinct with overpowering strength. The experience of every ethnologist contradicts such an assumption, and attack is therefore understandable. But if we were properly respectful of both the cultural and the biological and if we considered culture to be a stronger force than instinctive need, then it would not seem a paradox but an obvious matter of course that we ought to protect the weak, subtle, and tender instinctive needs if they are not to be overwhelmed by the tougher, more powerful culture, rather than the other way about. This could be so even though these same instinctive needs are in another sense strong—they persist, they demand gratification, their frustration produces highly pathological consequences, and so on.

To make the point, a paradox may help. We think of uncovering, insight, depth therapies—which include practically all but the hypnosis and behavior therapies—to be, from one point of view, an uncovering, a recovering, a strengthening of our weakened and lost instinct tendencies and instinct remnants, our painted-over animal selves, our subjective biology. This ultimate purpose is even more nakedly stated in the so-called personal growth workshops. These—both the therapies and the workshops—are expensive, painful, long drawn-out efforts, ultimately taking a whole lifetime of struggle, patience, and fortitude, and even then they may fail. But how many cats or dogs or birds need help to discover how to be a cat or a dog or a bird? Their impulse-voices are loud, clear, and unmistakable, where ours are weak, confused, and easily overlooked so that we need help to hear them.

This explains why animal naturalness is seen most clearly in self-actualizing people, least clearly in neurotic or "normally sick" people. We might go so far as to say that sickness often consists of just *exactly* the loss of one's animal nature. The clearest specieshood and animality is thus paradoxically seen in the *most* spiritual, the *most* saintly and sagacious, the *most* (organismically) rational.

Primitive Impulses

Another mistake derives from this focusing on animal instincts. For inscrutable reasons that only the intellectual historian may be able to unravel, Western civilization has generally believed that the animal in us is a bad animal, and that our most primitive impulses are evil, greedy, selfish, and hostile.[1]

The theologians have called it original sin, or the devil. The Freudians have called it id, and philosophers, economists, and educators all have called it by various names. Darwin was so identified with this view that he saw only competition in the animal world, completely overlooking the cooperation that is just as common and that Kropotkin saw so easily.

One expression of this world view has been to identify this animal within us with wolves, tigers, pigs, vultures, or snakes rather than with better, or at least milder, animals like the deer, elephant, dog, or chimpanzee. This we may call the bad-animal interpretation of our inner nature, and point out that if we *must* reason from animals to humans, it would be better if we chose those who were closest to us, the anthropoid apes.

Dichotomy of Instinct and Reason

We have seen that instincts and flexible, cognitive adaptation to the novel tend to be mutually exclusive in the phyletic scale. The more of one we find, the less of the other we may expect. Because of this the vital and even tragic mistake (in view of the historical consequences) has been made, from time immemorial, of dichotomizing instinctive impulse and rationality in the human being. It has rarely occurred to anyone that they might *both* be instinctlike in the human being, and more important, that their results or implied goals might be identical and synergic rather than antagonistic.

It is our contention that the impulses to know and to understand may be exactly as conative as the needs to belong or to love.

In the ordinary instinct-reason dichotomy or contrast, it is a badly defined instinct and a badly defined reason that are opposed to each other. If they were correctly defined in accordance with modern knowledge, they would be seen as not contrasting or opposing or even as strongly different from each other. Healthy reason, as definable today, and healthy instinctlike impulses point in the same direction and are *not* in opposition to each other in the healthy person (although they *may* be antagonistic in the unhealthy). As a single example, all the scientific

---

[1]"Is it not possible that the primitive and unconscious side of man's nature might be more effectively tamed, even radically transformed? If not, civilization is doomed" (Harding, 1947, p. 5). "Beneath the decent facade of consciousness with its disciplined, moral order and its good intentions, lurk the crude instinctive forces of life, like monsters of the deep—devouring, begetting, warring endlessly" (Harding, 1947, p. 1).

data now available indicate that it is psychiatrically desirable for children to be protected, accepted, loved, and respected. But this is precisely what children (instinctively) desire. It is in this very tangible and scientifically testable sense that we assert instinctlike needs and rationality to be probably synergic and not antagonistic. Their apparent antagonism is an artifact produced by an exclusive preoccupation with sick people. If this turns out to be true, we shall have thereby resolved the age-old problem of which should be master, instinct or reason—a question now as obsolete as which should be the boss in a good marriage, the husband or the wife?

Antagonism Between Instincts and Society

Weak instinctlike impulses need a beneficent culture for their appearance, expression, and gratification, and are easily blasted by bad cultural conditions. Our society, for instance, must be considerably improved before weak hereditary needs may expect gratification. To accept as intrinsic an antagonism between instincts and society, between individual interests and social interests, is a terrific begging of the question. Possibly its main excuse that in the sick society and in the sick individual, it actually tends to be true. But it *need* not be true.[2] And in the good society it *cannot* be true. Individual and social interests under healthy social conditions are synergic and *not* antagonistic. The false dichotomy persists only because erroneous conceptions of individual and social interests are the natural ones under bad individual and social conditions.

Separate Instincts

One lack in instinct theory, as in most other theories of motivation, has been the failure to realize that impulses are dynamically related to each other in a hierarchy of differential strength. If impulses are treated independently of each other, various problems must remain unsolved, and many pseudoproblems are created. For instance, the essentially holistic or unitary quality of the motivational life is obscured, and the insoluble problem of making lists of motives is created. In addition, the value or choice principle is lost that permits us to say one need is higher than another, or more important than another or even more basic than another. The *only* thing that a need, taken discretely, can do is press for gratification, which is to say, its own obliteration. This opens the theoretical door to instincts toward death, quiescence, homeostasis, complacency, and equilibrium.

  This neglects the obvious fact that the gratification of any need, while putting that need to rest, allows other weaker needs that have been pushed aside to come to the foreground to press their claims. Needing never ceases. The gratification of one need uncovers another.

Restraint of Instincts

Coordinate with the bad-animal interpretation of instincts was the expectation that they would be seen most clearly in the insane, the neurotic, the criminal, the

---

[2]See descriptions of synergistic societies in Benedict (1970) and Maslow (1964b, 1965b).

feeble-minded, or the desperate. This follows naturally from the doctrine that conscience, rationality, and ethics are no more than an acquired veneer, completely different in character from what lies beneath, and are related to that underneath as manacles to prisoner. From this misconception follows the phrasing of civilization and all its institutions—school, church, court, legislation—as bad-animality-restraining forces.

This mistake is so crucial, so tragedy laden, that it may be likened in historical importance to such mistakes as the belief in divine right of kings, in the exclusive validity of any one religion, in the denial of evolution, or in the belief that the earth is flat. Any belief that makes people mistrust themselves and each other unnecessarily and be unrealistically pessimistic about human possibilities must be held partly responsible for every war that has ever been waged, for every racial antagonism, and for every religious massacre.

Recognize instinctlike needs to be not bad, but neutral or good, and a thousand pseudoproblems solve themselves and fade out of existence.

As a single instance, the training of children would be revolutionized even to the point of not using a word with so many ugly implications as training. The shift to acceptance of legitimate animal demands would push us toward their gratification rather than toward their frustration.

In our culture, the averagely deprived child, not yet completely acculturated (i.e., not yet deprived of all healthy and desirable animality), keeps on pressing for admiration, for safety, autonomy, for love, and so on in whatever childish ways he or she can invent. The ordinary reaction of the sophisticated adult is to say, "Oh! he's just showing off" or "She's only trying to get attention," and thereupon to banish the child from the adult company. That is to say, this diagnosis is customarily interpreted as an injunction *not* to give the child what he or she is seeking, *not* to notice, *not* to admire, *not* to applaud.

If however, we should come to consider such pleas for acceptance, love, or admiration as legitimate demands or *rights* of the same order as complaints of hunger, thirst, cold, or pain, we should automatically become gratifiers rather than frustrators. A single consequence of such a regime would be that both children and parents would have more fun, would enjoy each other more, and would surely therefore love each other more.

BASIC NEEDS IN INSTINCT THEORY

All the foregoing considerations encourage us to the hypothesis that basic needs are in some sense, and to some appreciable degree, constitutional or hereditary in their determination. Such a hypothesis cannot be directly proved today, since the direct genetic or neurological techniques that are needed do not yet exist.

In the following pages and in Maslow, 1965a are presented such available data and theoretical considerations as can be marshaled in support of the hypothesis that basic human needs are instinctlike.

Uniquely Human Instincts

A complete understanding of instinct theory requires a recognition of man's continuity with the animal world as well as recognition of the profound differences between the human species and all others. While it is true that any impulse or need found in man *and* all other animals (e.g., feeding or breathing) is thereby proved to be instinctive, it does not disprove the possibility that some instinctive impulses may be found only in the human species. Chimpanzees, homing pigeons, salmon, and cats each have instincts peculiar to the species. Why could not the human species also have characteristics peculiar to it?

Frustration Is Pathogenic

Another reason for considering basic needs to be instinctlike in nature is that the frustration of these needs is psychopathogenic, all clinicians agree. This is not true for neurotic needs, for habits, for addictions, or for preferences.

If society creates and inculcates all values, why is it that only *some* and not others are psychopathogenic when thwarted? We learn to eat three times a day, say thank you, and use forks and spoons, table and chair. We are forced to wear clothes and shoes, to sleep in a bed at night, and to speak English. We eat cows and sheep but not dogs and cats. We keep clean, compete for grades, and yearn for money. And yet any and all of these powerful habits can be frustrated without hurt and occasionally even with positive benefit. Under certain circumstances, as on a canoe or camping trip, we acknowledge their extrinsic nature by dropping them all with a sigh of relief. But this can *never* be said for love, for safety, or for respect.

Clearly, therefore, the basic needs stand in a special psychological and biological status. There is something different about them. They *must* be satisfied or else we get sick.

Gratification Is Healthy

The gratification of basic needs leads to consequences that may be called variously desirable, good, healthy, or self-actualizing. The words *desirable* and *good* are used here in a biological rather than in an a priori sense and are susceptible to operational definition. These consequences are those that the healthy organism itself tends to choose and strives toward under conditions that permit it to choose.

These psychological and somatic consequences have already been sketched out in the chapter on basic need gratification and need not be examined further here except to point out that there is nothing esoteric or nonscientific about this criterion. It can easily be put on an experimental basis, or even on an engineering basis, if we remember only that the problem is not very different from choosing the right oil for a car. One oil is better than another if, with it, the car works better. It is the general clinical finding that the organism, when fed safety, love, and respect, works better (i.e., perceives more efficiently, uses intelligence more fully, thinks to correct conclusions more often, digests food more efficiently, is less subject to various diseases, etc.).

Requiredness

The requiredness of basic need gratifiers differentiates them from all other need gratifiers. The organism itself, out of its own nature, points to an intrinsic range of satisfiers for which no substitute is possible as is the case, for instance, with habitual needs or even with many neurotic needs.

Psychotherapy

The effects of psychotherapy are of considerable interest for our purpose. It seems to be true for all major types of psychotherapy that, to the degree that they consider themselves successful, they foster, encourage, and strengthen what we have called basic instinct needs while they weaken or expunge altogether the so-called neurotic needs.

Especially for those therapies that explicitly claim only to leave the person what he or she essentially and deep-down *is* (e.g., the therapies of Rogers, Jung, or Horney) this is an important fact, for it implies that the personality has some intrinsic nature of its own, and is not created de novo by the therapist, but is only *released* by him or her to grow and develop in its own style. If insight and the dissolution of repression make a reaction disappear, this reaction may reasonably thereafter be considered to have been foreign and not intrinsic. If insight makes it stronger, we may thereafter consider it to be intrinsic. Also, as Horney (1939) has reasoned, if the release of anxiety causes the patient to become more affectionate and less hostile, does this not indicate that affection is basic to human nature, while hostility is not?

There is here, in principle, a gold mine of data for the theory of motivation, of self-actualization, of values, of learning, of cognition in general, of interpersonal relations, of acculturation and deacculturation, and so on.

Encouragement of Instincts

The instinctlike nature of basic needs calls for a reconsideration of the relationship between culture and personality so as to give a greater importance to determination by intraorganismic forces. If a person is shaped without regard to this structuring, it is true that no bones are broken and no obvious or immediate pathology results. It is, however, completely accepted that the pathology *will come,* if not obviously, then subtly, and if not sooner, then later. It is not too inaccurate to cite the ordinary adult neurosis as an example of such early violence to the intrinsic (though weak) demands of the organism.

The resistance of the person to enculturation in the interests of his or her own integrity and own intrinsic nature is, then, or should be, a respectable area of study in the psychological and social sciences. A person who gives in eagerly to the distorting forces in the culture (i.e., a well-adjusted person) may occasionally be less healthy than a delinquent, a criminal, or a neurotic who may be demonstrating by his or her reactions that he or she has spunk enough left to resist the breaking of his or her psychological bones.

From this same consideration, furthermore, arises what seems at first to be a paradox. Education, civilization, rationality, religion, law, government, have all been interpreted by most as being primarily instinct-restraining and suppressing forces. But if our contention is correct that instincts have more to fear from civilization than civilization from instincts, perhaps it ought to be the other way about (if we wish to produce better people and better societies): Perhaps it should be at least one function of education, law, religion, and so on to safeguard, foster, and encourage the expression and gratification of the instinctive needs for safety, for love, for self-esteem, and for self-actualization.

Resolution of Dichotomies

The instinctlike nature of basic needs helps resolve and transcend many philosophical contradictions such as those of biology versus culture, innate versus learned, the subjective versus the objective, or the idosyncratic versus the universal. This is so because the uncovering, self-searching psychotherapies and the personal growth, "soul-searching" techniques are also a path to discovering one's objective, biological nature, one's animality and specieshood, that is, one's Being.

Most psychotherapists of whatever school assume that they are uncovering or releasing a more basic and truer and more real personality as they cut down through the neurosis to a core or nucleus that was somehow there all the time but was overlaid, concealed, inhibited by the sick surface layers. Horney's phrasing (1950) shows this very clearly when she speaks of getting through the pseudoself to the Real Self. Self-actualization phrasings also stress the making real or actual of what the person already is, though in a potential form. The search for Identity means very much the same thing, as does "becoming what one truly is" and as does becoming "fully functioning," or "fully human," or individuated, or authentically oneself (Grof, 1975).

Obviously, a central task here is to become aware of what one *is* biologically, temperamentally, and constitutionally as a member of a particular species. This is certainly what all the varieties of psychoanalysis try to do—to help one to become conscious of one's needs, impulses, emotions, pleasures, and pains. But this is a kind of phenomenology of one's own inner biology, of one's animality and specieshood, a discovery of biology by *experiencing* it, what one might call subjective biology, introspected biology, experienced biology, or something of the sort.

But this amounts to subjective discovery of the objective, that is, the species-specific characteristics of humanness. It amounts to individual discovery of the general and the universal, a personal discovery of the impersonal or transpersonal (and even the transhuman). In a word, the instinctlike can be studied *both* subjectively and objectively via "soul-searching" *and* via the more usual external observation of the scientist. Biology is not only an objective science; it can also be a subjective one.

To paraphrase Archibald MacLeish's poem a little, we could say:

> A person doesn't mean:
> A person is.

chapter 5

The Hierarchy of Needs

The higher needs and lower needs have different properties, but they are the same in that both higher needs as well as lower needs must be included in the repertory of basic and given human nature. They are not different from or opposed to human nature; they are part of human nature. The consequences for psychological and philosophical theory are revolutionary. Most civilizations, along with their theories of politics, education, religion, and so on, have been based on the exact contradictory of this belief. On the whole, they have assumed the biological animal, and instinctlike aspects of human nature to be severely limited to the physiological needs for food, sex, and the like. The higher impulses for truth, for love, for beauty were assumed to be intrinsically different in nature from these animal needs. Furthermore, these interests were assumed to be antagonistic, mutually exclusive, and in perpetual conflict with each other for mastery. All culture, with all its instruments, is seen from such a point of view as on the side of the higher and against the lower. It is therefore necessarily an inhibitor and a frustrator, and is at best an unfortunate necessity.

DIFFERENCES BETWEEN HIGHER AND LOWER NEEDS

The basic needs arrange themselves in a fairly definite hierarchy on the basis of the principle of relative potency. Thus the safety need is stronger than the love need because it dominates the organism in various demonstrable ways when both needs are frustrated. In this sense, the physiological needs (which are themselves ordered in a subhierarchy) are stronger than the safety needs, which are stronger than the love needs, which in turn are stronger than the esteem needs, which are stronger than those idiosyncratic needs we have called the need for self-actualization.

This is an order of choice or preference. But it is also an order that ranges from lower to higher in various other senses that are listed here.

1. *The higher need is a later phyletic or evolutionary development*. We share the need for food with all living things, the need for love with (perhaps) the higher apes, the need for self-actualization with nobody. The higher the need the more specifically human it is.

2. *Higher needs are later ontogenetic developments*. Any individual at birth shows physical needs and probably also, in a very inchoate form, safety needs (e.g., it can probably be frightened or startled, and probably thrives better when its world shows enough regularity and orderliness so that it can be counted on). It is only after months of life that an infant shows the first signs of interpersonal ties and selective affection. Still later we may see fairly definitely the urges to autonomy, independence, achievement, and for respect and praise over and above safety and parental love. As for self-actualization, even Mozart had to wait until he was three or four.

3. *The higher the need the less imperative it is for sheer survival, the longer gratification can be postponed, and the easier it is for the need to disappear permanently*. Higher needs have less ability to dominate, organize, and press into their service the autonomic reactions and other capacities of the organism (e.g., it is easier to be single-minded, monomaniac, and desperate about safety than about respect). Deprivation of higher needs does not produce so desperate a defense and emergency reaction as is produced by lower deprivations. Respect is a dispensable luxury when compared with food or safety.

4. *Living at the higher need level means greater biological efficiency, greater longevity, less disease, better sleep, appetite, and so on*. The psychosomatic researchers prove again and again that anxiety, fear, lack of love, domination, and so on tend to encourage undesirable physical as well as undesirable psychological results. Higher need gratifications have survival value and growth value as well.

5. *Higher needs are less urgent subjectively*. They are less perceptible, less unmistakable, more easily confounded with other needs by suggestion, imitation, by mistaken belief or habit. To be able to recognize one's own needs (i.e., to know what one really wants) is a considerable psychological achievement. This is doubly true for the higher needs.

6. *Higher need gratifications produce more desirable subjective results, that is, more profound happiness, serenity, and richness of the inner life*. Satisfactions of the safety needs produce at best a feeling of relief and relaxation. In any case they cannot produce the ecstasy, peak experiences, and happy delirium of satisfied love, or such consequences as serenity, understanding, nobility, and the like.

7. *Pursuit and gratification of higher needs represent a general healthward trend, a trend away from psychopathology*. The evidence for this statement is presented in Chapter 3.

8. *The higher need has more preconditions*. This is true if only because prepotent needs must be gratified before it can be. Thus it takes more

quanta of satisfactions for the love need to appear in consciousness than for the safety need. In a more general sense, it may be said that life is more complex at the level of the higher needs. The search for respect and status involves more people, a larger scene, a longer run, more means, and partial goals, more subordinate and preliminary steps than does the search for love. The same may be said in turn of this latter need when compared with the search for safety.

9. *Higher needs require better outside conditions to make them possible.* Better environmental conditions (familial, economic, political, educational, etc.) are all more necessary to allow people to love each other than merely to keep them from killing each other. *Very* good conditions are needed to make self-actualizing possible.

10. *A greater value is usually placed upon the higher need than upon the lower by those who have been gratified in both.* Such people will sacrifice more for the higher satisfaction, and furthermore will more readily be able to withstand lower deprivation. For example, they will find it easier to live ascetic lives, to withstand danger for the sake of principle, to give up money and prestige for the sake of self-actualization. Those who have known both universally regard self-respect as a higher, more valuable subjective experience than a filled belly.

11. *The higher the need level, the wider is the circle of love identification: the greater is the number of people love-identified with, and the greater is the average degree of love identification.* We may define love identification as, in principle, a merging into a single hierarchy of prepotency of the needs of two or more people. Two people who love each other well will react to each other's needs and their own indiscriminately. Indeed the other's need *is* one's own need.

12. *The pursuit and the gratification of the higher needs have desirable civic and social consequences.* To some extent, the higher the need the less selfish it must be. Hunger is highly egocentric; the only way to satisfy it is to satisfy oneself. But the search for love and respect necessarily involves other people. Moreover, it involves satisfaction for these other people. People who have enough basic satisfaction to look for love and respect (rather than just food and safety) tend to develop such qualities as loyalty, friendliness, and civic consciousness, and to become better parents, husbands, teachers, public servants, and so on.

13. *Satisfaction of higher needs is closer to self-actualization than is lower-need satisfaction.* If the theory of self-actualization be accepted, this is an important difference. Among other things, it means that we may expect to find, in people living at the higher need level, a larger number and greater degree of the qualities found in self-actualizing people.

14. *The pursuit and gratification of the higher needs leads to greater, stronger, and truer individualism.* This may seem to contradict the previous statement that living at higher need levels means more love identification, that is, more socialization. However it may sound logically, it is nevertheless an empirical reality. People living at the level of self-actualization are, in fact, found simultaneously to love mankind most and to be the most developed idiosyncratically. This completely supports Fromm's contention that self-love (or better, self-respect) is synergic with rather than antagonistic to love for others. His discussion of in-

dividuality, spontaneity, and robotization is also relevant (Fromm, 1941).

15. *The higher the need level the easier and more effective psychotherapy can be: at the lowest need levels it is of hardly any avail.* Hunger cannot be stilled by psychotherapy.

16. *The lower needs are far more localized, more tangible, and more limited than are the higher needs.* Hunger and thirst are much more obviously bodily than is love, which in turn is more so than respect. In addition, lower need satisfiers are much more tangible or observable than are higher need satisfactions. Furthermore, they are more limited in the sense that a smaller quantity of gratifiers is needed to still the need. Only so much food can be eaten, but love, respect, and cognitive satisfactions are almost unlimited.

CONSEQUENCES OF A HIERARCHY OF NEEDS

Recognizing the higher needs to be instinctlike and biological, precisely as biological as the need for food, has many repercussions of which we can list only a few.

1. Probably most important of all is the realization that the dichotomy between the cognitive and the conative is false and must be resolved. The needs for knowledge, for understanding, for a life philosophy, for a theoretical frame of reference, for a value system, are themselves a conative or impulsive part of our primitive and animal nature (we are very special animals). Since we know also that our needs are not completely blind, that they are modified by culture, by reality, and by possibility, it follows that cognition plays a considerable role in their development. It is John Dewey's claim that the very existence and definition of a need depends on the cognition of reality, of the possibility or impossibility of gratification.

2. Many age-old philosophical problems must be seen in a new light. Some of them perhaps may even be seen to be pseudoproblems resting on misconceptions about human motivational life. Here may be included, for instance, the sharp distinction between selfishness and unselfishness. If our instinctlike impulses, for instance, to love, arrange it so that we get more personal "selfish" pleasure from watching our children eat a special treat than from eating it ourselves, then how shall we define "selfish" and how differentiate it from "unselfish"? Are people who risk their lives for the truth any less selfish than those who risk their lives for food, if the need for truth is as animal as the need for food? Obviously also hedonistic theory must be recast if animal pleasure, selfish pleasure, personal pleasure can come equally from gratification of the needs for food, sex, truth, beauty, love, or respect. This implies that a higher need hedonism might very well stand where a lower need hedonism would fall. The romantic-classic opposition, the Dionysian-Apollonian contrast, must certainly be modified. In at least some of its forms, it has been based on the same illegitimate dichotomy between lower needs as animal and higher needs as nonanimal or antianimal.

Along with this must go considerable revision of the concepts of rational and irrational, the contrast between rational and impulsive, and the general notion of the rational life as opposed to the instinctive life.

3. The philosopher of ethics has much to learn from a close examination of human motivational life. If our noblest impulses are seen not as checkreins on the horses, but as themselves horses, and if our animal needs are seen to be of the same nature as our highest needs, how can a sharp dichotomy between them be sustained? How can we continue to believe that they could come from different sources? Furthermore, if we clearly and fully recognize that these noble and good impulses come into existence and grow potent primarily as a consequence of the prior gratification of the more demanding animal needs, we should certainly speak less exclusively of self-control, inhibition, discipline, and so on and more frequently of spontaneity, gratification, and self-choice. There seems to be less opposition than we thought between the stern voice of duty and the gay call to pleasure. At the highest level of living (i.e., of Being), duty *is* pleasure, one's "work" is loved, and there is no difference between working and vacationing.

4. Our conception of culture and of people's relation to it must change in the direction of "synergy," as Ruth Benedict (1970) called it. Culture can be basic need gratifying (Maslow, 1967, 1969b) rather than need inhibiting. Furthermore it is created not only for human needs but by them. The culture-individual dichotomy needs reexamination. There should be less exclusive stress on their antagonism and more on their possible collaboration and synergy.

5. The recognition that humanity's best impulses are appreciably intrinsic, rather than fortuitous and relative, must have tremendous implication for value theory. It means, for one thing, that it is no longer either necessary or desirable to deduce values by logic or to try to read them off from authorities or revelations. All we need do, apparently, is to observe and research. Human nature carries within itself the answer to the questions: How can I be good; how can I be happy; how can I be fruitful? The organism tells us what it needs (and therefore what it values) by sickening when deprived of these values and by growing when gratified.

6. A study of these basic needs has shown that though their nature is to an appreciable extent instinctlike, in many ways they are not like the instincts we know so well in lower animals. Most important of all these differences is the unexpected finding that in contradiction to the age-old assumption that instincts are strong, undesirable, and unchangeable, our basic needs, though instinctlike, are weak. To be impulse-aware, to know that we really want and need love, respect, knowledge, a philosophy, self-actualization, and so forth—this is a difficult psychological achievement. Not only this, but the higher they are, the weaker and more easily changed and suppressed they are. Finally they are not bad but are either neutral or good. We wind up with the paradox that our human instincts, what is left of them, are so weak that they need protection against culture, against education, against learning—in a word, against being overwhelmed by the environment.

7. Our understanding of the aims of psychotherapy (and of education, of

child rearing, of the formation of the good character in general) must shift considerably. To many it still means the acquisition of a set of inhibitions and controls of the intrinsic impulses. Discipline, control, suppression are the watchwords of such a regime. But if therapy means a pressure toward breaking controls and inhibitions, then our new key words must be spontaneity, release, naturalness, self-acceptance, impulse awareness, gratification, self-choice. If our intrinsic impulses are understood to be admirable rather than detestable, we shall certainly wish to free them for their fullest expression rather than to bind them into straitjackets.

8. If instincts can be weak and if higher needs are seen to be instinctlike in character, and if culture is seen as more, not less, powerful than instinctlike impulses, and if basic needs turn out to be good and not bad, then the improvement of human nature may come about via fostering of instinctlike tendencies as well as through fostering social improvements. Indeed, the point of bettering the culture will be seen as giving our inner biological tendencies a better chance to actualize themselves.

9. In the finding that living at the higher need level can sometimes become relatively independent of lower need gratification (and even of higher need gratification in a pinch), we may have a solution to an age-old dilemma of the theologians. They have always found it necessary to attempt to reconcile the flesh and the spirit, the angel and the devil—the higher and the lower in the human organism—but no one has ever found a satisfactory solution. Functional autonomy of the higher need life seems to be part of the answer. The higher develops only on the basis of the lower, but eventually, when well established, may become *relatively* independent of the lower (Allport, 1955).

10. In addition to Darwinian survival value, we may now also postulate "growth values." Not only is it good to survive, but it is also good (preferred, chosen, good for the organism) for the person to grow toward full humanness, toward actualization of potentialities, toward greater happiness, serenity, peak experiences, toward transcendence, toward richer and more accurate cognition of reality, and so on. No longer need we rest on sheer viability and survival as our only ultimate proof that poverty or war or domination or cruelty are bad, rather than good. We can consider them bad because they also degrade the quality of life, of personality, of consciousness, of wisdom.

chapter 6

Unmotivated Behavior

In this chapter we shall grope further toward a scientifically usable differentiation between striving (doing, coping, achieving, trying, purposiveness) and being-becoming (existing, expressing, growing, self-actualization). This distinction is, of course, a familiar one in Eastern cultures and religions, such as Taoism, and in our culture among some philosophers, theologians, aestheticians, students of mysticism, and increasingly among "humanistic psychologists," existential psychologists, and the like.

Western culture generally rests on the Judaic-Christian theology. The United States particularly is dominated by the Puritan and pragmatic spirit, which stresses work, struggle and striving, soberness and earnestness, and, above all, purposefulness.[1] Like any other social institution, science in general and psychology in particular are not exempt from these cultural climate and atmosphere effects. American psychology, by participation, is overpragmatic, over-Puritan, and over-

---

[1]"Idle associations, superfluous images, involved dreams, random explorations, play a part in development that could never be justified, in origin, on any principle of economy or by any direct expectation of usefulness. In a mechanistic culture like our own, these important activities have been either undervalued or overlooked. . . .

"Once we rid ourselves of the unconscious bias of mechanism, we must recognize that the 'superfluous' is just as essential to human development as the economic: that beauty, for example, has played as large a part in evolution as use and cannot be explained, as Darwin sought to, merely as a practical device for courtship or fertilization. In short, it is just as permissible to conceive nature, mythologically, as a poet, working in metaphors and rhythms, as to think of nature as a cunning mechanic, trying to save material, make both ends meet, do the job efficiently and cheaply. The Mechanistic interpretation is quite as subjective as the poetic one; and up to a point each is useful" (Mumford, 1951, p. 35).

purposeful. This is evident not only in its effects and avowed purposes but also in its gaps, in what it neglects. No textbooks have chapters on fun and gaiety, on leisure and meditation, on loafing and puttering, on aimless, useless, and purposeless activity, on aesthetic creation or experience, or on unmotivated activity. That is to say, American psychology is busily occupying itself with only half of life to the neglect of the other—and perhaps more important—half!

From the point of view of values, this may be described as a preoccupation with means to the exclusion of concern with ends. This philosophy is implicit in practically all American psychology (including orthodox and revisionist psychoanalysis), which uniformly neglects per se activity and end experience (which gets nothing done) in favor of coping, changing, effective, purposeful activity that gets something useful done. The culmination of this philosophy may be found in a quite explicit form in John Dewey's *Theory of Valuation* (1939), in which the possibility of ends is in effect denied; they are themselves only means to other means, to other means . . ., and so on (although in other of his writings, he *does* accept the existence of ends).

Because contemporary psychology is overly pragmatic, it abdicates from certain areas that should be of great concern to it. In its preoccupation with practical results, with technology and means, it has notoriously little to say, for example, about beauty, art, fun, play, wonder, awe, joy, love, happiness, and other "useless" reactions and end experiences. It is therefore of little or no service to the artist, the musician, the poet, the novelist, to the humanist, the connoisseur, the axiologist, the theologian, or to other end- or enjoyment-oriented individuals. This is the equivalent of an accusation against psychology that it offers little to the modern person whose most desperate need is a naturalistic or humanistic end or value system.

The distinction between the expressive (noninstrumental) and the coping (instrumental, adaptive, functional, purposive) components of behavior has not yet been properly exploited as a basis for value psychology.[2] By exploring and applying the differentiation between expression and coping—which is simultaneously a differentiation between "useless" and "useful" behavior—we may help to extend the jurisdiction of psychology in these directions.

The first part of this chapter discusses the differences between expression and coping. The latter part examines several examples of behaviors of expression rather than of coping, which could be considered *unmotivated behaviors*.

COPING VERSUS EXPRESSION

Here is a summary of the points of distinction between coping behaviors and expressive behaviors:

---

[2]We must be careful here to avoid sharp, either-or dichotomizing. Most acts of behavior have both an expressive and a coping component; for example, walking has simultaneously a purpose and a style. And yet we do not wish to exclude, as do Allport and Vernon (1933), the theoretical possibility of practically pure expressive acts, such as sauntering instead of walking; blushing; gracefulness; poor posture; whistling; a child's laughing in glee; private, noncommunicative artistic activity; pure self-actualization, and so on.

Purposive or unpurposive   Coping is by definition purposive and motivated; expression is often unmotivated.

Paradox of trying not to try   Coping is effortful; expression is effortless in most instances. Artistic expression is, of course, a special and in-between case because one *learns* to be spontaneous and expressive (if one is successful). One can *try* to relax.

External and internal determinants   Coping is more determined by external environmental and cultural variables; expression is largely determined by the state of the organism. A corollary is the much higher correlation of expression with deep-lying character structure. So-called projective tests might more accurately be called expressive tests.

Learned or unlearned   Coping is most often learned; expression is most often unlearned or released or disinhibited.

Possibility of control   Coping is more easily controlled (repressed, suppressed, inhibited, or acculturated); expression is more often uncontrolled and sometimes even uncontrollable.

Affecting the environment   Coping is usually designed to cause changes in the environment and often does; expression is not designed to do anything. If it causes environmental changes, it does so unwittingly.

Means and ends   Coping is characteristically means behavior, the end being need gratification of threat reduction. Expression is often an end in itself.

Conscious or unconscious   Typically, the coping component is conscious (although it may become unconscious); expression is more often not conscious.

Purposive or Unpurposive Behavior

Coping behavior always has among its determinants drives, needs, goals, purposes, functions, or aims. It comes into existence to get something done, such as walking to some destination, shopping for food, going to mail a letter, building a set of bookshelves, or doing the work for which we get paid. The term *coping* itself (Maslow and Mittelman, 1951) implies the attempt to solve a problem or at least to deal with it. It therefore implies a reference to something beyond itself; it is not self-contained. This reference may be either to immediate or to basic needs, to means as well as ends, to frustration-induced behavior as well as to goal-seeking behavior.

Expressive behavior of the type so far discussed by psychologists is generally unmotivated, although, of course, it is determined. (That is, though expressive behavior has many determinants, need gratification need not be one of them.) It simply mirrors, reflects, signifies, or expresses some state of the organism. Indeed, it most often is *part* of that state: the stupidity of the moron, the smile and the springy walk of the healthy person, the benevolent mien of the kind and affectionate, the beauty of the beautiful person, the slumping posture, lowered tonus, and hopeless expression of the depressed person, the style of handwriting, walking, gesturing, smiling, dancing, and so forth. These are nonpurposive. They have no aim or goal. They were not elaborated for the sake of need gratification.[3] They are epiphenomenal.

Paradox of Trying Not to Try

While all this is true as far as it goes, a special problem is raised by what at first glance seems a paradox, namely, the concept of motivated self-expression. The more sophisticated person can *try* to be honest, graceful, kind, or even artless. People who have been through psychoanalysis as well as people at the highest motivational levels know well how this is.

Indeed, it is their most basic single problem. Self-acceptance and spontaneity are among the easiest achievements (e.g., in healthy children) and the most difficult (e.g., in self-questioning, self-improving adults, especially those who have been or still are neurotic). Indeed, for some it is an impossible achievement; for example, in certain types of neurosis the individual is an actor who has no self at all in the ordinary sense, but only a repertoire of roles from which to choose.

We may take two examples, one simple and the other complex, to demonstrate the (apparent) contradictions involved in the concept of motivated, purposeful spontaneity, of Taoistic yielding and letting go, as with tight muscles or sphincters. The most desirable way to dance, at least for the amateur, is to be spontaneous, fluid, automatically responsive to the rhythm of the music and the unconscious wishes of the partner. Good dancers can let themselves go, becoming passive instruments fashioned by the music and played upon by it. They need have no wish, no criticism, no direction, no will. In a very real and useful sense of the word, they may become passive, even as they dance to the point of exhaustion. Such passive spontaneity or willing abandon can yield some of life's greatest pleasures, as in allowing the surf to tumble one about, or allowing oneself to be cared for and nursed, massaged, barbered, as in being made love to, or as in the mother who passively allows her baby to suckle, to bite, and to crawl over her. But few people can dance as well as this. Most will try, will be directed, self-controlled, and purposeful, will listen carefully to the rhythm of the music, and by a conscious act of choice fall in with it. They will be poor dancers from the point of view of the onlooker and from the subjective point of view as well, for they will never enjoy dancing as a profound experience of self-forgetfulness and voluntary renunciation of control unless they finally transcend trying and become spontaneous.

Many dancers become good without training. And yet education can be a

---

[3]This statement is independent of any particular phrasing of motivation theory. For instance, it applies as well to simple hedonism; thus we may rephrase our statement to say: Coping behavior is responsive to praise or blame, reward or punishment; expressive behavior is ordinarily not, at least so long as it remains expressive.

help here too. But it must be a different kind, an education in spontaneity and eager abandon, in being natural, nonvoluntary, noncritical, and passive in the Taoist style, trying not to try. One must "learn" for such purposes to be able to drop inhibitions, self-consciousness, will, control, acculturation, and dignity. ("When once you are free from all seeming, from all craving and lusting, then will you move of your own impulse, without so much as knowing that you move"—Lao Tse.)

More difficult problems are raised by an examination of the nature of self-actualization. Of people who are at this level of motivational development, it may be said that their actions and creations are in a very high degree spontaneous, guileness, open, self-disclosing, and unedited and therefore expressive (the "Easy State" we might call it, after Asrani). Furthermore, their motivations change in quality so much, and are so different from the ordinary needs for safety or love or respect, that they ought not even to be called by the same name. (I have suggested the word *metaneeds* to describe the motivations of self-actualizing people.)

If the wish for love be called a need, the pressure to self-actualize ought to be called by some name other than need because it has so many different characteristics. The one main difference most pertinent to our present task is that love and respect and the like may be considered as external qualities that the organism lacks and therefore needs. Self-actualization is not a lack or deficiency in this sense. It is not something extrinsic that the organism needs for health as, for example, a tree needs water. Self-actualization is intrinsic growth of what is already in the organism, or more accurately of what *is* the organism itself. Just as our tree needs food, sun, water from the environment, so does the person need safety, love, and respect from the social environment. But as in the first case, so also in the second, this is just where real development (i.e., of individuality) begins. All trees need sunlight and all human beings need love, and yet, once satiated with these elementary necessities, each tree and each human being proceeds to develop in its own style, uniquely, using these universal necessities to its own private purposes. In a word, development then proceeds from within rather than from without, and paradoxically the highest motive is to be unmotivated and nonstriving, that is, to behave purely expressively. Or, to say it in another way, self-actualization is growth-motivated rather than deficiency-motivated. It is a "second naivete," a wise innocence, an "Easy State."

One can try to go in the direction of self-actualization by solving the lesser, prerequisite motivational problems. Thereby one consciously and purposefully seeks spontaneity. Thus at the highest levels of human development, the distinction between coping and expression, like so many other psychological dichotomies, is resolved and transcended, and trying becomes a path to nontrying.[4]

---

[4]Gordon Allport stresses strongly and correctly that "being" is as effortful and active as is striving. His suggestions would lead us to contrast striving-to-make-up-deficiencies with striving-to-self-actualize rather than striving with being. This correction also serves to remove the too easily acquired impression that "being," unmotivated reactions and purposeless activity are easier, less energetic and less effortful than coping with external problems. That this *dolce far niente* interpretation of self-actualization is misleading is easily demonstrated by such examples of struggling self-development as Beethoven.

External and Internal Determinants

Coping behavior is characteristically more determined by relatively external de-terminants than is expressive behavior. It is most often a functional response to an emergency, a problem, or a need whose solution or gratification comes from the physical and/or cultural world. Ultimately, as we have seen, it is an attempt to make up internal deficiencies by external satisfiers.

Expressive behavior contrasts with coping behavior in its more exclusively characterological determination (see below). We may say that coping behavior is essentially an interaction of the character with the nonpsychic world, adjusting each to the other with mutual effect; expression is essentially an epiphenomenon or by-product of the nature of the character structure. In the former, therefore, may be detected the working of both the laws of the physical world and of the inner character; in the latter one detects primarily psychological or character-ological laws. An illustration could be the contrast between representational and nonrepresentational art.

Several corollaries follow. (1) It is certain that if one wishes to know about the character structure, the best behavior to study is expressive rather than coping behavior. This is supported by the now-extensive experience with projective (ex-pressive) tests. (2) With reference to the perennial debate about what is psychology and what is the best approach to its study, it is clear that adjustmental, purposive, motivated, coping behavior is not the only kind of behavior there is. (3) Our distinction may have some bearing on the question of the continuity or discon-tinuity of psychology with the other sciences. In principle the study of the natural world should help us to understand coping behavior but probably not expression. The latter seems to be more purely psychological, probably having its own rules and laws and therefore best studied directly rather than through the physical and natural sciences.

Learned or Unlearned Behavior

Ideal coping behavior is characteristically learned, while ideal expressive behavior is characteristically unlearned. We do not have to learn how to feel helpless or look healthy or be stupid or show anger, while we do ordinarily have to learn how to build bookshelves, ride a bicycle, or dress ourselves. This contrast may be clearly seen in the determinants of reaction to achievement tests on the one hand and to the Rorschach test on the other. Also, coping behavior tends to die out unless rewarded; expression often persists without reward or reinforcement. One is gratification-bent; the other is not.

Possibility of Control

Differential determination by inner and outer determinants shows itself also in a varying susceptibility to conscious or unconscious control (inhibition, repression, suppression). Spontaneous expression is very difficult to manage, to change, to conceal, to control, or to influence in any way. Indeed, control and expression are by definition antithetical. This is true even for the motivated self-expression spoken of above, for this is the end product of a series of efforts to learn how not to control.

Control of style of handwriting, dancing, singing, speaking, or emotional reacting may at best be kept up for only a short time. Supervision or criticism of one's reactions cannot be continuous. Sooner or later because of fatigue, distraction, redirection, or attention control slips, and deeper, less conscious, more automatic, more characterological determinants take over (Allport, 1961). Expression is not, in the full sense, voluntary behavior. Another aspect of this contrast is the effortlessness of expression. Coping is in principle effortful. (Again, the artist is a special case.)

Some warnings are called for here. An easy mistake here is to think of spontaneity and expressiveness as good always and control of any kind as bad and undesirable. This is not so. Certainly, much of the time, expressiveness *feels* better, is more fun, more honest, effortless, and so on, than self-control, so is in this sense desirable both for the person himself and for his interpersonal relationships, as for instance Jourard (1968) has shown. And yet there are several meanings of self-control, or of inhibition, and some of them are quite desirable and healthy, even apart from what is necessary for dealing with the outside world. Control need not mean frustration or renunciation of basic need gratifications. What I would call the "Apollonizing controls" do *not* call the gratification of needs into question at all; they make them *more* rather than less enjoyable by suitable delay (as in sex), by gracefulness (as in dancing or swimming), by aestheticizing (as with food and drink), by stylizing (as in sonnets), by ceremonializing, sacralizing, dignifying, by doing something well rather than just doing it.

And then too—what has to be repeated again and again—is that healthy persons are not only expressive. They must be able to be expressive when they wish to be. They must be able to let themselves go. They must be able to drop controls, inhibitions, defenses when they deem this desirable. But equally they must have the ability to control themselves, to delay their pleasures, to be polite, to avoid hurting, to keep their mouths shut, and to rein their impulses. They must be able to be either Dionysian or Apollonian, Stoic or Epicurean, expressive or coping, controlled or uncontrolled, self-disclosing or self-concealing, able to have fun and able to give up fun, able to think of the future as well as the present. Healthy or self-actualizing persons are essentially versatile; they have lost fewer of the human capacities than the average person has. They have a larger armamentarium of responses and moves toward full humanness as a limit; that is they have *all* the human capacities.

Affecting the Environment

Coping behavior characteristically originates as an attempt to change the world, and characteristically does so with more or less success. Expressive behavior, on the other hand, often has no effect on the environment. And where it does have such effect, it is not premeditated, willed, or purposed; it is unwitting.

As an example we may take a person in conversation. Conversation has purpose; for example, he or she is a salesperson trying to get an order, and the conversation is consciously and avowedly brought into being for this reason. But his or her style of speaking may be unconsciously hostile or snobbish or supercilious and may cause him or her to lose the order. Thus the expressive aspects of behavior may have environmental effects, but it is to be noted that the speaker did not want these effects, did not try to be supercilious or hostile, and was not even aware of giving this impression. The environmental effects of expression, when there are any at all, are unmotivated, unpurposed, and epiphenomenal.

Means and Ends

Coping behavior is always instrumental, always a means to a motivated end. Contrariwise, any means-end behavior (with the one exception, discussed above, of voluntarily giving up coping) must be coping behavior.

On the other hand, the various forms of expressive behavior either have nothing to do with either means or ends (e.g., style of handwriting), or else they come close to being ends-in-themselves behavior (e.g., singing, sauntering, painting, or extemporizing at the piano).[5]

Conscious or Unconscious Behavior

Expression in its purest forms is unconscious, or at least not fully conscious. We are ordinarily unaware of our style of walking, standing, smiling, or laughing. It is true that we may be made aware of them by moving pictures, phonograph records, caricatures, or imitations. But such are apt to be exceptions or at least uncharacteristic. Expressive acts that are conscious—choosing our clothes, furniture, hair style—are seen as special, unusual, or intermediate cases. But coping may be and characteristically is fully conscious. When it is unconscious, this is seen as exceptional or unusual.

EXPRESSIVE BEHAVIORS

Expression must be called relatively unmotivated and unpurposeful, in contrast with coping, which is both motivated and purposive. There are many examples of relatively unmotivated behaviors, and we shall now discuss some of them briefly. It should be observed that they are all relatively neglected areas of psychology, an excellent illustration for the student of science of the way in which a limited outlook on life creates a limited world. For the carpenter who is *only* a carpenter, the world is made of wood.

[5]In our overly pragmatic culture, the instrumental spirit can overtake even the end experiences: love ("It's the normal thing to do"), sport ("Good for the digestion"), ("Relaxation improves sleep"), beautiful weather ("Good for business"), reading ("I really should keep up with things"), affection ("Do you want your child to be neurotic?"), kindness ("Bread cast upon the waters . . ."), science ("National defense!"), art ("Has definitely improved American advertising"), kindness ("If you're not, they'll steal the silver").

Being

The expressive behaviors tend to occur when people are being themselves, developing, growing and maturing, not going anywhere (in the sense, e.g., of social climbing), not striving in the ordinary sense of straining and trying for a state of affairs other than that in which they are.[6] As a jumping-off point for thinking about just being, the concept of *waiting* is useful. The cat in the sun does *not* wait any more than a tree waits. Waiting implies wasted, unappreciated time that is empty of significance for the organism and is a by-product of a too exclusively means-oriented attitude toward life. It is most often a stupid, inefficient, and wasteful response, since (1) impatience usually does no good, even from the point of view of efficiency, and (2) even means experiences and means behaviors can be enjoyed, savored, and appreciated for their own sake at, so to speak, no extra charge. Travel is an excellent example of the way in which a piece of time can be either enjoyed as end experience or completely wasted. Educaton is another instance. So also are interpersonal relations in general.

Involved here also is a certain inversion of the concept of wasted time. For the use-oriented, purposeful, need-reducing kind of person that time is wasted that achieves nothing and serves no purpose. While this is a perfectly legitimate usage, we may suggest that an equally legitimate usage might be to consider that time wasted that does not carry end experience with it, that is, that is not ultimately enjoyed. "Time you enjoy wasting is not wasted time." "Some things that are not necessary may yet be essential."

An excellent illustration of the way in which our culture is unable to take its end experiences straight may be seen in strolling, canoeing, golfing, and the like. Generally these activities are extolled because they get people into the open, close to nature, out into the sunshine, or into beautiful surroundings. In essence, these are ways in which what *should be* unmotivated end activities and end experiences are thrown into a purposeful, achieving, pragmatic framework in order to appease the Western conscience.

Art

The creation of art may be relatively motivated (when it seeks to communicate, to arouse emotion, to show, to do something to another person) or it may be relatively unmotivated (when it is expressive rather than communicative, intrapersonal rather than interpersonal). The fact that expression may have unforeseen interpersonal effects (secondary gain) is beside the point.

Very much to the point, however, is the question "Is there a *need* for expression?" If there is, then artistic expression, as well as cathartic and release phenomena, are as motivated as food seeking or love seeking. We have indicated at various points in earlier chapters that we think the evidence will soon force us to recognize such a need to express in action whatever impulses have been aroused in the organism. That this will make paradoxes is clear from the fact that *any*

[6]Chapter 11, "Self-actualizing People: A Study of Psychological Health," documents this observation and elaborates it.

need or *any* capacity is an impulse and therefore seeks expression. Should it then be called a separate need or impulse or should it rather be considered to be a universal characteristic of *any* impulse?

At this point we need not opt for one or another of these alternatives, since our only purpose is to show that they are *all* neglected. Whichever one turns out to be most fruitful will force a recognition of (1) the category of unmotivation or (2) a tremendous reconstruction of all motivation theory.

Quite as important for the sophisticated person is the question of aesthetic experience. This is so rich and valuable an experience for so many people that they will simply scorn or sneer at any psychological theory that denies or neglects it, no matter what scientific grounds there may be for such neglect. Science must account for *all* reality, not only the impoverished and bloodless portions of it. The fact that the aesthetic response is useless and purposeless, and that we know nothing about its motivations, if indeed there *are* any in the ordinary sense, should indicate to us only the poverty of our official psychology.

Even the aesthetic perception, cognitively speaking, may be seen as relatively unmotivated by comparison with ordinary cognitions.[7] Taoistic, disinterested perceiving of the many-sidedness of a phenomenon (with especial reference not to usefulness but to its efficacy in producing end experiences) is one characteristic of the aesthetic perception.[8]

Appreciation

Not only the aesthetic experience but many others also are passively received and enjoyed by the organism. This enjoyment itself can hardly be said to be motivated; if anything it is the end or purpose of motivated activity, the epiphenomenon of need gratification.

The mystic experience, the experience of awe, of delight, of wonder, of mystery, and of admiration are all subjectively rich experiences of the same passive, aesthetic sort, experiences that beat their way in upon the organism, flooding it as music does. These too are end experiences, ultimate rather than instrumental,

---

[7]In Chapter 17, "Stereotyping Versus True Cognition," we see that categorized perception is at best partial; it is not so much an examination of all the attributes of an object as a classification of it on the basis of those few attributes that are useful to us, relevant to our concerns, and need gratifying or need threatening.

[8]"The brain serves to bring about this choice: it actualizes the useful memories, it keeps in the lower strata of the consciousness those which are of no use. One could say as much for perception. The auxiliary of action, it isolates *that part of reality as a whole that interests us; it shows us less the things themselves than the use we can make of them*. It classifies, it labels them beforehand; we scarcely look at the object, it is enough for us to know to which category it belongs. But now and then, by a lucky accident, men arise whose senses or whose consciousness are less adherent to life. Nature has forgotten *to attach their faculty of perceiving to their faculty of acting*. When they look at a thing, *they see it for itself, and not for themselves. They do not perceive simply with a view to action; they perceive in order to perceive—for nothing, for the pleasure of doing so*. In regard to a certain aspect of their nature, whether it be their consciousness or one of their senses, they are born *detached;* and according to whether this detachment is that of a certain particular sense, or of consciousness, they are painters or sculptors, musicians or poets. It is therefore a much more direct vision of reality that we find in the different arts; and *it is because the artist is less intent on utilizing his perception that he perceives a greater number of things*" (Bergson, 1944, pp. 162–163).

changing the outside world not at all. All this is true for leisure as well, if it is properly defined (Pieper, 1964).

Perhaps it is appropriate to speak here of two such ultimate pleasures: (1) function pleasure and (2) the pleasure of sheer living (biopleasure, zestful experiencing). Especially can we see these in the child who repeats and repeats his newly perfected skill out of sheer delight that comes with good and skillful functioning. Dancing may also be a good example. As for the basic life pleasure, any ailing or dyspeptic or nauseated person can testify to the reality of that most ultimate biological pleasure (zestful experiencing) that is an automatic, unsought-for, unmotivated by-product of being alive and healthy.

Play

Play may be either coping or expressive or both (see page 42) as is now quite clear from the literature on play therapy and play diagnosis. It seems quite probable that this general conclusion will supplant the various functional, purposive, and motivational theories of play put forward in the past. Since there is nothing to prevent us from using the coping-expressive dichotomy with animals, we may also reasonably look forward to more useful and realistic interpretations of animal play as well. All we have to do to open up this new area for research is to admit the possibility that play may be useless and unmotivated, a phenomenon of being rather than of striving, end rather than means. The same may probably be affirmed of laughter, hilarity, gaiety, having fun, joy, ecstasy, euphoria, and so on.

Intellectual Expression

Intellectual expression—ideology, philosophy, theology, cognition, and so on— is another area that has resisted the tools of official psychology. We think this is partly so because thinking in general has been automatically regarded since Darwin and Dewey as problem solving, that is, as functional and as motivated. In the good life lived by the healthy person, thinking, like perceiving, may be spontaneous and passive reception or production, an unmotivated, effortless, happy expression of the nature and existence of the organism, a *letting* things happen rather than making them happen, as much an example of being as the perfume of a flower or the apples on a tree.

two

PSYCHOPATHOLOGY AND NORMALITY

chapter 7

Origins of Pathology

The conception of motivation so far outlined contains some important cues for understanding the origins of psychopathology as well as the nature of frustration, conflict, and threat.

Practically all theories that propose to explain how psychopathology originates and how it maintains itself rest most heavily on the two concepts of frustration and conflict with which we shall now deal. Some frustrations do produce pathology; some do not. Some conflicts likewise do, and some do not. It will appear that recourse to basic need theory is necessary to unravel this puzzle.

DEPRIVATION AND THREAT

It is easy in the discussion of frustration to fall into the error of segmenting the human being; there is still a tendency to speak of the mouth or stomach being frustrated, or of a need being frustrated. We must remember always that only a whole human being is frustrated, never a part of a human being.

With this in mind, an important distinction becomes apparent, namely, the difference between deprivation and threat to the personality. The usual definitions of frustration are in terms simply of not getting what one desires, of interference with a wish, or with a gratification. Such a definition fails to make the distinction between a deprivation that is unimportant to the organism (easily substituted for, with few serious aftereffects) and, on the other hand, a deprivation that is at the same time a threat to the personality, that is, to the life goals of the individual, to the defensive system, to self-esteem, to self-actualization—to basic needs. It is our contention that only a *threatening* deprivation has the multitude of effects (usually undesirable) that are commonly attributed to frustration in general.

A goal object may have two meanings for the individual. First, it has its intrinsic meaning, and it may have also a secondary, symbolic value. Thus a certain child deprived of an ice-cream cone that she wanted may have lost simply an ice-cream cone. A second child, however, deprived of an ice-cream cone may have lost not only a sensory gratification, but may feel deprived of the love of his mother because she refused to buy it for him. For the second child the ice-cream cone not only has an intrinsic value, but may also be the carrier of psychological values. Being deprived merely of ice cream qua ice cream probably means little for a healthy individual, and it is questionable whether it should even be called by the same name, frustration, that characterizes other, more threatening deprivations. It is only when a goal object represents love, prestige, respect, or other basic needs that being deprived of it will have the bad effects ordinarily attributed to frustration in general.

It is possible to demonstrate very clearly this twofold meaning of an object in certain groups of animals and in certain situations. For instance, it has been shown that when two monkeys are in a dominance-subordination relationship a piece of food is (1) an appeaser of hunger and also (2) a symbol of dominance status. Thus if the subordinate animal attempts to pick up food, he will at once be attacked by the dominant animal. If, however, he can deprive the food of its symbolic dominance value, then his dominator allows him to eat it. This he can do very easily by a gesture of obeisance, i.e., sexual presentation as he approaches the food; this is as if to say, "I want this food only to still hunger, I do not want to challenge your dominance. I readily concede your dominance." In the same way we may take a criticism from a friend in two different ways. Ordinarily the average person will respond by feeling attacked and threatened (which is fair enough because so frequently criticism is an attack). She therefore bristles and becomes angry in response. But if she is assured that this criticism is not an attack or a rejection of herself, she will then not only listen to the criticism, but possibly even be grateful for it. Thus if she has already had thousands of proofs that her friend loves her and respects her, the criticism represents only criticism; it does not also represent an attack or threat (Maslow, 1936, 1940b).

Neglect of this distinction has created a great deal of unnecessary turmoil in psychiatric circles. An ever-recurring question is: Does sexual deprivation inevitably give rise to all or any of the many effects of frustration, such as aggression or sublimation? It is now well known that many cases are found in which celibacy has no psychopathological effects. In many other cases, however, it has many bad effects. What factor determines which shall be the result? Clinical work with nonneurotic people gives the clear answer that sexual deprivation becomes pathogenic in a severe sense only when it is felt by the individual to represent rejection by the opposite sex, inferiority, lack of worth, lack of respect, isolation, or other thwarting of basic needs. Sexual deprivation can be borne with relative ease by individuals for whom it has no such implications.

The unavoidable deprivations in childhood are also ordinarily thought of as frustrating. Weaning, elimination control, learning to walk, and in fact every new level of adjustment are conceived to be achieved by forcible pushing of the child. Here, too, the differentiation between mere deprivation and threat to the personality enjoins caution upon us. Observations of children who are completely assured of the love and respect of their parents have shown that deprivations, disciplines, and punishments can sometimes be borne with astonishing ease. There are few frustration effects if these deprivations are not conceived by the child to be threatening to fundamental personality, to main life goals, or to needs.

From this point of view, it follows that the phenomenon of threatening frustration is much more closely allied to other threat situations than it is to mere deprivation. The classic effects of frustration are also found frequently to be a consequence of other types of threat—traumatization, conflict, cortical damage, severe illness, actual physical threat, imminence of death, humiliation, or great pain.

This leads us to our final hypothesis that perhaps frustration as a single concept is less useful than the two concepts that crosscut it: (1) deprivation of nonbasic needs and (2) threat to the personality, that is, to the basic needs or to the various coping systems associated with them. Deprivation implies much less than is ordinarily implied by the concept of frustration; threat implies much more. Deprivation is not psychopathogenic; threat is.

CONFLICT AND THREAT

The single concept of conflict can be crosscut by the concept of threat just as we have done for frustration. We will look at several types of conflict.

Sheer choice is conflict in the simplest sense of all. The daily life of every human being is filled with numberless choices of this sort. We would conceive the difference between this kind of choice and the next type to be discussed to be as follows. The first type involves a choice between two paths to the same goal, this goal being relatively unimportant for the organism. The psychological reaction to such a choice situation is practically never a pathological one. As a matter of fact, most often there is no subjective feeling of conflict at all.

Another kind of conflict is a situation in which the goal itself is important but there are alternative ways of reaching this goal. The goal itself is not endangered. The importance or nonimportance of the goal is, of course, a matter to be determined for each individual organism. What is important for one may not be for another. When the decision is made the apparent feeling of conflict usually disappears. It is true, however, that when the goal is of great importance, the conflict of choosing between two or more paths to the same end may become very intense.

A threatening conflict is fundamentally different in kind from the two types of conflicts described above. It is still a choice situation but now it is a choice between two different goals, both vitally necessary. Here a choice reaction usually does not settle the conflict, since the decision means giving up something that is almost as necessary as what is chosen. Giving up a necessary goal or need satisfaction is threatening, and even after the choice has been made, threat effects persist. In a word, this sort of choice can eventuate only in chronic thwarting of a basic need. This is pathogenic.

Catastrophic conflict might better be called pure threat with no alternative or possibilities of choice. All the choices are equally catastrophic or threatening in their effects or else there is only one possibility and this is a catastrophic threat. Such a situation can be called a conflict situation only by an extension of the meaning of the word. This can be seen readily if we take the example of a man who is to be executed in a few minutes, or the animal who is forced in the direction of a decision that it knows to be a punishing one and in which all possibilities of escape, attack, or substitute behavior are cut off, as is the case in many experiments on animal neurosis (Maier, 1939).

Speaking from the point of view of psychopathology we must come to the same conclusion that we came to after our analysis of frustration. There are, in general, two types of conflict situations or conflict reactions, nonthreatening and threatening. The nonthreatening conflicts are quite unimportant since they are not ordinarily pathogenic; the threatening types of conflict are important because they very often are pathogenic.[1] Again it would seem that when we speak about a feeling of conflict as an originator of symptoms we should do better to speak rather about threat or threatening conflict, since there are types of conflict that do not create symptoms. Some actually strengthen the organism.

We may then proceed to a reclassification of our concepts in the general field of psychopathogenesis. We may speak first of deprivation and second of choice, and consider them both to be nonpathogenic and therefore unimportant concepts for the student of psychopathology. The one concept that is important is neither conflict nor frustration but the essential pathogenic characteristic of both, namely, threat of thwarting or actual thwarting of the basic needs and self-actualization of the organism.

INDIVIDUAL DEFINITION OF THREAT

General dynamic theory, as well as various specific empirical findings, indicates the necessity for individual definition of threat. That is, we must ultimately define a situation or threat not only in terms of species-wide basic needs but also in terms of the individual organism facing its particular problem. Thus frustration and conflict both have frequently been defined in terms of external situations alone rather than in terms of the organism's internal reaction to or perception of these external situations. Again it must be pointed out that a traumatic situation is not the same as a feeling of traumatization; a traumatic situation *may* be psychologically threatening but it does not *have* to be. It may indeed be educative and strengthening if well handled.

---

[1]Threat is not always pathogenic; there are healthy ways of handling it, as well as neurotic or psychotic solutions. Furthermore, an apparently threatening situation may or may not produce feelings of psychological threat in any particular individual. A bombardment or threat to life itself may not be so threatening as a sneer, a snub, the defection of a friend, an illness in one's child, or an act of injustice perpetrated against a total stranger miles away. In addition, threat may have strengthening effects.

How shall we know when any particular situation is perceived by the organism as a threat? For the human being, this can easily enough be determined by any technique that is adequate to describe the total personality, as, for instance, the psychoanalytic technique. Such techniques allow us to know what the person needs, what he or she is missing, and what endangers him or her. Healthy adults are less threatened by external situations in general than are average or neurotic adults. We must remember again that though this adult health has been produced by lack of threat through childhood or by threats successfully overcome, it becomes more and more impervious to threat as the years go by; for example, it is practically impossible to threaten the masculinity of the man who is *quite* sure of himself. Withdrawal of love is no great threat to one who has been well loved through her life and who feels loveworthy and lovable. Again the principle of functional autonomy must be invoked.

A last point that would certainly follow from dynamic theory is that we must always consider the feeling of threat to be in itself a dynamic stimulation to other reactions. No picture of threat is complete in any organism unless we know also what this threat feeling leads to, what it makes the individual do, and how the organism reacts to the threat. Certainly in the theory of neuroses it is absolutely necessary to understand both the nature of the feeling of threat and also the reaction of the organism to this feeling.

TRAUMA AND ILLNESS AS THREAT

It is necessary to point out that the concept of threat includes phenomena that are subsumed neither under the head of conflict nor under that of frustration as these words have been commonly used. Severe illness of certain types can by psychopathogenic. A person who has had a bad heart attack very frequently behaves in a threatened fashion. Illness or hospital experience in young children is often directly threatening, quite apart from the deprivations that are imposed thereby.

We can also add the effect of very basic and severe traumatization to our list of threat effects that are neither conflict nor frustration. The person who has gone through a very severe accident may conclude that he or she is not the master of his or her own fate and that death is ever at the door. In the face of such an overwhelmingly stronger and more threatening world, some people seem to lose confidence in their own abilities, even the simplest ones. Other milder traumata will of course be less threatening. We would add that such a reaction is to be expected more often in people with a certain kind of character structure that predisposes them to threat.

The imminence of death for whatever reasons also may (but not necessarily) put us in a state of threat for the reason that we may lose our basic self-confidence here. When we can no longer handle the situation, when the world is too much for us, when we are not masters of our own fate, when we no longer have control over the world or over ourselves, certainly we may speak of feelings of threat. Other situations in which "there is nothing we can do about it" are also sometimes felt to be threatening. Perhaps severe pain should be added in this category. This is certainly something that we can do nothing about.

Perhaps it is possible to extend the concept to include phenomena that are ordinarily included in a different category. For instance, we might speak of sudden intense stimulation, being dropped without foreknowledge, losing footing, anything unexplained or unfamiliar, the upset of routine or rhythm in the child as threatening to the child rather than as merely emotion producing.

We must of course also speak of the most nuclear aspects of threat, namely, the direct deprivation, or thwarting, or danger to the basic needs (humiliation, rejection, isolation, loss of prestige, loss of strength); these are all directly threatening. In addition, misuse or nonuse of the capacities threatens self-actualization directly. Finally, danger to the metaneeds or Being values can be threatening to the highly matured person.

INHIBITION OF SELF-ACTUALIZATION AS THREAT

In agreement with Goldstein (1939, 1940), we can understand most individual experiences of threat as situations that inhibit or threaten to inhibit development toward ultimate self-actualization. This emphasis on future as well as on contemporaneous damage has many serious consequences. As an instance we may cite Fromm's revolutionary conception of the "humanistic" conscience as perception of deviation from the path of growth or self-actualization. This phrasing throws into sharp relief the relativism and therefore the inadequacy of the Freudian conception of the superego.

We should also notice that synonymizing *threat* with *growth-inhibiting* creates the possibility of a situation being at this moment subjectively nonthreatening, but threatening or growth-inhibiting in the future. Children may now wish for gratification that will please, quiet, or make them grateful, but which will yet be growth-inhibiting. An example is seen in the parental submission to the child that produces the indulged psychopath.

THE SOURCE OF PATHOLOGY

Another problem that is created by identifying psychopathogenesis with ultimately faulty development arises from its monistic character. What we have implied is that all or most illnesses come from this single source; psychopathogenesis seems to be unitary rather than multiple. Where then do separate syndromes of illness come from? Perhaps not only pathogenesis but also psychopathology may be unitary. Perhaps what we now speak of as separate disease entities on the medical model are actually superficial and idiosyncratic reactions to a deeper general illness, as Horney claimed (1937). The S-I test of security-insecurity (Maslow, 1952) was built on just such a basic assumption and so far seems to have succeeded fairly well in picking out people who have psychological illness in general rather than hysteria or hypochondria or anxiety neurosis in particular.

Since the only aim here is to indicate that important problems and hypotheses are generated by this theory of psychopathogenesis, no effort will be made now to explore these hypotheses further. It is necessary only to underline its unifying, simplifying possibilities.

SUMMARY

We may summarize by saying that, in general, all the following are felt as threatening in our sense: danger of thwarting or actual thwarting of the basic needs and metaneeds (including self-actualization) or the conditions upon which they rest, threat to life itself, threat to the general integrity of the organism, threat to the integration of the organism, threat to the organism's basic mastery of the world, and threat to the ultimate values.

However we define threat, certainly there is one aspect that we must never neglect. An ultimate definition, no matter what else it might include, must certainly be related to the basic goals, values, or needs of the organism. This means that any theory of psychopathogenesis in turn must rest directly upon theory of motivation.

chapter 8

Is Destructiveness Instinctive?

On the surface, the basic needs (motives, impulses, drives) are not evil or sinful. There is nothing necessarily bad in wanting and needing food, safety, belonging-ness and love, social approval and self-approval, and self-actualization. On the contrary, most people in most cultures would consider these—in one local form or another—to be desirable and praiseworthy wishes. At our most scientifically cautious, we would still have to say that they are neutral rather than evil. Some-thing of the sort is true for most or all of the human species-specific capacities that we know about (the ability to abstract, to speak a grammatical language, to build philosophies, etc.), and for constitutional differences (activity or passivity, mesomorphy or ectomorphy, high or low energy levels, etc.). As for the meta-needs for excellence, truth, beauty, lawfulness, simplicity, and the like, it is prac-tically impossible in our culture, and in most cultures that we know, to call them intrinsically bad or evil or sinful.

The raw material of humanness and of human specieshood, therefore, does not in itself explain the huge amount of evil that is obvious in our world, in human history, and within our own individual characters. True, we already know enough to attribute much of what is called evil to sickness of the body and of the personality, to ignorance and stupidity, to immaturity, and to bad social and institutional arrangements. But it cannot be said that we know enough to say *how* much. We know that evil can be reduced by health and by therapy, by knowledge and wisdom, by chronological and psychological maturity, by good political, eco-nomic, and other social institutions and systems. But by how much? Can such measures ever reduce evil to zero? It can certainly be granted by now that our knowledge is sufficient to reject any claim that human nature is, in its essence, *primarily, biologically, fundamentally* evil, sinful, malicious, ferocious, cruel, or murderous. But we do not dare to say that there are *no* instinctlike tendencies at all to bad behavior. It is quite clear that we just do not know enough to make such an affirmation, and there is at least some evidence to contradict it. In any case it has become just as clear that such knowledge is attainable and that these questions can be brought into the jurisdiction of a suitably expanded humanistic science (Maslow, 1966; Polanyi, 1958).

This chapter is a sample of the empirical approach to one crucial question in this area of what has been called good and evil. Even though it makes no effort to be definitive, it is a reminder that knowledge of destructiveness *has* advanced, even though not yet to the point of final and conclusive answers.

ANIMALS

First of all, it is true that what looks like primary aggressiveness can be observed in some species of animals; not in all animals, nor even in many, but still in some. Some animals apparently kill for the sake of killing, and are aggressive for no observable external reason. A fox that enters a henhouse may kill more hens than it could eat, and the cat that plays with the mouse is proverbial. Stags and other ungulate animals at rutting will look for fights, sometimes even abandoning their mates to do so. In many animals, even the higher ones, onset of old age seems to make them more vicious for apparently constitutional reasons, and previously mild animals will attack without provocation. In various species killing is not for the sake of food alone.

A well-known study on the laboratory rat shows that it is possible to breed wildness, aggressiveness, or ferocity as one can breed anatomical characteristics. The tendency to ferocity, at least in this one species and possibly in others as well, can be a primarily inherited determinant of behavior. This is made more plausible by the general finding that the adrenal glands in wild and ferocious rats are much larger than in milder, tamer ones. Other species, of course, can be bred by the geneticists in just the opposite fashion, toward mildness and tameness and lack of ferocity. It is such examples and observations as these that permit us to advance and to accept the simplest of all possible explanations, namely, that the behavior in question comes from an ad hoc motivation, that there was a hereditary drive to just this particular kind of behavior.

However, many other instances of apparently primary ferocity in animals are not quite what they appear when analyzed more closely. Aggression can be evoked in many ways and by many situations in animals just as in human beings. For example, there is the determinant called territoriality (Ardrey, 1966), which may be illustrated in birds that nest on the ground. As they select their breeding place, it will be found that they attack any other birds that come within the radius that they have designated for themselves. But they will attack these trespassers and no others. They do not attack in general; they attack only trespassers. Certain species will attack any other animal, even of their own species, that does not have the odor or appearance of their particular group or clan. For example, the howler monkeys form a sort of closed corporation. Any other howler monkey that tries to join the group is repelled by noisy attack. If, however, it lingers long enough, it will eventually become part of the group, to attack in turn any stranger that comes along.

When the higher animals are studied, attacking is found to be correlated more and more with dominance. These studies are too complex to be quoted in detail, but it may be said that this dominance and the aggressiveness that sometimes evolves from it do have functional value or survival value for the animal. The animal's place in dominance hierarchy is in part determined by its successful aggression, and its place in the hierarchy determines in turn how much food it will get, whether or not it will have a mate, and other biological satisfactions. Practically all the cruelty manifested in these animals occurs only when it is necessary to validate dominance status or to make a revolution in dominance status. How true this is for other species I am not sure. But I do suspect that the phenomenon of territoriality, of attack on strangers, of jealous protection of the females, of attack on the weak or sick, and other phenomena that are often explained by instinctive aggression or cruelty are very often found to have been motivated by dominance rather than by a specific motivation to aggression for its own sake; this aggression may be means behavior rather than end behavior.

When the infrahuman primates are studied, it is discovered that aggression becomes less and less primary and more and more derived and reactive, more and more functional, more and more a reasonable, understandable reaction to a totality of motivations, of social forces, and immediate situational determinants. By the time one reaches the chimpanzees, that animal of all animals that is closest to the human being, no behavior at all is found that can even be remotely suspected of being aggressive for the sake of aggression. So likable and cooperative and friendly are these animals, especially when young, that in some groups one may not find cruel aggression of any kind for whatever reason. Something similar is true for gorillas as well.

At this point I may say that the whole argument from animal to man must certainly always be held suspect. But if it is accepted for the sake of argument, it must be concluded, if one reasons from the animals that are closest to humans, that they prove almost the opposite of what is usually considered to be the case. If humans have an animal heritage, it must be largely an anthropoid heritage, and anthropoid apes are more cooperative than aggressive.

This mistake is an instance of a general type of pseudoscientific thinking that can best be described as illegitimate animal centrism. The correct procedure for making this kind of a mistake is first to construct a theory or formulate a prejudice, and then to select from the whole evolutionary gamut that one animal that best illustrates the point. Second, we must deliberately blind ourselves to the behavior of all animals that do not fit into the theory. If one wishes to prove instinctive destructiveness, by all means choose the wolf and forget the rabbit. Third, it is necessary to forget that clear developmental trends can be seen if one studies the whole phyletic scale from low to high, instead of selecting some particular favorite species. For example, ascending the animal scale, appetites become more and more important and sheer hungers become less and less important. Moreover, variability becomes greater and greater; the period between fertilization and adulthood tends, with exceptions, to become longer and longer; and, perhaps most significantly, reflexes, hormones, and instincts become less and less important determiners and are increasingly replaced by intelligence, learning, and social determination.

The evidence from animals may be summarized by saying first that the argument from animal to human is always a delicate task to be executed with the greatest of caution; second, that a primary and inherited tendency to destructive or cruel aggression may be found in some species of animals, although probably in fewer than most people believe. It is missing completely in some species. Third, specific instances of aggressive behavior in animals, when carefully analyzed, are found more often than not to be secondary, derived reactions to various determinants and not just expressions of an instinct of aggressiveness for its own sake. Fourth, the higher the ascent in the phyletic scale and the closer the approach to man, the more clearly the evidence for a putative primary instinct of aggressiveness is seen to become weaker and weaker, until by the time one reaches the apes, it seems to be absent altogether. Fifth, if one studies most carefully the apes, our closest relatives among all the animals, little or no evidence of primary malicious aggression is found, but instead a great deal of evidence for friendliness, cooperativeness, and even altruism. A final point of importance comes from our tendency to assume motives when all we know is behavior. It is now generally agreed upon by students of animal behavior that most carnivores killing their prey are simply getting food rather than being sadistic, in about the same spirit that we get steaks for food rather than from the lust to kill. What all this means finally is that henceforth any evolutionary argument about our animal nature forcing us to aggressiveness or destructiveness for its own sake must be suspected or rejected.

CHILDREN

Observations and experimental studies and findings of children sometimes seem to resemble a kind of projective method, a Rorschach ink blot upon which adult hostility can be projected. One hears a great deal of talk about the innate selfishness and innate destructiveness of children, and there are far more papers dealing with these than with cooperation, kindness, sympathy, and the like. Furthermore, these latter studies, few in number though they have been, are usually overlooked. Psychologists and psychoanalysts often have conceived of the infant as a little devil, born with original sin and with hatred in its heart. Certainly this undiluted picture is false. I must admit that there is a regrettable lack of scientific material in this area. I base my judgment on only a few excellent studies, particularly that of Lois Murphy (1937) on sympathy in children. However, even such scanty evidence seems to be enough to throw doubt on the conclusion that children are primarily destructive, aggressive, hostile little animals who have to have some modicum of goodness knocked into them by discipline and punishment.

The facts, experimental and observational, seem to be that normal children are in fact often hostile, destructive, and selfish in a primitive sort of way as has been claimed. But they are also at other times, and perhaps as often, generous, cooperative, and unselfish in the same primitive style. The main principle that determines the relative frequency of the two types of behavior seems to be that the child who is insecure, basically thwarted, or threatened in his needs for safety, love, belongingness, and self-esteem is the child who will show more selfishness, hatred, aggression, and destructiveness. In children who are basically loved and respected by their parents, less destructiveness should be found, and in my opinion what evidence there is shows that less destructiveness actually *is* found. This implies a reactive, instrumental, or defensive interpretation of hostility rather than an instinctive one.

If one looks at a healthy and well-loved and cared-for infant, let us say up to the age of one year and perhaps later, then it is quite impossible to see anything that could be called evil, original sin, sadism, malice, pleasure in hurting, destructiveness, hostility for its own sake, or deliberate cruelty. On the contrary, careful and long-continued observation demonstrates the opposite. Practically every personality characteristic found in self-actualizing people, everything lovable, admirable, and enviable is found in such babies—that is, except knowledge, experience, and wisdom. One of the reasons that babies are loved and wanted so much must be just this—that they are without visible evil, hatred, or malice in the first year or two of their lives.

As for destructiveness, I am very doubtful that it ever occurs in normal children as a direct primary expression of a simple destructive drive. One example after another of apparent destructiveness can be analyzed away dynamically as it is examined more closely. The child who pulls the clock apart is not in his own eyes destroying the clock, but examining the clock. If one must speak of a primary drive here, curiosity would be a much more sensible choice than destructiveness. Many other examples that look like destructiveness to the distraught mother turn out to be not only curiosity but activity, play, exercise of the growing capacities and skills, and even sometimes actual creation, as when a child cuts her father's carefully typed notes into pretty little forms. I doubt that young children are deliberately destructive for the sheer pleasure of malicious destruction. A possible exception is pathological cases; for example, epilepsy and postencephalitis. Even in these so-called pathological examples it is not known that their destructiveness may not also have been reactive, a response to threats of one kind or another.

Sibling rivalry is a special and sometimes puzzling case. A two-year-old child can be dangerously aggressive to its newborn baby brother. Sometimes the hostile intent is expressed very naively and forthrightly. One reasonable explanation is that a two-year-old is simply not capable of the thought that his mother can love *two* children. He hurts not merely for the sake of hurting but to retain the love of his mother.

Another special case is the psychopathic personality whose aggression often seems unmotivated, that is, seems to be performed for its own sake. It is necessary to invoke a principle here first enunciated by Ruth Benedict (1970) in an effort to explain why secure societies could go to war. Her explanation was that secure, healthy people are not hostile or aggressive against people who are in a broad sense their brothers, people with whom they can identify. If certain ones are *not* seen as human beings, they can be snuffed out quite easily even by kind, loving, healthy people, in the same way that they are completely guiltless about killing annoying insects, or slaughtering animals for food.

It is helpful in understanding psychopaths to assume that they have no love identifications with other human beings and can therefore hurt them or even kill them casually, without hate, and without pleasure, precisely as they kill animals who have come to be pests. Some childish reactions that seem cruel probably also come from lack of identification of this sort before the child has matured enough to enter into interpersonal relations.

Finally, it seems to us that certain semantic considerations of considerable importance are also involved. To say it as succinctly as possible, aggression, hostility, and destructiveness are all adult words. They mean certain things to adults that they do *not* mean to children, and should therefore not be used without modification or redefinition.

For instance, children in the second year of life can play independently side by side without really interacting with each other. When selfish or aggressive interactions do occur in such children, it is not the same kind of interpersonal relationship that can occur between ten-year-olds; it may be without awareness of the other. If one such child then pulls away a toy from the other against resistance, this may be more like wrestling an object from a tight container than like adult selfish aggression.

So also for the active infant who finds the nipple snatched from its mouth and then yells in rage, or the three-year-old who strikes back at the punishing mother, or the angry five-year-old who shrieks "I wish you were dead," or the two-year-old who persistently roughs up his newborn brother. In none of these cases ought we treat the child as if he or she were an adult, nor ought we interpret the reaction as we would an adult's reaction.

Most such behaviors, dynamically understood in the child's own frame of reference, must probably be accepted as reactive. This is to say they most likely come from disappointment, rejection, loneliness, fear of loss of respect, or fear of loss of protection (i.e., thwarting of basic needs or threat of such thwarting) more than they do from an inherited, per se, drive to hate or hurt. Whether or not this reactive explanation accounts for *all* destructive behavior, and not merely most of it, our knowledge—or rather our lack of knowledge—simply does not permit us to say.

ANTHROPOLOGY

A discussion of the comparative data may be amplified through recourse to ethnology. We can say at once that even a cursory survey of the material would prove to any interested reader that the amount of hostility, aggression, or destructiveness in living, primitive cultures is not constant, but varies between the extremes of almost 0 to almost 100 percent. There are peoples like the Arapesh who are so mild, so friendly, so unaggressive that they have to go to extremes to find a man who is even self-assertive enough to organize their ceremonies. At the other extreme one can find people like the Chukchi and the Dobu who are so full of hatred that one wonders what keeps them from killing one another off altogether.

Of course, these are descriptions of behavior externally observed. We may still wonder about unconscious impulses that underlie these behaviors and that *may* be different from what we can *see*.

Apparently human beings need not be even as aggressive or destructive as the average person in American society, let alone those of some other parts of the world. There seems to be, in the anthropological evidence, a potent source for considering destructiveness, malice, or cruelty in human beings to be most probably a secondary, reactive consequence of thwarting of or threat to the basic human needs.

CLINICAL EXPERIENCE

The usual experience reported in the literature of psychotherapy is that violence, anger, hatred, destructive wishes, impulses to vengeance and the like all exist in great quantity in practically everyone, if not visibly then under the surface. Experienced therapists will refuse to take seriously anyone's claim that he or she has never felt hatred. They will simply assume that the person has suppressed or repressed it. They expect to find it in everyone.

Yet it is also the general experience in therapy that talking freely about one's violent impulses (without acting them out) tends to purge them, to reduce their frequency, and to eliminate their neurotic, unrealistic components. The general result of successful therapy (or a successful growth and maturing) tends to be approximately what is seen in self-actualizing people: (1) they experience hostility, hatred, violence, malice, destructive aggression much less often than do average people; (2) they do not *lose* their anger or aggression, but its quality tends to be changed into indignation, to self-affirmation, to resistance against being exploited, to anger against injustice, that is, from unhealthy to healthy aggression; and (3) healthier people seem much less afraid of their own angers and aggressions, and so are able to express them more wholeheartedly when they do express them at all. Violence has two opposites, not just one. The opposite of violence can be less violence, or control of one's violence, or efforts to be nonviolent. *Or* it can be an opposition between healthy and unhealthy violence.

These "data" do not settle our issue, however, and it is very instructive to learn that Freud and his loyalist followers consider violence to be instinctive, whereas Fromm, Horney, and other neo-Freudians conclude that it is not at all instinctive.

ENDOCRINOLOGY AND GENETICS

Anyone who wanted to put together all that is known about the sources of violence would also have to dig out the data that the endocrinologists have accumulated. Again, the situation is relatively simple in lower animals. There is little doubt that the sex hormones and the adrenal and pituitary hormones are unmistakable determiners of aggression, dominance, passivity, and wildness. But because all the endocrine glands are mutually determinative, some of these data are very complex and require special knowledge. This is even more true for the human species, in which the data are even more complex. And yet they dare not be bypassed. Again, there is evidence that the male hormones have something to do with self-affirmation, with readiness and ability to fight, and so on. There is some evidence that different individuals secrete different proportions of adrenaline and nonadrenaline, and that these chemicals have something to do with the individual's proneness to fight rather than flee, and so on. The new cross-disciplinary science of psychoendocrinology will undoubtedly teach us much about our problem.

Of course data from genetics, from the chromosomes and genes themselves, will obviously be of very special relevance. For instance, the discovery that males with a double male chromosome (a double dose of male heredity) tend to be almost uncontrollably violent itself makes a pure environmentalism impossible. In the most peaceful of societies, with the most perfect social and economic conditions, *some* people will have to be violent just because of the way they are constructed. This finding of course brings up the much discussed but not yet finally settled question: Does the male, especially the adolescent male, perhaps need some violence, something or someone to fight against, to have conflict with? There is some evidence to indicate that this may be so, not only for human adults but even for babies, and for monkey babies as well. The degree to which this is or is not intrinsically determined we must also leave to future researchers to decide.

THEORETICAL CONSIDERATIONS

As we have seen, a widely held view is that destructiveness or hurting is secondary or derived behavior rather than primary motivation. By this is meant the expectation that hostile or destructive behavior in the human being will practically always be found to result from an assignable reason of some sort, to be a reaction to another state of affairs, to be a product rather than an original source. The view with which this contrasts is that destructiveness is the direct and primary product, in whole or in part, of some instinct of destructiveness.

In any such discussion the most important single distinction that can be made is the one between motivation and behavior. Behavior is determined by many forces, of which internal motivation is only one. I might say very briefly that any theory of determination of behavior must include the study of at least the following determinants: (1) the character structure, (2) the cultural pressures, and (3) the immediate situation or field. In other words, the study of inner motivation is only part of one of three major areas involved in any study of the main determinants of behavior. With these considerations in mind, I may rephrase my question to read, How is destructive behavior determined? And then, Is the only determinant for destructive behavior some inherited, predetermined, ad hoc motivation? These questions of course answer themselves at once on an a priori basis alone. All possible motivations taken together, let alone a specific instinct, do not determine in themselves the occurrence of aggression or destructiveness. The culture in general must be involved, and the immediate situation or field in which the behavior occurs must also be considered.

There is still another way of stating the problem. It can be shown certainly for the human being that destructive behavior derives from so many different sources that it becomes ridiculous to speak of any single urge to destructiveness. This can be illustrated by a few examples.

Destructiveness may occur quite incidentally as one sweeps something out of his path to the goal. A child who is trying hard to reach some toy at a distance is not apt to notice that she is trampling other toys in her path (Klee, 1951).

Destructiveness may occur as one of the concomitant reactions to basic threat. Thus any threat of thwarting of the basic needs, any threat to the defensive or coping system, any threat to the general way of life is likely to be reacted to by anxiety-hostility, which means that hostile, aggressive, or destructive behavior may very frequently be expected in such reactions. This is ultimately defensive behavior, counterattack rather than attack for its own sake.

Any damage to the organism, any perception of organic deterioration, will probably arouse in the insecure person similar feelings of threat, and destructive behavior may therefore be expected, as in many cases of brain injury where the patient frantically attempts to support faltering self-esteem by a diversity of desperate measures.

One reason for aggressive behavior that is customarily overlooked, or if not then is phrased inaccurately, is the authoritarian view of life. If people were *actually* to live in a jungle in which all other animals were divided into two classes, those who could eat them and those they could eat, aggression would become a sensible and logical thing. People described as authoritarian must frequently tend unconsciously to envisage the world as just such a jungle. On the principle that the best defense is a good attack, these people are apt to lash out, to strike, to destroy with no apparent reason whatsoever, and the whole reaction remains meaningless until it is realized that this was simply in anticipation of an attack by the other person. There are also many other well-known forms of defensive hostility.

The dynamics of sadistic-masochistic reactions have now been fairly well analyzed, and it is generally understood that what looks like a simple aggression may actually have very complex dynamics behind it. These dynamics make an appeal to some putative instinct of hostility look far too simple. The same is true for the overwhelming drive for power over other people. Analysis by Horney (1939) has shown clearly that, in this area as well, recourse to instinctual explanation is unnecessary. World War II has taught us that the attack of the gangster and the defense of the righteously indignant are not the same psychologically.

This list could easily be expanded. I cite these few examples to illustrate my point that destructive behavior is very often a symptom, a type of behavior that can result from many factors. If one wishes to be truly dynamic, one must learn to be alert to the fact that these behaviors may appear alike despite the fact that they derive from different sources. The dynamic psychologist is not a camera or mechanical recorder. He or she is interested in knowing why things happen as well as what happens.

DESTRUCTIVENESS: INSTINCTIVE OR LEARNED?

We could mention data from history, sociology, management studies, semantics, medical pathologies of all sorts, politics, mythology, psychopharmacology, and other sources as well. But no more is necessary to make the point that the questions asked at the beginning of this chapter are *empirical* questions and may therefore be confidently expected to be answerable by further research. Of course the integration of data from many fields makes team research a probability, perhaps even a necessity. In any case, this casual sampling of data available should be enough to teach us to reject the extreme, black-white polarizing into *either* all instinct, heredity, biological fate *or else* all environment, social forces, learning. The old hereditarian versus environmental polemics are not yet dead, even though they should be. Clearly the determinants of destructiveness are pluralistic. It is absolutely clear even now that among these determinants we must count culture, learning, environment. It is less clear but still very probable that biological determinants also play an essential role, even though we cannot be quite sure what it is. At the very least, we must accept the inevitability of violence as part of the human essence, if only because basic needs are absolutely doomed to be frustrated at times, and we know that the human species is constructed in such a manner that violence, anger, retaliation are quite common consequences of such frustrations.

Finally it is not necessary to make a choice between all-powerful instincts and all-powerful culture. The position presented in this chapter transcends this dichotomy and makes it unnecessary. Hereditary or other biological determination is not all or none; it is a matter of degree, of little or much. In the human being the preponderance of the evidence indicates that there *are* biological and hereditary determinants, but that in most individuals they are quite weak and easily overwhelmed by learned cultural forces. Not only are they weak but also they are fragmented, remnants and pieces rather than the whole and complete instincts found in lower animals. Human beings have no instincts, but they *do* seem to have instinct remnants, instinctlike needs, intrinsic capacities and potentialities. Furthermore, clinical and personological experience generally suggests that these weak instinctlike tendencies are good, desirable, and healthy rather than malign or evil, that the great effort to save them from annihilation is both feasible and worthwhile, and, indeed, that this is a major function of any culture that would be called good.

chapter 9

Psychotherapy as Good Human Relationships

It is amazing that experimental psychologists have not turned to the study of phychotherapy as to an unworked gold mine. As a result of successful psychotherapy, people perceive differently, think differently, learn differently. Their motives change, as do their emotions. It is the best technique we have ever had for laying bare people's deepest nature as contrasted with their surface personalities. Their interpersonal relations and attitudes toward society are transformed. Their characters (or personalities) change both superficially and profoundly. There is even some evidence that their appearance changes, that physical health is improved, and so forth. In some cases, even the IQ goes up. And yet, the word *psychotherapy* is not even listed in the index of most books on learning, perception, thinking, motivation, social psychology, physiological psychology, and the like.

To take a single example, there is no question whatsoever that the theory of learning would, to say the least, profit by the study of the learning effects of such therapeutic forces as marriage, friendship, free association, resistance analysis, success in a job, not to mention tragedy, trauma, conflict, and suffering.

Another equally important set of unsolved problems is turned up by examining the psychotherapeutic relationships as simply a subexample of social or interpersonal relationships, that is, as a branch of social psychology. We can now describe at least three ways in which patients and therapists can relate to each other, the authoritarian, the democratic, and the laissez-faire, each having its special usefulness at various times. But precisely these three types of relationships are found in the social atmosphere of children's clubs and in styles of hypnosis, in types of political theory, in mother-child relationships (Maslow, 1957) and in kinds of social organization found in infrahuman primates (Maslow, 1940a).

Any thorough study of the aims and goals of therapy must expose very quickly the inadequate development of current personality theory, call into question the basic scientific orthodoxy that values have no place in science, lay bare the limitations of medical notions of health, disease, therapy, and cure, and reveal clearly that our culture still lacks a usable value system. No wonder people are afraid of the problem. Many other examples could be adduced to prove that psychotherapy is an important department of general psychology.

We may say that psychotherapy takes place in seven main ways: (1) by expression (act completion, release, catharsis); (2) by basic need gratification (giving support, reassurance, protection, love, respect); (3) by removing threat (protection, good social, political, and economic conditions); (4) by improved insight, knowledge, and understanding; (5) by suggestion or authority; (6) by direct attack on the symptoms, as in the various behavior therapies; and (7) by positive self-actualization, individuation, or growth. For the more general purposes of personality theory, this also constitutes a list of the ways in which personality changes in culturally and psychiatrically approved directions.

We are here specially interested in tracing a few of the interrelationships between the data of therapy and the theory of motivation so far presented in this book. It will be seen that gratification of the basic needs is an important (perhaps the *most* important) step along the path to the ultimate, positive goal of all therapy, namely, self-actualization.

It will also be pointed out that these basic needs are mostly satisfiable *only by other human beings,* and that therefore therapy must take place mostly on an interpersonal basis. The sets of basic needs whose gratifications constitute the basic therapeutic medications (e.g., safety, belongingness, love, and respect) can be obtained only from other people.

May I say at once that my own experience has been almost entirely confined to the briefer therapies. Those whose experience is primarily with psychoanalytic (deeper) therapy are much more likely to come to the conclusion that insight rather than need gratification is *the* important medicine. This is so because seriously sick people are incapable of accepting or assimilating satisfactions of basic needs until they have given up their infantile interpretations of self and others and become capable of perceiving and accepting personal and interpersonal reality as it is.

We could debate the matter if we wished, pointing out that the purpose of insight therapy is to make possible the acceptance of good interpersonal relations and the need gratifications that go with them. We know insight has been effective only because these motivational changes come to pass. However, acceptance for the time being of a crude differentiation between the simpler, briefer, need-gratification therapy and the deeper, longer, more laborious insight therapy has considerable heuristic value. As we shall see, need gratification is possible in many nontechnical situations, such as marriages, friendship, collaboration, or teaching. This opens a theoretical road to a much wider extension of therapeutic skills to all sorts of lay therapists. At present, insight therapy is definitely a technical matter, for which much training is necessary. The relentless pursuit of the theoretical consequences of this dichotomy between lay therapy and technical therapy will demonstrate its varied usefulness.

It is possible also to hazard the opinion that although the deeper insight therapies involve additional principles, they too can best be understood if we choose as our beginning point the study of the effects of thwarting and gratifying basic human needs. This is directly contrary to the practice now extant of deriving an explanation of the shorter therapies from a study of one or another variety of psychoanalysis (or other insight therapy). One by-product of this latter approach has been to make the study of psychotherapy and personal growth an isolated area in psychological theory, more or less sufficient unto itself, and governed by special or autochthonous laws peculiar to this field alone. This chapter explicitly rejects such implications, and proceeds from the conviction that there are no ad hoc laws in psychotherapy. That we have proceeded as if there were is due not only to the fact that most professional therapists have been trained medically rather than psychologically, but also to the curious blindness of experimental psychologists to the repercussions upon their own picture of human nature of the phenomena of psychotherapy. In short, we may contend not only that psychotherapy must ultimately base itself squarely on sound, general psychological theory, but also that psychological theory must enlarge itself to become adequate to this responsibility. Accordingly we shall deal first with the simpler therapeutic phenomena, postponing the problems of insight to a later part of this chapter.

PSYCHOTHERAPY AND NEED GRATIFICATION

We know many facts that, taken together, make impossible any theory of psychotherapy that is (1) purely cognitive or (2) purely impersonal, but that are nevertheless compatible with need-gratification theory and with an interpersonal approach to therapy and growth.

Shamanic Healing

Psychotherapy has always existed wherever there was a society. The shaman, the medicine man, the witch, the wise old woman of the community, the priest, the guru, and more recently in Western civilization the physician have always been able to achieve in some cases what we call today psychotherapy. Indeed the great religious leaders and organizations have been validated as such by their cures not only of gross and dramatic psychopathology, but also of subtler character and value disturbances. The explanations that these people offered for these achievements have nothing in common with each other and need not be considered seriously. We must accept the fact that though these miracles could be performed, the performers did not know *why* or *how* they were achieved.

Discrepancies Between Theories and Results

This discrepancy between theory and practice exists today also. The various schools of psychotherapy all disagree with each other, sometimes very violently.

And yet a psychologist in clinical work will, in a long enough period of time, run across patients who have been cured by representatives of each of these schools of thought. These patients will then be grateful and loyal proponents of the one or another brand of theory. But it is just as easy to collect instances of failure for each of these schools of thought. And to make the matter triply confusing, I have seen patients cured by physicians or even by psychiatrists who, to my certain knowledge, had never had any training of any kind in what could fairly be called psychotherapy (not to mention schoolteachers, ministers, nurses, dentists, social workers, and others).

It is true that we can criticize these various theoretical schools on empirical and scientific grounds and arrange them in a crude hierarchy of relative validity. And we may expect that in the future we shall be able to gather suitable statistics to show that one theoretical training produces a higher percentage of cure or growth than another, even though neither fails or succeeds all the time.

At this moment, however, we must accept the fact that therapeutic results may occur to some degree independently of theory or, for that matter, with no theory at all.

Good Results with Varying Techniques

Even within the confines of one school of thought, let us say classical Freudian psychoanalysis, it is well known and commonly admitted by the analysts that there are wide differences from analyst to analyst, not only in ability as ordinarily defined, but also in sheer efficacy at curing. Some brilliant analysts who make important contributions in teaching and writing, who admittedly know a great deal and who are sought after as teachers and lecturers and as training analysts, too often fail to cure their patients. And there are others who never write anything or make few if any discoveries, yet who cure their patients most of the time. Of course there is clearly some degree of positive correlation in these abilities to be brilliant and to cure patients, and yet the exceptions remain to be explained.

Therapists' Personalities

There have been through history some well-known cases in which the masters of a school of therapeutic thought, while extraordinarily capable as therapists, largely failed in teaching this ability to their students. If it were only a matter of theory, content, or knowledge, and if the personality of the therapist made no difference, students should eventually do as well or better than their teachers, if they were equally intelligent and assiduous.

Improvement Without "Therapy"

It is a common enough experience for any type of therapist to see patients for the first time, discuss a few external details with them (e.g., procedure, hours), and have them report or demonstrate improvement by the time of the second contact. In terms of what was overtly said or done, this result is absolutely incomprehensible. Sometimes therapeutic results occur without the therapist saying a word. In one instance, a college girl wanted advice about a personal problem. At the end of one hour, during which she talked and I said *not a single word,* she had settled the problem to her own satisfaction, thanked me gratefully for my advice, and left.

Therapeutic Effect of Life Experiences

For cases that are young enough and that are not too serious, the ordinary major life experiences can be therapeutic in the fullest sense of the word. A good marriage, success in a suitable job, developing good friendships, having children, facing emergencies, and overcoming difficulties—I have occasionally seen all of these produce deep character changes, get rid of symptoms, and so on without the help of a technical therapist. As a matter of fact, a case could be made for the thesis that good life circumstances are among the *ultimate* therapeutic agents and that technical psychotherapy often has the task only of enabling the individual to take advantage of them. Many psychoanalysts have observed that their patients progressed during gaps in their analysis and also after the analysis was completed.

Successful Treatments by Untrained Therapists

Perhaps most challenging of all is the very peculiar situation existing today in which the vast majority of cases are treated or at least handled by people who were never trained to be therapists or were inadequately trained. The training of the large majority of graduate students in psychology during the 1920s and 1930s was (and still is to a lesser extent) limited, sometimes to the point of sterility. Students coming into psychology because they liked human beings and wanted to understand and help them found themselves initiated into a peculiar cultlike atmosphere in which most of their time was spent on the phenomena of sensation, the ramifications of the conditioned reflex, the nonsense syllable, and the peregrinations of white rats through mazes. Along with this came a more useful but still philosophically limited and naive training in experimental and statistical methods.

And yet, to the layperson, a psychologist was a psychologist, a target for all the major life questions, a technician who was supposed to know why divorces occur, why hatred develops, or why people become psychotic. Often psychologists had to answer the best way they could. Especially was this true in the smaller cities and towns that had never seen a psychiatrist and never heard of psychoanalysis. The only alternative to a psychologist was a favorite aunt, the family physician or minister. Thus it was possible for untrained psychologists to assuage their guilty conscience. Also they could put their efforts down to necessary training.

What we wish to report, however, is that these fumbling efforts so often worked, to the complete amazement of the young psychologists. They were well enough prepared for their failures, which of course were more frequent, but how to explain successful results that they had not even hoped for?

Such phenomena as these are less often seen by the professional therapist than by the amateur. Indeed, it has become quite clear that some psychiatrists are simply not ready to believe the reports of such happenings as these. But this can all easily be checked and confirmed, since such experiences are common among psychologists and social workers, not to mention ministers, teachers, and physicians.

Summary

How to explain these phenomena? It seems to me that we can understand them only with the aid of a motivational, interpersonal theory. It is necessary apparently to stress not what was consciously said or done, but what was unconsciously done and unconsciously perceived. The therapist in all the cases cited was interested in the patients, concerned about them, and trying to help them, thereby proving to the patients that they had worth in the eyes of at least one person. Since the therapist was in all cases someone who was perceived as wiser, older, stronger, or healthier, the patients could also feel more safe and protected and therefore less vulnerable and less anxious. The willingness to listen, the lack of scolding, the encouragement of frankness, the acceptance and approval even after sinful revelations, gentleness and kindness, the feeling given to the patients of having someone on their side, all these in addition to the factors listed above help to produce in the patients the unconscious realization of being liked, protected, and respected. As has been pointed out already, these are all gratifications of basic needs.

It seems quite clear that if we supplement the better-known therapeutic determinants (suggestion, catharsis, insight, and, more recently, the behavior therapies, etc.) by assigning a much larger role to basic need gratifications, we can explain much more than we could with these known processes alone. Some therapeutic phenomena occur with these gratifications as their only explanation—presumably less serious cases. Others—more serious—that are sufficiently explained by the more complex therapeutic techniques alone *can* be even more fully understood by adding, as a determinant the basic need gratifications, which come almost automatically in good interpersonal relationships.

GOOD HUMAN RELATIONSHIPS

Any ultimate analysis of human interpersonal relationships (e.g., friendship, marriage, etc.) will show (1) that basic needs can be satisfied *only* interpersonally and (2) that the satisfactions of these needs are precisely those we have already spoken of as the basic therapeutic medicines, namely, the giving of safety, love, belongingness, feeling of worth, and self-esteem.

We should inevitably in the course of an analysis of human relations find ourselves confronted with the necessity, as well as the possibility, of differentiating good from poor relationships. Such a differentiation can very fruitfully be made on the basis of the degree of satisfaction of the basic needs brought about by the relationship. A relationship—friendship, marriage, parent-child relation—

would then be defined (in a limited fashion) as psychologically good to the extent that it supported or improved belongingness, security, and self-esteem (and ultimately self-actualization) and bad to the extent that it did not.

These cannot be satisfied by trees, mountains, or even dogs. Only from another human being can we get fully satisfying respect and protection and love, and it is only to other human beings that we can give these in the fullest measure. But these are precisely what we find good friends, good sweethearts, good parents and children, good teachers and students giving to each other. These are the very satisfactions that we seek for from good human relationship of *any* kind. And it is precisely these need gratifications that are the sine qua non preconditions for the production of good human beings, which in turn is the ultimate (if not immediate) goal of all psychotherapy.

The sweeping implications of our system of definitions would then be that (1) psychotherapy is not at its base a unique relationship, for some of its fundamental qualities are found in *all* "good" human relationships, and (2) if this is so, this aspect of psychotherapy must be subjected to a more thoroughgoing critique than it has ordinarily received, from the viewpoint of its nature as a good or bad human interpersonal relation.[1] Just as the major values of a good friendship may be entirely unconscious without much diminishing their worth, so can these same qualities be unconscious in a therapy relation without removing their influence. This is not a contradiction of the undoubted fact that a full awareness of these qualities with a conscious and voluntary direction of their use would increase their value tremendously.

Friendships: Loving and Being Loved

Taking then the good friendships (whether between wife and husband, parent and child, or person and person) as our paradigms of the good interpersonal relations and examining them a bit more closely, we find that they offer many more satisfactions than even those we have spoken of. Mutual frankness, trust, honesty, and lack of defensiveness can all be seen as having, in addition to their face value, an additional expressive, cathartic release value (see Chapter 6). A sound friendship permits also the expression of a healthy amount of passivity, relaxation, childishness, and silliness, since if there is no danger and we are loved and respected for ourselves rather than for any front we put on or role we play, we can be as we really are, weak when we feel weak, protected when we feel confused, childish when we wish to drop the responsibilities of adulthood. In addition, a really good relationship improves insight even in the Freudian sense, for a good friend or spouse is one who feels free enough to offer the equivalent of analytic interpretations for our consideration.

Nor have we spoken enough yet of what may broadly be called the educational value of a good human relationship. We have desires not only to be safe

---

[1]These conclusions are more readily acceptable if we confine ourselves for the moment to those milder cases who can receive love and respect directly (who are in a majority in our population, I believe). The question of neurotic need gratifications and their consequences must be postponed because of its great complexity.

and to be loved, but also to know more and more, to be curious, to unfold every wrapping and to unlock every door. Beyond this, we have to reckon also with our basically philosophical impulses to structure the world, to understand it deeply, and to have it make sense. While a fine friendship or parent-child relation should offer much in this area, these satisfactions are or should be achieved to a special degree in a good therapeutic relationship.

Finally it might be well to say a word about the obvious (and therefore neglected) fact that it is as great a delight to love as to be loved.[2] The open impulse to affection is as severely inhibited in our culture as the sexual and the hostile impulses—perhaps even more (Suttie, 1935). We are allowed open expression of affection in extraordinarily few relationships, perhaps in only three—the parent-child pair, the grandparent-grandchild pair, and in married people and sweethearts—and even in these we know how easily they can become strangulated and mixed with embarrassment, guilt, defensiveness, playing a role, and with a struggle for dominance.

It is not enough stressed that a therapeutic relationship permits, even encourages, open verbal expression of love and affection impulses. Only here (as well as in the various "personal growth" groups) are they taken for granted and expected, and only here are they consciously purged of their unhealthy admixtures and then, thus cleansed, put to the best of uses. Such facts as these point unmistakably to the necessity of reevaluating the Freudian concepts of transference and countertransference. These concepts rose out of a study of sickness, and are much too limited for dealing with health. They must be enlarged to include the sound as well as the crippled, the rational as well as the irrational.

Relationship: Precondition for Therapy

There can be differentiated at least three different qualities of human relationship, the dominant-subordinate, the equalitarian, and the aloof or laissez-faire. These have been demonstrated in diverse areas including the therapist-patient relationship.

A therapist can consider himself the active, deciding, managing boss of his patient, or she can relate herself to the patient as a partner in a common task, or finally, he can transform himself into a calm, emotionless mirror to the patient, never becoming involved, never coming humanly close, but always remaining detached. This last is the type that Freud recommended, but the other two types of relationship are the ones that actually prevail most often, although officially the only label available for any normal human feelings for the analysand is countertransference, that is, irrational, sick.

Now, if the relationship between the therapist and the patient is the medium through which the patient is to obtain his necessary therapeutic medicines—as the water is the medium in which the fish finds all its need objects—it must be

---

[2]We are particularly struck with this inexplicable oversight in the literature of child psychology. "The child must be loved," "The child will behave well in order to keep the love of his parents," and so on can all read, with equal validity, "The child must love," "The child will behave well *because* it loves its parents," and the like.

considered, not per se, but rather in the light of which medium is best for which patient. We must guard ourselves against choosing one for loyal backing, to the exclusion of others. There is no reason why all three, as well as others, perhaps yet to be discovered, should not be found in the armamentarium of the good therapist.

While it follows from what has been presented above that the average patient would thrive best in a warm, friendly, democratic partnership relation, there are too many for whom it will *not* be the best atmosphere to allow us to make it into a rule. This is particularly true for more serious cases of chronic stabilized neurosis.

Some more authoritarian characters, who will identify kindness with weakness, must not be allowed to develop an easy contempt for the therapist. Holding the reins tight and setting very definite limits to permissiveness may be desirable for the patient's ultimate good. This has been especially stressed by the Rankeans in their discussions of the limits of the therapeutic relation.

Others, who have learned to regard affection as a snare and a trap will recoil with anxiety to anything but aloofness. The deeply guilty may *demand* punishment. The rash and the self-destructive may need positive orders to keep them from harming themselves irreparably.

But there can be no exception to the rule that therapists ought to be as conscious as possible of the relationships they form with their patients. Granted that they will spontaneously tend to one type rather than another because of their own characters, they should be able to hold themselves in check when the patient's good is concerned.

In any case, if the relationship is bad, whether in general terms or in the terms of the individual patient, it is doubtful that any of the other resources of psychotherapy can have much effect. This is largely so because such a relationship is apt never to be entered into or soon broken off. But even if the patient stays with someone he or she deeply dislikes or resents or is anxious with, time is too apt to be taken with self-defense, with defiance, with the patient tempted to take as the main goal *dis*pleasing the therapist.

To sum up, even though forming a satisfactory human relationship may not be an end in itself but rather a means to an end, it must still be regarded as a necessary or highly desirable precondition for psychotherapy, since it is usually the best medium for dispensation of the ultimate psychological medicines that all human beings need.

Therapy: Training in Relationship

There are yet other interesting implications of this point of view. If psychotherapy consists, in ultimate essence, of supplying to a sick human being just those qualities that he or she should have gotten from other good human relations, this amounts to defining the psychologically sick person as one who has never had enough good relationships with other people. This does not contradict our previous definition of sick people as those who have not got enough of love, respect, and so on, since they can get these only from other people. Though these definitions are thus shown to be tautologous, each leads us off in different directions and opens our eyes to different aspects of therapy.

One consequence of this second definition of sickness is that it throws the psychotherapeutic relationship into another light. It is by most considered to be a desperate measure, a last recourse, and because mostly sick people enter into it, it has come to be regarded as itself weird, abnormal, sick, unusual, an unfortunate necessity like surgery, even by the therapists themselves.

Surely this is not the attitude with which people enter into other beneficial relationships such as marriage, friendship, or partnership. But, by theory at least, psychotherapy is as similar to friendship as it is to surgery. It ought then to be looked upon as a healthy, desirable relation, even to some extent and in some respects, as one of the *ideal* relationships between human beings. By theory, it ought to be looked forward to, eagerly entered upon. This is what *should* follow from previous considerations. In actuality, however, we know that this is not the case very often. This contradiction, of course, is well recognized but is not fully explained by the neurotic's necessity for hanging on to the illness. It must also be explained by misunderstanding of the fundamental nature of therapeutic relations, not only by patients, but also by many therapists. We have found potential patients more ready to go into therapy when it was explained to them as we have done above than when the explanation was of the more usual sort.

Another consequence of an interpersonal definition of therapy is that it makes it possible to phrase one of its aspects as training in the technique of establishing a good human relationship (something a chronic neurotic cannot do without special help), of proving this to be a possibility, of discovering how enjoyable and fruitful it is. The hope would be then that the patient could now form deeply good friendships with others by a kind of transfer of training. Presumably, he or she could then get all necessary psychological medicines, as most of us do, from our friendships, our children, our wives or husbands, and our colleagues. From this point of view, therapy can be defined in still another way, namely, as preparing patients to set up on their own the good human relationships that all human beings want and in which relatively healthy people get many of the psychological medicines that they need.

Another deduction from foregoing considerations would be that patients and therapists ideally should *choose* each other and that furthermore this choice should be made not alone on the basis of reputation, size of fee, technical training, skill, and the like, but also on the basis of ordinary human liking for each other. It could easily be demonstrated logically that this should at least shorten the time necessary for treatment, make it easier for both patient and therapist, make possible a closer approach to ideal cure, and make the whole experience more rewarding for both. Various other corollaries of such a conclusion would be that the backgrounds, level of intelligence, experiences, religion, politics, values, and so on of both should be more rather than less similar, ideally.

It must by now be clear that the personality or character structure of therapists is, if not all-important, certainly one of the crucial considerations. They must be individuals who can enter easily into the ideally good human relationship that is psychotherapy. Furthermore, they must be able to do this with many different kinds of people or even with all human beings. They must be warm and sympathetic, and they must be sure enough of themselves to be able to give respect to other human beings. They ought to be essentially democratic persons, in the psychological sense that they look on other human beings with essential respect simply because they are human and unique. In a word, they should be emotionally secure and they should have healthy self-esteem. In addition their life situation ought *ideally* to be so good that they are not absorbed with their own problems. They should be happily married, be financially successful, have good friends, like life, and generally be capable of having a good time.

Finally, all this implies that we might very well throw open for additional consideration the prematurely closed question (by the psychoanalysts) of continued social contacts between therapist and patient after the formal therapeutic sessions are closed or even while they are going on.

Daily Life as Therapy

Because we have expanded and generalized the phrasing of the ultimate goals of psychotherapy and the specific medicines that produce these end effects, we have become logically committed to an obliteration of the walls that fence off psychotherapy from other human relationships and life happenings. Those happenings and those relationships in the life of ordinary individuals that help them make progress toward the ultimate ends of technical psychotherapy may fairly be called psychotherapeutic even though they occur outside an office and without benefit of a professional therapist. It follows that a wholly proper part of the study of psychotherapy is examination of the everyday miracles produced by good marriages, good friendships, good parents, good jobs, good teachers, and so on. An example of a theorem deriving directly from such consideration would be that technical therapy ought to rely much more than it has on steering patients into just such therapeutic relationships as soon as the patient can accept and handle them.

Certainly we need not be afraid as professionals of putting into the hands of amateurs these important psychotherapeutic tools: protection, love, and respect for other human beings. While they are certainly powerful tools, they are not therefore dangerous ones. We may expect that ordinarily we cannot hurt people by loving and respecting them (except occasional neurotic individuals, who are, in any case, badly off already). It is fair to expect that care, love, and respect are forces almost always for good and not for harm.

Accepting this, it must be our clear conviction that not only is every good human being potentially an unconscious therapist, but also we must accept the conclusion that we should approve of this, encourage it, and teach it. At least these fundamentals of what we may call lay psychotherapy can be taught from childhood on to any human being at all. One clear task for public psychotherapy (using the analogy of contrast between public health and private medicine) is to teach just these facts, to broadcast them far and wide, to be certain that every teacher, every parent, and ideally every human being be given the chance to understand them and to apply them. Human beings have always gone for advice and help to others whom they respected and loved. There is no reason why this historical phenomenon should not be formalized, verbalized, and encouraged to the point of universality by psychologists as well as religionists. Let people realize clearly that every time they threaten someone or humiliate or hurt unnecessarily or dominate or reject another human being, they become forces for the creation of psychopathology, even if these be small forces. Let them recognize also that every person who is kind, helpful, decent, psychologically democratic, affectionate, and warm is a psychotherapeutic force, even though a small one.

Self-therapy

One implication of the theory presented here is that self-therapy has at the same time greater possibilites and also greater limitations than have been commonly realized. If all human beings learn to know what they lack, learn what their fundamental desires are, and learn in broad outline the symptoms that indicate the lack of satisfaction of these fundamental desires, they can consciously go about trying to make up for these lacks. We may fairly say that by this theory most human beings have within their own power greater possiblity than they have realized for curing themselves of the multitude of mild maladjustments that are so common in our society. Love, safety, belongingness, and respect from other people are almost panaceas for the situational disturbances and even for some of the mild character disturbances. If individuals know that they should have love, respect, self-respect, and so on, they can consciously seek them out. Certainly everyone will agree that seeking them out consciously will be better and more effective than trying to make up for their lack unconsciously.

But at the same time that this hope is offered to a good many individuals and that they are given a wider possibility for self-therapy than has ordinarily been thought to be possible, there are certain problems for which they must necessarily seek help only from professional hands. For one thing, in severe character disturbances or existential neuroses a clear understanding of the dynamic forces originating, precipitating, and maintaining the disturbance are absolutely necessary before anything can be done for the patient beyond mere amelioration. It is here that all the tools that are necessary to bring conscious insight must be used, tools for which there are as yet no substitutes and that are at present usable only by professionally trained therapists. Once a case is recognized as severe, help from the layman, from the wise old woman, becomes in nine cases out of ten completely useless so far as permanent cure is concerned. This is the essential limitation upon self-therapy.[3]

---

[3]Since this was first written, the interesting books on self-analysis by Horney (1942) and Farrow (1942) have appeared. Their contention is that individuals, by their own efforts, can come to achieve the kind—but not the degree—of insight achieved by professional analysis. This is not denied by most analysts, but is considered impracticable because of the extraordinary drive, patience, courage, and persistence required of such patients. Something similar is true, I believe, for many of the books on personal growth. They can certainly be helpful but must not be counted on for great transformations without help from a professional or from a "guide," guru, leader, or the like.

Group Therapy

A final implication of our approach of psychotherapy is a greater respect for group therapies as well as T-groups and the like. We have stressed so much the fact that psychotherapy and personal growth is an interpersonal relationship that on a priori grounds alone we should feel that an extension from pairing into a larger grouping might very well be beneficial. If ordinary therapy may be conceived of as a miniature ideal society of two, then group therapy may be seen as a miniature ideal society of ten. We already have a strong motivation for experimenting with group therapy, namely, economy of money and time and a wider availability of psychotherapy to more and more patients. But in addition we now have empirical data that indicate that group therapy and T-groups can do some things that individual psychotherapy cannot. We know already that it is very easy to get rid of the sense of uniqueness, of isolation, of guilt or sin when patients find out that the other members of the group are made of about the same kind of stuff as they are, that their goals, their conflicts, their satisfactions and dissatisfactions, their hidden impulses and thoughts are apt to be almost universal in the society taken at large. This reduces the psychopathogenic effect of these secretive conflicts and impulses.

Another therapeutic expectation is also borne out by actual practice. In individual psychotherapy patients learn to make a good human relationship with at least one individual—the therapist. It is then hoped that they can transfer this ability over to their social life in general. Often they can, but sometimes they cannot. In group therapy they not only learn how to establish this good relationship with at least one person, but actually proceed under the eye of the therapist to practice this ability with a whole group of other people as well. In general the results from experiments already available, while not startling, are certainly encouraging.

It is because of such empirical data as well as because of deductions from theory that we should urge more research with group psychotherapy, not only because it is a promising lead for technical psychotherapy, but also because it will surely teach us much about general psychological theory and even about broad social theory as well.

So also for T-groups, basic encounter groups, sensitivity training, and all the other kinds of groups now categorized as personal growth groups or affective education seminars and workshops. Though quite different in procedure, they may yet be said to have the same *far* goals of all psychotherapies, that is, self-actualization, full-humanness, fuller use of species and personal potentials, and so on. Like any of the psychotherapies, they can do wonders when well run by competent people. But we now have enough experience to know that they can be useless or harmful when under bad management. Therefore much more research is needed. This of course is not a startling conclusion because exactly the same is true for surgeons and for all other professionals. Nor have we solved the problem of just *how* a layperson or an amateur can choose the competent therapist (or physician or dentist, or guru, guide, or teacher) and avoid the incompetent one.

THE GOOD SOCIETY

What Is a Good Society?

As a parallel to the previously discussed definition of good human relationships, we can explore the implications of the (by now) obviously called-for definition of the good society as one that gives to its members the greatest possibility of becoming sound and self-actualizing human beings. This in turn means that the good society is the one that has its institutional arrangements set up in such a way as to foster, encourage, reward, and produce a maximum of good human relationships and a minimum of bad human relationships. A corollary from foregoing definitions and identities would be that good society is synonymous with psychologically healthy society, while bad society is synonymous with psychologically sick society, which in turn means basic need gratifying and basic need thwarting respectively (i.e., not enough love, affection, protection, respect, trust, and truth and too much hostility, humiliation, fear, contempt, and domination).

It should be stressed that social and institutional pressures *foster* therapeutic or pathogenic consequences (make them easier, more advantageous, more probable, give them greater primary and secondary gains). They do not absolutely *fate* them or make them absolutely inevitable. We know enough of the range of personality in both simple and complex societies to respect, on the one hand, the plasticity and resilience of human nature and, on the other hand, the peculiar stubbornness of the already formed character structure in exceptional individuals that makes it possible for them to resist and even flout social pressures (see Chapter 11). Always the anthropologist seems to be able to find one kind person in the cruel society, one fighter in the pacific society. We know enough now not to blame *all* human ills on social arrangements à la Rousseau, nor dare we hope that all human beings can be made happy, healthy, and wise by social improvements alone.

So far as our society is concerned we can look at it from various points of view, all useful for one or another purpose. For instance we can strike a sort of average for our or any other society and label it fairly sick, extremely sick, and so on. More useful for us, however, would be a gauging and balancing against each other of the sickness-fostering and the health-fostering forces. Our society clearly has much of both teetering in a precarious balance, with control going now to one set of forces, now another. There is no reason why these forces should not be measured and experimented with.

Leaving such general considerations and turning to the individual-psychological ones, we deal first with the fact of subjective interpretation of the culture. From this point of view, we may fairly say of neurotic people that, *for them,* the society is sick, for they see in it preponderantly danger, threat, attack, selfishness, humiliation, and coldness. It is of course understood that their neighbors, looking at the same culture and the same people, may find the society to be a healthy one. These conclusions do not contradict each other *psychologically.* They can both exist psychologically. Thus every deeply sick person lives subjectively in a sick society. The conclusion from the conjoining of this statement and our previous discussion of the psychotherapeutic relationship is that therapy may be phrased as an attempt to set up a miniature good society. This same phrasing may be used even where the society is sick from the point of view of a large majority of its members. We must beware of a too extreme subjectivism here. The society that is sick for the sick patient is also bad in a more objective sense (even for healthy people), if only because it can produce neurotic people.

How Does Society Affect Human Nature?

Theoretically, then, psychotherapy socially amounts to running counter to the basic stresses and tendencies in a sick society. Or in a more generalized form, no matter what the degree of general health or sickness of a society, therapy amounts to fighting against the sickness-producing forces in that society on an individual scale. It tries, so to speak, to turn the tide, to bore from within, to be revolutionary or radical in an ultimate etymological sense. All psychotherapists, then, are or should be fighting in the small rather than in the large, the psychopathogenic forces in their society, and if these be fundamental and primary, they are actually fighting their society.

Clearly if psychotherapy could be tremendously extended, if, instead of dealing with a few dozen patients a year, psychotherapists could deal with several million patients a year, then these small forces against the nature of our society would become quite perceptible to the naked eye. That the society would change there can be no doubt. First would come changes here and there in the flavor of human relationships with respect to such qualities as hospitality, generosity, friendliness, and the like, but when enough people became more hospitable, more generous, more kind, more social, then we may rest assured that they would force legal, political, economic, and sociological changes as well (Mumford, 1951). Perhaps the rapid spread of T-groups, encounter groups, and many other kinds of "personal growth" groups and classes may have perceptible effects on the society.

It seems to us that no society, however good, could completely eliminate sickness. If threats do not come from other human beings, they will always come from nature, from death, from frustration, from sickness, even from the mere fact that by living together in a society, though we advantage ourselves thereby, we must also necessarily modify the form of satisfying our desires. Nor dare we forget that human nature itself generates much evil, if not from inborn malice, then from ignorance, stupidity, fear, miscommunications, clumsiness, and so on (see Chapter 8).

This is a terribly complicated set of interrelations and it is very easy to be misunderstood or to say things in such a way as to invite misunderstanding. Perhaps I can guard against this, without writing at very great length, by referring the reader to a paper I prepared for my students in a seminar on Utopian Social Psychology (1968b). It stresses the empirical, the actually attainable (rather than unattainable fantasies), and it also insists on statements of degree rather than either/or statements. The task is structured by the questions: How good a society does human nature permit? How good a human nature does society permit? How good a human nature can we hope for considering the built-in limitations of human nature that we already know about? How good a society dare we hope for in view of the difficulties inherent in the very nature of society itself?

My personal judgments are that no perfect human being is possible or even conceivable, but that human beings are *far* more improvable than most people believe. As for the perfect society, this seems to me to be an impossible hope, especially in view of the obvious fact that it is close to impossible even to make a perfect marriage, a friendship, or parent-child relationship. If untainted love is so difficult to achieve in a pair, a family, a group, how much more difficult for 200 million? For 3 billion? And yet again it is clear that pairings, groupings, and societies, though not perfectible, are very clearly improvable and can range from very good to very bad.

Furthermore, I feel we know enough about improving pairs, groups, and societies to reject the likelihood of quick or easy changes. Improving a single person—so that it lasts—can be a matter of years of therapeutic work, and even then the main aspect of the "improvement" is that it permits the person to go about the lifelong task of improving her- or himself. Instant self-actualization in a great moment of conversion or insight or awakening *does* happen, but it is extremely rare and should not be counted upon. The psychoanalysts have long since learned not to rely on insight alone, but now stress "working through," the long, slow, painful, repeated effort to use and to apply the insights. In the East, spiritual teachers and guides will generally also make this same point that to improve oneself is a lifelong effort. The same lesson is now slowly dawning upon the more thoughtful and sober of the leaders of T-groups, basic encounter groups, personal growth groups, affective education, and the like, who are now in the painful process of giving up the "Big Bang" theory of self-actualization.

All formulations in this area would have to be degree formulas of course, as in the following examples. (1) The healthier the general society, the less necessity there should be for individual psychotherapy, since fewer individuals would be sick. (2) The healthier the general society, the more likely will it be that a sick person can be helped or cured without technical therapeutic intervention, that is, by the good life experiences. (3) The healthier the general society, the easier will it be for the therapist to cure the sick patient, since simple gratification therapy is more likely to be acceptable to the patient. (4) The healthier the general society, the easier will it be for insight therapy to cure, because there will be so many supporting good life experiences, good relationships, and so on, as well as relative absence of war, unemployment, poverty, and other sociopathogenic influences. Obviously, dozens of theorems of this easily testable sort are possible.

Some such phrasing of the relationship between individual sickness, individual therapy, and the nature of the society is necessary to help solve the often-stated pessimistic paradox: How can health or improvement of health be possible in a sick society that created the ill health in the first place? Of course the pessimism implied in this dilemma is contradicted by the very presence of self-actualizing people and by the existence of psychotherapy, which proves its possibility by actually existing. It is helpful, even so, to supply a theory of *how* it is possible, if only to throw the whole question open to empirical research.

PROFESSIONAL PSYCHOTHERAPY

Techniques

As illness becomes more and more severe, it becomes less and less accessible to benefit from need gratification. There comes a point in this continuum where (1) basic need gratifications are often not even sought for or wanted, having been given up in favor of neurotic need gratifications, and (2) even when they are offered, the patient cannot use them. It is no use offering affection, for he or she is afraid of it, mistrusts it, misinterprets it, and finally refuses it.

It is at this point that professional (insight) therapy becomes not only necessary but irreplaceable. No other therapy will do, neither suggestion, nor catharsis, nor symptom cure, nor need gratification. Therefore, beyond this point we enter, so to speak, into another country—an area governed by its own laws, an area in which all principles so far discussed in this chapter cease to apply unless modified and qualified.

The differences between technical and lay therapy are vast and important. Psychological developments in this century, starting with the revolutionary discoveries of Freud, Adler, and others have been transforming psychotherapy from an unconscious art into a consciously applied science. There are now available psychotherapeutic tools that are not automatically available to the good human being, but are available only to people of sufficient intellect who have in addition been rigorously trained to use these new techniques. They are artificial techniques, not spontaneous or unconscious ones. They can be taught in a way that is to some extent independent of the character structure of the psychotherapist.

We wish to speak here only about the most important, the most revolutionary of these techniques: the bringing of insight to patients, that is, making consciously available to them their unconscious desires, impulses, inhibitions, and thoughts (genetic analysis, character analysis, resistance analysis, analysis of the transference). It is primarily this tool that gives the professional psychotherapist who also has the requisite good personality a tremendous advantage over the person who has merely the good personality and not the professional techniques.

How is this insight brought about? So far most if not all the techniques for bringing it about have not gone very much beyond those that Freud elaborated. Free associations, dream interpretation, and interpretation of the meaning behind everyday behavior are the major paths by which therapists help patients to gain conscious insight into themselves. A few other possibilities are ready to hand but they are much less important. Relaxation techniques and various techniques that induce some form of dissociation and then take advantage of it are not so important as the so-called Freudian techniques, even though they might very well be used more than they are today.

Within limits these techniques can be acquired by anybody with a decent intelligence who is willing to go through a suitable course of training provided by psychiatric and psychoanalytical institutes, graduate departments of clinical psychology, and so on. It is true that, as we might have expected, there are individual differences in the efficiency of their use. Some students of insight therapy seem to have better intuition than others. We may suspect also that the kind of person we have labeled as the good personality will be able to use them far more efficiently than the therapist who does not have this kind of personality. All institutes of psychoanalysis include a personality requirement for their students.

Another new and great discovery given to us by Freud is the recognition of the necessity for self-understanding by the psychotherapist himself. While the necessity for this kind of insight by the therapist is recognized by the psychoanalysts, it is not yet formally recognized by psychotherapists of other persuasions. This is a mistake. It follows from the theory presented here that any force that will make therapists into better personalities will thereby make them better therapists. Psychoanalysis or other profound therapy of therapists *can* help to do this. If it sometimes fails to cure altogether, at least it can make therapists aware of what is likely to threaten them, of the major areas of conflict and frustration within them. Consequently, when they deal with their patients, they can discount these forces within themselves and correct for them. Being always conscious of them, they can make them subject to their intelligence.

In the past, as we have said, the character structure of therapists was far more important than any theories they held, or even more important than the conscious techniques that they used. But this must become less and less so as technical therapy becomes more and more sophisticated. In the total picture of the good psychotherapist character structure has slowly receded in importance and will certainly continue to do so in the future, while training, intelligence, techniques, and theories have steadily become more and more important until, we may rest assured, some time in the future they will become all-important. We have lauded the wise old woman technique of psychotherapy for the simple reasons that in the past these were the only psychotherapists available, and second because even in the present and in the future they will always be important in what we have called lay psychotherapy. No longer, however, is it sensible or justified to toss a coin to decide whether to go to the minister or to the psychoanalyst. The good professional psychotherapist has left the intuitive helper far behind.

We may expect that in the not too distant future, especially if the society improves, the professional psychotherapist will not be used for purposes of reassurance, support, and other need gratifications, because we will get these from our fellow laypersons. An individual will come for maladies that lie beyond the reach of simple gratification therapy or release therapy, but that are accessible only to professional techniques that are not used by the lay therapist.

Paradoxically a completely contrary deduction is also possible from the foregoing theories. If relatively healthy people are so much more readily touched by therapy, it is quite possible that much technical therapeutic time will be reserved for the most healthy instead of the least healthy on the sensible grounds that improving ten people a year is better than improving one, especially if these few are themselves in key lay therapeutic positions (e.g., teachers, social workers, and physicians). This is already happening to a considerable extent. A large proportion of the time of experienced psychoanalysts and existential analysts is occupied with training and teaching and analyzing young therapists. It is also very common now for a therapist to be teaching physicians, social workers, psychologists, nurses, ministers, and teachers.

Insight and Need Gratification

Before leaving the subject of insight therapy, it would be well to resolve the dichotomy so far implied between insight and need gratification. Purely cognitive or rationalistic insight (cold, unemotional knowledge about) is one thing; organismic insight is another. The full insight that Freudians sometimes speak about is a recognition of the fact that mere knowledge about one's symptoms, even when we add knowledge about where they come from and the dynamic role they play in the contemporary psychic economy, is frequently not in itself curative. There ought to be an emotional experience simultaneously, an actual reliving of the experience, a catharsis, a reaction. That is, a full insight is not only a cognitive but also an emotional experience.

Somewhat more subtle is the contention that this insight is often a conative, need gratifying, or frustrating experience as well, an actual feeling of being loved, or abandoned, or despised, or rejected, or protected. The emotion that the analysts speak of then is better seen as the reaction to realization, for example, that father really loved him after all as one vividly relives a 20-year-old experience, repressed or wrongly understood until now, or that she suddenly realizes, by actually experiencing the appropriate emotion, that she hated the mother she had always assumed she loved.

This rich experience, simultaneously cognitive, emotional, and conative, we may call the organismic insight. But supposing we have been studying *emotional* experiences primarily? Again we should have to expand the experience more and more to include conative elements, and we should ultimately find ourselves speaking of the organismic or holistic emotion, and so on. So also for the conative experience; it too would expand to a nonfaculty experience of the total organism. The final step would be to realize that there was no difference between organismic insight, organismic emotion, and organismic conation except the angle of approach of the student, and the original dichotomies would be clearly seen to be artifacts of a too atomistic approach to the subject.

chapter 10

Approaches to Normality and Health

The words *normal* and *abnormal* cover so many different meanings that they have become just about useless. The strong tendency today is for psychologists and psychiatrists to substitute for these very general words the more specific concepts that are included under these heads. This is what we mean to do in this chapter.

In general the attempts to define normality have been either statistical, or culturally relative, or biological-medical. However, these are the *formal* definitions only, the "company" or Sunday definitions, not the everyday ones. The informal meaning carried by the word is just as definite as the professional ones. Most people have something else in mind when they ask "What is normal?" For most people, even for the professionals in their informal moments, this is a value question, and in effect asks what we should value, what is good and bad for us, what we should worry about, and what we ought to feel guilty or virtuous about. I choose to interpret the title of this chapter in the lay sense as well as in the professional sense. It is my impression that most of the technicians in the field do the same thing although they do not admit it most of the time. There is a good deal of discussion about what normal ought to mean and rather little about what it *does* mean in context, in normal conversation. In my therapeutic work I have always interpreted the question about normality and abnormality in the speaker's context rather than in the technical context. When a mother has asked me whether her child was normal, I understood her to be asking ought she worry about it or not, should she change her efforts to control her child's behavior, or should she let it slide and not bother. When people after a lecture have asked about the normality and abnormality of sexual behavior, I have understood their question in the same way, and my answer very frequently implied "Do worry about it" or "Do not worry about it."

I think that the real reason for currently revived interest in this problem among psychoanalysts, psychiatrists, and psychologists is the feeling that this is *the* great value question. When, for instance, Erich Fromm talks about normality, he places it in the context of goodness, desirability, and value. So increasingly have most other writers in this area. This kind of work now and for some time past has been very frankly an effort to construct a psychology of values that might ultimately serve as a practical guide for ordinary people as well as a theoretical frame of reference for professors of philosophy and other technicians.

I can go even further than this. For many of these psychologists this whole effort is more and more (for most) admitted to be an attempt to do what the formal religions have tried to do and failed to do, that is, to offer people an understanding of human nature in relationship to itself, to other people, to society in general, and to the world in general, a frame of reference in which they could understand when they ought to feel guilty and when they ought not to feel guilty. That is to say, we are working up what amounts to a scientific ethics. I am perfectly willing that my remarks in this chapter be understood as moving in this direction.

STANDARD CONCEPTS

Now before we get to this important subject let us turn first to the various technical attempts to describe and define normality that have not worked well.

Statistical Averages

Statistical surveys of human behavior tell us simply what is the case and what actually exists, and are supposed to be completely devoid of evaluation. Fortunately, most people, even scientists, are simply not strong enough to resist the temptation to approve of the average, of what is most common and most frequent, especially in our culture, which is so strong for the common man. For instance, Kinsey's excellent survey of sexual behavior is highly useful for the raw information that it gives. But Dr. Kinsey and others simply cannot avoid talking about what is normal (meaning desirable). It is average in our society to have a sick, pathological sexual life (from the psychiatric point of view). This does not make it desirable or healthy. We must learn to say average when we mean average.

Another example is the Gesell table of norms of baby development, which are certainly useful for scientists and physicians to have. But most mothers are apt to get worried if their baby is below the average in the development of walking or drinking out of a cup, as if this were bad or frightening. Apparently after we find out what is average, we must still ask, "Is the average desirable?"

Social Conventions

The word *normal* often is used as an unconscious synonym for *traditional* or *habitual* or *conventional,* and is usually meant to cloak the tradition in approval.

I remember the turmoil over women smoking when I went to college. It was not normal, our dean of women said, and forbade it. At that time it was also not normal for college women to wear slacks or to hold hands in public. Of course what she meant was "This is not traditional," which was perfectly true, and this implied for her "This is abnormal, sick, intrinsically pathological," which was perfectly false. A few years later the traditions changed and she was fired, because by that time *her* ways were not "normal."

A variant of this usage is to cloak tradition in theological approval. So-called sacred books are interpreted very frequently as setting norms for behavior, but the scientist pays as little attention to these traditions as to any other.

Cultural Norms

Finally, the culturally relative may also be considered to be obsolete as a source of definition of normal, desirable, good, or healthy. The anthropologists of course did us a great service at first in making us aware of our ethnocentrism. We had been as a culture trying to set up as absolute and species-wide criteria all sorts of local cultural habits, such as wearing pants or eating cows rather than dogs. A wider ethnological sophistication has dispelled many of these notions, and it is generally recognized that ethnocentrism is a serious danger. Nobody can speak for the whole species now unless he or she is able to rise above his or her own culture or stand aside from it, and is thereby more able to judge the human species as a species and not as a neighborhood group.

Passive Adjustment

The main variant of this mistake is found in the idea of the well-adjusted person. It may puzzle the lay reader to discover how hostile psychologists have become to this seemingly sensible and obvious idea. After all everyone wants his or her children to be well adjusted and part of the group, popular, admired, and loved by the friends of their own age. Our big question is: Adjusted to *which* group? Nazis, criminals, delinquents, drug addicts? Popular with whom? Admired by whom? In H. G. Well's wonderful short story "The Valley of the Blind," where all are blind the sighted man is maladjusted.

Adjustment means a passive shaping of oneself to one's culture, to the external environment. But supposing it is a sick culture? Or to give another example, we are slowly learning not to prejudge juvenile delinquents as being necessarily bad or undesirable on psychiatric grounds. Crime and delinquency and bad behavior in children may sometimes represent psychiatrically and biologically *legitimate* revolt against exploitation, injustice, and unfairness.

Adjustment is a passive rather than active process; its ideal is attained in anyone who can be happy without individuality, even the well-adjusted lunatic or prisoner.

This extreme environmentalism implies infinite malleability and flexibility in the human being and unchangeability in reality. It is therefore status quo and fatalistic. It is also untrue. Human beings are *not* infinitely malleable, and reality *can* be changed.

Absence of Disease

In a completely different tradition is the medical-clinical custom of applying the word *normal* to the absence of lesion, disease, or obvious malfunctions. The internist who cannot find anything physically wrong after a thorough examination will say the patient is normal, even though he is in pain still. What the internist means is, "By *my* techniques I cannot discover what is wrong with you."

The physician with some psychological training, the so-called psychosomaticist, can see still more and will use the word normal much less often. Indeed many psychoanalysts go so far as to say no one is normal, meaning completely free of sickness. That is to say, no one is without blemish. Which is true enough, but again does not help us much in our ethical pursuit.

NEW CONCEPTS

What is taking the place of these various conceptions that we have learned to reject? The new frame of reference that this chapter is concerned with is still in process of development and construction. It cannot be said to be clearly seen yet or reliably supported by incontestable evidence at the moment. It is fair to characterize it rather as a slowly developing concept or theory that seems more and more probably to be the true direction of future development.

Specifically my prediction or guess about the future of the normality idea is that some form of theory about generalized, species-wide psychological health will soon be developed that will hold for all human beings no matter what their culture and no matter what their time. This is taking place on empirical as well as on theoretical grounds. This new form of thinking has been forced by new facts, new data of which we shall speak later.

Drucker (1939) has presented the thesis that Western Europe since the beginning of Christianity has been dominated by some four successive ideas or concepts as to the ways in which individual happiness and welfare should be sought. Each of these concepts or myths held up a certain type of man as ideal, and generally assumed that if only this ideal were followed, individual happiness and welfare would be sure to result. The spiritual man was regarded as ideal during the middle ages, the intellectual man during the Renaissance. Then, with the rise of capitalism and Marxism, the economic man has tended to dominate ideal thinking. More recently, and especially in the fascist countries, it might also be fair to speak of a similar and parallel myth, namely, that of heroic man (heroic in the Nietzchean sense).

It looks now as if all these myths have failed and are now giving way to a new one that is slowly developing in the minds of the most advanced thinkers and researchers on the subject, and that may fairly be expected to come into flower in the next decade or two, namely, the concept of the psychologically healthy person, or the eupsychic person, who is also in effect the "natural" person. I expect that this concept will affect our era as profoundly as have the ones mentioned by Drucker.

Now let me try to present briefly and at first dogmatically the essence of this newly developing conception of the psychologically healthy person. First of all and most important of all is the strong belief that individuals have essential natures of their own, some skeleton of psychological structure that may be treated and discussed analogously with their physical structure, and that they have some needs, capacities, and tendencies that are in part genetically based, some of which are characteristic of the whole human species, cutting across all cultural lines, and some of which are unique to the individual. These basic needs are on their face good or neutral rather than evil. Second, there is involved the conception that full health and normal and desirable development consist in actualizing this nature, in fulfilling these potentialities, and in developing into maturity along the lines that this hidden, covert, dimly seen essential nature dictates, growing from within rather than being shaped from without. Third, it is now seen clearly that most psychopathology results from the denial or the frustration or the twisting of essential human nature.[1]

By this concept what is good? Anything that conduces to this desirable development in the direction of actualization of inner human nature. What is bad or abnormal? Anything that frustrates or blocks or denies essential human nature. What is psychopathological? Anything that disturbs or frustrates or twists the course of self-actualization. What is psychotherapy, or for that matter any therapy or growth of any kind? Any means of any kind that helps to restore the person to the path of self-actualization and of development along the lines that his or her inner nature dictates.

WHAT WE MAY BECOME

I suppose that if I had to put into a single phrase the contrast between traditional concepts of normality and the new concept that is emerging, I would maintain that the essential difference is that we can now see not only what humans are, but also what they may become. That is to say that we can see not only surface, not only the actualities, but the potentialities as well. We know better now what

---

[1]At first blush, this conception reminds us a great deal of the Aristotelian and Spinozist ideas of the past. In truth, we must say that this new conception has much in common with the older philosophies. But we must also point out that we now know a great deal more than Aristotle and Spinoza about the true nature of the human being. We may agree with Aristotle when he assumed that the good life consisted in living in accordance with the true nature of man, but we must add that he simply did not know enough about the true nature of the human being. All that Aristotle could do in delineating this essential nature, or inherent design of human nature, was to look about him, to study people, to observe what they were like. But if one observes human beings only on the surface, which was all Aristotle could do, one must ultimately wind up with what amounts to a static conception of human nature. The only thing that Aristotle could do was to build a picture of the good man in his own culture and in that particular period of time. You remember that in his conception of the good life, Aristotle accepted completely the fact of slavery and made the fatal mistake of assuming that just because a man was a slave that this was his essential nature and therefore it was good for him to be a slave. This exposes completely the weakness of resting on a mere surface observation in the attempt to build up the idea of what the good person or the normal person or the healthy person is like.

lies hidden in humans, what lies suppressed, neglected, and unseen. We are now able to judge the essential nature of humans in terms of what their possibilities, potentialities, and highest possible development may be, instead of relying only on external observations of what is the case at this moment. This approach sums up to this: History has practically always sold human nature short.

Another advantage that we have over Aristotle is that we have learned from these same dynamic psychologists that self-realization cannot be attained by intellect or rationality alone. You remember that Aristotle had a hierarchy of human capacities in which reason took the top place. Along with this went inevitably the notion that reason contrasted with, struggled with, and was at odds with human emotional and instinctive nature. But we have learned from the study of psychopathology and psychotherapy that we must modify considerably our picture of the psychological organism to respect equally rationality, emotionality, and the conative or wishing and driving side of our nature. Furthermore, from our empirical studies of the healthy person we have learned that these are definitely not at odds with each other, that these sides of human nature are not necessarily antagonistic but can be cooperative and synergic. The healthy person is all of a piece, integrated, we might say. It is the neurotic person who is at odds with himself, whose reason struggles with his emotions. The result of this split has been that not only the emotional life and the conative have been misunderstood and badly defined, but that also we realize now that the conception of rationality that we inherited from the past is also wrongly understood and wrongly defined. As Erich Fromm has said, "Reason by becoming a guard set to watch its prisoner, human nature, has become a prisoner itself and thus both sides of human nature, reason and emotion, were crippled" (Fromm, 1947). We must all agree with Fromm that the realization of the self occurs not only by acts of thinking but rather by the realization of the total human personality, which includes the active expression not only of the intellectual but also the emotional and instinctlike capacities.

Once granted reliable knowledge of what people *can* be under certain conditions that we have learned to call good, and granted that they are happy, serene, self-accepting, unguilty, and at peace with themselves only when they are fulfulling themselves and becoming what they can be, it is possible and reasonable to speak about good and right and bad and wrong and desirable and undesirable.

It may be objected by the technical philosopher "How can you prove that it is better to be happy than unhappy?" Even this question can be answered empirically, for if we observe human beings under sufficiently wide conditions, we discover that they, *they* themselves, *not* the observer, choose spontaneously to be happy rather than unhappy, comfortable rather than pained, serene rather than anxious. In a word, human beings choose health rather than illness, all other things being equal (with the proviso that *they* choose for themselves that they be not too sick and that the conditions be of a kind that will be discussed later).

This answers also the customary philosophical objection to the means-end value propositions with which all are familiar (*If* you want end *x,* you *ought* to do means *y;* "You ought to eat vitamins, if you want to live longer"). We now have a different approach to this proposition. We know *empirically* what the human species wants—love, safety, absence of pain, happiness, prolongation of life, knowledge, and so on. We can then say *not* "If you wish to be happy, then. . .," but "If you are a sound member of the human species, then. . . ."

This is all true in the same empirical sense that we casually say a dog prefers meat to salad, or that goldfish need fresh water, or that flowers prosper best in the sun. I maintain firmly then that we have been making descriptive, scientific statements rather than purely normative ones.

What we *can* be = what we ought to be, and is much better language than *ought to be*. Observe that if we are being descriptive and empirical, then *ought* is completely out of place, as can be clearly seen if we ask about flowers or animals, what *they* ought to be. What sense does *ought* make here (or *should*)? What *ought* a kitten become? The answer to this question and the spirit in which it is put is the same for human children.

Even a stronger way of saying this is that it is today possible to distinguish in a single moment of time what a person *is* and what he or she *could* be. We are all familiar with the fact that the human personality is organized into layers, or depths. That which is unconscious and that which is conscious coexist, even though they may contradict each other. One *is* (in one sense); the other also *is* (in another deeper sense) and *could* one day come to the surface, become conscious, and then *be* in *that* sense.

In this frame of reference, you can understand that people who behave badly may yet be loving deep down. If they manage to actualize this species-wide potentiality they become healthier people and, in this special sense, more normal.

The important difference between humans and all other beings is that their needs, preferences, and instinct remnants are *weak* and not strong, equivocal not unequivocal, that they leave room for doubt, uncertainty, and conflict, that they are all too easily overlaid and lost to sight by culture, by learning, by the preferences of other people. Through the ages we have been so used to thinking of instincts as univocal, unmistakable, strong, and powerful (as they *are* in animals) that we never saw the possibility of *weak* instincts.

We *do* have a nature, a structure, a shadowy bone structure of instinctlike tendencies and capacities, but it is a great and difficult achievement to know it in ourselves. To be natural and spontaneous, to know what one is and what one *really* wants, is a rare and high culmination that comes infrequently, and that usually takes long years of courage and hard work.

INHERENT HUMAN NATURE

Let us sum up then. What has been affirmed is that humans' inherent design or inner nature seems to be not only their anatomy and physiology, but also their most basic needs, yearnings, and psychological capacities. And second, this inner nature is usually not obvious and easily seen, but is rather hidden and unfulfilled, weak rather than strong.

And how do we know that these needs and constitutional potentialities *are* inherent design? Of the 12 separate lines of evidence and techniques of discovery listed in Chapter 4 (see also Maslow, 1965a), we shall mention now only the 4 most important. First, frustration of these needs and capacities is psychopathogenic (i.e., it makes people sick). Second, their gratification is healthy character fostering (eupsychogenic), as neurotic need gratifications are not. That is, it makes people healthy and better. Third, they spontaneously show themselves as choices under free conditions. Fourth, they can be directly studied in relatively healthy people.

If we wish to differentiate basic from nonbasic, we cannot look alone to introspection of conscious needs or even to description of unconscious needs because, phenomenologically, neurotic needs and inherent needs may all feel much alike. They press equally for gratification, for the monopolizing of consciousness, and their introspected qualities are not different enough from each other to enable the introspector to differentiate them except perhaps at the end of life and in retrospect (as did Tolstoy's Ivan Ilyitch), or in moments of speical insight.

No, we must have some other external variable to correlate with, to covary with. In effect this other variable has been the neurosis-health continuum. We are now pretty well convinced that nasty aggressiveness is reactive rather than basic, effect rather than cause, because as a nasty person gets healthier in psychotherapy, he gets less vicious; and as a healthier person gets more sick, she changes in the direction of *more* hostility, *more* venom, and *more* viciousness.

Furthermore, we know that giving gratification to neurotic needs does *not* breed health as does gratification of basic inherent needs. Giving neurotic power seekers all the power they want does not make them less neurotic, nor is it possible to satiate their neurotic need for power. However much they are fed they still remain hungry (because they're really looking for something else). It makes little difference for ultimate health whether a neurotic need be gratified or frustrated.

It is very different with basic needs like safety or love. Their gratification *does* breed health, their satiation *is* possible, their frustration *does* breed sickness.

The same seems to be true for individual potentialities like intelligence or strong tendency to activity. (The only data we have here are clinical.) Such a tendency acts like a drive that demands fulfillment. Gratify it and the person develops nicely; frustrate it and block it and various subtle troubles, not yet very well known, develop at once.

The most obvious technique of all, however, is the direct study of people who are *actually* healthy. We certainly know enough now to be able to select *relatively* healthy people. Granted that perfect specimens do not exist, still it may be expected that we can learn more about the nature, for example, of radium when it is relatively concentrated than when it is relatively dilute.

The investigation reported in Chapter 11 has demonstrated the possibility that a *scientist* could study and describe normality in the sense of excellence, perfection, ideal health, and the fulfillment of human possibilities.

DIFFERENTIATING THE INHERENT FROM THE ACCIDENTAL

The most fully studied example of inherent design is the love need. With this we can illustrate all four of the techniques so far mentioned for differentiating the inherent and universal in human nature from the accidental and local.

1. It is agreed by practically all therapists that when we trace a neurosis back to its beginnings we shall find with great frequency a deprivation of love in the early years. Several semiexperimental studies have confirmed this in infants and babies to such a point that radical deprivation of love is considered dangerous even to the life of the infant. That is to say, the deprivation of love leads to illness.

2. These illnesses, if they have not gone so far as to be irreversible, are now known to be curable, especially in young children, by giving affection and loving kindness. Even in adult psychotherapy and analysis of more serious cases, there is now good reason to believe that one thing that the therapy does is to make it possible for the patient to receive and utilize the love that heals. Also there is a mounting mass of evidence to prove a correlation between affectionate childhood and a healthy adulthood. Such data add up to the generalization that love is a basic need for healthy development of the human being.

3. Children in the situation where they are permitted free choice, and granted that they are not yet warped and twisted, prefer affection to nonaffection. We have no true experiments yet to prove this, but we have a huge amount of clinical data and *some* ethnological data to support this conclusion. The common observation that children prefer an affectionate teacher or parent or friend to the hostile or cold teacher or parent or friend illustrates what we mean. The crying of infants tells us that they prefer affection to nonaffection, for instance in the Balinese situation. The adult Balinese does not need love as the adult American does. Balinese children are taught by bitter experiences not to ask for it and not to expect it. But they do not *like* this training; the children weep bitterly while being trained not to ask for love.

4. Finally, what do we find descriptively in healthy adults? That practically all (though not quite all) have led loving lives, have loved and been loved. Furthermore, they are *now* loving people. And finally and paradoxically they *need* love *less* than the average person does, apparently because they already have enough.

A perfect parallel that makes these points more plausible and more commonsense is supplied by *any* other of the deficiency diseases. Supposing an animal lacks salt. First, this produces pathology. Second, extra salt taken into the body cures or helps these sicknesses. Third, a white rat or a human that lacks salt when given a choice will prefer salt-laden foods, that is, will eat salt in unusually large quantities and in the case of the human will report subjective cravings for salt and will report that it tastes especially good. Fourth, we find that healthy organisms, already having enough salt, do *not* specially crave it or need it.

We may therefore say that just as an organism needs salt in order to attain health and avoid illness, so also does it need love for the same reasons. In other words, we can say that the organism is so designed that it needs salt and love, in the same way that automobiles are so designed that they need gas and oil.

We have spoken much of good conditions, of permissiveness, and the like. These refer to the special conditions of observation that are so often necessary in scientific work and are the equivalent of saying "This is true under such and such circumstances."

CONDITIONS FOR HEALTH

Let us turn to this problem of what constitutes good conditions for the revelation of original nature to see what contemporary dynamic pshychology has to offer on the subject.

If the upshot of what we have already said is that the organism has a vaguely delineated, intrinsic nature of its own, it is quite clear that this inner nature is a very delicate and subtle something rather than being strong and overpowering as it is in lower animals, who are never in any doubt about what they are, what they want, and what they do not want. The human needs for love, for knowledge, or for a philosophy are weak and feeble rather than unequivocal and unmistakable; they whisper rather than shout. And the whisper is easily drowned out.

In order to discover what human beings need and what they *are*, it is necessary to set up special conditions that foster expression of these needs and capacities that encourage and make them possible. In general these conditions may all be summed up under the one head of permissiveness to gratify and to express. How do we know what is best for pregnant white rats to eat? We give them free choice from among a wide range of possibilities, and we let them eat whatever they want, whenever they want it, and in any quantities or patterns they choose. We know it is best for human infants to be weaned in an individual fashion, that is, whenever it is best for *them*. How do we determine this? Certainly we cannot ask the infant, and we have learned not to ask the old-school pediatrician. We give babies a choice; we let them decide. We offer them both the liquid and the solid food. If the solid food appeals to them they will spontaneously wean themselves from the breast. In the same way we have learned to let children tell us when they need love, or protection, or respect, or control by setting up a permissive, accepting, gratifying atmosphere. We have learned that this is the best atmosphere for psychotherapy, indeed, the *only* possible one, in the long run. Free choice from among a wide range of possibilities has been found useful in such diverse social situations as choosing roommates in institutions for delinquents, choosing teachers and courses in college, choosing bombardier crews, and the like. (I leave aside the knotty but important question of *desirable* frustration, of discipline, of setting limits to gratification. I wish to point out only that while permissiveness may be best for our experimental purpose, it need not also be sufficient in itself for teaching consideration of others and awareness of *their* needs or of what may be necessary in the future.)

From the point of view, then, of fostering self-actualization or health, a good environment (in theory) is one that offers all necessary raw materials and then gets out of the way and stands aside to let the (average) organism itself utter its wishes and demands and make its choices (always remembering that it often chooses delay, renunciation in favor of others, etc., and that *other* people also have demands and wishes).

ENVIRONMENT AND PERSONALITY

There is another important problem that confronts us as we struggle to understand this newer conception of normality and its relationship to environment. One theoretical consequence would seem to be that perfect health needs a perfect world to live in and to make it possible. In actual research, it does not seem to work out that way exactly.

It *is* possible to find extremely healthy individuals in our society, which is very far from perfection. Certainly these individuals are not perfect, but they certainly are as fine people as we can now conceive. Perhaps at this time and in this culture we just do not know enough about how perfect people can get.

In any case, research has established an important point in discovering that individuals can be healthier, even *much* healthier, than the culture in which they grow and live. This is possible primarily because of the ability of healthy people to be detached from their surroundings, which is the same as saying that they live by their inner laws rather than by outer pressures.

Our culture is democratic and pluralistic enough to give a very wide latitude to individuals to have the characters that they please, so long as their external behavior is not too threatening or frightening. Healthy individuals are not usually externally visible; they are not marked off by unusual clothes, or manners, or behavior. It is an *inner* freedom that they have. So long as they are independent of the approval and disapproval of other people, and seek rather *self*-approval, so long may they be considered to be psychologically autonomous, that is, relatively independent of the culture. Tolerance and freedom of taste and opinion seem the key necessities.

To sum up, what research we have points to the conclusion that while a good environment fosters good personalities, this relationship is far from perfect, and furthermore, the definition of *good* environment has to change markedly to stress spiritual and psychological as well as material and economic forces.

PSYCHOLOGICAL UTOPIA

It has been my pleasure to work up a speculative description of a psychological Utopia in which all people are psychologically healthy. Eupsychia, I call it (pronounced Yew-sigh-key-a). From what we know of healthy people, could we predict the kind of culture that they would evolve if 1000 healthy families migrated to some deserted land where they could work out their own destiny as they pleased? What kind of education would they choose? Economic system? Sexuality? Religion?

I am very uncertain of some things—economics in particular. But of other things I am *very* sure. One of them is that this would almost surely be a (philosophically) anarchistic group, a Taoistic but loving culture, in which people (young people too) would have much more free choice than we are used to, and in which basic needs and metaneeds would be respected much more than they are in our society. People would not bother each other so much as we do, would be much less prone to press opinions or religions or philosophies or tastes in clothes or food or art on their neighbors. In a word, the inhabitants of Eupsychia would tend to be more Taoistic, nonintrusive, and basic need gratifying (whenever possible), would frustrate only under certain conditions that I have not attempted to describe, would be more honest with each other than we are, and would permit people to make free choices wherever possible. They would be far less controlling, violent, contemptuous, or overbearing than we are. Under such conditions, the deepest layers of human nature could show themselves with greater ease.

I must point out that adult human beings constitute a special case. The free choice situation does not necessarily work for people in general—only for intact ones. Sick, neurotic people make the wrong choices; they do not know what they want, and even when they do, have not courage enough to choose correctly. When we speak of free *choice* in human beings, we refer to sound adults or children who are not yet twisted and distorted. Most of the good experimental work with free choice has been done with animals. We have also learned a great deal about it at the clinical level from the analysis of psychotherapeutic processes.

THE NATURE OF NORMALITY

Now coming back to the question with which we started, the nature of normality, we have come close to identifying it with the highest excellence of which we are capable. But this ideal is not an unattainable goal set out far ahead of us; rather it is actually within us, existent but hidden, as potentiality rather than as actuality.

Furthermore, it is a conception of normality that I claim is discovered rather than invented, based on empirical findings rather than on hopes or wishes. It implies a strictly naturalistic system of values that can be enlarged by further empirical research with human nature. Such research should be able to give us answers to the age-old questions "How can I be a good person?" "How can I live a good life?" "How can I be fruitful?" "Happy?" "At peace with myself?" If the organism tells us what it needs—and therefore what it values—by sickening and withering when deprived of these values, this is the same as telling us what is good for it.

One last point. The key concepts in the newer dynamic psychology are spontaneity, release, naturalness, self-choice, self-acceptance, impulse awareness, gratification of basic needs. They *used* to be control, inhibition, discipline, training, and shaping, on the principle that the depths of human nature were dangerous, evil, predatory, and ravenous. Education, family training, bringing up children, and acculturation in general were all seen as a process of bringing the darker forces within us under control.

See how different are the ideal conceptions of society, law, education, and family that are generated by these two different conceptions of human nature. In the one case they are restraining and controlling forces; in the other they are gratifying and fulfilling. Again I must stress that there are two kinds of restraint and control. One kind frustrates basic needs and fears them. The other kind (Apollonizing controls), such as delaying the sexual climax, eating elegantly, or swimming skillfully, *enhances* the gratification of basic needs. Of course, this is an oversimple, either-or contrast. It is unlikely that either conception is totally correct or totally incorrect. Yet the contrast of ideal types is useful in sharpening our perceptions.

In any case, if this conception that identifies normality with ideal health holds up, we shall have to change not only our conceptions of individual psychology but also our theories of society.

three

SELF-ACTUALIZATION

chapter *11*

Self-actualizing People: A Study of Psychological Health

The study to be reported in this chapter is unusual in various ways. It was not planned as an ordinary research; it was not a social venture but a private one, motivated by my own curiosity and pointed toward the solution of various personal moral, ethical, and scientific problems. I sought only to convince and to teach myself rather than to prove or to demonstrate to others. [Editor's note: Maslow's study of self-actualizing people was an informal personal inquiry that he continued throughout his life.]

Quite unexpectedly, however, these studies have proved to be so enlightening to me, and so laden with exciting implications, that it seems fair that some sort of report should be made to others in spite of its methodological shortcomings.

In addition, I consider the problem of psychological health to be so pressing that *any* suggestions, *any* bits of data, however moot, are endowed with great heuristic value. This kind of research is in principle so difficult—involving as it does a kind of lifting oneself by one's own norms—that if we were to wait for conventionally reliable data, we should have to wait forever. It seems that the necessary thing to do is not to fear mistakes, to plunge in, to do the best that one can, hoping to learn enough from blunders to correct them eventually. At present the only alternative is simply to refuse to work with the problem. Accordingly, for whatever use can be made of it, the following report is presented with due apologies to those who insist on conventional reliability, validity, sampling, and the like.

THE STUDY

Subjects and Methods

The subjects were selected from among personal acquaintances and friends, and from among public and historical figures. In addition, in a first research with young people, three thousand college students were screened, but yielded only one immediately usable subject and a dozen or two possible future subjects ("growing well").

I had to conclude that self-actualization of the sort I had found in my older subjects perhaps was not possible in our society for young, developing people.

Accordingly, in collaboration with E. Raskin and D. Freedman, a search was begun for a panel of *relatively* healthy college students. We arbitrarily decided to choose the healthiest 1 percent of the college population. This research, pursued over a two-year period as time permitted, had to be interrupted before completion, but it was, even so, very instructive at the clinical level.

It was also hoped that figures created by novelists or dramatists could be used for demonstration purposes, but none were found that were usable in our culture and our time (in itself a thought-provoking finding).

The first clinical definition, on the basis of which subjects were finally chosen or rejected, had a positive as well as a merely negative side. The negative criterion was an absence of neurosis, psychopathic personality, psychosis, or strong tendencies in these directions. Possibly psychosomatic illness called forth closer scrutiny and screening. Wherever possible, Rorschach tests were given, but turned out to be far more useful in revealing concealed psychopathology than in selecting healthy people. The positive criterion for selection was positive evidence of self-actualization (SA), as yet a difficult syndrome to describe accurately. For the purposes of this discussion, it may be loosely described as the full use and exploitation of talents, capacities, potentialities, and the like. Such people seem to be fulfilling themselves and to be doing the best that they are capable of doing, reminding us of Nietzsche's exhortation, "Become what thou art!" They are people who have developed or are developing to the full stature of which they are capable. These potentialities may be either idiosyncratic or species-wide.

This criterion implies also gratification, past or present, of the basic needs for safety, belongingness, love, respect, and self-respect, and of the cognitive needs for knowledge and for understanding, or in a few cases, conquest of these needs. This is to say that all subjects felt safe and unanxious, accepted, loved and loving, respect-worthy and respected, and that they had worked out their philosophical, religious, or axiological bearings. It is still an open question as to whether this basic gratification is a sufficient or only a prerequisite condition of self-actualization.

In general, the technique of selection used was that of *iteration,* previously used in studies of the personality syndromes of self-esteem and of security and described in Chapter 18. This consists briefly in starting with the personal or cultural nontechnical state of belief, collating the various extant usages and definitions of the syndrome, and then defining it more carefully, still in terms of actual usage (what might be called the lexicographical stage), with, however, the elimination of the logical and factual inconsistencies customarily found in folk definitions.

On the basis of the corrected folk definition, the first groups of subjects are selected, a group who are high in the quality and a group who are low in it. These people are studied as carefully as possible in the clinical style, and on the basis of this empirical study the original corrected folk definition is further changed and corrected as required by the data now in hand. This gives the first clinical definition. On the basis of this new definition, the original group of subjects is reselected, some being retained, some being dropped, and some new ones being added. This second level group of subjects is then in its turn clinically and, if possible, experimentally and statistically studied, which in turn causes modification, correction, and enrichment of the first clinical definition, with which in turn a new group of subjects is selected and so on. In this way an originally vague and unscientific folk concept can become more and more exact, more and more operational in character, and therefore more scientific.

Of course, external, theoretical, and practical considerations may intrude into this spiral-like process of self-correction. For instance, early in this study, it was found that folk usage was so unrealistically demanding that no living human being could possibly fit the definition. We had to stop excluding a possible subject on the basis of single foibles, mistakes, or foolishness; or to put it in another way, we could not use perfection as a basis for selection, since no subject was perfect.

Another such problem was presented by the fact that in all cases it was impossible to get full and satisfactory information of the kind usually demanded in clinical work. Possible subjects, when informed of the purpose of the research, became self-conscious, froze up, laughed off the whole effort, or broke off the relationship. As a result, since this early experience, all older subjects have been studied indirectly, indeed almost surreptitiously. Only younger people can be studied directly.

Since living people were studied whose names could not be divulged, two desiderata or even requirements of ordinary scientific work became impossible to achieve: namely, repeatability of the investigation and public availability of the data upon which conclusions were made. These difficulties are partly overcome by the inclusion of public and historical figures, and by the supplementary study of young people and children who could conceivably be used publicly.

The subjects have been divided into the following categories:[1]

CASES: Seven fairly sure and two highly probable contemporaries (interviewed)

Two fairly sure historical figures (Lincoln in his last years and Thomas Jefferson)

[1]See also Bonner (1961, p. 97), Bugental (1965, pp. 264–276), and the Manual and Bibliography for Shostrom's POI Test of Self-Actualization (1963, 1968).

Seven highly probable public and historical figures (Albert
Einstein, Eleanor Roosevelt, Jane Addams, William James,
Albert Schweitzer, Aldous Huxley, and Benedict de Spi-
noza)

PARTIAL CASES: Five contemporaries who fairly certainly fall short somewhat but who can yet be used for study[2]

Collection and Presentation of Data

Data here consist not so much in the usual gathering of specific and discrete facts
as in the slow development of a global or holistic impression of the sort that we
form of our friends and acquaintances. It was rarely possible to set up a situation,
to ask pointed questions, or to do any testing with my older subjects (although
this *was* possible and was done with younger subjects). Contacts were fortuitous
and of the ordinary social sort. Friends and relatives were questioned where this
was possible.

Because of this and also because of the small number of subjects as well
as the incompleteness of the data for many subjects, any quantitative presentation
is impossible: only composite impressions can be offered for whatever they may
be worth.

THE OBSERVATIONS

Holistic analysis of the total impressions yields the following characteristics of
self-actualizing people for further clinical and experimental study: perception of
reality, acceptance, spontaneity, problem centering, solitude, autonomy, fresh appreciation, peak experiences, human kinship, humility and respect, interpersonal
relationships, ethics, means and ends, humor, creativity, resistance to enculturation, imperfections, values, and resolution of dichotomies.

Perception of Reality

The first form in which this capacity was noticed was as an unusual ability to
detect the spurious, the fake, and the dishonest in personality, and in general to
judge people correctly and efficiently. In an informal experiment with a group of
college students, a clear tendency was discerned for the more secure (the more
healthy) to judge their professors more accurately than did the less secure students,
that is, high scorers in the S-I test (Maslow, 1952).

As the study progressed, it slowly became apparent that this efficiency ex-

---

[2]Potential or possible cases that have been suggested or studied by others are G. W. Carver,
Eugene V. Debs, Thomas Eakins, Fritz Kreisler, Goethe, Pablo Casals, Martin Buber, Danilo Dolci,
Arthur E. Morgan, John Keats, David Hilbert, Arthur Waley, D. T. Suzuki, Adlai Stevenson, Sholom
Aleichem, Robert Browning, Ralph Waldo Emerson, Frederick Douglass, Joseph Schumpeter, Bob
Benchley, Ida Tarbell, Harriet Tubman, George Washington, Karl Muenzinger, Joseph Haydn, Camille
Pissarro, Edward Bibring, George William Russell (A. E.), Pierre Renoir, Henry Wadsworth Long-
fellow, Peter Kropotkin, John Altgeld, Thomas More, Edward Bellamy, Benjamin Franklin, John Muir,
and Walt Whitman.

tended to many other areas of life—indeed *all* areas that were observed. In art and music, in things of the intellect, in scientific matters, in politics and public affairs, they seemed as a group to be able to see concealed or confused realities more swiftly and more correctly than others. Thus an informal survey indicated that their predictions of the future from whatever facts were in hand at the time seemed to be more often correct, because less based upon wish, desire, anxiety, fear, or upon generalized, character-determined optimism or pessimism.

At first this was phrased as good taste or good judgment, the implication being relative and not absolute. But for many reasons (some to be detailed below), it has become progressively more clear that this had better be called perception (not taste) of something that was absolutely there (reality, not a set of opinions). It is hoped that this conclusion—or hypothesis—can one day be put to the experimental test.

If this is so, it would be impossible to overstress its importance. Money-Kyrle (1944), an English psychoanalyst, has indicated that he believes it possible to call neurotic people not only *relatively* but *absolutely* inefficient, simply because they do not perceive the real world so accurately or so efficiently as do healthy persons. Neurotics are not emotionally sick—they are cognitively *wrong*! If health and neurosis are, respectively, correct and incorrect perceptions of reality, propositions of fact and propositions of value merge in this area, and, in principle, value propositions should then be empirically demonstrable rather than merely matters of taste or exhortation. For those who have wrestled with this problem it will be clear that we may have here a partial basis for a true science of values, and consequently of ethics, social relations, politics, religion, and so forth.

It is definitely possible that maladjustment or even extreme neurosis would disturb perception enough to affect acuity of perception of light or touch or odor. But it is *probable* that this effect can be demonstrated in spheres of perception removed from the merely physiological. It should also follow that the effects of wish, desire, or prejudice upon perception as in many recent experiments should be very much less in healthy people than in sick. A priori considerations encourage the hypothesis that this superiority in the perception of reality eventuates in a superior ability to reason, to perceive the truth, to come to conclusions, to be logical, and to be cognitively efficient, in general.

One particularly impressive and instructive aspect of this superior relationship with reality will be discussed at length in Chapter 13. It was found that self-actualizing people distinguished far more easily than most the fresh, concrete, and idiographic from the generic, abstract, and categorized. The consequence is that they live more in the real world of nature than in the human-made mass of concepts, abstractions, expectations, beliefs, and stereotypes that most people confuse with the world. They are therefore far more apt to perceive what is there rather than their own wishes, hopes, fears, anxieties, their own theories and beliefs, or those of their cultural group. "The innocent eye," Herbert Read has very effectively called it.

The relationship with the unknown seems to be of exceptional promise as another bridge between academic and clinical psychology. Our healthy subjects are generally unthreatened and unfrightened by the unknown, being therein quite different from average people. They accept it, are comfortable with it, and, often are even *more* attracted by it than by the known. They not only tolerate the ambiguous and unstructured (Frenkel-Brunswik, 1949); they like it. Quite characteristic is Einstein's statement, "The most beautiful thing we can experience is the mysterious. It is the source of all art and science."

These people, it is true, are the intellectuals, the researchers, and the scientists, so that perhaps the major determinant here is intellectual power. And yet we all know how many scientists with high IQ, through timidity, conventionality, anxiety, or other character defects, occupy themselves exclusively with what is known, with polishing it, arranging and rearranging it, classifying it, and otherwise puttering with it instead of discovering, as they are supposed to do.

Since for healthy people the unknown is not frightening, they do not have to spend any time laying the ghost, whistling past the cemetery, or otherwise protecting themselves against imagined dangers. They do not neglect the unknown, or deny it, or run away from it, or try to make believe it is really known, nor do they organize, dichotomize, or categorize it prematurely. They do not cling to the familiar, nor is their quest for the truth a catastrophic need for certainty, safety, definiteness, and order, such as we see in an exaggerated form in Goldstein's brain-injured patients (1939) or in the compulsive-obsessive neurotic. They can be, when the total objective situation calls for it, comfortably disorderly, sloppy, anarchic, chaotic, vague, doubtful, uncertain, indefinite, approximate, inexact, or inaccurate (all, at certain moments in science, art, or life in general, quite desirable).

Thus it comes about that doubt, tentativeness, uncertainty, with the consequent necessity for abeyance of decision, which is for most a torture, can be for some a pleasantly stimulating challenge, a high spot in life rather than a low.

Acceptance

A good many personal qualities that can be perceived on the surface and that seem at first to be various and unconnected may be understood as manifestations or derivatives of a more fundamental single attitude, namely, of a relative lack of overriding guilt, of crippling shame, and of extreme or severe anxiety. This is in direct contrast with the neurotic person who in every instance may be described as crippled by guilt and/or shame and/or anxiety. Even the normal member of our culture feels unnecessarily guilty or ashamed about too many things and has anxiety in too many unnecessary situations. Our healthy individuals find it possible to accept themselves and their own nature without chagrin or complaint or, for that matter, even without thinking about the matter very much.

They can accept their own human nature in the stoic style, with all its shortcomings, with all its discrepancies from the ideal image without feeling real concern. It would convey the wrong impression to say that they are self-satisfied. What we must say rather is that they can take the frailties and sins, weaknesses, and evils of human nature in the same unquestioning spirit with which one accepts the characteristics of nature. One does not complain about water because it is wet, or about rocks because they are hard, or about trees because they are green. As children look out upon the world with wide, uncritical, undemanding, innocent eyes, simply noting and observing what is the case, without either arguing the matter or demanding that it be otherwise, so do self-actualizing people tend to look upon human nature in themselves and in others. This is of course not the same as resignation, but resignation too can be observed in our subjects, especially in the face of illness and death.

Be it observed that this amounts to saying in another form what we have already described; namely, that the self-actualized person sees reality more clearly: our subjects see human nature as it *is* and not as they would prefer it to be. Their eyes see what is before them without being strained through spectacles of various sorts to distort or shape or color the reality (Bergson, 1944).

The first and most obvious level of acceptance is at the so-called animal level. Those self-actualizing people tend to be good animals, hearty in their appetites and enjoying themselves without regret or shame or apology. They seem to have a uniformly good appetite for food; they seem to sleep well; they seem to enjoy their sexual lives without unnecessary inhibition and so on for all the relatively physiological impulses. They are able to accept themselves not only on these low levels, but at all levels as well; for example, love, safety, belongingness, honor, self-respect. All of these are accepted without question as worth while, simply because these people are inclined to accept the work of nature rather than to argue with it for not having constructed things to a different pattern. This shows itself in a relative lack of the disgusts and aversions seen in average people and especially in neurotics, such as food annoyances, disgust with body products, body odors, and body functions.

Closely related to self-acceptance and to acceptance of others is (1) their lack of defensiveness, protective coloration, or pose, and (2) their distaste for such artificialities in others. Cant, guile, hypocrisy, front, face, playing a game, trying to impress in conventional ways: these are all absent in themselves to an unusual degree. Since they can live comfortably even with their own shortcomings, these finally come to be perceived, especially in later life, as not shortcomings at all, but simply as neutral personal characteristics.

This is not an absolute lack of guilt, shame, sadness, anxiety, or defensiveness; it is a lack of unnecessary or neurotic (because unrealistic) guilt, and the like. The animal processes (e.g., sex, urination, pregnancy, menstruation, growing old, etc.) are part of reality and so must be accepted.

What healthy people *do* feel guilty about (or ashamed, anxious, sad, or regretful) are (1) improvable shortcomings (e.g., laziness, thoughtlessness, loss of temper, hurting others); (2) stubborn remnants of psychological ill health (e.g., prejudice, jealousy, envy); (3) habits, which, though relatively independent of character structure, may yet be very strong, or (4) shortcomings of the species or of the culture or of the group with which they have identified. The general formula seems to be that healthy people will feel bad about discrepancies between what is and what might very well be or ought to be (Adler, 1939; Fromm, 1947; Horney, 1950).

Spontaneity

Self-actualizing people can all be described as relatively spontaneous in behavior and far more spontaneous than that in their inner life, thoughts, impulses, and so on. Their behavior is marked by simplicity and naturalness, and by lack of artificiality or straining for effect. This does not necessarily mean consistently unconventional behavior. If we were to take an actual count of the number of times that self-actualizing people behaved in an unconventional manner the tally would not be high. Their unconventionality is not superficial but essential or internal. It is their impulses, thought, and consciousness that are so unusually unconventional, spontaneous, and natural. Apparently recognizing that the world of people in which they live could not understand or accept this, and since they have no wish to hurt them or to fight with them over every triviality, they will go through the ceremonies and rituals of convention with a good-humored shrug and with the best possible grace. Thus I have seen a man accept an honor he laughed at and even despised in private, rather than make an issue of it and hurt the people who thought they were pleasing him.

That this conventionality is a cloak that rests very lightly upon their shoulders and is easily cast aside can be seen from the fact that self-actualizing people infrequently allow convention to hamper them or inhibit them from doing anything that they consider very important or basic. It is at such moments that their essential lack of conventionality appears, and not as with the average Bohemian or authority-rebel, who makes great issues of trivial things and who will fight against some unimportant regulation as if it were a world issue.

This same inner attitude can also be seen in those moments when such persons become keenly absorbed in something that is close to one of their main interests. They can then be seen quite casually to drop off all sorts of rules of behavior to which at other times they conform; it is as if they have to make a conscious effort to be conventional; as if they were conventional voluntarily and by design.

Finally, this external habit of behavior can be voluntarily dropped when in the company of people who do not demand or expect routine behavior. That this relative control of behavior is felt as something of a burden is seen by our subjects' preference for such company as allows them to be more free, natural, and spontaneous, and that relieves them of what they find sometimes to be effortful conduct.

One consequence or correlate of this characteristic is that these people have codes of ethics that are relatively autonomous and individual rather than conventional. The unthinking observer might sometimes believe them to be unethical, since they can break down not only conventions but laws when the situation seems to demand it. But the very opposite is the case. They are the most ethical of people even though their ethics are not necessarily the same as those of the people around them. It is this kind of observation that leads us to understand very assuredly that the ordinary ethical behavior of the average person is largely conventional behavior rather than truly ethical behavior (e.g., behavior based on fundamentally accepted principles, which are perceived to be true).

Because of this alienation from ordinary conventions and from the ordinarily accepted hypocrisies, lies, and inconsistencies of social life, they sometimes feel like spies or aliens in a foreign land and sometimes behave so.

I should not give the impression that they try to hide what they are like. Sometimes they let themselves go deliberately, out of momentary irritation with customary rigidity or with conventional blindness. They may, for instance, be trying to teach someone or they may be trying to protect someone from hurt or injustice or they may sometimes find emotions bubbling up from within them that are so pleasant or even ecstatic that it seems almost sacrilegious to suppress them. In such instances I have observed that they are not anxious or guilty or ashamed of the impression that they make on the onlooker. It is their claim that they usually behave in a conventional fashion simply because no great issues are involved or because they know people will be hurt or embarrassed by any other kind of behavior.

Their ease of penetration to reality, their closer approach to an animallike or childlike acceptance and spontaneity imply a superior awareness of their own impulses, desires, opinions, and subjective reactions in general (Fromm, 1947; Rand, 1943; Reik, 1948). Clinical study of this capacity confirms beyond a doubt the opinion of, for example, Fromm (1941) that average, normal, well-adjusted people often have not the slightest idea of what they are, of what they want, of what their own opinions are.

It was such findings as these that led ultimately to the discovery of a most profound difference between self-actualizing people and others; namely, that the motivational life of self-actualizing people is not only quantitatively different but also qualitatively different from that of ordinary people. It seems probable that we must construct a profoundly different psychology of motivation for self-actualizing people, such as metamotivation or growth motivation, rather than deficiency motivation. Perhaps it will be useful to make a distinction between living and *preparing* to live. Perhaps the ordinary concept of motivation should apply *only* to nonself-actualizers. Our subjects no longer strive in the ordinary sense, but rather develop. They attempt to grow to perfection and to develop more and more fully in their own style. The motivation of ordinary people is a striving for the basic need gratifications that they lack. But self-actualizing people in fact lack none of these gratifications; and yet they have impulses. They work, they try, and they are ambitious, even though in an unusual sense. For them motivation is just character growth, character expression, maturation, and development; in a word self-actualization. Could these self-actualizing people be more human, more revealing of the original nature of the species, closer to the species type in the taxonomical sense? Ought a biological species to be judged by its crippled, warped, only partially developed specimens, or by examples that have been overdomesticated, caged, and trained?

Problem Centering

Our subjects are in general strongly focused on problems outside themselves. In current terminology they are problem centered rather than ego centered. They generally are not problems for themselves and are not generally much concerned about themselves (e.g., as contrasted with the ordinary introspectiveness that one finds in insecure people). These individuals customarily have some mission in life, some task to fulfill, some problem outside themselves which enlists much of their energies (Bühler & Massarik, 1968; Frankl, 1969).

This is not necessarily a task that they would prefer or choose for themselves; it may be a task that they feel is their responsibiliy, duty, or obligation. This is why we use the phrase "a task that they must do" rather than the phrase "a task that they want to do." In general these tasks are nonpersonal or unselfish, concerned rather with the good of humanity in general, or of a nation in general, or of a few individuals in the subject's family.

With a few exceptions we can say that our objects are ordinarily concerned with basic issues and eternal questions of the type that we have learned to call philosophical or ethical. Such people live customarily in the widest possible frame of reference. They seem never to get so close to the trees that they fail to see the forest. They work within a framework of values that are broad and not petty, universal and not local, and in terms of a century rather than the moment. In a word, these people are all in one sense or another philosophers, however homely.

Of course, such an attitude carries with it dozens of implications for every area of daily living. For instance, one of the main presenting symptoms originally worked with (bigness, lack of smallness, triviality, or pettiness) can be subsumed under this more general heading. This impression of being above small things, of having a larger horizon, a wider breadth of vision, of living in the widest frame of reference, *sub specie aeternitatis,* is of the utmost social and interpersonal importance; it seems to impart a certain serenity and lack of worry over immediate concerns that make life easier not only for themselves but for all who are associated with them.

Solitude

For all my subjects it is true that they can be solitary without harm to themselves and without discomfort. Furthermore, it is true for almost all that they positively *like* solitude and privacy to a definitely greater degree than the average person.

It is often possible for them to remain above the battle, to remain unruffled, undisturbed by that which produces turmoil in others. They find it easy to be aloof, reserved, and also calm and serene; thus it becomes possible for them to take personal misfortunes without reacting violently as the ordinary person does. They seem to be able to retain their dignity even in undignified surroundings and situations. Perhaps this comes in part from their tendency to stick by their own interpretation of a situation rather than to rely upon what other people feel or think about the matter. This reserve may shade over into austerity and remoteness.

This quality of detachment may have some connection with certain other qualities as well. For one thing it is possible to call my subjects more objective (in *all* senses of that word) than average people. We have seen that they are more problem centered than ego centered. This is true even when the problem concerns themselves, their own wishes, motives, hopes, or aspirations. Consequently, they have the ability to concentrate to a degree not usual for ordinary people. Intense concentration produces as a by-product such phenomena as absent-mindedness, the ability to forget and to be oblivious of outer surroundings. Examples are the ability to sleep soundly, to have undisturbed appetite, and to be able to smile and laugh through a period of problems, worry, and responsibility.

In social relations with most people, detachment creates certain troubles and problems. It is easily interpreted by "normal" people as coldness, snobbishness, lack of affection, unfriendliness, or even hostility. By contrast, the ordinary friendship relationship is more clinging, more demanding, more desirous of reassurance, compliment, support, warmth, and exclusiveness. It is true that self-actualizing people do not need others in the ordinary sense. But since this being needed or being missed is the usual earnest of friendship, it is evident that detachment will not easily be accepted by average people.

Another meaning of autonomy is self-decision, self-government, being an active, responsible, self-disciplined, deciding agent rather than a pawn, or helplessly "determined" by others, being strong rather than weak. My subjects make up their own minds, come to their own decisions, are self-starters, and are responsible for themselves and their own destinies. It is a subtle quality, difficult to describe in words, and yet profoundly important. They taught me to see as profoundly sick, abnormal, or weak what I had always taken for granted as humanly normal; namely, that too many people do not make up their own minds, but have their minds made up for them by salesmen, advertisers, parents, propagandists, TV, newspapers, and so on. They are pawns to be moved by others rather than self-moving, self-determining individuals. Therefore they are apt to feel helpless, weak, and totally determined; they are prey for predators, flabby whiners rather than self-determining, responsible persons. What this nonresponsibility means for self-choice politics and economics is of course obvious; it is catastrophic. Democratic self-choice society must have self-movers, self-deciders, self-choosers who make up their own minds, free agents, free-willers.

The extensive experiments by Asch (1956) and by McClelland (McClelland, 1961, 1964; McClelland & Winter, 1969) permit us to guess that self-determiners come to perhaps 5 percent to 30 percent of our population depending on the particular circumstances. Of my self-actualizing subjects, 100 percent are self-movers.

Finally I must make a statement, even though it will certainly be disturbing to many theologians, philosophers, and scientists: self-actualizing individuals have more "free will" and are less "determined" than average people are. However the words *free will* and *determinism* may come to be operationally defined, in this investigation they are empirical realities. Furthermore, they are degree concepts, varying in amount; they are not all-or-none packages.

Autonomy

One of the characteristics of self-actualizing people, which to a certain extent crosscuts much of what we have already described, is their relative independence of the physical and social environment. Since they are propelled by growth motivation rather than by deficiency motivation, self-actualizing people are not dependent for their main satisfactions on the real world, or other people or culture or means to ends or, in general, on extrinsic satisfactions. Rather they are dependent for their own development and continued growth on their own potentialities and latent resources. Just as the tree needs sunshine and water and food, so do most people need love, safety, and the other basic need gratifications that can come only from without. But once these external satisfiers are obtained, once these inner deficiencies are satiated by outside satisfiers, the true problem of individual human development begins, namely self-actualization.

This independence of environment means a relative stability in the face of hard knocks, blows, deprivations, frustrations, and the like. These people can maintain a relative serenity in the midst of circumstances that would drive other people to suicide; they have also been described as "self-contained."

Deficiency-motivated people *must* have other people available, since most of their main need gratifications (love, safety, respect, prestige, belongingness) can come only from other human beings. But growth-motivated people may actually be *hampered* by others. The determinants of satisfaction and of the good life are for them now inner-individual and *not* social. They have become strong enough to be independent of the good opinion of other people, or even of their affection. The honors, the status, the rewards, the popularity, the prestige, and the love they can bestow must have become less important than self-development and inner growth (Huxley, 1944; Northrop, 1947; Rand, 1943; Rogers, 1961). We must remember that the best technique we know, even though not the only one, for getting to this point of relative independence from love and respect is to have been given plenty of this very same love and respect in the past.

Fresh Appreciation

Self-actualizing people have the wonderful capacity to appreciate again and again, freshly and naively, the basic goods of life, with awe, pleasure, wonder, and even ecstasy, however stale these experiences may have become to others—what C. Wilson has called "newness" (1969). Thus, for such a person, any sunset may be as beautiful as the first one, any flower may be of breath-taking loveliness, even after a million flowers have been seen. The thousandth baby seen is just as miraculous a product as the first. A man remains as convinced of his luck in marriage 30 years after his marriage and is as surprised by his wife's beauty when she is 60 as he was 40 years before. For such people, even the casual workaday, moment-to-moment business of living can be thrilling, exciting, and ecstatic. These intense feelings do not come all the time; they come occasionally rather than usually, but at the most unexpected moments. The person may cross the river on the ferry ten times and at the eleventh crossing have a strong recurrence of the same feelings, reaction of beauty, and excitement as when riding the ferry for the first time (Eastman, 1928).

There are some differences in choice of beautiful objects. Some subjects go primarily to nature. For others it is primarily children, and for a few subjects it has been primarily great music; but it may certainly be said that they derive ecstasy, inspiration, and strength from the basic experiences of life. No one of them, for instance, will get this same sort of reaction from going to a night club or getting a lot of money or having a good time at a party.

Perhaps one special experience may be added. For several of my subjects the sexual pleasures and particularly the orgasm provided not passing pleasure alone, but some kind of basic strengthening and revivifying that some people derive from music or nature. I shall say more about this in the section on the mystic experience.

It is probable that this acute richness of subjective experience is an aspect of closeness of relationship to the concrete and fresh, per se reality discussed above. Perhaps what we call staleness in experience is a consequence of categorizing or ticketing off a rich perception into one or another category or rubric as it proves to be no longer advantageous, or useful, or threatening, or otherwise ego involved (Bergson, 1944).

I have also become convinced that getting used to our blessings is one of the most important nonevil generators of human evil, tragedy, and suffering. What we take for granted we undervalue, and we are therefore too apt to sell a valuable birthright for a mess of pottage, leaving behind regret, remorse, and a lowering of self-esteem. Wives, husbands, children, friends are unfortunately more apt to be loved and appreciated after they have died than while they are still available. Something similar is true for physical health, for political freedoms, for economic well-being; we learn their true value after we have lost them.

Herzberg's studies of "hygiene" factors in industry (1966), Wilson's observations on the St. Neot's margin (1967, 1969), and my study of "low grumbles, high grumbles, and metagrumbles" (1965b) all show that life could be vastly improved if we could count our blessings as self-actualizing people can and do, and if we could retain their constant sense of good fortune and gratitude for it.

Peak Experiences

Those subjective expressions that have been called the mystic experience and described so well by William James (1958) are a fairly common experience for our subjects, though not for all. The strong emotions described in the previous section sometimes get strong, chaotic, and widespread enough to be called mystic experiences. My interest and attention in this subject was first enlisted by several of my subjects who described their sexual orgasms in vaguely familiar terms, which later I remembered had been used by various writers to describe what *they* called the mystic experience. There were the same feelings of limitless horizons opening up to the vision, the feeling of being simultaneously more powerful and also more helpless than one ever was before, the feeling of great ecstasy and wonder and awe, the loss of placing in time and space with, finally, the conviction that something extremely important and valuable had happened, so that the subject is to some extent transformed and strengthened even in daily life by such experiences.

It is quite important to dissociate this experience from any theological or supernatural reference, even though for thousands of years they have been linked.

Because this experience is a natural experience, well within the jurisdiction of science, I call it the peak experience.

We may also learn from our subjects that such experiences can occur in a lesser degree of intensity. The theological literature has generally assumed an absolute, qualitative difference between the mystic experience and all others. As soon as it is divorced from supernatural reference and studied as a natural phenomenon, it becomes possible to place the mystic experience on a quantitative continuum from intense to mild. We discover then that the *mild* mystic experience occurs in many, perhaps even most, individuals, and that in the favored individual it occurs often, perhaps even daily.

Apparently the acute mystic or peak experience is a tremendous intensification of *any* of the experiences in which there is loss of self or transcendence of it, such as problem centering, intense concentration, intense sensuous experience, or self-forgetful and intense enjoyment of music or art.

I have learned through the years since this study was first begun in 1935 to lay far greater stress than I had at first on the differences between "peakers" and "nonpeakers." Most likely this is a difference of degree or amount, but it is a very important difference. Some of its consequences are set forth in considerable detail in Maslow, 1969b. If I had to sum it up very briefly, I would say that the nonpeaking self-actualizers seem so far to tend to be practical, effective people, mesomorphs living in the world and doing very well in it. Peakers seem *also* to live in the realm of Being; of poetry, aesthetics; symbols; transcendence; "religion" of the mystical, personal, noninstitutional sort; and of end experiences. My prediction is that this will turn out to be one of the crucial characterological "class differences," crucial especially for social life because it looks as though the "merely healthy" nonpeaking self-actualizers seem likely to be the social world improvers, the politicians, the workers in society, the reformers, the crusaders, whereas the transcending peakers are more apt to write the poetry, the music, the philosophies, and the religions.

Human Kinship

Self-actualizing people have a deep feeling of identification, sympathy, and affection for human beings in general. They feel kinship and connection, as if all people were members of a single family. One's feelings toward siblings would be on the whole affectionate, even if they were foolish, weak, or even if they were sometimes nasty. They would still be more easily forgiven than strangers. Because of this, self-actualizing people have a genuine desire to help the human race.

If one's view is not general enough and if it is not spread over a long period of time, then one may not see this feeling of identification with mankind. Self-actualizing people are after all very different from other people in thought, impulse, behavior, and emotion. When it comes down to it, in certain basic ways they are like aliens in a strange land. Very few really understand them, however much they may like them. They are often saddened, exasperated, and even enraged by the shortcomings of the average person, and while these are ordinarily no more than a nuisance, they sometimes become bitter tragedy. However far apart they are at times, they nevertheless feel a basic underlying kinship with these creatures whom they must regard with, if not condescension, at least the knowledge that they themselves can do many things better than others can, that they can see things that others cannot see, and that the truth that is so clear to them is for most people veiled and hidden.

Humility and Respect

All my subjects without exception may be said to be democratic people in the deepest possible sense. I say this on the basis of a previous analysis of authoritarian (Maslow, 1943) and democratic character structures that is too elaborate to present here; it is possible only to describe some aspects of this behavior in short space. These people have all the obvious or superficial democratic characteristics. They can be and are friendly with anyone of suitable character regardless of class, education, political belief, race, or color. As a matter of fact it often seems as if they are not even aware of these differences, which are for the average person so obvious and so important.

They have not only this most obvious quality but their democratic feeling goes deeper as well. For instance they find it possible to learn from anybody who has something to teach them—no matter what other characteristics he or she may have. In such a learning relationship they do not try to maintain any outward dignity or to maintain status or age prestige or the like. It should even be said that my subjects share a quality that could be called humility of a certain type. They are all quite well aware of how little they know in comparison with what *could* be known and what *is* known by others. Because of this it is possible for them without pose to be honestly respectful and even humble before people who can teach them something that they do not know or who have a skill they do not possess. They give this honest respect to a carpenter who is a good carpenter, or for that matter to anybody who is a master of his own tools or his own craft.

The careful distinction must be made between this democratic feeling and a lack of discrimination in taste, of an undiscriminating equalizing of any one human being with any other. These individuals, themselves elite, select for their friends elite, but this is an elite of character, capacity, and talent, rather than of birth, race, blood, name, family, age, youth, fame, or power.

Most profound, but also most vague is the hard-to-get-at tendency to give a certain quantum of respect to *any* human being just because he or she is a human individual; our subjects seem not to wish to go beyond a certain minimum point, even with scoundrels, of demeaning, of derogating, of robbing of dignity. And yet this goes along with their strong sense of right and wrong, of good and evil. They are *more* likely rather than less likely to counterattack against evil people and evil behavior. They are far less ambivalent, confused, or weak-willed about their own anger than average people are.

Interpersonal Relationships

Self-actualizing people have deeper and more profound interpersonal relations than any other adults (although not necessarily deeper than those of children). They are capable of more fusion, greater love, more perfect identification, more obliteration of the ego boundaries than other people would consider possible. There are, however, certain special characteristics of these relationships. In the first place, it is my observation that the other members of these relationships are likely to be healthier and closer to self-actualization than the average, often *much* closer. There is high selectiveness here, considering the small proportion of such people in the general population.

One consequence of this phenomenon and of certain others as well is that self-actualizing people have these especially deep ties with rather few individuals. Their circle of friends is rather small. The ones that they love profoundly are few in number. Partly this is for the reason that being very close to someone in this self-actualizing style seems to require a good deal of time. Devotion is not a matter of a moment. One subject expressed it like this: "I haven't got time for many friends. Nobody has, that is, if they are to be *real* friends." This exclusiveness of devotion can and does exist side by side with a widespreading human warmth, benevolence, affection, and friendliness (as qualified above). These people *tend* to be kind or at least patient to almost everyone. They have an especially tender love for children and are easily touched by them. In a very real even though special sense, they love or rather have compassion for all humanity.

This love does not imply lack of discrimination. The fact is that they can and do speak realistically and harshly of those who deserve it, and especially of the hypocritical, the pretentious, the pompous, or the self-inflated. But the face-to-face relationships even with these people do not always show signs of realistically low evaluations. One explanatory statement was about as follows: "Most people, after all, do not amount to much but they *could* have. They make all sorts of foolish mistakes and wind up being miserable and not knowing how they got that way when their intentions were good. Those who are not nice are usually paying for it in deep unhappiness. They should be pitied rather than attacked."

Perhaps the briefest possible description is to say that their hostile reactions to others are (1) deserved, and (2) for the good of the person attacked or for someone else's good. This is to say, with Fromm, that their hostility is not character based, but is reactive or situational.

All the subjects for whom I have data show in common another characteristic that is appropriate to mention here, namely, that they attract at least some admirers, friends, or even disciples or worshippers. The relation between the individual and his or her train of admirers is apt to be rather one-sided. The admirers are apt to demand more than our individual is willing to give. And, furthermore, these devotions can be rather embarrassing, distressing, and even distasteful to the self-actualizing person, since they often go beyond ordinary bounds. The usual picture is of our subject being kind and pleasant when forced into these relationships, but ordinarily trying to avoid them as gracefully as possible.

Ethics

I have found none of my subjects to be chronically unsure about the difference between right and wrong in their actual living. Whether or not they could verbalize the matter, they rarely showed in their day-to-day living the chaos, the confusion, the inconsistency, or the conflict that are so common in the average person's ethical dealings. This may be phrased also in the following terms: these individuals are strongly ethical, they have definite moral standards, they do right and do not do wrong. Needless to say, their notions of right and wrong and of good and evil are often not the conventional ones.

One way of expressing the quality I am trying to describe was suggested by Dr. David Levy, who pointed out that a few centuries ago these would all have been described as men who walk in the path of God or as godly men. A few say that they believe in a God, but describe this God more as a metaphysical concept than as a personal figure. If religion is defined only in social-behavioral terms, then these are all religious people, the atheists included. But if more conservatively we use the term *religion* to stress the supernatural element and institutional orthodoxy (certainly the more common usage) then our answer must be quite different, for then very few of them are religious.

Means and Ends

Self-actualizing people most of the time behave as though, for them, means and ends are clearly distinguishable. In general, they are fixed on ends rather than on means, and means are quite definitely subordinated to these ends. This, however, is an overly simple statement. Our subjects make the situation more complex by often regarding as ends in themselves many experiences and activities that are, for other people, only means. Our subjects are somewhat more likely to appreciate for its own sake, and in an absolute way, the doing itself; they can often enjoy for its own sake the getting to some place as well as the arriving. It is occasionally possible for them to make out of the most trivial and routine activity an intrinsically enjoyable game or dance or play. Wertheimer pointed out that most children are so creative that they can transform hackneyed routine, mechanical, and rote experiences (e.g., as in one of his experiments, transporting books from one set of shelves to another) into a structured and amusing game of a sort by doing this according to a certain system or with a certain rhythm.

Humor

One very early finding that was quite easy to make, because it was common to all my subjects, was that their sense of humor is not of the ordinary type. They do not consider funny what the average person considers to be funny. Thus they do not laugh at hostile humor (making people laugh by hurting someone) or superiority humor (laughing at someone else's inferiority) or authority-rebellion humor (the unfunny, Oedipal, or smutty joke). Characteristically what they consider humor is more closely allied to philosophy than to anything else. It may also be called the humor of the real because it consists in large part in poking fun at human beings in general when they are foolish, or forget their place in the universe, or try to be big when they are actually small. This can take the form of poking fun at themselves, but this is not done in any masochistic or clownlike way. Lincoln's humor can serve as a suitable example. Probably Lincoln never made a joke that hurt anybody else; it is also likely that many or even most of his jokes had something to say, had a function beyond just producing a laugh. They often seemed to be education in a more palatable form, akin to parables or fables.

On a simple quantitative basis, our subjects may be said to be humorous less often than the average of the population. Punning, joking, witty remarks, gay repartee, persiflage of the ordinary sort is much less often seen than the rather thoughtful, philosophical humor that elicits a smile more usually than a laugh, that is intrinsic to the situation rather than added to it, that is spontaneous rather than planned, and that very often can never be repeated. It should not be surprising that average people, accustomed as they are to joke books and belly laughs, considers our subjects to be rather on the sober and serious side.

Such humor can be very pervasive; the human situation, human pride, seriousness, busy-ness, bustle, ambition, striving and planning can all be seen as amusing, humorous, even funny. I once understood this attitude, I thought, in a room full of "kinetic art," which seemed to me to be a humorous parody of human life, with the noise, movement, turmoil, hurry and bustle, all of it going no place. This attitude also rubs off on professional work itself, which in a certain sense is also play, and which, though taken seriously, is somehow also taken lightly.

Creativity

This is a universal characteristic of all the people studied or observed (see Chapter 13, "Creativity in Self-actualizing People"). There is no exception. Each one shows in one way or another a special kind of creativeness or originality or inventiveness that has certain peculiar characteristics. These special characteristics can be understood more fully in the light of discussion later in this chapter. For one thing, it is different from the special-talent creativeness of the Mozart type. We may as well face the fact that the so-called geniuses display ability that we do not understand. All we can say of them is that they seem to be specially endowed with a drive and a capacity that may have rather little relationship to the rest of the personality and with which, from all evidence, the individuals seem to be born. Such talent we have no concern with here since it does not rest upon psychic health or basic satisfaction. The creativeness of the self-actualized person seems rather to be kin to the naive and universal creativeness of unspoiled children. It seems to be more a fundamental characteristic of common human nature— a potentiality given to all human beings at birth. Most human beings lose this as they become enculturated, but some few individuals seem either to retain this fresh and naive, direct way of looking at life, or if they have lost it, as most people do, they later in life recover it. Santayana called this the "second naiveté," a very good name for it.

This creativeness appears in some of our subjects not in the usual forms of writing books, composing music, or producing artistic objects, but rather may be much more humble. It is as if this special type of creativeness, being an expression of healthy personality, is projected out upon the world or touches whatever activity the person is engaged in. In this sense there can be creative shoemakers or carpenters or clerks. Whatever one does can be done with a certain attitude, a certain spirit that arises out of the nature of the character of the person performing the act. One can even *see* creatively as the child does.

This quality is differentiated out here for the sake of discussion, as if it were something separate from the characteristics that precede it and follow it, but this is not actually the case. Perhaps when we speak of creativeness here we are simply describing from another point of view, namely, from the point of view of consequences, what we have described above as a greater freshness, penetration, and efficiency of perception. These people seem to see the true and the real more easily. It is because of this that they seem to other more limited men creative.

Furthermore, as we have seen, these individuals are less inhibited, less constricted, less bound, in a word, less enculturated. In more positive terms, they are more spontaneous, more natural, more human. This too would have as one of its consequences what would seem to other people to be creativeness. If we assume, as we may from our study of children, that all people were once spontaneous, and perhaps in their deepest roots still are, but that these people have in addition to their deep spontaneity a superficial but powerful set of inhibitions, then this spontaneity must be checked so as not to appear very often. If there were no choking-off forces, we might expect that every human being would show this special type of creativeness (Anderson, 1959; Maslow, 1958).

Resistance to Enculturation

Self-acutalizing people are not well adjusted (in the naive sense of approval of and identification with the culture). They get along with the culture in various ways, but of all of them it may be said that in a certain profound and meaningful sense they resist enculturation and maintain a certain inner detachment from the culture in which they are immersed. Since in the culture-and-personality literature very little has been said about resistance to molding by the culture, and since, as Riesman (1950) has clearly pointed out, the saving remnant is especially important for American society, even our meager data are of some importance.

On the whole the relationship of these healthy people with their much less healthy culture is a complex one; from it can be teased out at least the following components.

1. All these people fall well within the limits of apparent conventionality in choice of clothes, of language, of food, of ways of doing things in our culture. And yet they are not *really* conventional, certainly not fashionable or smart or chic. The expressed inner attitude is usually that it is ordinarily of no great consequence which folkways are used, that one set of traffic rules is as good as any other set, that while they make life smoother they do not really matter enough to make a fuss about. Here again we see the general tendency of these people to accept most states of affairs that they consider unimportant or unchangeable or not of primary concern to them as individuals. Since choice of shoes, or style of haircut or politeness, or manner of behaving at a party are not of primary

concern to any of the individuals studied, they are apt to elicit as a reaction only a shrug of the shoulders. These are not moral issues. But since this tolerant acceptance of harmless folkways is not warm approval with identification, their yielding to convention is apt to be rather casual and perfunctory, with cutting of corners in favor of directness, honesty, saving of energy, and so on. In the pinch, when yielding to conventions is too annoying or too expensive, the apparent conventionality reveals itself for the superficial thing that it is, and is tossed off as easily as a cloak.

2. Hardly any of these people can be called authority rebels in the adolescent or hot sense. They show no active impatience or moment-to-moment, chronic, long-time discontent with the culture or preoccupation with changing it quickly, although they often enough show bursts of indignation with injustice. One of these subjects, who was a hot rebel in his younger days, a union organizer in the days when this was a highly dangerous occupation, has given up in disgust and hopelessness. As he became resigned to the slowness of social change (in this culture and in this era) he turned finally to education of the young. All the others show what might be called a calm, long-time concern with culture improvement that seems to me to imply an acceptance of slowness of change along with the unquestioned desirability and necessity of such change. This is by no means a lack of fight. When quick change is possible or when resolution and courage are needed, it is available in these people. Although they are not a radical group of people in the ordinary sense, I think they easily *could* be. First of all, this is primarily an intellectual group (it must be remembered who selected them), most of whom already have a mission and feel that they are doing something really important to improve the world. Second, they are a realistic group and seem to be unwilling to make great but useless sacrifices. In a more drastic situation it seems very likely that they would be willing to drop their work in favor of radical social action (e.g., the anti-Nazi underground in Germany or in France). My impression is that they are not against fighting but only against ineffective fighting. Another point that came up very commonly in discussion was the desirability of enjoying life and having a good time. This seems to all but one to be incompatible with hot and full-time rebelliousness. Furthermore, it seems to them that this is too great a sacrifice to make for the small returns expected. Most of them have had their episodes of fighting, impatience, and eagerness in youth, and in most cases have learned that their optimism about quick change was unwarranted. What they settled down to as a group was an accepting, calm, good-humored everyday effort to improve the culture, usually from within, rather than to reject it wholly and fight it from without.

3. An inner feeling of detachment from the culture is not necessarily conscious but is displayed by almost all, particularly in discussions of the American culture as a whole, in various comparisons with other cultures, and in the fact that they very frequently seem to be able to stand off from it as if they did not quite belong to it. The mixture of varying proportions of affection or approval and hostility or criticism indicated that they select from American culture what is good in it by their lights and reject what they think bad in it. In a word they weigh it, assay it,

taste it, and then make their own decisions. This is certainly very different from the ordinary sort of passive yielding to cultural shaping displayed for instance by the ethnocentric subjects of the many studies of authoritarian personalities. It is also different from the total rejection of what after all is a relatively good culture, that is, when compared with other cultures that actually *exist,* rather than fantasied heavens of perfection (or as one lapel button put it, Nirvana *Now*!). Detachment from the culture is probably also reflected in our self-actualizing subjects' detachment from people and their liking for privacy, which has been described above, as also in their less than average need for the familiar and customary.

4. For these and other reasons they may be called autonomous, that is, ruled by the laws of their own character rather than by the rules of society. It is in this sense that they are not only or merely Americans, but also, to a greater degree than others, members at large of the human species. To say that they are above or beyond the American culture would be misleading if interpreted strictly, for after all they speak American, act American, have American characters, and so forth. And yet if we compare them with the oversocialized, the robotized, or the ethnocentric, we are irresistibly tempted to hypothesize that this group is not simply another subcultural group, but rather less enculturated, less flattened out, less molded. This implies degree, and placing on a continuum that ranges from relative acceptance of the culture to relative detachment from it. If this turns out to be a tenable hypothesis, at least one other hypothesis can be deduced from it: that those individuals in different cultures who are more detached from their own culture should not only have less national character but also should be more like each other in certain respects than they are like the less developed members of their own societies.

In summary the perennial question "Is it possible to be a good or healthy man in an imperfect culture?" has been answered by the observation that it *is* possible for relatively healthy people to develop in the American culture. They manage to get along by a complex combination of inner autonomy and outer acceptance that of course will be possible only so long as the culture remains tolerant of this kind of detached withholding from complete cultural identification.

Of course this is not ideal health. Our imperfect society clearly forces inhibitions and restraints upon our subjects. To the extent that they have to maintain their little secrecies, to that extent is their spontaneity lessened and to that extent are some of their potentialities not actualized. And since only few people can attain health in our culture (or perhaps in *any* culture), those who do attain it are lonely for their own kind and are therefore less spontaneous and less actualized.[3]

Imperfections

The ordinary mistake that is made by novelists, poets, and essayists about good human beings is to make them so good that they are caricatures, so that nobody

[3] I am indebted to Dr. Tamara Dembo for her help with this problem.

would like to be like them. The individual's own wishes for perfection and guilt and shame about shortcomings are projected upon various kinds of people from whom average people demand much more than they themselves give. Thus teachers and ministers are sometimes conceived to be rather joyless people who have no mundane desires and who have no weaknesses. It is my belief that most of the novelists who have attempted to portray good (healthy) people did this sort of thing, making them into stuffed shirts or marionettes or unreal projections of unreal ideals, rather than into the robust, hearty, lusty individuals they really are. Our subjects show many of the lesser human failings. They too are equipped with silly, wasteful, or thoughtless habits. They can be boring, stubborn, irritating. They are by no means free from a rather superficial vanity, pride, partiality to their own productions, family, friends, and children. Temper outbursts are not rare.

Our subjcts are occasionally capable of an extraordinary and unexpected ruthlessness. It must be remembered that they are very strong people. This makes it possible for them to display a surgical coldness when this is called for, beyond the power of average people. The man who found that a long-trusted acquaintance was dishonest cut himself off from this friendship sharply and abruptly and without any observable pangs whatsoever. A woman who was married to someone she did not love, when she decided on divorce, did it with such decisiveness that looked almost like ruthlessness. Some of them recover so quickly from the death of people close to them as to seem heartless.

We may mention one more example that arises primarily from the absorption of our subjects in an impersonal world. In their concentration, in their fascinated interest, in their intense concentration on some phenomenon or question, they may become absent-minded or humorless and forget their ordinary social politeness. In such circumstances, they are apt to show themselves more clearly as essentially not interested in chatting, gay conversation, party-going, or the like; they may use language or behavior that may be very distressing, shocking, insulting, or hurtful to others. Other undesirable (at least from the point of view of others) consequences of detachment have been listed above.

Even their kindness can lead them into mistakes, such as marrying out of pity, getting too closely involved with neurotics, bores, or unhappy people and then being sorry for it, allowing scoundrels to impose on them for a while, or giving more than they should so that occasionally they encourage parasites and psychopaths.

Finally, it has already been pointed out that these people are *not* free of guilt, anxiety, sadness, self-castigation, internal strife, and conflict. The fact that these arise out of nonneurotic sources is of little consequence to most people today (even to most psychologists) who are therefore apt to think them *un*healthy for this reason.

What this has taught me I think all of us had better learn. *There are no perfect human beings*! Persons can be found who are good, very good indeed, in fact, great. There do in fact exist creators, seers, sages, saints, shakers, and movers. This can certainly give us hope for the future of the species even if they *are* uncommon and do *not* come by the dozen. And yet these very same people can at times be boring, irritating, petulant, selfish, angry, or depressed. To avoid disillusionment with human nature, we must first give up our illusions about it.

Values

A firm foundation for a value system is automatically furnished to self-actualizers by their philosophic acceptance of the nature of self, of human nature, of much of social life, and of nature and physical reality. These acceptance values account for a high percentage of the total of their individual value judgments from day to day. What they approve of, disapprove of, are loyal to, oppose or propose, what pleases them or displeases them can often be understood as surface derivations of this source trait of acceptance.

Not only is this foundation automatically (and universally) supplied to *all* self-actualizers by their intrinsic dynamics (so that in at least this respect fully developed human nature may be universal and cross-cultural); other determniners are supplied as well by these same dynamics. Among these are (1) their peculiarly comfortable relationships with reality, (2) their feelings of human kinship, (3) their basically satisfied condition from which flow, as epiphenomena, various consequences of surplus, of wealth, overflowing abundance, (4) their characteristically discriminating relations to means and ends, and so on (see above).

One most important consequence of this attitude toward the world—as well as a validation of it—is the fact that conflict and struggle, ambivalence and uncertainty over choice lessen or disappear in many areas of life. Apparently much so-called morality is largely an epiphenomenon of nonacceptance or dissatisfaction. Many problems are seen to be gratuitous and fade out of existence in the atmosphere of pagan acceptance. It is not so much that the problem is solved as that it becomes clearly seen that it never was an intrinsic problem in the first place, but only a sick-person-created one, such as card playing, dancing, wearing short dresses, exposing the head (in some churches) or *not* exposing the head (in others), drinking wine, or eating some meats and not others, or eating them on some days but not on others. Not only are such trivialities deflated; the process also goes on at a more important level, such as in the relations between the sexes, attitudes toward the structure of the body and toward its functioning, and toward death itself.

The pursuit of this finding to more profound levels has suggested to the writer that much else of what passes for morals, ethics, and values may be simple by-products of the pervasive psychopathology of the average. Many conflicts, frustrations, and threats (which force the kind of choice in which value is expressed) evaporate or resolve for self-actualizing people in the same way as do, let us say, conflicts over dancing. For them the seemingly irreconcilable battle of the sexes becomes no conflict at all but rather a delightful collaboration. The antagonistic interests of adults and children turn out to be not so antagonistic after all. Just as with sex and age differences, so also is it with natural differences, class and caste differences, political differences, role differences, religious differences, and the like. As we know, these are each fertile breeding grounds for anxiety, fear, hostility, aggression, defensiveness, and jealousy. But it begins to appear that they *need not be,* for our subjects' reaction to differences is much less often of this undesirable type. They are more apt to enjoy differences than to fear them.

To take the teacher-student relationship as a specific paradigm, our teacher subjects behaved in a very unneurotic way simply by interpreting the whole situation differently, for example, as a pleasant collaboration rather than as a clash of wills, of authority, of dignity, and so on; the replacement of artificial dignity—which is easily and inevitably threatened—with the natural simplicity, which is *not* easily threatened; the giving up of the attempt to be omniscient and omnipotent; the absence of student-threatening authoritarianism; the refusal to regard the students as competing with each other or with the teacher; the refusal to assume the professor stereotype and the insistence on remaining as realistically human as, say, a plumber or a carpenter; all of these create a classroom atmosphere in which suspicion, wariness, defensiveness, hostility, and anxiety tend to disappear. So also do similar threat responses tend to disappear in marriages, in families, and in other interpersonal situations when threat itself is reduced.

The principles and the values of the desperate person and of the psychologically healthy person must be different in at least some ways. They have profoundly different perceptions (interpretations) of the physical world, the social world, and the private psychological world, whose organization and economy is in part the responsibility of the person's value system. For basically deprived people the world is a dangerous place, a jungle, an enemy territory populated by (1) those whom they can dominate and (2) those who can dominate them. Their value systems are of necessity, like those of any jungle denizen, dominated and organized by the lower needs, especially the creature needs and the safety needs. Basically satisfied people are a different case. They can afford out of their abundance to take these needs and their satisfaction for granted and can devote themselves to higher gratifications. This is to say that their value systems are different, in fact *must* be different.

The topmost portion of the value system of the self-actualized person is entirely unique and idiosyncratic-character-structure-expressive. This must be true by definition, for self-actualization is actualization of a self, and no two selves are altogether alike. There is only one Renoir, one Brahms, one Spinoza. Our subjects had very much in common, as we have seen, and yet at the same time were more completely individualized, more unmistakably themselves, less easily confounded with others than any average control group could possibly be. That is to say, they are simultaneously very much alike and very much unlike each other. They are more completely individual than any group that has ever been described, and yet are also more completely socialized, more identified with humanity than any other group yet described. They are closer to *both* their specieshood and to their unique individuality.

Resolution of Dichotomies

At this point we may finally allow ourselves to generalize and underscore a very important theoretical conclusion derivable from the study of self-actualizing people. At several points in this chapter—and in other chapters as well—it was concluded that what had been considered in the past to be polarities or opposites or dichotomies were so *only in less healthy people*. In healthy people, these dichotomies were resolved, the polarities disappeared, and many oppositions thought to be intrinsic merged and coalesced with each other to form unities. See also Chenault (1969).

For example the age-old opposition between heart and head, reason and instinct, or cognition and conation was seen to disappear in healthy people where they become synergic rather than antagonists, and where conflict between them disappears because they say the same thing and point to the same conclusion. In a word in these people, desires are in excellent accord with reason. St. Augustine's "Love God and do as you will" can easily be translated "Be healthy and then you may trust your impulses."

The dichotomy between selfishness and unselfishness disappears altogether in healthy people because in principle every act is *both* selfish and unselfish. Our subjects are simultaneously very spiritual and very pagan and sensual even to the point where sexuality becomes a *path* to the spiritual and "religious." Duty cannot be contrasted with pleasure nor work with play when duty *is* pleasure, when work *is* play, and people doing their duty and being virtuous are simultaneously seeking their pleasure and being happy. If the most socially identified people are themselves also the most individualistic people, of what use is it to retain the polarity? If the most mature are also childlike? And if the most ethical and moral people are also the lustiest and most animal?

Similar findings have been reached for kindness-ruthlessness, concreteness-abstractness, acceptance-rebellion, self-society, adjustment-maladjustment, detachment from others-identification with others, serious-humorous, Dionysian-Apollonian, introverted-extraverted, intense-casual, serious-frivolous, conventional-unconventional, mystic-realistic, active-passive, masculine-feminine, lust-love, and Eros-Agape. In these people, the id, the ego, and the superego are collaborative and synergic; they do not war with each other nor are their interests in basic disagreement as they are in neurotic people. So also do the cognitive, the impulsive, and the emotional coalesce into an organismic unity and into a non-Aristotelian interpenetration. The higher and the lower are not in opposition but in agreement, and a thousand serious philosophical dilemmas are discovered to have more than two horns or, paradoxically, no horns at all. If the war between the sexes turns out to be no war at all in matured people, but only a sign of crippling and stunting of growth, who then would wish to choose sides? Who would deliberately and knowingly choose psychopathology? Is it necessary to choose between the good woman and the bad, as if they were mutually exclusive, when we have found that the really healthy woman is both at the same time?

In this, as in other ways, healthy people are so different from average ones, not only in degree but in kind as well, that they generate two very different kinds of psychology. It becomes more and more clear that the study of crippled, stunted, immature, and unhealthy specimens can yield only a cripple psychology and a cripple philosophy. The study of self-actualizing people must be the basis for a more universal science of psychology.

chapter 12

Love in
Self-actualizing People

It is amazing how little the empirical sciences have to offer on the subject of love. Particularly strange is the silence of the psychologists, for one might think this to be their particular obligation. Probably this is just another example of the besetting sin of the academicians, that they prefer to do what they are easily able rather than what they ought, like the not-so-bright kitchen helper I knew who opened every can in the hotel one day because he was so *very* good at opening cans.

I must confess that I understand this better now that I have undertaken the task myself. It is an extraordinarily difficult subject to handle in any tradition. And it is triply so in the scientific tradition. It is as if we were at the most advanced position in no man's land, at a point where the conventional techniques of orthodox psychological science are of very little use.

Our duty is clear here. We *must* understand love; we must be able to teach it, to create it, to predict it, or else the world is lost to hostility and to suspicion. The research, the subjects, and the major findings have already been described in the previous chapter. The specific question before us now is what have these people to teach us about love and sex?

OPENNESS

Theodor Reik (1957) has defined one characteristic of love as the absence of anxiety. This is seen with exceptional clearness in healthy individuals. There is little question about the tendency to more and more complete spontaneity, the dropping of defenses, the dropping of roles, and of trying and striving in the relationship. As the relationship continues, there is a growing intimacy and honesty and self-expression, which at its height is a rare phenomenon. The report from these people is that with a beloved person it is possible to be oneself, to feel natural; "I can let my hair down." This honesty also includes allowing one's faults, weaknesses, and physical and psychological shortcomings to be freely seen by the partner.

One of the deepest satisfactions coming from the healthy love relationship reported by my subjects is that such a relationship permits the greatest spontaneity, the greatest naturalness, the greatest dropping of defenses and protection against threat. In such a relationship it is not necessary to be guarded, to conceal, to try to impress, to feel tense, to watch one's words or actions, to suppress or repress. My people report that they can be themselves without feeling that there are demands or expectations upon them; they can feel psychologically (as well as physically) naked and still feel loved and wanted and secure. These conclusions are further supported by the greater freedom of hostility and anger expression in our subjects as well as in their lowered need for conventional politeness with each other.

TO LOVE AND BE LOVED

My subjects were loved and were loving, and are loved and are loving. In practically all (not quite all) my subjects where data were available, this tended to point to the conclusion that (all other things being equal) psychological health comes from being loved rather than from being deprived of love. Granted that the ascetic path is a possible one and that frustration has some good effects, yet basic need gratification seems to be much more the usual precursor or foundation of health in our society. This seems to be true not only for being loved but for loving as well.

It is also true of our self-actualizing people that they *now* love and are loved. For certain reasons it had better be said that they have the power to love and the ability to *be* loved. (Even though this may sound like a repetition of the sentence before, it is really not.) These are clinically observed facts, and are quite public and easily confirmed or disconfirmed.

Menninger (1942) makes the very acute statement that human beings really *do* want to love each other but just do not know how to go about it. This is much less true for healthy people. *They* at least know how to love, and can do so freely and easily and naturally and without getting wound up in conflicts or threats or inhibitions.

However, my subjects used the word love warily and with circumspection. They applied it only to a few rather than to many, tending to distinguish sharply between loving someone and liking the person or being friendly or benevolent or familial. It described for them an intense feeling, not a mild or disinterested one.

SEXUALITY

We can learn a very great deal from the peculiar and complex nature of sex in the love life of self-actualizing people. It is by no means a simple story; there are many interwoven threads. Nor can I say that I have many data. Information of this sort is hard to come by in private people. On the whole, however, their sex life, as much as I know of it, is characteristic and can be described in such a way as to make possible guesses, both positive and negative, about the nature of sex as well as about the nature of love.

For one thing it can be reported that sex and love can be and most often are more perfectly fused with each other in healthy people. Although it is perfectly true that these are separable concepts, and although no purpose would be served in confusing them with each other unnecessarily (Reik, 1957; Suttie, 1935), still it must be reported that in the life of healthy people, they tend to become joined and merged with each other. As a matter of fact we may also say that they become less separable and less separate from each other in the lives of the people we have studied. Self-actualizing men and women tend on the whole not to seek sex for its own sake, or to be satisfied with it alone when it comes. I am not sure that my data permit me to say that they would rather not have sex at all if it came without affection, but I am quite sure that I have a fair number of instances in which for the time being at least sex was given up or rejected because it came without love or affection.

In self-actualizing people the orgasm is simultaneously more important and less important than in average people. It is often a profound and almost mystical experience, and yet the absence of sexuality is more easily tolerated by these people. This is not a paradox or a contradiction. It follows from dynamic motivation theory. Loving at a higher need level makes the lower needs and their frustrations and satisfactions less important, less central, more easily neglected. But it also makes them more wholeheartedly enjoyed when gratified.

Sex can be wholeheartedly enjoyed, enjoyed far beyond the possibility of the average person, even at the same time that it does not play any central role in the philosophy of life. It is something to be enjoyed, something to be taken for granted, something to build upon, something that is very basically important like water or food, and that can be enjoyed as much as these; but gratification should be taken for granted. I think such an attitude as this resolves the apparent paradox in the self-actualizing person's simultaneously enjoying sex so much more intensely than the average person, yet at the same time considering it so much less important in the total frame of reference.

It should be stressed that from this same complex attitude toward sex arises the fact that the orgasm may bring on mystical experiences, and yet at other times may be taken rather lightly. This is to say that the sexual pleasure of self-actualizing people may be very intense or not intense at all. This conflicts with the romantic attitude that love is a divine rapture, a transport, a mystic experience. It is true that it may be also a delicate pleasure rather than an intense one, a gay and light-hearted, playful sort of thing rather than a serious and profound experience or even a neutral duty. These people do not always live on the heights— they usually live at a more average level of intensity, and lightly and mildly enjoy sex as a titillating, pleasant, playful, enjoyable, tickling kind of experience instead of a plumbing of the most intense depths of ecstatic emotionality.

Self-actualizing people appear much more free than the average to admit to the fact of sexual attraction to others. My impression is that there tends to be a rather easy relationship with the opposite sex, along with casual acceptance of the phenomenon of being attracted to other people, at the same time that these individuals do rather less about this attraction than other people.

Another characteristic I found in the attitudes about sexuality among healthy people is that they made no really sharp differentiation between the roles and personalities of the two sexes. That is, they did not assume that the female was passive and the male active, whether in sex or love or anything else. These people were all so certain of their maleness or femaleness that they did not mind taking on some of the cultural aspects of the opposite sex role. It was especially noteworthy that they could be both active and passive lovers and this was the clearest in the sexual act and in physical love-making. Kissing and being kissed, being above or below in the sexual act, taking the initiative, being quiet and receiving love, teasing and being teased—these were all found in both sexes. The reports indicated that both were enjoyed at different times. It was considered to be a shortcoming to be limited to just active love-making or passive love-making. Both have their particular pleasures for self-actualizing people.

This agrees with the thesis that erotic and agapean love are basically different but merge in the best people. D'Arcy's thesis posits two kinds of love, which are ultimately masculine or feminine, active or passive, self-centered or self-effacing, and it is true that in the general public these seem to contrast and to be at opposite poles. However, it is different in healthy people. In these individuals the dichotomies are resolved, and the individual becomes both active and passive, both selfish and unselfish, both masculine and feminine, both self-interested and self-effacing.

EGO-TRANSCENDENCE

One important aspect of a good love relationship is what may be called need identification, or the pooling of the hierarchies of basic needs in two persons into a single hierarchy. The effect of this is that one person feels another's needs as if they were his or her own and for that matter also feels his or her own needs to some extent as if they belonged to the other. An ego now expands to cover two people, and to some extent the two people have become for psychological purposes a single unit, a single person, a single ego.

In the history of theorizing about love relations as well as about altruism, patriotism, and the like, much has been said about the transcendence of the ego. An excellent modern discussion of this tendency at the technical level is afforded in a book by Angyal (1965), in which he discusses various examples of a tendency to what he calls homonomy, and which he contrasts with the tendency to autonomy, to independence, to individuality, and the like. More and more clinical and historical evidence accumulates to indicate that Angyal was right in demanding that some room be made in a systematic psychology for these various tendencies to go out beyond the limits of the ego. Furthermore, it seems quite clear that this need to go out beyond the limits of the ego may be a need in the same sense that we have needs for vitamins and minerals, that is, that if the need is not satisfied, the person becomes sick in one way or another. I should say that one of the most satisfying and most complete examples of ego transcendence is a healthy love relationship. (See also Harper, 1966; Maslow, 1967.)

FUN AND GAIETY

The love and sex life of healthy people, in spite of the fact that it frequently reaches great peaks of ecstasy, is nevertheless also easily compared to the games of children and puppies. It is cheerful, humorous, and playful. It is not primarily a striving; it is basically an enjoyment and a delight, which is another thing altogether.

RESPECT FOR OTHERS

All serious writers on the subject of ideal or healthy love have stressed the affirmation of the other's individuality, the eagerness for the growth of the other, the essential respect for his or her individuality and unique personality. This is confirmed very strongly by the observation of the self-actualizing people, who have in unusual measure the rare ability to be pleased rather than threatened by the partner's triumphs. They do indeed respect their partners in a very profound and basic way that has many, many implications.

Respect for another person acknowledges him or her as an independent entity and as a separate and autonomous individual. Self-actualizing people will not casually use, control, or disregard the wishes of another. They will allow the respected person a fundamental irreducible dignity, and will not unnecessarily humiliate the person. This is true not only for interadult relationships but also in self-actualizing people's relationships to children. It is possible for them, as for practically nobody else in our culture, to treat a child with real respect.

One amusing aspect of this respect relationship between the sexes is that it is very frequently interpreted in just the opposite way as a lack of respect. For example, we know well that a good many of the so-called signs of respect for ladies are in fact hangovers from a nonrespecting past, and possibly even at this time are for some unconscious representations of a deep contempt for women. Such cultural habits as standing up when a lady enters a room, giving a lady the chair, helping her with her coat, allowing her to go first through the door, giving her the best of everything and the first choice of everything—these all imply historically and dynamically the opinion that the woman is weak and incapable of taking care of herself, for these all imply protection, as for the weak and incapable. Generally women who respect themselves strongly tend to be wary of these signs of respect, knowing full well that they may mean just the opposite. Self-actualizing men who tend really and basically to respect and to like women as partners, as equals, as pals, and as full human beings rather than as partial members of the species are apt to be much more easy and free and familiar and impolite in the traditional sense.

LOVE AS ITS OWN REWARD

The fact that love has many good effects does not mean that it is motivated by those effects or that people fall in love *in order* to achieve them. The love that is found in healthy people is much better described in terms of spontaneous admiration and of the kind of receptive and undemanding awe and enjoyment that we experience when struck by a fine painting. There is too much talk in the psychological literature of rewards and purposes, of reinforcements and gratifications, and not nearly enough of what we may call the end experience (as contrasted with the means experience) or awe before the beautiful that is its own reward.

Admiration and love in my subjects are most of the time per se, undemanding of rewards and conducive to no purposes, experienced concretely and richly, for their own sake.

Admiration asks for nothing and gets nothing. It is purposeless and useless. It is more passive than active and comes close to simple receiving in the Taoist sense. Awed perceivers do little or nothing to the experience; rather, it does something to them. They watch and stare with the innocent eye, like a child who neither agrees nor disagrees, approves nor disapproves, but who, fascinated by the intrinsic attention-attracting quality of the experience, simply lets it come in and achieve its effects. The experience may be likened to the *eager* passivity with which we allow ourselves to be tumbled by waves just for the fun that is in it; or perhaps better, to the impersonal interest and awed, unprojecting appreciation of the slowly changing sunset. There is little we can inject into a sunset. In this sense we do not project ourselves into the experience or attempt to shape it as we do with the Rorschach. Nor is it a signal or symbol for anything; we have not been rewarded or associated into admiring it. It has nothing to do with milk, or food, or other body needs. We can enjoy a painting without wanting to own it, a rosebush without wanting to pluck from it, a pretty baby without wanting to kidnap it, a bird without wanting to cage it, and so also can one person admire and enjoy another in a nondoing or nongetting way. Of course awe and admiration lie side by side with other tendencies that *do* involve individuals with each other; it is not the *only* tendency in the picture, but it is definitely part of it.

Perhaps the most important implication of this observation is that we thereby contradict most theories of love, for most theorists assume that people are *driven* into loving another rather than *attracted* into it. Freud (1930) speaks of aim-inhibited sexuality, Reik (1957) speaks of aim-inhibited power, and many speak of dissatisfaction with the self forcing us to create a projected hallucination, an unreal (because overestimated) partner.

But it seems clear that healthy people fall in love the way one appreciates great music—one is awed by it, overwhelmed by it and loves it. This is so even though there was no prior need to be overwhelmed by great music. Horney in a lecture has defined unneurotic love in terms of regarding others as per se, as ends in themselves rather than as means to ends. The consequent reaction is to enjoy, to admire, to be delighted, to contemplate and appreciate, rather than to use. St. Bernard said it very aptly: "Love seeks no cause beyond itself and no limit; it is its own fruit, its own enjoyment. I love because I love; I love in order that I may love" (Huxley, 1944).

ALTRUISTIC LOVE

Similar statements are available in abundance in the theological literature. The effort to differentiate godly love from human love was often based on the assumption that disinterested admiration and altruistic love could be only a superhuman ability and not a natural human one. Of course, we must contradict this; human beings at their best, fully grown, show *many* characteristics once thought, in an earlier era, to be supernatural prerogatives.

It is my opinion that these phenomena are best understood in the framework of various theoretical considerations presented in previous chapters. In the first place, let us consider the differentiation between deficiency motivation and growth motivation. I have suggested that self-actualizers can be defined as people who are no longer motivated by the needs for safety, belongingness, love, status, and self-respect because these needs *have already been satisfied*. Why then should a love-gratified person fall in love? Certainly not for the same reasons that motivate love-deprived people, who fall in love because they need and crave love, they lack it, and are impelled to make up this pathogenic deficiency.

Self-actualizers have no serious deficiencies to make up and must now be looked upon as freed for growth, maturation, development, in a word, for the fulfillment and actualization of their highest individual and species nature. What such people do emanates from growth and expresses it without striving. They love because they are loving persons, in the same way that they are kind, honest, and natural, that is, because it is their nature to be so spontaneously, as a strong man is strong without willing to be, as a rose emits perfume, as a cat is graceful, or as a child is childish. Such epiphenomena are as little motivated as is physical growth or psychological maturation.

There is little of the trying, straining, or striving in the loving of the self-actualizer that so dominates the loving of the average person. In philosophical language, it is an aspect of being as well as of becoming and can be called B-love, that is, love for the Being of the other.

DETACHMENT AND INDIVIDUALITY

A paradox seems to be created at first sight by the fact that self-actualizing people maintain a degree of individualtiy, detachment, and autonomy that seems at first glance to be incompatible with the kind of identification and love that I have been describing. But this is only an apparent paradox. As we have seen, the tendencies to detachment and to need identification and to profound interrelationships with another person can coexist in healthy people. The fact is that self-actualizing people are simultaneously the most individualistic and the most altruistic and social and loving of all human beings. The fact that we have in our culture put these qualities at opposite ends of a single continuum is apparently a mistake that must now be corrected. These qualities go together and the dichotomy is resolved in self-actualizing people.

We find in our subjects a healthy selfishness, a great self-respect, a disinclination to make sacrifices without good reason.

What we see in the love relationship is a fusion of great ability to love and at the same time great respect for the other and great respect for oneself. This shows itself in the fact that these people cannot be said in the ordinary sense of the word to *need* each other as do ordinary lovers. They can be extremely close together and yet go apart when necessary without collapsing. They do not cling to each other or have hooks or anchors of any kind. One has the definite feeling that they enjoy each other tremendously but would take philosophically a long separation or death, that is, would remain strong. Throughout the most intense and ecstatic love affairs, these people remain themselves and remain ultimately masters of themselves as well, living by their own standards even though enjoying each other intensely.

Obviously, this finding, if confirmed, will necessitate a revision or at least an extension in the definition of ideal or healthy love in our culture. We have customarily defined it in terms of a complete merging of egos and a loss of separateness, a giving up of individuality rather than a strengthening of it. While this is true, the fact appears to be at this moment that the individuality is strengthened, that the ego is in one sense merged with another, but yet in another sense remains separate and strong as always. The two tendencies, to transcend individuality and to sharpen and strengthen it, must be seen as partners and not as contradictories. Furthermore, it is implied that the best way to transcend the ego is via having a strong identity.

chapter 13

Creativity in Self-actualizing People[1]

I first had to change my ideas about creativity about 15 years ago when I began studying people who were positively healthy, highly evolved and matured; self-actualizing. These ideas have been evolving ever since, and will, I suppose, continue to change. This is, therefore, a report of progress which should be of interest, not only because of the specific subject under discussion, but also because side by side with it has gone a change in my conception of what psychology is and should be.

PRECONCEPTIONS

I had to give up my stereotyped notion that health, genius, talent, and productivity were synonymous. A large proportion of my subjects, though healthy and creative in a special sense that I am going to describe, were *not* productive in the ordinary sense, nor did they have great talent or genius, nor were they poets, composers, inventors, artists, or creative intellectuals. And it was obvious that some of the greatest talents of mankind were certainly not psychologically healthy people, Wagner, for example, or Van Gogh or Degas or Byron. Some were and some weren't, it was clear. I very early had to come to the conclusion that great talent was not only more or less independent of goodness or health of character but also that we know very little about it. For instance, there is some evidence that great

[1]Four years after the first publication of *Motivation and Personality,* Maslow spoke about creativity and self-actualization in a creativity symposium sponsored by Michigan State University. This chapter is an unedited version of his lecture given in East Lansing, Michigan, on February 28, 1958, with headings added for clarity.

musical talent and mathematical talent are more inherited than acquired. It seemed clear then that health and special talent were separate variables, maybe only slightly correlated, maybe not. And at this time, we may as well admit that psychology knows very little about special talent of the genius type. I shall say nothing more about it, confining myself instead to that more widespread kind of creativeness which is the universal heritage of every human being that is born, and which covaries with psychological health. Furthermore, I soon discovered that I had, like most other people, been thinking of creativeness in terms of products, and secondly I had unconsciously confined creativeness to certain conventional areas only of human endeavor. That is, I unconsciously assumed that *any* painter was leading a creative life, *any* poet, *any* composer. Theorists, artists, scientists, inventors, writers could be creative. Nobody else could be. You were in or you were out, all or none, as if creativeness were the sole prerogative of certain professionals.

NEW MODELS

But these expectations were broken up by various of my subjects. For instance, one woman, uneducated, poor, a full-time housewife and mother, did none of these conventionally creative things and yet was a marvelous cook, mother, wife, and homemaker. With little money, her home was somehow always beautiful. She was a perfect hostess. Her meals were banquets. Her taste in linens, silver, glass, crockery, and furniture was impeccable. She was in all these areas original, novel, ingenious, unexpected, inventive. I just *had* to call her creative. I learned from her and others like her to think that a first-rate soup is more creative than a second-rate painting, and that generally cooking or parenthood or making a home could be creative while poetry need not be: It could be uncreative.

Another of my subjects devoted herself to what had best be called social service in the broadest sense, bandaging up wounds, helping the downtrodden, not only in a personal way, but in an organizational way as well. One of her "creations" is an organization which helps many more people than she could individually.

Another was a psychiatrist, a "pure" clinician who never wrote anything or created any theories or researches but who delighted in his everyday job of helping people to create themselves. This man approached each patient as if he were the only one in the world, without jargon, expectations, or presuppositions, with innocence and naiveté and yet with great wisdom, in a Taoistic fashion. Each patient was a unique human being and therefore a completely new problem to be understood and solved in a completely novel way. His great success even with very difficult cases validated his "creative" (rather than stereotyped or orthodox) way of doing things. From another man I learned that constructing a business organization could be a creative activity. From a young athlete, I learned that a perfect tackle could be as aesthetic a product as a sonnet and could be approached in the same creative spirit. In other words, I learned to apply the word *creative* (and also the word *aesthetic*) not only to products but also to people in a characterological way, and to activities, processes, and attitudes. And furthermore, I had come to apply the word *creative* to many products other than the standard and conventionally accepted poems, theories, novels, experiments, or paintings to which I had hitherto restricted the word.

SELF-ACTUALIZING CREATIVENESS

The consequence was that I found it necessary to distinguish "special talent creativeness" from "self-actualizing creativeness," which sprang much more directly from the personality, which showed itself widely in the ordinary affairs of life, and which showed itself not only in great and obvious products, but also in many other ways, in a certain kind of humor, a tendency to do *anything* creatively: for instance, teaching and so forth.

Perception

Very frequently, it appeared that an essential aspect of self-actualizing creativeness was a special kind of perceptiveness that is exemplified by the child in the fable who saw that the king had no clothes on. (This, too, contradicts the notion of creativity as products). These people can see the fresh, the raw, the concrete, the ideographic, as well as the generic, the abstract, the rubricized, the categorized and classified. Consequently, they live far more in the real world of nature than in the verbalized world of concepts, abstractions, expectations, beliefs, and stereotypes that most people confuse with the real world. This is well expressed in Rogers's phrase "openness to experience."

Expression

All my subjects were relatively more spontaneous and expressive. They were able to be more "natural" and less controlled and inhibited in their behavior; it seemed to be able to flow out more easily and freely and with less blocking and self-criticism. This ability to express ideas and impulses without strangulation and without fear of ridicule from others turned out to be a very essential aspect of self-actualizing creativeness. Rogers has used the excellent phrase "fully functioning person" to describe this aspect of health.

"Second Naiveté"

Another observation was that creativeness in self-actualized people was in many respects like the creativeness of *all* happy and secure children. It was spontaneous, effortless, innocent, easy, a kind of freedom from stereotypes and cliches. And again it seemed to be made up largely of "innocent" freedom of perception and "innocent," uninhibited spontaneity and expressiveness. Almost any child can perceive more freely, without a prior expectation about what ought to be there or what must be there, or what has always been there. And almost any child can compose a song or a poem or a dance or a painting or a play or a game on the spur of the moment, without planning or previous intent.

It was in this childlike sense that my subjects were creative. Or to avoid misunderstanding, since my subjects were after all not children (they were all people in their 50s or 60s), let us say that they had either retained or regained at least two main aspects of childlikeness; namely, they were nonrubricizing or "open to experience" and they were easily spontaneous and expressive. These are certainly different in quality from what is found in children. If children are naive, then my subjects had attained a "second naiveté," as Santayana called it. Their innocence of perception and expressiveness was combined with sophisticated minds.

In any case, this all sounds as if we are dealing with a fundamental characteristic, inherent in human nature, a potentiality given to all or most human beings at birth, which most often is lost or buried or inhibited as the person gets enculturated.

Affinity for the Unknown

My subjects were different from the average person in another characteristic that makes creativity more likely. Self-actualizing people are relatively unfrightened by the unknown, the mysterious, the puzzling, and often are positively attracted by it; that is, selectively pick it out to puzzle over, to meditate on, and to be absorbed with. I quote from my description: "They do not neglect the unknown, or deny it, or run away from it, or try to make believe it is really known, nor do they organize, dichotomize, or categorize it prematurely. They do not cling to the familiar, nor is their quest for the truth a catastrophic need for certainty, safety, definiteness, and order, such as we see in an exaggerated form in Goldstein's brain-injured patients (1939) or in the compulsive-obsessive neurotic. They can be, when the total objective situation calls for it, comfortably disorderly, sloppy, anarchic, chaotic, vague, doubtful, uncertain, indefinite, approximate, inexact, or inaccurate (all, at certain moments in science, art, or life in general, quite desirable)."

Thus it comes about that doubt, tentativeness, uncertainty, with the consequent necessity for abeyance of decision, which is for most a torture, can be for some a pleasantly stimulating challenge, a high spot in life rather than a low.

RESOLUTION OF DICHOTOMIES

One observation I made has puzzled me for many years but it begins to fall into place now. It was what I described as the resolution of dichotomies in self-actualizing people. Briefly stated, I found that I had to see differently many oppositions and polarities that all psychologists had taken for granted as straight line continua. For instance, to take the first dichotomy that I had trouble with, I couldn't decide whether my subjects were selfish or unselfish. Observe how spontaneously we fall into an either-or here. The more of one, the less of the other is the implication of the style in which I put the question. But I was forced by sheer pressure of fact to give up this Aristotelian style of logic. My subjects were very unselfish in one sense and very selfish in another sense. And the two fused together, not like incompatibles, but rather in a sensible, dynamic unity or synthesis very much like what Fromm has described in his classical paper on self-love; that is, on healthy selfishness. My subjects had put opposites together in such a way as to make me realize that regarding selfishness and unselfishness as contradictory and mutually exclusive is itself characteristic of a lower level of personality development. So also in my subjects were many other dichotomies resolved into unities; cognition versus conation (heart versus head, wish versus fact) had become cognition "structured with" conation, just as instinct and reason had come to the same conclusions. Duty became pleasure and pleasure merged with duty. The distinction between work and play became shadowy. How could selfish hedonism be opposed to altruism, when altruism became selfishly pleasurable? These most mature of all people were also strongly childlike. These same people, the strongest egos ever described and the most definitely individual, were also precisely the ones who could be most easily ego-less, self-transcending, and problem-centered.

But this is precisely what the great artist does. He is able to put together clashing colors, forms that fight each other, dissonances of all kinds, into a unity. And this is also what the great theorist does when he puts puzzling and inconsistent facts together so that we can see that they really belong together. And so also for the great statesman, the great therapist, the great philosopher, the great parent, the great lover, the great inventor. They are all integrators, able to put separate and even opposites together into unity.

We speak here of the ability to integrate and of the play back and forth between integration within the person, and his ability to integrate whatever it is he is doing in the world. To the extent that creativeness is constructive, synthesizing, unifying, and integrative, to that extent does it depend in part on the inner integration of the person.

ABSENCE OF FEAR

In trying to figure out why all this was so, it seemed to me that much boiled down to the relative absence of fear in my subjects. They were certainly less enculturated; that is, they seemed to be less afraid of what other people would say or demand or laugh at. It was this approval and acceptance of their deeper selves that made it possible to perceive bravely the real nature of the world and also made their behavior more spontaneous (less controlled, less inhibited, less planned, less "willed" and designed). They were less afraid of their own thoughts even when they were "nutty" or silly or crazy. They were less afraid of being laughed at or of being disapproved of. They could let themselves be flooded by emotion. By contrast, average and neurotic people walled off through fear much that lay within themselves. They controlled, they inhibited, they repressed, and they suppressed. They disapproved of their deeper selves and expected that others did, too.

What I am saying in effect is that the creativity of my subjects seemed to be an epiphenomenon of their greater wholeness and integration, which is what self-acceptance implies. The civil war within the average person between the forces of the inner depths and the forces of defense and control seems to have been resolved in my subjects and they are less split. As a consequence, more of themselves is available for use, for enjoyment, and for creative purposes. They waste less of their time and energy protecting themselves against themselves.

PEAK EXPERIENCES

Another later investigation on "peak experiences" supported and enriched these conclusions. What I did was to question many persons (not only healthy ones) about the most wonderful, most ecstatic experiences of their lives. This had started out as an attempt to make a generalized, all-inclusive theory of the changes of cognition which had been described in the various specific literatures on the creative experience, the esthetic experience, the lover experience, the insight experience, the orgasmic experience, the mystic experience. The generalized word I used for all these happenings was "peak experience." It was my impression that each of these experiences changed the person and his perception of the world in similar or parallel ways. And I was impressed by the fact that these changes often seemed to parallel my already-described self-actualization, or at least a transient unifying of the splits within the person.

So it turned out. But here, too, I learned that some comfortable beliefs I had held had to be given up. For one thing, I had to respect constitutional differences of the Sheldonian sort more than I had, as Charles Morris has also discovered. Different kinds of people get their peak experiences from different kinds of happenings. But no matter where they get them from the subjective experience is described in about the same way. And I assure you that it was a very startling thing for me to hear a woman describing her feelings as she gave birth in the same words used by Bucke to describe cosmic consciousness or by Huxley to describe the mystic experience in all cultures and eras or by Ghiselin to describe the creative process or by Suzuki to describe the Zen satori experience. It opened up for me also the possibility of different kinds of creativeness, as well as of health, and so on.

However, the main finding relevant to our present topic was that an essential aspect of the peak experience is integration within the person and therefore between the person and the world. In these states of being, the person becomes unified; for the time being, the splits, polarities, and dissociations within him tend to be resolved; the civil war within is neither won nor lost but transcended. In such a state, the person becomes far more open to experience and far more spontaneous and fully functioning, essential characteristics, as we have already seen, of self-actualizing creativeness.

> One aspect of the peak experience is a complete, though momentary loss of fear, anxiety, inhibition, defense and control, a giving up of renunciation, delay and restraint. The fear of disintegration and dissolution, the fear of being overwhelmed by the "instincts," the fear of death and of insanity, the fear of giving in to unbridled pleasure and emotion, all tend to disappear or go into abeyance for the time being. This, too, implies a greater openness of perception since fear distorts.

It may be thought of as pure gratification, pure expression, pure elation. But since it is "in the world," it represents a kind of fusion of the Freudian "pleasure principle" and "reality principle."

Observe that these fears are all of our own depths. It is as if in the peak experience we accepted and embraced our deeper selves instead of controlling and fearing them.

For one thing, not only the world but also he himself becomes more a unity, more integrated, and self-consistent. This is another way of saying that he becomes more completely himself, idiosyncratic, unique. And since he is so, he can be more easily expressive and spontaneous without effort. All his powers then come together in their most efficient integration and coordination, organized and coordinated much more perfectly than usual. Everything then can be done with unusual ease and lack of effort. Inhibition, doubt, control, self-criticism, diminish toward a zero point and he becomes the spontaneous, coordinated, efficient organism, functioning like an animal without conflict or split, without hesitation or doubt, in a great flow of power that is so peculiarly effortless, that it may become like play, masterful, virtuoso-like. In such a moment, his powers are at their height and he may be startled (afterwards) by his unsuspected skill, confidence, creativeness, perceptiveness and virtuosity of performance. It is all so easy that it can be enjoyed and laughed with. Things can be dared that would be impossible at other times.

To put it simply, he becomes more whole and unified, more unique and idiosyncratic, more alive and spontaneous, more perfectly expressive and uninhibited, more effortless and powerful, more daring and courageous (leaving fears and doubts behind), more ego-transcending and self-forgetful.

And since almost everyone I questioned could remember such experiences, I had to come to the tentative conclusion that many, perhaps more, people are capable of temporary states of integration, even of self-actualization and therefore of self-actualizing creativeness. (Of course, I must be very tentative in view of my very casual and inadequate sampling).

LEVELS OF CREATIVITY

Classical Freudian theory is of little use for our purposes and as a matter of fact is partially contradicted by our data. It is (or was) essentially an id psychology, an investigation of the instinctive impulses and their vicissitudes, and the basic Freudian dialectic is seen to be ultimately between impulses and defenses against them. But far more crucial than repressed impulses for understanding the sources of creativity (as well as play, love, enthusiasm, humor, imagination, and fantasy) are the so-called primary processes, which are essentially cognitive rather than conative. As soon as we turn our attention to this aspect of human depth psychology, at once we find much agreement between the psychoanalytic ego psychology (Kris, Milner, Ehrenzweig), the Jungian psychology, and the American self-and-growth psychology.

The normal adjustment of the average, commonsense, well-adjusted man implies a continued successful rejection of much of the depths of human nature, both conative and cognitive. To adjust well to the world of reality means a splitting of the person. It means that the person turns his back on much in himself because it is dangerous. But it is now clear that by so doing, he loses a great deal, too, for these depths are also the source of all his joys, his ability to play, to love, to laugh, and, most important for us, to be creative. By protecting himself against the hell within himself, he also cuts himself off from the heaven within. In the extreme instance, we have the obsessional person, flat, tight, rigid, frozen, controlled, cautious, who can't laugh or play or love or be silly or trusting or childish. His imagination, his intuitions, his softness, his emotionality tend to be strangulated or distorted.

Primary Level

The goals of psychoanalysis as a therapy are ultimately integrative. The effort is to heal this basic split by insight, so that what has been repressed becomes conscious or preconscious. But here again we can make modifications as a consequence of studying the depth sources of creativeness. Our relation to our primary processes is not in all respects the same as our relation to unacceptable wishes. The most important difference that I can see is that our primary processes are not as dangerous as the forbidden impulses. To a large extent they are not repressed or censored but rather are forgotten, as Schachtel (1959) has shown, or else turned away from, suppressed (rather than repressed) as we have to adjust to a harsh reality which demands a purposeful and pragmatic striving rather than reverie, poetry, play. Or to say it in another way, in a rich society, there must be far less resistance to primary thought processes. I expect that education processes, which are known to do rather little for relieving repression of "instinct," can do very much to accept and integrate the primary processes into conscious and preconscious life. Education in art, poetry, dancing, can in principle do much in this direction. And so also can education in dynamic psychology; for instance, Deutsch and Murphy's (1967) *Clinical Interview*, which speaks in primary process language, and can be seen as a kind of poetry. Marion Milner's (1967) extraordinary book *On Not Being Able to Paint* perfectly makes my point.

The kind of creativeness I have been trying to sketch out is best exemplified by the improvisation, as in jazz or in childlike paintings rather than by the work or art designated as "great."

Secondary Level

In the first place, the great work needs great talent which, as I found, turned out to be irrelevant for my concern. In the second place, the great work needs not only the flash, the inspiration, the peak experience, it also needs hard work, long training, unrelenting criticism, perfectionistic standards. In other words, succeeding upon the spontaneous is the deliberate; succeeding upon total acceptance comes criticism; succeeding upon intuition comes rigorous thought; succeeding upon daring comes caution; succeeding upon fantasy and imagination comes reality testing. Now come the questions "Is it true?" "Will it be understood by the other?" "Is its structure sound?" "Does it stand the test of logic?" "How will it do in the world?" "Can I prove it?"

Now come the comparisons, the judgments, the evaluations, the cold, calculating morning-after thoughts, the selections, and the rejections.

If I may say it so, the secondary processes now take over from the primary, the Apollonian from the Dionysian, the "masculine" from the "feminine." The voluntary regression into our depths is now terminated, the necessary passivity and receptivity of inspiration or of peak experience must now give way to activity, control, and hard work. A peak experience happens *to* a person; but the person *makes* the great product. It could be described as a masculine phase succeeding upon a feminine one.

Strictly speaking, I have investigated this first phase only, that which comes easily and without effort as a spontaneous expression of an integrated person, or of a transient unifying within the person. It can come only if a person's depths are available to him, only if he is not afraid of his primary thought processes.

Integrated Creativity

I shall call "primary creativity" that which proceeds from and uses the primary process much more than the secondary processes. The creativity which is based mostly on the secondary thought processes I shall call "secondary creativity." This latter type includes a large proportion of production-in-the-world, the bridges, the houses, the new automobiles, even many scientific experiments and much literary work which are essentially the consolidation and exploitation of other people's ideas. It parallels the difference between the commando and the military police behind the lines, the pioneer and the settler. That creativity which uses *both* types of process easily and well in good fusion or in good succession I shall call "integrated creativity." It is from this kind that comes the great work of art, or philosophy, or science.

The upshot of all of these developments can, I think, be summarized as an increased stress on the role of integration (or self-consistency, unity, wholeness) in the theory of creativeness. Resolving a dichotomy into a higher, more inclusive unity amounts to healing a split in the person and making him more unified. Since the splits I have been talking about are within the person, they amount to a kind of civil war, a setting of one part of the person against another part. In any case, so far as self-actualizing creativeness is concerned, it seems to come more immediately from fusion of primary and secondary processes rather than from working through repressive control of forbidden impulses and wishes. It is, of course, probably that defenses arising out of fears of these forbidden impulses also push down primary processes in a kind of total, undiscriminating, panicky war on *all* the depths. But it seems that such lack of discrimination is not in principle necessary.

CREATIVITY AND SELF-ACTUALIZATION

To summarize, self-actualizing creativeness stresses first the personality rather than its achievements, considering these achievements to be epiphenomena emitted by the personality and therefore secondary to it. It stresses characterological qualities like boldness, courage, freedom, spontaneity, perspicuity, integration, self-acceptance, which make possible the kind of generalized creativeness I've been talking about, which expresses itself in the creative life, or the creative attitude, or the creative person. I have also stressed the expressive or Being quality of self-actualizing creativeness rather than its problem-solving or product-making quality. Self-actualizing creativeness is "emitted," like radioactivity, and hits all of life, regardless of problems, just as a cheerful person emits cheerfulness without purpose or design or even consciousness. It is emitted like sunshine; it spreads all over the place; it makes some things grow (which are growable) and is wasted on rocks and other ungrowable things.

As I come to the end I am quite aware that I have been trying to break up widely accepted concepts of creativity without being able to offer in exchange a nice, clearly defined, clean-cut substitute concept. Self-actualizing creativeness is hard to define because sometimes it seems to be synonymous with health itself, as Moustakas has suggested. And since self-actualization or health must ultimately be defined as the coming to pass of the fullest humanness, or as the Being of the person, it is as if self-actualizing creativity were almost synonymous with, or a sine qua non aspect of, or a defining characteristic of, essential humanness.

four

METHODOLOGIES FOR
A HUMAN SCIENCE

chapter *14*

Questions for
a New Psychology[1]

The formulation of a problem is far more often essential than its solution, which may be merely a matter of mathematical or experimental skill. To raise new questions, new possibilities, to regard old problems from a new angle requires creative imagination and marks real advance in science.

ALBERT EINSTEIN AND L. INFELD
The Evolution of Physics, 1938

There is now available the beginnings of another philosophy of science. It is a positive, value-based conception of knowledge and of cognizing, including the holistic as well as the atomistic, the unique as well as the repetitive, the human and personal as well as the mechanical, the changing as well as the stable, the transcendent as well as the positivistic. This chapter is a beginning survey of the questions that emerge from this new approach to human psychology.

LEARNING

How do people learn to be wise, mature, kind, to have good taste, to be inventive, to have good characters, to be able to fit themselves to a new situation, to detect

[1] I am leaving this chapter with only minor corrections because (1) most of the suggestions are still pertinent and (2) it will be interesting to the student to see just how much progress has been made in these directions in 15 years. [Editor's note: Now, 15 years since Maslow added this remark, some of these questions have become recognized fields of study, while many of them remain provocative and unanswered.]

the good, to seek the truth, to know the beautiful, and the genuine, that is, intrinsic rather than extrinsic learning?

Learning from unique experiences, from tragedy, marriage, having children, success, triumphy, falling in love, being ill, death, and the like.

Learning from pain, illness, depression, tragedy, failure, old age, death.

Much that passes for associative learning is actually intrinsic and required by reality rather than being relative, arbitrary, and fortuitous.

With self-actualizing people, repetition, contiguity, and arbitrary reward become less and less important. Probably advertising of the usual sort is ineffective with them. They are much less susceptible to arbitrary association, to prestige suggestion, to snob appeals and to simple, senseless repetition. Perhaps even these have negative effect, that is, make them *less* likely to buy rather than more likely.

Why does so much of educational psychology concern itself with means (e.g., grades, degrees, credits, diplomas), rather than with ends (e.g., wisdom, understanding, good judgment, good taste)?

We do not know enough about the acquisition of emotional attitudes, of tastes, of preferences. The "learning of the heart" has been neglected.

Education in practice too often adapts children to the convenience of adults by making them less nuisances and little devils. More positively oriented education concerns itself more with the growth and future self-actualization of the child. What do we know about teaching children to be strong, self-respecting, righteously indignant, resistant to domination and exploitation, to propaganda and blind enculturation, to suggestion and to fashion?

We know very little about purposeless, unmotivated learning, that is, latent learning, learning out of sheer, intrinsic interest, and the like.

PERCEPTION

Perception is too much the limited study of mistakes, distortion, illusions, and the like. Wertheimer would have called it the study of psychological blindness. Why not add to it the study of intuition, of subliminal perception, of unconscious and preconscious perception? Would not the study of good taste enter here? Of the genuine, of the true, and the beautiful? How about the aesthetic perception? Why do some people perceive beauty and others not? Under this same heading of perception we may also include the constructive manipulation of reality by hope, dreams, imagination, inventiveness, organizing, and ordering.

Unmotivated, disinterested, unselfish perception. Appreciation. Awe. Admiration. Choiceless awareness.

Plenty of studies of stereotypes, but very little scientific study of fresh, concrete, Bergsonian reality.

Free-floating attention of the type that Freud spoke about.

What are the factors that make it possible for healthy people to perceive reality more efficiently, to predict the future more accurately, to perceive more easily what people really are like, that make it possible for them to endure or to enjoy the unknown, the unstructured and ambiguous, and the mysterious?

Why do the wishes and hopes of healthy people have so little power to distort their perceptions?

The healthier people are, the more their capacities are interrelated. This holds also for the sensory modalities that make synaesthesia in principle a more basic study than the isolated study of separate senses. Not only is this so, but the sensory equipment as a whole is related to the motor aspects of the organism. These interrelations need more study: So also do unitive consciousness, B-cognition, illumination, transpersonal and transhuman perceiving, the cognitive aspects of mystic experiences and peak experiences, and the like.

EMOTIONS

The positive emotions (i.e., happiness, calm, serenity, peace of mind, contentment, acceptance) have not been studied sufficiently. Neither have compassion, pity, charity.

Fun, joy, play, games, sport, are not sufficiently understood.

Ecstacy, elation, zest, exhilaration, gaiety, euphoria, well-being, the mystic experience, the conversion experience in politics and religion, the emotions generated by orgasm.

The difference between the struggle, conflict, frustration, sadness, anxiety, tension, guilt, shame, and so on of the psychopathological person and of the healthy person. In the healthy person these are or can be good influences.

The organizing effects and other good and desirable effects of emotion have been less studied than its disorganizing effects. Under which circumstances does it correlate with *increased* efficiency of perception, of learning, of thinking, and so on?

The emotional aspects of cognition, for example, the lift that comes with insight, the calming effect of understanding, the acceptance and forgiveness that are products of deeper understanding of bad behavior.

The affective side of love and friendship, the satisfactions and pleasures that they bring.

In healthy people, cognition, conation, and affect are much more synergic than antagonistic or mutually exclusive. We must discover why this is so, and what the underlying mechanical arrangements are, for example, are hypothalamic-cerebral interrelations different in the healthy? We must learn how, for instance, conative and affective mobilization helps cognition, how cognitive and conative synergism supports affect, emotions, and so on. These three aspects of psychic life should be studied in their interrelations, rather than separately.

The connoisseur has been unreasonably neglected by psychologists. Simple enjoyment of eating, of drinking, of smoking, or of the other sensuous gratifications has a definite place in psychology.

What are the impulses behind the construction of utopias? What is hope? Why do we imagine and project and create ideas of heaven, of the good life, of a better society?

What does admiration mean? Awe? Amazement?

Study of inspiration? How can we inspire people to greater efforts? To better goals?

Why does pleasure disappear more rapidly than pain? Are there ways to refreshen pleasure, gratification, happiness? Can we learn to appreciate our blessings instead of taking them for granted?

MOTIVATION

The parental impulses: Why do we love our children, why do people want children at all, why do they make so many sacrifices for them? Or rather, why does what looks like a sacrifice to someone else not feel like a sacrifice to the parent? Why are babies lovable?

The study of justice, equality, liberty, the desire for liberty, for freedom, and for justice. Why is it that people will fight for justice at great cost to themselves or even give up their lives? Why is it that some with nothing to gain for themselves come to the aid of the downtrodden, of the unjustly treated, and the unhappy?

Human beings to some extent yearn for their goals, purposes, and ends, *rather* than being driven by blind impulses and drives. The latter of course also happens but not exclusively. The full picture requires both.

So far we have studied only the pathogenic effects of frustration, neglecting its "healthogenic" effects.

Homeostasis, equilibrium, adaptation, self-preservation, defense, and adjustment are merely negative concepts and must be supplemented by positive concepts. "Everything seems directed towards preserving life and very little towards making it worth living." H. Poincaré said that his problem was not to earn his meals but to keep from being bored between them. If we were to define functional psychology as the study of usefulness from the point of view of self-preservation, then by extension a *meta*functional psychology would study usefulness from the point of view of self-perfection.

The neglect of higher needs and neglect of the differences between lower and higher needs dooms people to disappointment when wanting continues even after a need is gratified. In the healthy person, gratification produces, not cessation of desire, but after a temporary period of contentment, substitution of higher desires and higher frustration levels, along with the same old restlessness and dissatisfaction.

Appetites and preferences and tastes, as well as the brute, life-and-death, desperate hungers.

Urge to perfection, truth, justice (same as straightening a crooked picture? Or completing an incompleted task? Or perseveration of an unsolved problem?). The Utopian impulse, the desire to improve the external world, to set wrong things right.

Neglect of cognitive needs, for example by Freud (Aronoff, 1962) as well as by the academic psychologists.

The conative side of aesthetics, the aesthetic needs.

We do not sufficiently understand the motivations of the martyr, the hero, the patriot, the unselfish man. The Freudian nothing-but, reductive explanations do not explain healthy people.

How about the psychology of right and wrong, the psychology of ethics and of morality?

The psychology of science, of the scientist, of knowledge, of the search for knowledge, of the impulses behind the search for knowledge, of the philosophical impulse.

Appreciation, contemplation, meditation.

Sex is customarily discussed as if it were a problem of avoiding the plague. The preoccupation with the dangers of sex has obscured the obvious that it can be or should be a very enjoyable pastime and possibly also a very profoundly therapeutic and educational one.

INTELLIGENCE

Must we rest content with a definition of intelligence that is derived from what is the case, rather than what should be the case? The whole concept of IQ has nothing to do with wisdom; it is a purely technological concept. For example, Goering had a high IQ but was in a very real sense a stupid man. He was certainly a vicious man. We do not think there is any great harm in separating out the specific concept of high IQ. The only trouble is that in a psychology that limits itself so, the more important subjects—wisdom, knowledge, insight, understanding, common sense, good judgment—are neglected in favor of the IQ because it is technologically more satisfactory. For the humanist, of course, it is a highly irritating concept.

What are the influences that raise the IQ—effective intelligence, common sense, good judgment? We know much about what harms them, little about what improves them. Could there be a psychotherapy of the intelligence.

An organismic conception of intelligence?

To what extent are the intelligence tests culture-bound?

COGNITION AND THINKING

Change of mind. Conversion. Psychoanalytic insight. Sudden understanding. The perception of principle. Illumination. Satori. Awakening.

Wisdom. What are the relations with good taste, with good morals, kindness, and the like?

The characterological and therapeutic effects of sheer knowledge.

The study of creativeness and of productiveness should have an important place in psychology. In thinking we should pay more attention to the study of novelty, of inventiveness, of the production of new ideas, rather than to the finding of solutions to predetermined puzzles of the type so far used in thinking studies. Since thinking at its best is creative, why not study it at its best?

The psychology of science and scientists, of philosophy and philosophers.

Thinking in the healthiest people—if they are also intelligent—is not only of the Dewey type, that is, stimulated by some disequilibrating problem or nuisance, and disappearing when the problem is solved. It is also spontaneous, sportive, and pleasurable, and *is* often emitted, or produced without effort, automatically, as the liver secretes bile. Such people *enjoy* being thinking animals, they do not have to be harassed into it.

Thinking is not always directed, organized, motivated, or goal-bent. Fantasy, dreaming, symbolism, unconscious thinking, infantile, emotional thinking, psychoanalytic free association, are all productive in their own way. Healthy people come to many of their conclusions and decisions with the aid of these techniques, traditionally opposed to rationality but in actuality synergic with it.

The concept of objectivity. Disinterestedness. Passive response to the nature of reality per se without injecting any personal or ego elements. Problem-centered rather than ego-centered cognition. Taoistic objectivity, love-objectivity versus spectator-objectivity.

CLINICAL PSYCHOLOGY

In general, we should learn to see as psychopathology *any* failure to achieve self-actualization. The average or normal person is just as much a case as the psychotic, even though less dramatic, and less urgent.

The aims and goals of psychotherapy should be positively seen. (This is of course true also for the goals of education, of the family, of medicine, of religion and philosophy.) The therapeutic values of good and successful life experiences should be stressed, as, for example, marriage, friendship, economic success, and the like.

Clinical psychology is not the same as abnormal psychology. Clinical psychology may be the personal, individual case study of successful and happy and healthy individuals as well. Clinical psychology can study health as well as illness, the strong, the courageous, and the kind as well as the weak, the cowardly, and the cruel.

Abnormal psychology should not be limited to the study of schizophrenia, but should also include such subjects as cynicism, authoritarianism, anhedonia, the loss of values, prejudice, hatred, greed, selfishness, and the like. These are *the* serious diseases from the point of view of values. Dementia praecox, manic depression, obsession-compulsion, and the like are the serious diseases of mankind *from the point of view of technology,* that is, in the sense that they limit efficiency. But it would have been a blessing, not a curse, if Hitler or Mussolini or Stalin had broken down with obvious schizophrenia. What we should study from the point of view of positive and value-oriented psychology are those disturbances that make people bad or limited in the value sense. Cynicism, then, is certainly more important socially than depression.

We spend a great amount of time studying criminality. Why not study also law-abidingness, identification with society, philanthropy, social conscience?

In addition to studying the psychotherapeutic effects of the good life experiences, such as marriage, success, having children, falling in love, education, and so on, we should also study the psychotherapeutic effects of bad experiences, particularly of tragedy, but also, illness, deprivation, frustration, conflict, and the like. Healthy people seem able to turn even such experiences to good use.

The study of interest (as contrasted with the study of boredom). Those who have vitality, wish for life, resistance to death, zest.

Our present knowledge of personality dynamics, of health, and adjustment comes almost entirely from the study of sick people. Not only will the study of healthy people correct this and teach us directly about psychological health, but we are sure it will also teach us much more than we know now about neurosis, psychosis, psychopathy, and psychopathology in general.

The clinical study of ability, capacity, skills, craftsmanship. Vocation, calling, mission.

The clinical study of genius and talent. We spend far more time and money on feeble-minded people than on intelligent people.

Frustration theory as usually conceived is a good example of cripple psychology. In too many theories of child raising, the child is conceived of in the original Freudian fashion, as a completely conservative organism, hanging on to already achieved adjustments; it has no urge to go on to a new adjustment, to grow, and to develop in its own style.

To this day, the psychodiagnostic techniques are used to diagnose pathology, not health. We have no good Rorschach or TAT or MMPI norms for creativeness, ego strength, health, self-actualization, hypnosis, resistance to disease. Most personality questionnaires are still modeled on the original Woodworth model; they list many symptoms of sickness, and a good or healthy score is the *absence* of responses to these list of symptoms.

Since psychotherapy improves people, we miss an opportunity to see people at their best by failing to study the posttherapeutic personality.

The study of peakers and nonpeakers, that is, those who do and those who do not have peak experiences.

ANIMAL PSYCHOLOGY

In animal psychology, the stress has been on hunger and thirst. Why not study the higher needs? We actually do not know whether the white rat has anything to compare with our higher needs for love, beauty, understanding, status, and the like. With the techniques now available to animal psychologists, how could we know? We must get over the psychology of the *desperate* rat, the rat who is pushed to the point of starvation, or who is pushed by pain or electric shock into an extreme situation, one so extreme that human beings seldom find themselves in it. (Some such work has been done with monkeys and apes.)

The study of understanding and insight should be more stressed than the study of rote, blind association learning, the higher levels of intelligence as well as the lower, the more complex, as well as the less complex; the higher limits of animal performance have been neglected in favor of averages.

When Husband (1929) showed that a rat could learn a maze almost as well as a human being, the maze should have been dropped once and for all as an instrument for the study of learning. We know in advance that the human being learns better than the rat. Any technique that cannot demonstrate this is like measuring people who are bent over in a room with a low ceiling. What we are measuring is the ceiling, not the people. All that a maze does is to measure a low ceiling and not the height to which learning and thinking may go, not even in the rat.

It seems very probable that the use of higher animals rather than lower animals would teach us much more about human psychology.

It should always be kept in mind that the use of animals guarantees in advance the neglect of just those capacities that are uniquely human, for example, martyrdom, self-sacrifice, shame, symbols, language, love, humor, art, beauty, conscience, guilt, patriotism, ideals, the production of poetry or philosophy or music or science. Animal psychology is necessary for learning about those human characteristics that humans share with all primates. It is useless in the study of those characteristics that humans do *not* share with other animals or in which they are vastly superior, such as latent learning.

SOCIAL PSYCHOLOGY

Social psychology should be more than a study of imitation, suggestion, prejudice, hatred, hostility. These are minor forces in healthy people.

Theory of democracy, of anarchism. Democratic, interpersonal relationship. The democratic leader. Power in a democracy and among democratic people and in the democratic leader. The motivations of the unselfish leader. Sound people *dislike* having power over other people. Social psychology is too much dominated by a low-ceiling, lower-animal conception of power.

Competition is studied more than cooperation, altruism, friendliness, unselfishness.

The study of freedom and of free people has little or no place in social psychology today.

How is culture improved? What are the good effects of the deviant? We know that culture can never advance or be improved without deviants. Why have they not been more studied? Why are they generally considered to be pathological? Why not healthy?

Brotherhood and equalitarianism deserves as much attention as class and caste and domination in the social sphere. Why not study the religious brotherhoods? The consumers' and producers' cooperatives? Intentional and Utopian communities?

The culture-personality relationship is usually studied as if culture were the prime mover, as if its shaping force were inexorable. But it can be and is resisted by stronger and healthier people. Acculturation and enculturation work only to an extent with some people. The study of freedom *from* the environment is called for.

Opinion polling is based on the uncritical acceptance of a low conception of human possibilities, for example, the assumption that people's votes will be determined by selfishness or by sheer habit. This is true, but only in the unhealthy 99 percent of the population. Healthy human beings vote or buy or form judgments at least partially on the basis of logic, common sense, justice, fairness, reality, and so on, even when this is against their own interests, narrowly and selfishly considered.

Why is there so much neglect of the fact that leadership in democracies is very often sought for the opportunity of service rather than to have power over other people? This has been completely neglected even though it has been a profoundly important force in American history and in world history as well. It is quite clear that Jefferson never wanted power or leadership for any selfish benefits that might come from it, but that he felt rather that he should sacrifice himself because he could do a good job that needed to be done.

The sense of duty, of loyalty, obligation to society, responsibility, the social conscience. The good citizen, the honest person. We spend much time studying the criminal, why not these?

The crusader. The fighter for principle, for justice, for freedom, for equality. The idealist.

The good effects of prejudice, of unpopularity, of deprivation, and of frustration. There is little effort among psychologists to get the full many-sidedness of even pathological phenomena like prejudice. There are certain *good* consequences of excluding or ostracizing. This is especially so if the culture is a doubtful one or a sick or a bad one. Ostracism from such a culture is a good thing for the person, even though it may cost much pain. Self-actualizing people often ostracize themselves by withdrawing from subcultures of which they disapprove.

We do not know as much about the saint, the knight, the do-gooder, the hero, the unselfish leader as we do about the tyrant, the criminal, the psychopath.

Conventionality has its good side and its desirable effects. The good conventions. The contrasting value of conventions in a healthy and in a sick society. The same for "middle-class" values.

Kindness, generosity, benevolence, and charity have too little place in the social psychology textbooks.

The rich liberals like Franklin Roosevelt, or Thomas Jefferson, who, quite in contradiction to the dictates of their own pocketbooks, fight against their own economic interest, in the interest of fairness, and justice, and so forth.

While there is much written about anti-Semitism, anti-Negroism, racism, and xenophobia, there is very little recognition of the fact that there is also such a thing as philo-Semitism, Negrophilia, and sympathy for the underdog. This illustrates how we concentrate more on hostility than on altruism, or sympathy or concern for people who are treated badly.

The study of sportsmanship, of fairness, of the sense of justice, of concern for the other person.

In textbooks of interpersonal relations or of social psychology the study of love, marriage, friendships, and the therapeutic relationship might very well be paradigmatic for all the chapters that followed. As of today, however, they are rarely taken seriously by extant textbooks.

Sales resistance, advertising resistance, propaganda resistance, opinion-of-other-people resistance, maintenance of autonomy, suggestion resistance, imitation resistance, prestige resistance are all high in healthy people and low in average people. These symptoms of health should be more extensively studied by applied social psychologists.

Social psychology must shake itself free of that variety of cultural relativism which stresses too much human passivity, plasticity, and shapelessness and too little autonomy, growth tendencies, and the maturation of inner forces. It should study the active agent as well as the pawn.

Either psychologists and social scientists will supply empirical value systems for humanity or no one will. This task alone generates a thousand problems.

From the point of view of the positive development of human potentiality, psychology was very largely a complete failure during World War II. It was used by very many psychologists as a technology only and was allowed to apply only what was already known. Practically nothing new in psychological theory has come out of the war yet, though there may be later developments. This meant that many psychologists and other scientists allied themselves with the short-sighted people who stressed only the winning of the war and neglected the winning of the peace afterward. They neglected entirely the point of the whole war, making it into a technological game rather than a value struggle, which it actually was, or at least was supposed to be. There was little in the body of psychology to prevent them from making this mistake, no philosophy for instance that separated technology from science, no value theory that enabled them to understand clearly what democratic people are really like, what the fighting was all about, and what its emphases were or should have been. They addressed themselves generally to means-questions rather than end-questions and could have been put to as good use by the Nazis as by the democracies. Their efforts were of little avail in preventing the growth of authoritarianism even in our own country.

Social institutions, and indeed culture itself, are customarily studied as shapers, forcers, inhibitors, rather than as need gratifiers, happiness producers, self-actualization fosterers. "Is culture a set of problems or a set of opportunities?" (A. Meiklejohn). The culture-as-shaper concept is probably a consequence of too exclusive experience with pathological cases. The use of healthier subjects suggests rather culture-as-reservoir-of-gratifications. The same may probably be affirmed for the family, which is also seen too often to be a shaping, training, molding force exclusively.

PERSONALITY

The concept of the well-adjusted personality or of good adjustment sets a low ceiling upon the possibility for advancement and for growth. The cow, the slave, the robot may all be well adjusted.

The superego of the child is ordinarily conceived of as introjection of fear, punishment, loss of love, abandonment, and so on. The study of children and adults who are safe, loved, and respected indicates the possibility of an intrinsic conscience built on love identification, the desire to please and to make others happy, as well as on truth, logic, justice, consistency, right, and duty.

The behavior of the healthy person is less determined by anxiety, fear, insecurity, guilt, shame, and more by truth, logic, justice, reality, fairness, fitness, beauty, rightness, and the like.

Where are the researches on unselfishness? Lack of envy? Will power? Strength of character? Optimism? Friendliness? Realism? Self-transcendence? Boldness, courage? Lack of jealousy? Sincerity? Patience? Loyalty? Reliability? Responsibility?

Of course the most pertinent and obvious choice of subject for a positive psychology is the study of psychological health (and other kinds of health, aesthetic health, value health, physical health, and the like). But a positive psychology also calls for more study of the good person, of the secure and of the confident, of the democratic character, of the happy man, of the serene, the calm, the peaceful, the compassionate, the generous, the kind, of the creator, of the saint, of the hero, of the strong person, of the genius, and of other good specimens of humanity.

What produces the socially desirable characteristics of kindliness, social conscience, helpfulness, neighborliness, identification, tolerance, friendliness, desire for justice, righteous indignation?

We have a very rich vocabulary for psychopathology but a very meager one for health or transcendence.

Deprivation and frustration have some good effects. The study of just as well as of unjust discipline is indicated, as is also study of the self-discipline that comes from being allowed to deal directly with reality, learning from its intrinsic rewards and punishments, its feedback.

The study of idiosyncrasy and individuality (*not* individual differences in the classical sense). We must develop an idiographic science of personality.

How do people get to be unlike each other instead of like each other (acculturated, ironed out by the culture, etc.)?

What is dedication to a cause? What produces the dedicated, devoted person who identifies himself with an ego-transcending cause or mission?

The contented, happy, calm, serene, peaceful personality.

The tastes, values, attitudes, and the choices of self-actualizing people are to a great extent on an intrinsic and reality-determined basis, rather than on a relative and extrinsic basis. It is therefore a taste for the right rather than wrong, for the true rather than the false, for the beautiful rather than the ugly. They live within a system of stable values and *not* in a robot world of *no values at all* (only fashions, fads, opinions of others, imitation, suggestion, prestige).

Frustration level and frustration tolerance may very well be *much* higher in self-actualizing people. So also guilt level, conflict level, and shame level.

Child-parent relationships have usually been studied as if they *were* only a set of problems, *only* a chance to make mistakes. They are primarily a pleasure and a delight, and a great opportunity to enjoy. This is true even for adolescence, too often treated as if akin to a plague.

chapter 15

A Psychological Approach to Science

A psychological interpretation of science begins with the acute realization that science is a human creation, rather than an autonomous, nonhuman, or per se "thing" with intrinsic rules of its own. Its origins are in human motives, its goals are human goals, and it is created, renewed, and maintained by human beings. Its laws, organization, and articulations rest not only on the nature of the reality that it discovers, but also on the nature of the human nature that does the discovering. The psychologist, especially if he or she has had any clinical experience, will quite naturally and spontaneously approach any subject matter in a personal way by studying people, rather than the abstractions they produce, scientists as well as science.

The misguided effort to make believe that this is not so, the persistent attempt to make science completely autonomous and self-regulating and to regard it as a disinterested game, having intrinsic, arbitrary chesslike rules, the psychologist must consider unrealistic, false, and even antiempirical.

In this chapter, I wish to spell out some of the more important implications and consequences of the recognition that science is first of all a human creation that must be examined psychologically.

STUDYING THE SCIENTIST

The study of scientists is clearly a basic, even necessary, aspect of the study of science. Since science as an institution is partly a magnified projection of certain aspects of human nature, any increment in the knowledge of these aspects will be automatically multiplied many times. For instance, every science and every theory within every science will be affected by improved knowledge of (1) the nature of bias and objectivity, (2) the nature of the abstracting process, (3) the nature of creativity, (4) the nature of enculturation and of the scientist's resistance to enculturation, (5) the contamination of perception by wishes, hopes, anxieties, expectations, (6) the nature of the scientist's role or status, (7) anti-intellectualism in our culture, and (8) the nature of belief, conviction, faith, certainty, and so forth.

SCIENCE AND HUMAN VALUES

Science is based on human values and is itself a value system (Bronowski, 1956). Human emotional, cognitive, expressive, and aesthetic needs give science its origins and its goals. The gratification of any such need is a "value." This is true of the love of safety as it is of the love of truth, or of certainty. The aesthetic satisfactions of succinctness, parsimony, elegance, simplicity, precision, neatness, are values to the mathematician and to the scientist as they are to the craftsman, the artist, or the philosopher.

These are quite apart from the fact that as scientists we share the basic values of our culture and probably will always have to, at least to some extent—for example, honesty, humanitarianism, respect for the individual, social service, democratic respect for the right of individuals to make their own decisions even when mistaken, the preservation of life and health, the relief of pain, giving credit where credit is due, sharing credit, sportsmanship, "fairness," and the like.

Clearly "objectivity" and "disinterested observations" are phrases that need redefining. "Excluding values" meant originally excluding theological and other authoritarian dogmas that prejudged the facts. This exclusion is quite as necessary today as it was at the time of the Renaissance because we still want our facts as uncontaminated as possible. If organized religion today is only a feeble threat to science in our country, we still have strong political and economic dogmas to contend with.

UNDERSTANDING VALUES

However, the only way we now know of preventing contamination of our perception of nature, of society, or of ourselves by human values is to be very conscious of these values at all times, to understand their influence on perception, and with the aid of such understanding to make the necessary corrections. (By contamination I mean the confusion of psychic determinants with reality determinants, when it is the latter we seek to perceive.) The study of values, of needs and wishes, of bias, of fears, of interests, and of neurosis must become a basic aspect of all scientific studies.

Such a statement must include also the most generalized tendencies of all human beings to abstract, to classify, to see similarities and differences, and in general to pay selective attention to reality and to shuffle and reshuffle it in accordance with human interests, needs, wishes, and fears. To organize our perceptions under various rubrics and categories in this way is desirable and useful in some ways and is undesirable and harmful in other ways, for, while it throws some aspects of reality into sharp relief, it simultaneously throws other aspects of reality into shadow. We must understand that while nature gives us clues to classification, and that it sometimes has "natural" lines of cleavage, often these clues are only minimal or ambiguous. We must often create or impose a classification upon nature. This we do in accordance not only with nature's suggestions but also in accordance with our own human nature, our own unconscious values, biases, and interests. Granted that the ideal of science is to reduce to a minimum these human determinants of theory, this will never be achieved by denying their influence, but only by knowing them well.

It should reassure the uneasy pure scientist to know that the point of all this disquieting talk about values is to achieve more efficiently the goal of science, namely, the improvement of our knowledge of nature, the decontamination of our knowledge of the known by study of the knower (Polanyi, 1958, 1964).

HUMAN AND NATURAL LAWS

The laws of human psychology and of nonhuman nature are in some respects the same, but are in some respects utterly different. The fact that humans live in the natural world does not mean that their rules and laws need to be the same. The human being, living in the real world, certainly has to make concessions to it, but this in itself is not a denial of the fact that the human being has intrinsic laws, which are not those of natural reality. Wishes, fears, dreams, hopes, all behave differently from pebbles, wires, temperatures, or atoms. A philosophy is not constructed in the same way as a bridge. A family and a crystal must be studied in different ways. All our talk about motives and values does not imply a wish to subjectivize or psychologize nonhuman nature, but, of course, we *must* psychologize *human* nature.

This nonhuman reality is independent of the wishes and needs of human beings, being neither beneficent nor malevolent, having no purposes, aims, goals, or functions (only living beings have purposes), no conative and no affective tendencies. This is the reality that would persist if all human beings disappeared—a not impossible happening.

To know this reality as it is rather than as we should like it to be is desirable from *any* point of view, either of "pure," disinterested curiosity, or of concern for predicting and controlling reality for immediate human ends. Kant was certainly correct in claiming that we can never fully know nonhuman reality, yet it *is* possible to get closer to it, to know it more truly, or less truly.

SOCIOLOGY OF SCIENCE

The study of the sociology of science and of scientists deserves more attention than it is now getting. If scientists are determined in part by cultural variables, then so also are the products of these scientists. To what extent science needs the contribution of people of other cultures, to what extent the scientist must stand aloof from culture in order to perceive more validly, to what extent the scientist must be an internationalist rather than, for example, an American, to what extent the products of scientists are determined by their class and caste affiliation—these are questions of the type that must be asked and answered for fuller understanding of the "contaminating" effect of culture upon perception of nature.

DIFFERENT APPROACHES TO REALITY

Science is only one means of access to knowledge of natural, social, and psychological reality. The creative artist, the philosopher, the literary humanist, or, for that matter, the ditch digger can also be the discoverer of truth, and should be encouraged as much as the scientist.[1] They should not be seen as mutually exclusive or even as necessarily separate from each other. The scientist who is also something of a poet, philosopher, and even a dreamer is almost certainly an improvement over more constricted colleagues.

If we are led by this psychological pluralism to think of science as an orchestration of diverse talents, motives, and interests, the line between the scientist and the nonscientist grows shadowy. The philosopher of science who occupies himself with criticism and analysis of the concepts of science is surely closer to the scientist who is also interested in pure theory than the latter is to the purely technological scientist. The dramatist or poet who presents an organized theory of human nature is certainly closer to the psychologist than the latter is to the engineer. The historian of science may be either a historian or a scientist, it does not matter which. The clinical psychologist or the physician who makes a careful study of the individual case may get more nutrition from the novelist than from abstracting, experimenting colleagues.

I see no way of sharply defining off scientists from nonscientists. One cannot even use as a criterion the pursuit of experimental research, because so many people who are down on the payrolls as scientists have never performed and never will perform a true experiment. The person who teaches chemistry in a junior college considers himself a chemist even though he or she has never discovered anything new in chemistry, but has simply read the chemical journals and repeated the experiments of others in a cookbook fashion. He or she may be less a scientist than a bright 12-year-old student who is systematically curious in the basement at home or a skeptical consumer who checks on the doubtful claims of advertisers.

In what respect does the chair of a research institute remain a scientist? His or her time may be completely occupied with administrative and organizational work, and yet there may be a wish to refer to oneself as a scientist.

If the ideal scientist combines the creative hypothesizer, the careful checker-experimenter, the philosophical system builder, the historical scholar, the tech-

---

[1]Perhaps the main differences today between the idealized artist and the idealized scientist can be phrased in the following way: the former is usually a specialist in knowledge or discovery of the idiographic (the unique, the idiosyncratic, the individual), whereas the latter is a specialist in the nomothetic (the generalized, the abstract). Second, the artist is closer to the scientist as problem discoverer, questioner, or hypothesizer than to the scientist as problem solver, checker, and certainty maker. These last functions deal with what is verifiable and testable, and are ordinarily the exclusive responsibility of the scientist.

nologist, the organizer, the educator-writer-publicist, the applier, and the appreciator, then we can easily conceive that the ideal team might be composed of at least nine individual specialists in these different functions, *no one of whom need be a scientist in the rounded sense!*

But while this makes the point that the scientist-nonscientist dichotomy is too simple, we must also take into account the general finding that one who overspecializes is usually not much good for anything in the long run, since the person suffers as a whole human being. The generalized, rounded, and healthy person can do most things better than the generalized, crippled human being; the person who tries to be *too* pure a thinker by stifling impulses and emotions paradoxically winds up being a sick person who can think only in a sick fashion, that is, becomes a bad thinker. In a word we may expect the scientist who is also a bit of an artist to be a better scientist than a colleague who is not also a bit of an artist.

If we use the case history method, this becomes very clear. Our great scientific figures ordinarily have had extensive interests and certainly have not been narrow technologists. From Aristotle to Einstein, from Leonardo to Freud, the great discoverer has been versatile and many-sided, with humanistic, philosophical, social, and aesthetic interests.

We must conclude that a psychological pluralism in science teaches us that there are many paths to knowledge and truth, that the creative artist, the philosopher, the literary humanist, either as individuals or as aspects within the single individual, can also be discoverers of truth.

PSYCHOLOGICAL HEALTH

All other things being equal, we may expect the scientist (or artist, or machinist, or executive) who is happy, secure, serene, and healthy to be a better scientist (or artist, or machinist, or executive) than if the person were unhappy, insecure, troubled, and unhealthy. The neurotic person distorts reality, makes demands upon it, imposes premature conceptualizations upon it, is afraid of the unknown and of novelty, is too much determined by his intrapersonal needs to be a good reporter of reality, is too easily frightened, is too eager for other people's approval, and so on.

There are at least three implications of this fact. First of all the scientist (or better, truth seeker in general) ought to be psychologically healthy rather than unhealthy to do the best work. Second, it may be expected that as a culture improves, thereby improving the health of all its citizens, truth seeking should

---

[2]For those readers who recognize that this is a revolutionary statement, and who feel the obligation to read further, I would urge struggling through *the* great book in the field, *Personal Knowledge* by Michael Polanyi (1958). If you have not studied this book, you dare not consider yourself prepared for the next century. If you don't have the time, the will, or the strength for this giant of a book, then I recommend my *Psychology of Science: A Reconnaissance* (Maslow, 1966) which has the virtue of being short and readable while making similar points. This chapter, these two books, and the other books touted in their bibliographies represent well enough the new humanistic *Zeitgeist* as it is reflected in the field of science.

improve, and third, we should expect that psychotherapy would improve the individual scientist in his or her individual function.

We already acknowledge as a fact that better social conditions tend to help the searcher for knowledge by our pressure for academic freedom, tenure, better salaries, and the like.[2]

chapter 16

Means Centering Versus Problem Centering

More and more attention has been given to the shortcomings and sins of "official" science. With the one major exception of Lynd's brilliant analysis (1939), discussion of the sources of these failings has, however, been neglected. This chapter will attempt to show that many of the weaknesses of orthodox science and particularly of psychology are consequences of a means- or technique-centered approach to the defining of science.

By *means centering,* I refer to the tendency to consider that the essence of science lies in its instruments, techniques, procedures, apparatus, and its methods rather than in its problems, questions, functions, or goals. In its unsophisticated form, means centering confuses scientists with engineers, physicians, dentists, laboratory technicians, glass blowers, urinanalysts, machine tenders, and so on. Means centering at the highest intellectual levels usually takes the form of making synonyms of science and scientific method.

OVERSTRESS ON TECHNIQUE

Inevitable stress on elegance, polish, technique, and apparatus has as a frequent consequence a playing down of meaningfulness, vitality, and significance of the problem and of creativeness in general. Almost any candidate for the Ph.D. in psychology will understand what this means in practice. A methodologically satisfactory experiment, whether trivial or not, is rarely criticized. A bold, groundbreaking problem, because it may be a "failure," is too often criticized to death before it is ever begun. Indeed criticism in the scientific literature seems usually to mean only criticism of method, technique, logic, and so forth. I do not recall seeing, in the literature with which I am familiar, any paper that criticized another paper for being unimportant, trivial, or inconsequential.[1]

The tendency is growing therefore to say that the dissertation problem itself does not matter—only so it be well done. In a word, it need no longer be a contribution to knowledge. Ph.D. candidates are required to know the techniques of their field and the already accumulated data in it. It is not usually stressed that good research ideas are also desirable. As a consequence it is possible for completely and obviously uncreative people to become "scientists."

At a lower level—in the teaching of science in the high school and college—similar results can be seen. The student is encouraged to identify science with directed manipulations of apparatus and with rote procedures learned out of a cook book—in a word, following other people's leads and repeating what other people have already discovered. Nowhere is it taught that a scientist is different from a technician or from a reader of books about science.

It is easy to misunderstand the point of these contentions. I do not wish to underplay method; I wish only to point out that even in science, means may easily be confused with ends. It is only the goals or ends of science that dignify and validate its methods. Working scientists must, of course, be concerned with their techniques, but only because they can help them achieve their proper ends, namely, the answering of important questions. Once they forget this, they become like the man spoken of by Freud who spent all his time polishing his glasses instead of putting them on and seeing with them.

Means centering tends to push into a commanding position in science the technicians and the "apparatus men," rather than the "question askers" and the problem solvers. Without wishing to create an extreme and unreal dichotomy, it is still possible to point out a difference between those who know only *how* to do and those who also know *what* to do. These former individuals, of whom there are always a large number, tend inevitably to become a class of priests in science, authorities on protocol, on procedure, and, so to speak, on ritual and ceremonial. While such people have been no more than a nuisance in the past, now that science becomes a matter of national and international policy, they may become an active danger. This trend is doubly dangerous because lay people understand manipulators far more easily than they do creators and theorists.

Means centering tends strongly to overvalue quantification indiscriminately and as an end in itself. This must be true because of the greater stress of means-centered science on *how* statements are made rather than on what is said. Elegance and precision are then counterposed to pertinence and breadth of implication.

Means-centered scientists tend, in spite of themselves, to fit their problems to their techniques rather than the contrary. Their beginning question tends to be Which problems can I attack with the techniques and equipment I now possess? rather than what it should more often be, Which are the most pressing, the most

---

[1]"But even the scholars were likely to work most at big monographs on little subjects. Original research they called it. What mattered was that the facts that they found had not been known before, not that they were worth knowing. Some other specialist might sooner or later make use of them. The specialists in all the universities wrote for one another, with the patience of mound builders, for mysterious ends" (Van Doren, 1936, p. 107). A "sportsman" is a man who sits and *watches* athletes.

crucial problems I could spend my time on? How else explain the fact that most run-of-the-mill scientists spend their lifetimes in a small area whose boundaries are defined, not by a basic question about the world, but by the limits of a piece of apparatus or of a technique? In psychology, few people see any humor in the concept of an "animal psychologist" or a "statistical psychologist," that is, individuals who do not mind working with *any* problem so long as they can use, respectively, their animals or their statistics. Ultimately this must remind us of the famous drunk who looked for his wallet, not where he had lost it, but under the street lamp, "because the light is better there," or of the doctor who gave all his patients fits because that was the only sickness he knew how to cure.

Means centering tends strongly to create a hierarchy of sciences, in which, quite perniciously, physics is considered to be more "scientific" than biology, biology than psychology, and psychology than sociology. Such an assumption of hierarchy is possible only on the basis of elegance, success, and precision of technique. From the point of view of a problem-centered science, such a hierarchy would never be suggested, for who could maintain that questions about unemployment, or race prejudice, or love are, in any intrinsic way, less important than questions about stars, or sodium, or kidney function?

Means centering tends to compartmentalize the sciences too strongly, to build walls between them that divide them into separate territories. Jacques Loeb, when asked whether he was a neurologist, a chemist, a physicist, a psychologist, or a philosopher, answered only, "I solve problems." Certainly this ought to be a more usual answer. And it would be well for science if it had more people like Loeb. But these desiderata are clearly discouraged by the philosophy that makes the scientist into a technician and an expert rather than a venturesome truth seeker, into one who *knows* rather than one who is *puzzled*.

If scientists looked on themselves as question askers and problem solvers rather than specialized technicians, there would now be something of a rush to the newest scientific frontier, to the psychological and social problems about which we know least and should know most. Why is it that there is so little traffic across these departmental borders? How does it happen that a hundred scientists prosecute physical or chemical research for every dozen who pursue the psychological problems? Which would be better for humanity, to put a thousand fine minds to producing better bombs (or even better penicillin) or to set them to work on the problems of nationalism or psychotherapy or exploitation?

Means centering in science creates too great a cleavage between scientists and other truth seekers, and between their various methods of searching after truth and understanding. If we define science as a search for truth, insight, and understanding, and as a concern with important questions, we must be hard put to differentiate between the scientists on the one hand, and the poets, artists, and philosophers on the other hand.[2] Their avowed problems may be the same. Ultimately, of course, a semantically honest differentiation should be made, and it

---

[2]"You must love the questions themselves."—Rilke.
   "We have learned all the answers, all the answers:
It is the questions that we do not know."—A. MacLeish, *The Hamlet of A. MacLeish*, Houghton Mifflin.

must be admitted that it would have to be mostly on the basis of difference in method and in techniques of guarding against mistakes. And yet it would clearly be better for science if this gap between the scientist and the poet and the philosopher were less abysmal than it is today. Means centering simply puts them into different realms; problem centering would conceive of them as mutually helpful collaborators. The biographies of most great scientists show that the latter is more nearly true than the former. Many of the greatest scientists have themselves been also artists and philosophers, and have often derived as much sustenance from philosophers as from their scientific colleagues.

MEANS CENTERING AND SCIENTIFIC ORTHODOXY

Means centering tends inevitably to bring into being a scientific orthodoxy, which in turn creates a heterodoxy. Questions and problems in science can rarely be formulated, classified, or put into a filing system. The questions of the past are no longer questions, but answers. The questions of the future have not yet come into existence. But it *is* possible to formulate and classify the methods and techniques of the past. These then are termed the "laws of scientific method." Canonized, crusted about with tradition, loyalty, and history, they tend to become binding upon the present day (rather than merely suggestive or helpful). In the hands of the less creative, the timid, the conventional, these "laws" become virtually a demand that we solve our present problems *only* as our forebears solved theirs.

Such an attitude is especially dangerous for the psychological and social sciences. Here the injunction to be truly scientific is usually translated as: Use the techniques of the physical and life sciences. Hence we have the tendency among many psychologists and social scientists to imitate old techniques rather than to create and invent the new ones made necessary by the fact that their degree of development, their problems, and their data are intrinsically different from those of the physical sciences. Tradition in science can be a dangerous blessing. Loyalty is an unqualified peril.

One main danger of scientific orthodoxy is that it tends to block the development of new techniques. If the laws of scientific method have already been formulated, it remains only to apply them. New methods, new ways of doing things, must inevitably be suspect, and have usually been greeted with hostility, for example, psychoanalysis, Gestalt psychology, Rorschach testing. The expectation of such hostility probably is partly to blame for the fact that there have not yet been invented the relational, holistic, and syndrome logics, statistics, and mathematics demanded by the new psychological and social sciences.

Ordinarily, the advance of science is a collaborative product. How else could limited individuals make important, even great, discoveries? When there is no collaboration, the advance is apt to stop dead until there shows up some giant who needs no help. Orthodoxy means the denial of help to the heterodox. Since few (of the heterodox, as well as of the orthodox) are geniuses, this implies continuous, smooth advance only for orthodox science. We may expect heterodox ideas to be held up for long periods of weary neglect or opposition, to break through rather suddenly (if they are correct), and then to become in turn orthodox.

Another, probably more important, danger of the orthodoxy fostered by means centering is that it tends to limit more and more the jurisdiction of science. Not only does it block the development of new techniques, it also tends to block the asking of many questions, on grounds that the reader might well expect by now that such questions cannot be answered by currently available techniques (e.g., questions about the subjective, questions about values, questions about religion). It is only such foolish grounds that make possible that unnecessary confession of defeat, that contradiction in terms, the concept of the "unscientific problem," as if there were *any* question that we dared not ask, and try to answer. Surely, anyone who had read and understood the history of science would not dare to speak of an *unsolvable* problem; he or she would speak only of problems that had not yet been solved. Phrased in this latter way, we have a clear incentive to action, to further exercise of ingenuity and inventiveness. Phrased in terms of current scientific orthodoxy—What can we do with scientific method (as we know it)?—we are encouraged to the opposite—to voluntarily imposed self-limitations, to abdication from huge areas of human interest. This tendency can go to the most incredible and dangerous extremes. It has even happened in recent discussions of congressional efforts to set up national research foundations that some physicists suggested the exclusion from its benefits of all the psychological and social sciences on the grounds that they were not "scientific" enough. On what possible basis could this statement have been made if not an exclusive respect for polished and successful techniques, and a complete lack of awareness of the question-asking nature of science and its rooting in human values and motives? How shall I as a psychologist translate this and other similar jibes from my physicist friends? Ought I to use their techniques? But these are useless for my problems. How would that get the psychological problems solved? Ought they not be solved? Or ought scientists to abdicate from the field completely and give it back to the theologians? Or is there perhaps an ad hominem sneer? Is it implied that the psychologists are stupid and the physicists intelligent? But on what grounds can such an inherently improbable statement be made? Impressions? Then I must report *my* impression that there are as many fools in any one scientific group as in any other. Which impression is more valid?

I am afraid that I can see no other possible explanation except one that covertly gives the primary place to technique—perhaps the only place.

Means-centered orthodoxy encourages scientists to be "safe and sound" rather than bold and daring. It makes the normal business of scientists seem to be moving ahead inch by inch on the well-laid-out road rather than cutting new paths through the unknown. It forces conservative rather than radical approaches to the not-yet-known. It tends to make them into settlers rather than pioneers.[3]

The proper place for scientists—once in a while at least—is in the midst of the unknown, the chaotic, the dimly seen, the unmanageable, the mysterious,

---

[3]"Geniuses are panzer-spearheads; their lightning advance into no-man's-land necessarily leaves their flanks unprotected" (Koestler, 1945, p. 241).

the not-yet-well-phrased. This is where a problem-oriented science would have them be as often as necessary. And this is where they are discouraged from going by a means-stressing approach to science.

Overstress on methods and techniques encourages scientists to think (1) that they are more objective and less subjective than they actually are and (2) that they need not concern themselves with values. Methods are ethically neutral; problems and questions may not be, for sooner or later, they involve all the knotty arguments about values. One way of avoiding the problem of values is to stress the techniques of science rather than the goals of science. Indeed, it seems probable that one of the main roots of the means-centered orientation in science is the strenuous effort to be as objective (nonvalued) as possible.

But as we have seen in Chapter 15, science was not, is not, and cannot be completely objective, which is to say, independent of human values. Furthermore, it is highly debatable whether it ought even to *try* to be (that is, *completely* objective rather than as objective as it is possible for human beings to be). All the mistakes listed in this chapter attest to the dangers of attempting to neglect the shortcomings of human nature. Not only do neurotics pay a huge subjective price for their vain attempts, but ironically enough, they also become progressively poorer and poorer thinkers.

Because of this fancied independence of values, standards of worth become steadily more blurred. If means-centering philosophies were extreme (which they rarely are), and if they were quite consistent (which they dare not be for fear of obviously foolish consequences), there would be no way to distinguish between an important experiment and an unimportant one. There could be only technically well-prosecuted experiments and technically poorly prosecuted experiments.[4] Using only methodological criteria, the most trivial research could demand as much respect as the most fruitful one. Of course, this does not actually happen in an extreme way, but this is only because of appeal to criteria and standards other than methodological ones. However, although this mistake is rarely seen in a blatant form, it *is* often enough seen in a less obvious form. The journals of science are full of instances that illustrate the point, that what is not worth doing is not worth doing well.

If science were no more than a set of rules and procedures, what difference would there be between science on the one hand, and on the other, chess, alchemy, "umbrellaology," or the practice of dentistry?[5]

---

[4] "A scientist is called 'great' not so much because he has solved a problem as because he has posed a problem the solution of which . . . will make for real progress" (Cantril, 1950).

[5] Sir Richard Livingstone, of Corpus Christi College, Oxford, has defined a technician as "a man who understands everything about his job except its ultimate purpose and its place in the order of the universe." Someone else, in similar vein, has defined an expert as a person who avoids all the small errors while sweeping on to the grand fallacy.

chapter 17

Stereotyping Versus True Cognition

Even where it (reason) confesses that it does not know the object presented to it, it believes that its ignorance consists only in not knowing which one of its time-honored categories suits the new object. In what drawer, ready to open, shall we put it? In what garment, already cut out, shall we clothe it? Is it this, or that, or the other thing? And "this," and "that," and "the other thing" are always something already conceived, already known. The idea that for a new object we might have to create a new concept, perhaps a new method of thinking, is deeply repugnant to us. The history of philosophy is there, however, and shows us the eternal conflict of systems, the impossibility of satisfactorily getting the real into the ready-made garments of our ready-made concepts, the necessity of making to measure.

HENRI BERGSON
Creative Evolution, 1944, pp. 55–56

There is an important difference for various fields of psychology between stereotyped cognition and fresh, humble, receptive, Taoistic cognition of the concrete, the idiosyncratic, the unique, innocent cognition without preconceptions and expectations, and without the intrusion of wishes, hopes, fears, or anxieties. Most acts of cognition, it would seem, are stale, careless recognitions and catalogings of stereotypes. Such a lazy classifying under preexisting rubrics is profoundly different from actual, concrete perceiving with full and undivided attention of the many-sidedness of the unique phenomenon. It is only from such cognition that full appreciation and savoring of any experience can come.

In this chapter I shall discuss some of the problems of cognition in the light of these theoretical considerations. The writer especially hopes to communicate some of his conviction that much of what passes for cognition is actually a sub-stitute for it, a second-hand trick made necessary by the exigencies of living in a flux-and-process reality without being willing to acknowledge this fact. Because reality is dynamic, and because the average Western mind can cognize well only what is static, much of our attending, perceiving, learning, remembering, and thinking actually deals with staticized abstractions from reality or with theoretical constructions rather than with reality itself.

Lest this chapter be taken as a polemic against abstractions and concepts, let me make it clear that we cannot possibly live without concepts, generalizations, and abstractions. The point is that they must be experientially based rather than empty or helium-filled. They must be rooted in concrete reality and tied to it. They must have meaningful content rather than being mere words, mere labels, mere abstractions. This chapter deals with pathological abstracting, "reduction to the abstract," and with the dangers of abstracting.

ATTENTION

Insofar as the concept of attending differs at all from the concept of perceiving, it is in a relatively greater stress on selective, preparatory, organizing, and mo-bilizing acions. These need not be pure and fresh responses that are determined entirely by the nature of the reality attended to. It is a commonplace that attending is determined as well by the nature of the individual organism, by the person's interests, motives, prejudices, past experiences, and so forth.

What is more to our point, however, is the fact that it is possible to discern in the attending responses the difference between fresh, idiosyncratic attending to the unique event, and stereotyped, categorized recognition in the outside world of a set of categories that already exist in the mind of the attending person. That is, attending may be no more than a recognition or discovery in the world of what we ourselves have already put there—a sort of prejudging of experience before it happens. It may be, so to speak, a rationalization for the past, or an attempt to maintain the status quo, rather than a true recognition of change, novelty, and flux. This can be achieved by attending only to that which is already known, or by forcing the new into the shape of the familiar.

The advantages and disadvantages for the organism of this stereotyping of attention are equally obvious. It is evident that full attention is not needed for mere classification of an experience, which in turn means saving of energy and effort. Categorizing is definitely less fatiguing than whole-hearted attending. Furthermore, it does not call for concentration, it does not demand *all* the re-sources of the organism. Concentrated attention, which is necessary for the per-ceiving and understanding of an important or novel problem is, as we all know, extremely wearing, and is therefore relatively rare. Testimomy for this conclusion is found in the common preference for streamlined reading, condensed novels, digest magazines, stereotyped movies, cliché-laden conversation, and, in general, avoidance of real problems, or at least a strong preference for stereotyped pseu-dosolutions.

Rubricizing or categorizing is a partial, token, or nominal response rather than a total one. This makes possible automaticity of behavior (i.e., doing several things at the same time), which in turn means making possible higher activities by permitting lower activities to be carried on in a reflexlike fashion. In a word, we do not have to notice or pay attention to the familiar elements of experience.[1]

There is a paradox involved here, for it is simultaneously true that (1) we tend *not* to notice that which does not fit into the already constructed set of rubrics (i.e., the strange) and (2) it is the unusual, the unfamiliar, the dangerous, or threatening that are *most* attention compelling. An unfamiliar stimulus may be either dangerous (a noise in the dark) or not (new curtains on the windows). Fullest attention is given to the unfamiliar-dangerous; least attention is given to the familiar-safe; an intermediate amount is given to the unfamiliar-safe or else it is transformed into the familiar-safe, that is, categorized.[2]

There is an interesting speculation that proceeds from the curious tendency that the novel and strange either attract no attention at all or attract it overwhelmingly. It would seem that a large proportion of our (less healthy) population responds with attention only to threatening experiences. It is as if attention were to be regarded only as a response to danger and as a warning of the necessity for an emergency response. These people brush aside experiences that are nonthreatening and not dangerous as therefore not being worthy of attention or any other response, cognitive or emotional. For them, life is either a meeting of dangers or relaxation between dangers.

But there are some people for whom this is not so. These are the people who will respond not only to dangerous situations. Probably feeling more secure and self-confident, they can afford the luxury of responding to, noticing, and even thrilling with experiences that are not dangerous but pleasantly exciting, and so on. It has been pointed out that this positive response, whether mild or strong, whether a slight titillation or an overwhelming ecstasy, is, like the emergency response, a mobilization by the autonomic nervous system, involving the viscera and the rest of the organism. The main difference between these experiences is that one seems to be felt introspectively as pleasant, the other as unpleasant. With this observation, we see that human beings not only adapt to the world in a passive way but also enjoy it and even impose themselves upon it actively. The factor whose variation seems to account for most of these differences is what may loosely be called mental health. For relatively anxious people, attending is more exclusively an emergency mechanism, and the world tends somewhat to be divided simply into the dangerous and the safe.

The truest contrast with categorizing attention is probably furnished by Freud's concept of "free floating attention."[3] Observe that Freud recommends pas-

---

[1] For experimental examples, see Bartlett's excellent study (1932).

[2] "Nothing is more congenial from babyhood to the end of life than to be able to assimilate the new to the old, to meet each threatening violator or burster of our well known series of concepts, as it comes in, see through its unwontedness and ticket it off as an old friend in disguise. . . . We feel neither curiosity nor wonder concerning things so far beyond us that we have no concepts to refer them to or standards by which to measure them" (James, 1890, Vol. II, p. 110).

[3] "For as soon as attention is deliberately concentrated in a certain degree, one begins to select from the material before one; one point will be fixed in the mind with particular clearness and some other consequently disregarded, and in this selection one's expectations of one's inclinations will be

sive rather than active attending on the grounds that active attention tends to be an imposition of a set of expectations upon the real world. Such expectations can drown out the voice of reality, if it be weak enough. Freud recommends that we be yielding, humble, passive, interested only in finding out what reality has to say to us, concerned only to allow the intrinsic structure of the material to determine that which we perceive. This all amounts to saying that we must treat the experience as if it were unique and unlike anything else in the world and that our only effort must be to apprehend it in its own nature, rather than to try to see how it fits into our theories, our schemes, and our concepts. This is in the most complete sense a recommendation to problem centering and against ego centering. To the fullest extent possible the ego, its experiences, and its preconceptions, its hopes, and its fears are to be put aside if we are to apprehend the per se intrinsic nature of the experience before us.

It may be helpful to make the familiar (even stereotyped) contrast between the approach to an experience by the scientist and by the artist. If we may allow oursleves to think of such abstractions as the true scientist and the true artist, it is probably accurate to contrast their approach to any experience by saying that the scientist fundamentally seeks to classify the experience, to relate it to all other experiences, to put it into its place in a unitary philosophy of the world, to look for the respects in which this experience is similar to and different from all other experiences. Scientists tend to put a name or a label upon the experience, tend to put it into its place, in a word, to classify it. Artists are most interested in the unique and idiosyncratic character of their experience. They treat each experience as an individual. Each apple is unique, different, and so also each model, each tree, each head—no one is quite like any other. As a critic said of a certain artist, "He sees what others only look at." They are in no way interested in classifying the experience or placing it in any mental card catalog that they may have. It is their task to see the experience fresh, and then if they have the talent, to freeze the experience in some way so that perhaps less perceptive people may also see it fresh. Simmel said it nicely: "The scientist *sees* something because he *knows* something—the artist, however, *knows* something because he *sees* it."

Like all stereotypes, these are dangerous. It is an implied point of this chapter that scientists would do well to become more intuitive, more artistic, and more appreciative and respectful of raw, direct experience. Likewise, the study

---

followed. This is just what must not be done, however; if one's expectations are followed in this selection there is the danger of never finding anything but what is already known, and if one follows one's inclinations anything which is to be perceived will most certainly be falsified. It must not be forgotten that the meaning of the thing one hears is, at all events, for the most part, only recognizable later on.

"It will be seen, therefore, that the principle of evenly-distributed attention is the necessary corollary to the demand on the patient to communicate everything that occurs to him without criticism or selection. If the physician behaves otherwise he is throwing aside most of the advantage to be gained by the patients' obedience to the 'fundamental rule of psycho-analysis.' For the physicians the rule may be expressed thus: All conscious exertion is to be withheld from the capacity for attention, and one's 'unconscious memory' is to be given full play; or to express it in terms of technique, pure and simple: One has simply to listen and not to trouble to keep in mind anything in particular" (Freud, 1924, pp. 324–325).

and understanding of reality as seen by science should deepen the artist's reactions to the world, in addition to making them more valid and adult. The injunction to both artist and scientist is actually the same: "See reality whole."

PERCEPTION

Stereotyping is a concept that can apply not only to the social psychology of prejudice, but also to the basic process of perceiving. Perceiving may be something other than the absorption or registration of the intrinsic nature of the real event. It is more often a classifying, ticketing, or labeling of the experience rather than an examination of it, and ought therefore to be called by a name other than true perceiving. What we do in stereotyped perceiving is parallel to the use of clichés and hackneyed phrases in speaking. For instance, it is possible in being introduced to another human being to react to her or him freshly, to try to understand or to perceive this individual as a unique individual, not quite like anybody else living. More often what we do, however, is to ticket or label or place the person. We place the person in a category, not as a unique individual, but as an example of some concept or as a representation of a category. In other words, the person engaged in stereotyped perceiving ought to be compared, if we wish to be honest, to a file clerk rather than a camera.

Among the many examples of stereotyping in perceiving, we may cite the tendency to perceive

1. The familiar and hackneyed rather than the unfamiliar and fresh
2. The schematized and abstract rather than the actual
3. The organized, structured, the univalent rather than the chaotic, unorganized, and ambiguous
4. The named or namable rather than the unnamed and unnamable
5. The meaningful rather than the meaningless
6. The conventional rather than the unconventional
7. The expected rather than the unexpected

Furthermore, where the event is unfamiliar, concrete, ambiguous, unnamed, meaningless, unconventional, or unexpected, we show a strong tendency to twist or force or shape the event into a form that is more familiar, more abstract, more organized, and so on. We tend to perceive events more easily as representatives of categories than in their own right, as unique and idiosyncratic.

Numerous illustrations of each of these tendencies can be found in the Rorschach test, the literatures of Gestalt psychology, of projective testing, and of the theory of art. Hayakawa (1949, p. 103), in this last area, cites the example of an art teacher who "is in the habit of telling his pupils that they are unable to draw any individual arm because they think of it as *an* arm; and because they think of it as an arm they think they know what it ought to be." Schachtel's book is full of fascinating examples (1959).

It is obvious that one needs to know less about a stimulus object for the purpose of filing it in an already constructed system of categories than for the purpose of understanding and appreciating it. True perception, which would encompass the object as unique, play over all of it, soak it in, and understand it, would obviously take infinitely more time than the fraction of a second that is all that is necessary for labeling and cataloging.

It is also probable that categorizing is far less efficient than the fresh perception, mostly because of this already mentioned characteristic of being possible in a fraction of a second. Only the most outstanding characteristics can then be used to determine the reaction, and these can very easily give a false lead. Categorizing perception then is an invitation to mistakes.

These mistakes become doubly important because categorizing perception also makes it less probable that any original mistake will be corrected. A thing or person that has been placed in a category tends to be kept there, because any behavior that contradicts the stereotype can be regarded simply as an exception that need not be taken seriously. For instance, if we have become convinced for some reason that a person is dishonest, and if then, in one particular card game, we try to catch him, only to fail, we ordinarily continue to call him a thief, assuming that he was honest for ad hoc reasons, perhaps out of fear of detection or out of laziness or the like. If we are profoundly enough convinced of his dishonesty, it may make no difference if we *never* catch him in a dishonest act. He might then be regarded simply as a thief who happens to be afraid to be dishonest with us. Or contradictory behavior may be regarded as interesting, in the sense of being not characteristic of the essence of the person but rather only superficially put on.

Indeed it may be that the concept of stereotyping may furnish us with a good part of the answer to the age-old problem of how people can continually believe in falsehood even when truth stares them in the face year after year. We know it is customary to consider this imperviousness to evidence as entirely explained by repression, or in general, motivational forces. There is no doubt that this statement is also true. The question is whether it is the whole truth, and in and of itself a sufficient explanation. Our discussion indicates that there are also other reasons for being blind to evidence. When we ourselves are on the receiving end of a stereotyping attitude, we get some inkling of the violence that can be done by such a process. We feel insulted and unappreciated if we are casually put into a parcel with a lot of other people from whom we feel different in many ways. But it is impossible to improve on William James's statement on the subject: "The first thing the intellect does with an object is to class it along with something else. But any object that is infinitely important to us and awakens our devotion feels to us also as if it must be *sui generis* and unique. Probably a crab would be filled with a sense of personal outrage if it could hear us class it without ado or apology as a crustacean, and thus dispose of it. 'I am no such thing,' it would say; 'I am *myself, myself* alone' " (1958, p. 10).

LEARNING

A habit is an attempt to solve a present problem by using a previously successful solution. This implies that there must be (1) a placing of the present problem in a certain category of problems, and (2) a selection of the most efficient problem solution for this particular category of problems. Classification is therefore inevitably involved.

The phenomenon of habit illustrates best a point that is also true of categorized attention, perceiving, thinking, expression, and the like, namely that they are, in effect, attempts to "freeze the world." In actuality, the world is a perpetual flux and all things are in process. In theory, nothing in the world is static (even though for *practical* purposes, many things are). If we are to take theory quite seriously, then each experience, each event, each behavior is in some way or other (whether important or unimportant) different from every other experience, behavior, and so on that has occurred in the world before or will ever occur again.[4]

It would seem reasonable, then, as Whitehead has repeatedly pointed out, to base our theories and philosophies of science and common sense squarely on this basic and unavoidable fact. The truth is that most of us do not do this. Even though our most sophisticated scientists and philosophers have long ago discarded the old concepts of empty space and enduring things pushed around aimlessly in it, these verbally discarded concepts still live on as a basis for all our less intellectual reactions. Though the world of change and growth is and must be accepted, this is rarely done emotionally and with enthusiasm. We are still deeply Newtonian.

All actions of categorization may then be understood as efforts to freeze or staticize or stop the motion of a moving, changing process world in order to be able to handle it, for it is as if we could handle this world only when it is not in motion. An example of this tendency is the ingenious trick that static-atomistic mathematicians have invented in order to treat motion and change in a motionless way, namely, the calculus. For the purposes of this chapter, psychological examples are more pertinent, however, and it is necessary to pound home the thesis that habits, and indeed all reproductive learning, are examples of this tendency by statically minded people to freeze a process world into temporary immobility, since they cannot manage or cope with a world in a flux.

To the extent that rubricizing is a premature freezing of conclusions because the person is afraid of the unknown, it is motivated by the hope of anxiety reduction and avoidance. Persons who have comfortable relations with the unknown, or what is almost the same thing, can tolerate ambiguity (Frenkel-Brunswik, 1949), are therefore less motivated in their perceptions. The close tie between motivation and perception had best be regarded as a somewhat psychopathological phenomenon, rather than as healthy. Very bluntly put, this tie is symptomatic of a slightly sick organism. In self-actualizing people it is at a minimum; in neurotic and psychotic people it is at a maximum, as in delusions and hallucinations. One

---

[4]"No two things are alike, and no one stays the same. If you are clearly aware of this, it is quite all right to act as though some things were alike, and to act as though some things stayed the same—to act according to habit. It is all right, because a difference to be a difference, must make a difference, and some differences don't, sometimes. So long as you realize that there always are differences nonetheless, and that you have to judge whether they do make any difference, you can be trusted with a habit, because you will know when to set it aside. No habit is foolproof. Habits are useful to people who do not depend on them or insist on following them, regardless of circumstances; for less judicious individuals, habits tend to make for inefficiency, stupidity, and danger" (Johnson, 1946, p. 199).

way of describing this difference is to say that cognition in the healthy is relatively unmotivated; in the sick it is relatively motivated.

Habits are then conservative mechanisms, as James long ago pointed out (1890). Why is this so? For one thing, because any learned reaction, merely by existing, blocks the formation of other learned reactions to the same problem. But there is another reason, just as important, but ordinarily neglected by the learning theorists, namely, that learning is not only of muscular responses but of affective preferences as well. Not only do we learn to speak English but we learn to like and prefer it (Maslow, 1937).[5] Learning is not then a completely neutral process. We cannot say, "If this reaction is a mistake, it is easy enough to unlearn it or replace it with the right reaction," for by learning, we have, to some degree, committed ourselves and our loyalties. Thus if it is our desire to learn to speak French well, it may be better not to learn it at all if the only available teacher has a bad accent; it could be more efficient to wait until a good teacher is available. For this same reason we must disagree with those in science who are very airy in their attitude toward hypotheses and theories. "Even a false theory is better than none," they say. The true situation is not as simple as this, if the foregoing considerations have any validity. As a Spanish proverb says, "Habits are at first cobwebs, then cables."

These criticisms by no means apply to all learning; they apply only to atomistic and reproductive learning, that is, recognition and recall of isolated ad hoc reactions. Many psychologists write as if this were the only way in which the past could have an influence upon the present, or in which the lessons of past experience may profitably be used to solve present problems. This is a naive assumption, for much of what is actually learned in the world (e.g., the most important influences of the past) is neither atomistic nor reproductive. The most important influence of the past, the most influential type of learning, is what we may call character or intrinsic learning (Maslow, 1968a), that is, all the effects on character of all our experiences. Thus, experiences are not acquired by the organism one by one like so many coins; if they have any deep effect at all, they change the whole person. Thus the influence of some tragic experience would be to change him or her from an immature person to a more mature adult, wiser, more tolerant, more humble, better able to solve *any* of the problems of adult life. The contrasting theory would be that he or she had changed in no way except by the ad hoc acquisition of a technique of managing or solving such and such

---

[5]*Anthologistics*

"Since one anthologist put in his book
Sweet things by Morse, Bone, Potter, Bliss and Brook,
All subsequent anthologists, of course,
Have quoted Bliss, Brook, Potter, Bone and Morse.
For, should some rash anthologist make free
To print selections, say, from you and me,
Omitting with a judgment all his own
The classic Brook, Morse, Potter, Bliss and Bone,
Contemptuous reviewers, passing by
Our verses, would unanimously cry,
'What manner of anthology is this
That leaves out Bone, Brook, Potter, Morse and Bliss!' " (Guiterman, 1939)

a particular type of problem (e.g., the death of mother). Such an example is far more important, far more useful, far more paradigmatic than the usual examples of blind association of one nonsense syllable with another, which experiments, in our opinion, have to do with nothing in the world except other nonsense syllables.[6]

If the world is in process, every moment is a new and unique one. Theoretically speaking, *all* problems must be novel. The typical problem, according to process theory, is the problem that has never been faced before and that is, in essential ways, unlike any other problem. That problem that very much resembles past problems is then, according to this theory, to be understood as a special case rather than a paradigmatic one. If this is so, recourse to the past for ad hoc solutions is as likely to be dangerous as helpful. My belief is that actual observation will show this to be practically as well as theoretically true. In any case, nobody, whatever his or her theoretical bias, will argue about the fact that at least *some* of the problems of life are novel and must therefore have novel solutions.

From the biological point of view, habits play a double role in adaptation because they are simultaneously necessary and dangerous. They necessarily imply something which is not true, that is, a constant, unchanging, static world, and yet are commonly regarded as one of the human being's most efficient tools of adaptation, which certainly implies a changing, dynamic world. A habit is an already formed reaction to a situation or answer to a problem. Because it is already formed, it develops a certain inertia and resistance to change. But when a situation changes, our reaction to it should also change or be ready to change quickly. Therefore, the presence of a habit may be worse than no reaction at all, since the habit guarantees resistance to and delay in building up the newly necessary reaction to the new situation.

It may help to make this clearer if we describe this paradox from another point of view. We may then say that habits are built up to save time, effort, and thought in dealing with recurrent situations. If a problem comes up again and again in similar form, we certainly can save a good deal of thought by having available some habitual answer that can automatically be trotted out to deal with this recurrent problem whenever it arises. Thus a habit is a response to a repetitive, unchanging, familiar problem. This is why it is possible to say that a habit is an as-if reaction—"as if the world were static, unchanging, and constant." This interpretation is borne out, of course, by the uniform stress upon repetition by those psychologists who are impressed with the primary importance of habit as an adjustive mechanism.

---

[6]"Memory, as we have tried to prove, is not a faculty of putting away recollections in a drawer, or of inscribing them in a register. There is no register, no drawer; there is not even, properly speaking, a faculty, for a faculty works intermittently, when it will or when it can, whilst the piling up of the past upon the past goes without relaxation. . . .

"But, even though we may have no distinct idea of it, we feel vaguely that our past remains present to us. What are we, in fact, what is our *character,* if not the condensation of the history that we have lived from our birth—nay, even before our birth, since we bring with us prenatal dispositions? Doubtless we think with only a small part of our past, but it is with our entire past, including the original bent of our soul, that we desire, will and act. Our past, then, as a whole, is made manifest to us in its impulse; it is felt in the form of idea" (Bergson, 1944, pp. 7–8).

A good deal of the time this is just as it should be, for there is no doubt that many of our problems are actually repetitive, familiar, and relatively unchanging. The person who is engaged in what are called the higher activities, thinking, inventing, creating, finds that these activities demand, as a prerequisite, elaborate sets of innumerable habits that automatically solve the petty problems of everyday life, so that the creator is free to give energy to the so-called higher problems. But a contradiction is involved—even a paradox. In actual fact, the world is not static, familiar, repetitive, and unchanging. Instead, it is constantly in flux, ever new, always developing into something else, shifting, and changing. We need not argue as to whether this is a fair characterization of every aspect of the world; we can avoid unnecessary metaphysical debate by assuming for the sake of argument that some aspects of the world are constant, while some are not. If this is granted, then it must also be granted that however useful habits may be for the constant aspects of the world, they are positively a hindrance and an impediment when the organism has to deal with the changing, fluctuating aspects of the world with problems which are unique, novel, never before met with.[7]

Here then we have the paradox. Habits are simultaneously necessary and dangerous, useful and harmful. They undoubtedly save us time, effort, and thought, but at a big expense. They are a prime weapon of adaptation and yet they hinder adaptation. They are problem solutions and yet in the long run they are the antonyms of fresh, uncategorized thinking, that is to say, of solutions to new problems. Though useful in adjusting ourselves to the world,[8] they often hinder us in our inventiveness and creativeness, which is to say they tend to prevent our adjusting the world to ourselves. Finally, they tend to *replace*, in a lazy way, true and fresh attending, perceiving, learning, and thinking.

THINKING

In this area, categorizing consists of (1) having only stereotyped problems, and/ or (2) using only stereotyped techniques for solving these problems, and/or (3) having, in advance of all life's problems, sets of ready-made, cut and dried solutions and answers. These three tendencies add up to an almost complete guarantee against creativeness or inventiveness.[9]

---

[7]"The picture is one of human beings confronted by a world in which they can live and be masters only as they learn to match its infinite diversity by increasing delicacy of response, and as they discover ways to escape from the complete sway of immediate circumstances" (Bergson, 1944, p. 301).

"Our freedom, in the very moments by which it is affirmed, creates the growing habits that will stifle it if it fails to renew itself by a constant effort: it is dogged by automatism. The most living thought becomes frigid in the formula that expresses it. The word turns against the idea. The letter kills the spirit" (Bergson, 1944, p. 141).

[8]It might be added that reproductive memory is much more difficult *unless* a set of categories (frame of reference) is available. The interested reader is referred to Bartlett's excellent book (1932) for experimental support for this conclusion. Schachtel (1959) is brilliant on the subject.

[9]"Clarity and orderliness enable the possessor to deal with foreseen situations. They are necessary foundations for the maintenance of existing social situations. And yet they are not enough. Transcendence of mere clarity and order is necessary for dealing with the unforeseen, for progress,

Stereotyped Problems

To start with, the first effort of that person who tends strongly to categorize will ordinarily be to avoid or overlook problems of any kind. In most extreme form this is exemplified by those compulsive-obsessive patients who regulate and order every corner of their lives because they dare not face anything unexpected. Such people are severely threatened by any problem that demands more than a ready-made answer, that is, that demands self-confidence, courage, security.

If the problem *must* be perceived, the first effort is to place the problem and to see it as a representative of a familiar category (since the familiar does not produce anxiety). The attempt is to discover, "Into which class of previously experienced problems can this particular one be placed?" or "Into which category of problems does this fit—or can it be squeezed?" Such a placing reaction is possible, of course, only on the basis of perceived resemblances. I do not wish to go into the difficult problem of similarity; it is sufficient to point out that this perception of resemblances need not be a humble, passive registration of the intrinsic nature of the realities perceived. This is proved by the fact that various individuals, classifying in terms of idiosyncratic sets of categories, can nevertheless *all* be successful in stereotyping the experience. Such people do not like to be at a loss and will classify all experiences that cannot be overlooked, even if they find it necessary to cut, squeeze, or distort the experience.

Stereotyped Techniques

Generally, one of the main advantages of categorizing is that along with successful placing of the problem goes an automatically available set of techniques for handling this problem. This is not the only reason for categorizing. That the tendency to place a problem is very deeply motivated is seen, for instance, in the physician who feels more easy in the presence of a known, though incurable, disease than in the presence of a completely mysterious set of symptoms.

If one has handled this same problem many times before, the proper machinery will be well oiled and ready to use. Of course, this means a strong tendency to do things as they have been done before, and as we have seen, habitual solutions carry disadvantages as well as advantages. As advantages we may cite again ease of execution, energy saving, automaticity, affective preference, anxiety saving, and so on. The main disadvantages are loss of flexibility, adaptability, and creative inventiveness, that is, the usual consequences of assuming that this dynamic world can be treated as if it were static.

---

for excitement. Life degenerates when enclosed within the shackles of mere conformation. A power of incorporating vague and disorderly elements of experience is essential for the advance into novelty" (Whitehead, 1938, p. 108).

"The essence of life is to be found in the frustrations of established order. The Universe refuses the deadening influence of complete conformity. And yet in its refusal, it passes toward novel order as a primary requisite for important experience. We have to explain the aim at forms of order, and the aim at novelty of order, and the measure of success, and the measure of failure" (Whitehead, 1938, p. 119).

Stereotyped Conclusions

Probably the best-known example of this process is rationalization. This and similar processes may be defined for our purposes as having a ready-made idea or foregone conclusion and then devoting a good deal of intellectual activity to supporting this conclusion or finding evidence for it. ("I don't like that fellow and I'm going to find a good reason why.") This is the kind of activity that has only a thinking-like facade. It is not thinking in the best sense because it comes to its conclusions irrespective of the nature of the problem. The knitting of the brow, the heated discussions, the straining after evidence are all so many smoke screens; the conclusion was fated before the thinking ever began. Often enough even the facade is lacking; people may simply *believe* without even making the gesture of seeming to think. This takes even less effort than rationalizing.

It is possible for a person to live by a set of ready-made ideas that were acquired complete and entire during the first decade of life and that have never and shall never be changed in the slightest degree. It is true that such a person may have a high IQ. He or she may therefore be able to spend a good deal of time in intellectual activity, selecting out from the world whatever bits of evidence support his or her ready-made ideas. We cannot deny that this sort of activity may occasionally be of some use to the world, and yet it seems clearly desirable to make some sort of verbal differentiation between productive, creative thinking on the one hand and even the most skillful rationalizing on the other. The occasional advantages of rationalizing are a small matter when weighed against the more impressive phenomena of blindness to the real world, imperviousness to new evidence, distortion in perceiving and remembering, the loss of modifiability and adaptability to a changing world, and other indications that the mind has ceased to develop.

But rationalization need not be our only example. It is also categorizing when the problem is used as a stimulus to associations from among which are chosen those that best fit the particular occasion.

It would seem that categorized thinking has a special affinity for and relationship to reproductive learning. The three types of processes that we have listed could easily be dealt with as special forms of habit activity. There is clearly involved a special reference to the past. Problem solving becomes little more than a technique of classifying and solving any new problem in the light of past experience. Thinking of this type then often amounts to no more than a shuffling about and rearrangement of previously acquired habits and memories of the reproductive type.

The contrast with more holistic-dynamic thinking can be seen more clearly when we understand that this latter type of thinking is more clearly allied to the perceptual processes than to the memory processes. The main effort in holistic thinking is perceiving as clearly as possible the intrinsic nature of the problem with which one is confronted. The problem is examined carefully in its own right and in its own style almost as if no other such problem had been met before. The effort is to ferret out its own intrinsic, per se nature, "to perceive *in* a problem its solution" (Katona, 1940; see also Wertheimer, 1959), whereas in associative thinking it is rather to see how one problem relates to or resembles other problems previously experienced.

In a practical sense, in terms of behavior, this principle can be reduced to a sort of motto: "I don't know—let's see." That is to say, whenever one is confronted by a new situation one does not unhesitatingly respond to it in some way definitely decided upon in advance. It is rather as though one were to say, "I don't know—let's see," with a sensitiveness to any respects in which *this* situation might be different from previous ones, and with a readiness to make appropriate reactions accordingly.

This is not to imply that past experience is not used in holistic thinking. Of course it is. The point is that it is used in a different way, as has been described in the discussion of character or intrinsic learning in the preceding section, "Learning." That associative thinking occurs there is no doubt. The debate is rather over which kind of thinking shall be used as the centering point, as the paradigm, as the ideal model. The contention of the holistic-dynamic theorists is that thinking activity, if it carries any meaning at all, by definition has the meaning of creativeness, uniqueness, ingenuity, and inventiveness. Thinking is the technique whereby humanity creates something new, which in turn implies that thinking must be revolutionary in the sense of occasionally conflicting with what has already been concluded. If it conflicts with an intellectual status quo it is then the *opposite* of habit, or memory, or what we have already learned, for the simple reason that it must *by definition* contradict what we have already learned. If our past learning and our habits work well, we can respond automatically, habitually, and familiarly. That is to say, we do not have to think. From this point of view, thinking is seen as the opposite of learning, rather than as a type of learning. If we were permitted a slight exaggeration, thinking might almost be defined as the ability to *break* our habits and to *disregard* our past experiences.

Another dynamic aspect is involved in the kind of truly creative thinking exemplified by the great achievements of human history. This is its characteristic boldness, daring, and courage. If these words are not *quite* apropos in this connection, they come close enough, as we can see if we think of the contrast between a timid child and a brave child. The timid child must cling closer to its mother, who represents safety, familiarity, and protection; the bolder child is freer to venture forth and can go farther from home base. The thinking process that parallels the timid clinging to the mother is the equally timid clinging to habit. The bold thinker—which is almost a redundancy, like saying a thinking thinker—must be able to break free of the past, of habit, expectation, learning, custom, and convention, and to be free of anxiety whenever venturing out of the safe and familiar harbor.

Another type of stereotyped conclusion is furnished by those instances in which individuals' opinions are formed by imitation and/ or prestige suggestion. These are generally considered to be underlying and basic trends in healthy human nature. It would probably be more accurate to consider them examples of mild psychopathology, or at least something very close to it. When important enough problems are involved, they are primarily responses to an unstructured situation, which has no fixed frame of reference, by overanxious, overconventionalized, or overlazy people (people without an opinion of their own, people who do not know what their opinion is, people who mistrust their own opinions).[10]

It would seem that a fairly large proportion of the conclusions and problem solutions that we come to in the most basic areas of life seem to be of this sort, in which, while we think, we look out of the corner of our eyes to see what conclusion the other people are coming to so that we can also come to it. Obviously such conclusions are not thoughts in the truest sense of the word, that is, dictated by the nature of the problem, but rather stereotyped conclusions picked up whole from other people whom we trust more than ourselves.

As might be expected, such a position has certain implications for helping us to understand why conventional education in this country falls so far short of its goals. We shall stress only one point here, namely, that education makes little effort to teach individuals to examine reality directly and freshly. Rather it gives them a complete set of prefabricated spectacles with which to look at the world in every aspect, such as what to believe, what to like, what to approve of, what to feel guilty about. Rarely is each person's individuality made much of, rarely is he or she encouraged to be bold enough to see reality in his or her own style, or to be iconoclastic or different. Proof for the contention of stereotyping in higher education can be obtained in practically any college catalog, in which all of shifting, ineffable, and mysterious reality is neatly divided into three credit slices which, by some miraculous coincidence, are exactly 15 weeks long, and which fall apart neatly, as a tangerine does, into completely independent and mutually exclusive departments.[11] If ever there was a perfect example of a set of categories imposed *upon* reality rather than *by* reality, this is it.

This is all obvious enough, but what is less obvious is what to do about it. One idea strongly suggested by an examination of stereotyped thinking is a decreased absorption with categories and an increased concern with fresh experiences, with concrete and particular realities. On this point we cannot improve on Whitehead's statements.

> My own criticism of our traditional educational methods is that they are far too much occupied with intellectual analysis, and with the acquirement of formularized information. What I mean is, that we neglect to strengthen habits of concrete appreciation of the individual facts in their full interplay of emergent values, and that we merely emphasize abstract formulations which ignore this aspect of the interplay of diverse values.

> At present our education combines a thorough study of a few abstractions, with a slighter study of a large number of abstractions. We are too exclusively

[10]An excellent discussion of the dynamics of the situation is found in Fromm (1941). This same theme is also discussed in novel form in *The Fountainhead,* by Ayn Rand (1943). In this connection, *1066 and All That* (Yeatman & Sellar, 1931) is both funny and instructive.

[11]"Science is taught as something fixed and stable, not as a system of knowledge whose life and value depends on its mobility and readiness to revise at a moment's notice its most cherished constructions when new facts or a new point of view suggests the possibility of alternative ones."

"I am Master of this College;
And what I know not,
Is not knowledge" (Whitehead, 1938, p. 59).

bookish in our scholastic routine. The general training should aim at eliciting our concrete apprehensions, and should satisfy the itch of youth to be doing something. There should be some analysis even here, but only just enough to illustrate the ways of thinking in diverse spheres. In the Garden of Eden, Adam saw the animals before he named them: in the traditional system, children named the animals before they saw them.

This professional training can only touch one side of education. Its centre of gravity lies in the intellect, and its chief tool is the printed book. The centre of gravity of the other side of training should lie in intuition without an analytical divorce from the total environment. Its object is immediate apprehension with the minimum of eviscerating analysis. The type of generality, which above all is wanted, is the appreciation of variety of value (Whitehead, 1938, pp. 284–286).

LANGUAGE

Language is primarily an excellent means of experiencing and communicating nomothetic information, that is, an excellent means of categorizing. Of course, it attempts also to define and communicate the idiosyncratic or idiographic, but for ultimate theoretical purposes, it often fails.[12] All it can do with the idiosyncratic is to give it a name, which after all does not describe it or communicate it, but only labels it. The only way to know the idiosyncratic fully is to experience it fully and to experience it oneself. Even naming the experience may screen it off from further appreciation.

To the extent that language forces experiences into categories it is a screen between reality and the human being. In a word, we pay for its benefits.

If all this is true for language at its theoretical best, the situation must be far worse when language gives up altogether the struggle to be idiosyncratic, and degenerates completely into the use of stereotypes, platitudes, mottoes, slogans, clichés, battle cries, and epithets. It is then very obviously and frankly a means for obviating thought, for dulling the perceptions, stunting mental growth, and stultifying the human being. Language then has in truth "the function of concealing thought rather than of communicating it."

Therefore, while using language, as we must of necessity, we should be aware of its shortcomings. One suggestion would be that scientists learn to respect poets. Scientists usually think of their own language as being exact and of other languages as being inexact, but often the poets' language is paradoxically, if not more exact, at any rate more true. Sometimes it is even more exact. For instance, it is possible to say, if one is talented enough, in a very condensed way what the intellectual professor needs ten pages to say. The following story, attributed to Lincoln Steffens (in Baker, 1945, p. 222) illustrates this point.

[12]Poetry is an attempt to communicate, or at least express, an idiosyncratic experience that most people "have no art to say." It is a putting into words of emotional experiences that are in essence wordless. It is an attempt to describe a fresh and unique experience with schematizing labels that are themselves neither fresh nor unique. About all poets can do in such a hopeless situation is to use these words to make parallels, figures of speech, new word patterns, and the like, with which, though they cannot describe the experience itself, they hope to touch off a similar experience in the reader. That they sometimes succeed is simply a miracle.

"Satan and I," said Steffens, "were walking down Fifth Avenue together when we saw a man stop suddenly and pick up a piece of Truth out of the air—right out of the air—a piece of living Truth."

"Did you see that?," I asked Satan.

"Doesn't it worry you? Don't you know that it is enough to destroy you?"

"Yes, but I am not worried. I'll tell you why. It is a beautiful living thing now, but the man will first name it, then he will organize it, and by that time it will be dead. If he would let it live, and live it, it would destroy me. I'm not worried."

One other characteristic of language that helps to make trouble is that it is outside of space-time—or at least particular words may be. The word *England* over a period of 1000 years does not grow, age, develop, evolve, or change as the nation itself does. And yet such words as this are all we have to describe events in space-time. What does it mean to say, "There will always be an England"? As Johnson has it, "The moving finger of actuality writes faster than the tongue can herald. The structure of language is less fluid than the structure of reality. Just as the thunder we hear is no longer sounding, so the reality we speak about exists no more" (Johnson, 1946, p. 119).

THEORY

Theories built upon categories are almost always abstractive, that is to say, they emphasize certain qualities of phenomena as more important than others or at least more worthy of notice. Thus any such theory, or any other abstraction for that matter, is apt to derogate or neglect or overlook some of the qualities of phenomena, that is, to omit part of the truth. Because of these principles of rejection and selection, any theory must be expected to give no more than a partial, pragmatically biased view of the world. It is probably true, also, that all theories combined never give a full view of phenomena and of the world. The full subjective richness of an experience seems to come more often to artistically and emotionally sensitive people than to theorizers and intellectuals. It may even be that the so-called mystic experience is the perfect and extreme expression of this sort of full appreciation of all the characteristics of the particular phenomenon.

These considerations should by contrast show up another characteristic of particularized, individual experience, namely, its nonabstractive character. This is not the same as saying it is concrete in Goldstein's sense. Brain-injured patients, when they behave concretely, are actually *not* seeing all the sensuous characteristics of an object or experience. They see and are able to see only one such characteristic, that determined by the particular context; for example, a bottle of wine is *just* that and nothing else, not, for instance, a weapon, or a decoration, or a paperweight, or a fire extinguisher. If we define abstracting as selective attention, for any of various reasons, to some rather than others of the numberless characteristics of an event, Goldstein's patients might actually be said to be abstracting.

There is then a certain contrast between classifying experiences and appreciating them, between using them and enjoying them, between cognizing them in one way and cognizing them in another way. All writers on the mystic and religious experiences have emphasized this as few technical psychologists have. For instance, Aldous Huxley says: "As the individual grows up, his knowledge becomes more conceptual and systematic in form, and its factual, utilitarian content is enormously increased. But these gains are offset by a certain deterioration in the quality of immediate apprehension, a blunting and a loss of intuitive power" (1944, vii).[13]

However, since appreciation is certainly not our only relationship with nature, being in fact the least pressing biologically of all such relationships, we must not maneuver ourselves into the foolish position of stigmatizing theories and abstractions because of their dangers. Their advantages are great and obvious, especially from the point of view of communication and of practical manipulation of the world. If it were our function to make recommendations, we should probably phrase it in some such fashion as this: The ordinary cognitive processes of the working intellectual, the scientist, and so on can be made even more powerful than they are if it be remembered that these processes are not the only possible weapons in the armory of the researchers. There are others as well. If they have ordinarily been relegated to the poet and the artist this is because it was not understood that these neglected styles of cognition gave access to that portion of the real world which is hidden from the exclusively abstracting intellectual.

Furthermore, as we shall see in Chapter 18, holistic theorizing is also possible, in which things are not dissected and separated from each other, but are seen intact in their interrelations as facets of a whole, contained within it, seen as figure against ground, or at different levels of magnification.

---

[13]For references on mysticism, see Aldous Huxley's *The Perennial Philosophy* (1944) and William James's *The Varieties of Religious Experience* (1958).

chapter *18*

A Holistic Approach to Psychology[1]

HOLISTIC-DYNAMIC APPROACH

The Fundamental Psychological Datum

It is difficult to say just what this fundamental datum is, but it is easy to say what it is not. There have been many "nothing but" attempts, but all reductive efforts have failed. We know that the fundamental psychological datum is not a muscle twitch, not a reflex, nor an elementary sensation, nor a neuron, nor even an observable bit of overt behavior. It is a much larger unit, and more and more psychologists think that it is at least as large a unit as an adjustive or coping act, which necessarily involves an organism, a situation, and a goal or purpose. In view of what we have said about unmotivated reactions and pure expression, even this looks too limited.

[1]This chapter presents a set of theoretical conclusions emerging directly from research on the roles of self-esteem and security in the organization of human personality. It is documented in the following papers and tests.

The authoritarian character structure, *J. Social Psychol.*, 1943, *18,* 401–411.

A clinically derived test for measuring psychological security-insecurity, *J. Gen. Psychol.*, 1945, *33,* 21–51. (with E. Birsh, E. Stein, and I. Honigmann). Published by Consulting Psychologists Press, Palo Alto, Calif., 1952.

Comments on Prof. McClelland's paper. In M. R. Jones (ed.), *Nebraska Symposium on Motivation, 1955,* Lincoln: University of Nebraska Press, 1955.

The dominance drive as a determiner of the social and sexual behavior of infra-human primates, I, II, III, IV, *J. Genet. Psychol.*, 1936, *48,* 261–277; 278–309 (with S. Flanzbaum); 310–338; 1936, *49,* 161–198.

In a word, we wind up with the paradoxical conclusion that the fundamental datum of psychology is the original complexity that psychologists had set themselves to analyze into elements or fundamental units. If we use the concept of fundamental datum at all, it is certainly a peculiar sort of concept, for it refers to a complex and not a simplex, a whole rather than a part.

If we ponder this paradox, we must soon come to understand that the search for a fundamental datum is itself a reflection of a whole world view, a scientific philosophy that assumes an atomistic world—a world in which complex things are built up out of simple elements. The first task of such a scientist then is to reduce the so-called complex to the so-called simple. This is to be done by analysis, by finer and finer separating until we come to the irreducible. This task has succeeded well enough elsewhere in science, for a time at least. In psychology it has not.

This conclusion exposes the essentially theoretical nature of the entire reductive effort. It must be understood that this effort is *not* of the essential nature of science in general. It is simply a reflection or implication in science of an atomistic, mechanical world view that we now have good reason to doubt. Attacking such reductive efforts is then not an attack on science in general, but rather on one of the possible attitudes toward science. We still have, however, the original problem with which we started. Let us now rephrase it so as to ask, not What is the fundamental (irreducible) datum of psychology?, but rather, What is the subject matter of psychological study? and What is the nature of psychological data and how can they be studied?

Holistic Methodology

How shall we study our individuals if not by reducing them to their "simple parts"? It can be demonstrated that this is a much simpler problem than it is considered to be by some who reject the reductive effort.

It is necessary to understand first that objection is made not to analysis in general but only to the particular kind of analysis that we have called reduction. It is not at all necessary to deny the validity of the concepts of analysis, of parts, and the like. We need simply redefine these concepts so that they may allow us to do our work more validly and more fruitfully.

Dominance-feeling, behavior, and status, *Psychol. Rev., 1937, 44*, 404–429.

Dominance-feeling, personality, and social behavior in women, *J. Social Psychol., 1939, 10*, 3–39.

Dominance-quality and social behavior in infra-human primates, *J. Social Psychol., 1940, 11*, 313–324.

The dynamics of psychological security-insecurity, *Character and Pers., 1942, 10*, 331–344.

Individual psychology and the social behavior of monkeys and apes, *Int. J. Individ. Psychol., 1935, 1*, 47–59.

Liberal leadership and personality, *Freedom, 1942, 2*, 27–30.

Some parallels between the dominance and sexual behavior of monkeys and the fantasies of patients in psychotherapy, *J. Nervous Mental Disease, 1960, 131*, 202–212 (with H. Rand and S. Newman).

Self-esteem (dominance-feeling) and sexuality in women, *J. Social Psychol., 1942, 16*, 259–294.

A test for dominance-feeling (self-esteem) in women, *J. Social Psychol., 1940, 12*, 255–270.

If we take an example, such as blushing or trembling or stammering, it is easy to see that we may study this behavior in two different ways. On the one hand we may study it as if it were an isolated, discrete phenomenon, self-contained and understandable in itself. On the other hand, we may study it as one expression of the whole organism, attempting to understand it in its richness of interrelationships with the organism and with other expressions of the organism. This distinction can be made clearer if we make the analogy with the two possible ways of studying an organ like the stomach: (1) it can be cut out of the cadaver and laid on the dissecting table, or (2) it can be studied in situ, that is, in the living, functioning organism. The results that are obtained by these two approaches are different in many ways, anatomists now realize. Knowledge obtained by the second approach is more valid and more useful than the results obtained by the equivalent of in vitro techniques. Of course dissection and isolated study of the stomach are not stigmatized by modern anatomists. These techniques are used, but only against the broad background of in situ knowledge, of knowledge that the human body is not a collection of separate organs, of the realization that organization in the cadaver is not the same as that in the living body. In a word, anatomists do all that was done in the past but (1) they do it with a different attitude, and (2) they do more—they use techniques in addition to those used traditionally.

Just so can we turn to our study of personality with two different attitudes. We can conceive either that we are studying a discrete entity, or that we are studying a part of a whole. The former method we may call reductive-analytic. The latter we may call holistic-analytic. One essential characteristic of holistic analysis of the personality in actual practice is that there be a preliminary study or understanding of the total organism, and that we then proceed to study the role that our part of the whole plays in the organization and dynamics of the total organism.

In the two series of researches upon which this chapter is based (studies of the self-esteem syndrome and of the security syndrome) this holistic-analytic method was used. Actually these results may be phrased not so much as studies of self-esteem or of security in themselves, but as studies of the role of self-esteem or of security in the total personality. In methodological terms this means that the writer found it necessary to understand each subject as a whole, functioning, adjusting individual before he could attempt to find out specifically about the self-esteem of the subject. Thus, before any questions were asked specifically about self-esteem, explorations were made of the subject's relations to his or her family, to the kind of subculture he or she lived in, of the general style of adjusting to main life problems, his or her hopes for the future, ideals, frustrations, and conflicts. This procedure continued until the writer felt that he understood the subject as well as was possible with the simple techniques being used. Only then did he feel that he could understand the actual psychological meaning for self-esteem of specific bits of behavior.

We can indicate by example the necessity of this background of understanding for proper interpretations of a specific behavior. In general, people with low self-esteem tend to be more religious than people with high self-esteem, but obviously there are many other determinants of religiosity as well. To discover whether, in a specific individual, religious feeling means a necessity to lean on some other source of strength, one must know the individual's religious training, the various external compulsions for and against religion that play on the subject, whether or not the religious feeling is superficial or deep, whether it is external or sincere. In a word, we must understand what religion means for the person as an individual. So people who go to church regularly may actually be rated as *less* religious than those who do not go to church at all, because perhaps (1) they go to avoid social isolation, or (2) they go to please their parents, or (3) religion represents for them not humbleness but a weapon of domination over others, or (4) it marks them as members of a superior group, or (5) as for Clarence Day's father, "It is good for the ignorant masses and I must play along," or . . . , and so on. They may in a dynamic sense be not at all religious and still behave as if they were. We must obviously know what religion means for them as individuals before we can assay its role in the personality. Sheer behavioral going to church can mean practically anything, and therefore, for us, practically nothing.

Another example, perhaps more striking, because the same behavior may mean exactly opposite things psychologically, is that of political-economic radicalism. If it is taken per se, that is to say behaviorally, discretely, out of context, we get the most confusing results when we study its relation to security feelings. Some radicals are at the extreme of security, others are at the extreme of insecurity. But if we analyze this radicalism in its total context we can learn easily that some people may be radicals because life is not good for them, because they are bitter, disappointed, or frustrated, because they do not have what others have. Careful study of such people often shows them to be very hostile to their fellow humans in general, sometimes consciously, sometimes unconsciously. It has been said aptly of this kind of person that they tend to perceive their personal difficulties as a world crisis.

But there is another type of radical who is a very different *kind* of individual even though he or she votes, behaves, and talks in the same way as the one we have just described. For such people, however, radicalism may have a completely different, even opposite motivation or meaning. These people are secure, happy, personally contented people who, however, out of a deep love for their fellow humans, feel impelled to improve the lot of the less fortunate, to fight injustice even if it does not touch them directly. Such people may express this urge in any one of a dozen ways: through personal philanthropy, or religious exhortation, or patient teaching, or radical political activity. Their political beliefs tend to be independent of fluctuations of income, of personal calamity, and the like.

In a word, radicalism is a form of expression that may come from completely different underlying motivations, from opposite types of character structure. In one person it may spring essentially from hate for his fellows, in another it may spring essentially from love for her fellows. If radicalism is studied in itself, such a conclusion is not likely to be arrived at.[2]

---

[2]A rather commonly used holistic technique (not so labeled ordinarily) is the technique of iteration used in constructing personality tests. I have also used this technique in my investigations

The general point of view that is being propounded here is holistic rather than atomistic, functional rather than taxonomic, dynamic rather than static, dynamic rather than causal, purposive rather than simple-mechanical. I have found that those who think dynamically find it easier and more natural to think also holistically rather than atomistically, purposively rather than mechanically, and so on. This point of view we shall call the holistic-dynamic point of view. It could also be called organismic in Goldstein's sense (1939, 1940).

Opposed to this interpretation is found an organized and unitary viewpoint that is simultaneously atomistic, taxonomic, static, causal, and simple-mechanical. The atomistic thinker finds it much more natural to think also statically rather than dynamically, mechanically rather than purposively, and so forth. This general point of view we shall call arbitrarily general-atomistic. We have no doubt that it is possible to demonstrate not only that these partial views *tend* to go together but that they *must* logically go together.

The Limits of Causality Theories

A few special remarks on the causality concept are necessary at this point since it is an aspect of the general-atomistic theory that seems to us to be centrally important and that psychological writers have slurred or neglected altogether. This concept lies at the very heart of the general-atomistic point of view and is a natural, even necessary, consequence of it. If one sees the world as a collection of intrinsically independent entities, there remains to be solved the very obvious phenomenal fact that these entities nevertheless have to do with each other. The first attempt to solve this problem gives rise to the notion of the simple billiard-ball kind of causality in which one separate thing does something to another separate thing, but in which the entities involved continue to retain their essential identity. Such a view is easy enough to maintain, and actually seemed absolute so long as the old physics gave us our world theory. But the advance in physics and chemistry made modification necessary. For instance, the usually more sophisticated phrasing today is in terms of multiple causation. It is recognized that the interrelationships holding within the world are too complex, too intricate to describe in the same way as we do the clicking of billiard balls on a table. But the answer is most often simply a complexifying of the original notion rather than a basic restructuring of it. Instead of one cause, there are many, but they are conceived to act in the same way—separately and independent of each other. The billiard ball is now hit not by one other ball, but by ten simultaneously, and we simply have to use a somewhat more complicated arithmetic to understand what happens. The essential procedures are still addition of separate entities into an "and-sum," to use Wertheimer's phrase. No change is felt to be necessary in the

---

of personality syndromes. Starting with a vague grasped whole, we analyze its structure into subdivisions, parts, and so on. Through this analysis we discover difficulties with our original conception of the whole. The whole is then reorganized, redefined, and rephrased more exactly and more efficiently, and is, as before, subjected to analysis. Again this analysis makes possible a better, more precise whole, and so on.

fundamental envisagement of the complex happenings. No matter how complex the phenomenon may be, no essentially new thing is happening. In this way the notion of cause is stretched more and more to fit new needs until sometimes it seems to have no relation but a historical one to the old concept. Actually, however, different though they may seem, they remain in essence the same, since they continue to reflect the same world view.

It is particularly with personality data that the causality theory falls down most completely. It is easy to demonstrate that within any personality syndrome, relationship other than causal exists. That is to say, if we had to use causal vocabulary we should have to say that every part of the syndrome is both a cause and an effect of every other part as well as of any grouping of these other parts, and that furthermore we should have to say that each part is both a cause and effect of the whole of which it is a part. Such an absurd conclusion is the only one that is possible if we use only the causality concept. Even if we attempt to meet the situation by introducing the newer concept of circular or reversible causaltiy we could not completely describe the relations within the syndrome nor the relations of the part to the whole.

Nor is this the only shortcoming of causality vocabulary with which we must deal. There is also the difficult problem of the description of the interaction or interrelation between a syndrome as a whole and all the forces bearing upon it from the "outside." The syndrome of self-esteem, for instance, has been shown to tend to change as a whole. If we try to change Johnny's stammering and address ourselves specifically to this and only this, the chances are very great that we shall find either (1) that we have changed nothing at all, or else (2) that we have changed not Johnny's stammering alone but rather Johnny's self-esteem in general, or even Johnny as a whole individual. External influences usually tend to change the whole human being, not just a bit or a part of the person.

There are yet other peculiarities in this situation that defy description by the ordinary causal vocabulary. There is one phenomenon in particular that is very difficult to describe. The nearest I can come to expressing it is to say that it is as if the organism (or any other syndrome) "swallows the cause, digests it, and emits the effect." When an effective stimulus, a traumatic experience let us say, impinges upon the personality, there are certain consequences of this experience. But these consequences practically never bear a one-to-one or a straight-line relationship to the original causal experience. What actually happens is that the experience, if it is effective, changes that whole personality. This personality, now different from what it was before, expresses itself differently and behaves differently from before. Let us suppose that this effect would be that a facial twitch gets a little worse. Has this 10 percent increase of the tic been caused by the traumatic situation? If we say it has, it can be shown that we must, if we wish to be consistent, say that every single effective stimulus that has ever impinged on the organism has also caused this 10 percent increase in the facial tic. For every experience is taken into the organism, in the same sense that food is digested and by intussusception becomes the organism itself. Is the sandwich I ate an hour ago the cause of the words I now set down, or was it the coffee I drank, or what I ate yesterday, or was it the lesson in writing I got years ago, or the book I read a week ago?

It would certainly seem obvious that any important expression, such as writing a paper in which one is deeply interested, is not caused by anything in particular, but is an expression of, or a creation of the whole personality, which in turn is an effect of almost everything that has ever happened to it. It should seem just as natural for the psychologist to think of the stimulus or cause as being taken in by the personality by means of a readjustment, as to think of it as hitting the organism and pushing it. The net result here would be, not a cause and effect remaining separate, but simply a new personality (new by however little).

Still another way of demonstrating the inadequacy for psychology of conventional cause-effect notions is to show that the organism is not a passive agent to which causes or stimuli *do* something, but that it is an active agent entering into a complex mutual relationship with the cause, doing something to it as well. For readers of the psychoanalytic literature this is a commonplace, and it is necessary only to remind the reader of the facts that we can be blind to stimuli, we can distort them, reconstruct, or reshape them if they are distorted. We can seek them out or avoid them. We can sift them out and select from among them. Or finally, we can even create them if need be.

The causality concept rests on the assumption of an atomistic world with entities that remain discrete, even though they interact. The personality, however, is not separate from its expressions, effects, or the stimuli impinging upon it (causes) and so at least for psychological data it must be replaced by another conception.[3] This conception—holistic-dynamics—cannot be stated simply, since it involves fundamental reorganization of viewpoint, but must be expounded step by step.

THE CONCEPT OF PERSONALITY SYNDROME

Granted that a more valid type of analysis is possible, how then can we proceed further in this study of the whole organism? It is clear that the answer to this question must depend on the nature of the organization of the data to be analyzed and we must now ask: How is the personality organized? As an antecedent to a full answer to this question must come an analysis of the syndrome concept.

Medical Usage

In attempting to describe the interrelated nature of the personality, we have borrowed the term *syndrome* from medicine. In this field it is used to mean a complex

[3]More sophisticated scientists and philosophers have now replaced the causality notion with an interpretation in terms of "functional" relationships, that is, A is a function of B, *or* If A, then B. By so doing, it seems to us that they have given up the nuclear aspects of the concept of cause, that is to say, of necessity, and of acting upon. Simple linear coefficients of correlations are examples of functional statements, which are, however, often used as *contrasting* with cause-effect relationships. It serves no purpose to retain the word *cause* if it means the very opposite of what it used to mean. In any case, we are then left with the problems of necessary or intrinsic relationship, and of the ways in which change comes about. These problems must be solved, not abandoned or denied or liquidated.

of symptoms that are usually found to occur together and that are therefore given a unifying name. Used thus, the word has its shortcomings as well as its advantages. For one thing it usually connotes disease and abnormality rather than health or normality. We shall not use it in any such special sense, considering it rather to be a general concept that refers only to a type of organization without reference to the "value" of this organization.

Further, in medicine it has often been used in a merely additive sense, as a list of symptoms rather than as an organized, interdependent, structured group of symptoms. We shall of course use it in the latter sense. Finally, it has been used in medicine in a causal context. Any syndrome of symptoms was conceived to have a putative, single cause. Once something like this was found, such as the microorganism in tuberculosis, researchers tended to rest content and consider their labors finished. By so doing they neglected many problems that we should consider central. Examples of such problems are (1) the failure of tuberculosis to develop more often in view of the ubiquity of the tuberculosis bacillus, (2) the frequent nonappearance of many of the symptoms of the syndrome, (3) the interchangeability of these symptoms, (4) the unexplained and unpredictable mildness or severity of the disease in specific individuals, and so on. In a word, we should demand a study of *all* the factors involved in the production of tuberculosis, not only the most dramatic or the most powerful single one.

Our preliminary definition of a personality syndrome is that it is a structured, organized complex of apparently diverse specificities (behaviors, thoughts, impulses to action, perceptions, etc.) which, however, when studied carefully and validly are found to have a common unity that may be phrased variously as a similar dynamic meaning, expression, "flavor," function, or purpose.

Dynamically Interchangeable Parts

Since these specificities have the same source or function or aim, they are interchangeable and may actually be thought to be psychological synonyms of one another (all "saying the same thing"). For example temper tantrums in one child and enuresis in another may come from the same situation (e.g., rejection) and may be attempts to achieve the same end (e.g., attention or love from the mother). Thus, though they are quite different behaviorally, they may be identical dynamically.[4]

In a syndrome we have a group of feelings and behaviors that seem behaviorally different, or at least have different names, which, however, overlap, intertwine, interdepend, and may be said to be dynamically synonymous. We may thus study them either in their diversity as parts or specificities or we may study them in their unity or wholeness. The problem of language is a difficult one here. How shall we label this unity in diversity? There are various possibilities.

[4]Interchangeability may be defined in these terms of behavioral difference and dynamic similarity of aim. It may also be defined in terms of probability. If symptoms *a* and *b* have the same probability of being found or not found in syndrome *X* in an individual case, they may be called interchangeable.

Flavor of the Personality

We may introduce the concept of "psychological flavor," using as an example a dish composed of different elements and yet having a character of its own (e.g., a soup, a hash, a stew, etc.).[5] In a stew we have a concoction of many elements that nevertheless has a unique flavor. Its flavor permeates all the elements of the stew and may be spoken of apart from its isolated ingredients. Or, if we take the human physiognomy we recognize readily that a man may have a misshapen nose, too-small eyes, too-large ears, and still be handsome. (A witticism says, "He has an ugly face, but on him it looks good.") Here again we may consider either the separate elements taken additively, or the whole, which, though composed of parts, yet has a "flavor" different from anything brought to the whole by any single part. The definition of syndrome that we might derive here is that it is organized of diversities that have a common psychological flavor.

Psychological Meaning

A second approach to the problem of definitions could be in terms of psychological meaning, a concept that is made much of in current dynamic psychopathology. When disease symptoms are said to have the same meaning (night sweating, loss of weight, certain sounds in breathing, etc., all mean tuberculosis) the implication is that they are all diverse expressions of the unifying putative cause spoken of above. Or in psychological discussions the symptoms of feeling of isolation and of feeling of being disliked both mean insecurity because they are seen as being included in this larger, more inclusive concept. That is to say, two symptoms will mean the same thing if they are both parts of the same whole. A syndrome may then be defined in a somewhat circular fashion as an organized collection of diversities, all of which have the same psychological meaning. These concepts of interchangeability, flavor, and meaning, useful though they may be (for instance in the description of the pattern of a culture), have certain specific theoretical and practical difficulties that impel further search for a satisfactory phrasing. Some of these difficulties can be solved if we introduce into our considerations the functional concepts of motivations, goals, purposes, or coping aims. (But still other problems require the concept of expression, or unmotivation for their solution.)

Response to a Problem

From the point of view of functional psychology the unified organism is seen as always facing problems of certain kinds and attempting to solve them in various ways permitted by the nature of the organism, the culture, and the external reality. The key principle or the centering of all personality organization is then seen by the functional psychologist in terms of the answers of the organism in a world of problems. The alternative phrasing is that the organization of the personality is

---

[5]"I have had to tell the story, not as one draws a line from left to right, marking birth at the left, and death at the right; but as one ponders while he turns a relic over and over in his hands." (Taggard, 1934, p. 15.)

to be understood in terms of the problems facing it and what it is trying to do about them. Most organized behaviors then must be doing something about something.[6] In the discussion of personality syndromes we should then characterize two specific behaviors as belonging to the same syndrome if they have the same coping aims with respect to a certain problem, that is to say, if they were doing the same thing about the same something. We might then say of the self-esteem syndrome, for instance, that it is the organized answer of the organism to the problem of acquiring, losing, keeping, and defending self-esteem, and similarly for the security syndrome that it is the organism's answer to the problem of gaining, losing, and keeping the love of others.

That we have here no final simple answer is indicated by the fact that the usual finding, when a single behavior is analyzed dynamically, is that it has not one, but several coping aims. Also, the organism ordinarily has more than one answer to an important life problem.

We might add also that quite apart from the facts about character expression, purpose cannot, in any case be made a principal characteristic of *all* syndromes.

We cannot speak of the purpose of an organization in the world outside the organism. The Gestalt psychologists have demonstrated abundantly the ubiquity of organization in perceived, learned, and thought-about materials. These materials, of course, cannot all be said to have coping aims in the sense in which we have used the word.

In general it may be said that the Gestalt psychologists have agreed with Wertheimer's original definition, that a whole is meaningful when a demonstrable, mutual dependency exists among its parts, and there are certain obvious similarities between our definition of a syndrome and the various definitions of a Gestalt offered by Wertheimer, Köhler, Koffka, and others. The two Ehrenfels criteria are also paralleled in our definition.

Meaning of the Whole Inherent in the Parts

Ehrenfels's first criterion of an organized mental phenomenon was that the separate stimuli (e.g., the single notes of a melody), presented singly to a number of persons, would be lacking something that would be experienced by an individual given the organized totality of stimuli (e.g., the whole melody). In other words, the whole is something else than the additive sum of the parts. So also the syndrome is something else than the additive sum of its isolated reduced parts.[7] But there is also an important difference. In our definition of the syndrome, the main quality that characterizes the whole (meaning, flavor, or aim) can be seen in any of its parts if these parts are understood not reductively, but holistically. Of course this is a theoretical statement and we may expect to find operational difficulties with it. Most of the time we shall be able to discover the flavor or aim of the

---

[6]For exceptions to this rule, see Chapter 6, "Unmotivated Behavior."

[7]It is a question, however, whether the syndrome is something else than the sum of its parts taken holistically. Parts by reduction can add up only to an and-sum; parts of a whole may, however, very well be thought of as adding up to the organized whole if the various terms of this statement are defined in a specific way.

specific behavior only by understanding the whole of which it is a part. And yet, there are enough exceptions to this rule to convince us that the aim or flavor inheres in the part as well as in the whole. For instance, often we can deduce or infer the whole from a single given part; for example, we hear a person laugh just once and we are almost certain that the individual feels insecure, or we can know much about people's self-esteem in general simply by their choice of clothes. It is of course granted that such a judgment from a part is usually not so valid as a judgment from the whole.

Transposing the Parts

The second Ehrenfels criterion was that of transposability of elements within a whole. Thus a melody retains its identity even when played in a different key with all the single notes being different in the two cases. This resembles the interchangeability of the elements in a syndrome. Elements that have the same aim are interchangeable or dynamically synonymous with each other; so also are different notes that have the same role in a melody.[8]

Focus on the Human Organism

The Gestalt psychologists have worked mostly with the organization of the phenomenal world, of the "field" of "materials" primarily outside the organism. It is, however, the human organism itself that is most highly organized and intradependent, as Goldstein has amply proved. The basic phenomena of motivation, purpose, aim, expression, and direction all show up clearly in the organism. A definition of the personality syndrome in terms of coping aims at once creates the possibility of unifying the otherwise isolated theories of functionalism, Gestalt psychology, purposivism (not teleology), the kind of psychodynamics espoused by the psychoanalysts, Adlerians, and so on, and the organismic holism of Goldstein. That is to say, the syndrome concept properly defined can be a theoretical basis for the unified world view that we have called the holistic-dynamic point of view and that we contrast with general-atomistic point of view.

CHARACTERISTICS OF PERSONALITY SYNDROMES

Interchangeability

The parts of a syndrome are interchangeable or equivalent in the dynamic sense which has been discussed in previous paragraphs, namely in the sense that two behaviorally different parts or symptoms, since they have the same aim, can substitute for each other, can do the same job, have equal expectancy of appearing, or may be predicted with equal probability or confidence.

In a hysterical person symptoms are clearly interchangeable in this sense. In the classical cases a paralyzed leg could be "cured" by hypnosis or other suggestion techniques but would almost inevitably be replaced later by some other

[8]See, however, Köhler's criticism of the Ehrenfels criteria (1961, p. 25).

symptom, a paralyzed arm perhaps. Throughout the Freudian literature as well, there are encountered many examples of symptom equivalents; for example, fear of a horse may mean, or substitute for, a repressed fear of the father. In a secure person all behavior expressions are interchangeable in the sense that they all express the same thing, that is, security. In the example of secure radicalism mentioned before, general desire to help humanity may eventuate *either* in radicalism or philanthropy or kindness to neighbors or in giving nickels to beggars and tramps. In an unknown case, of which we know only that a person is secure, one may predict with great certainty that he or she will show *some* expression of kindness or social interest; but what exactly it will be cannot be predicted. Such equivalent symptoms or expressions may be called interchangeable.

Circular Determination

The best descriptions of this phenomenon have come from psychopathological studies, for example, Horney's (1937) concept of the vicious circle that is a special case of circular determination. Horney's is one attempt to describe the continual flux of dynamic interaction within a syndrome, whereby any one part is always affecting every other part in some way and is in turn being affected by all other parts, the entire action going on simultaneously.

Complete neurotic dependence implies expectations that must be thwarted. This necessary thwarting creates anger additional to that probably already involved by the admission of weakness and helplessness implicit in complete dependence. This anger, however, tends to be directed against the very person on whom one is dependent and through whose help one hopes to avoid catastrophe, and such anger feelings immediately lead to guilt, anxiety, fear of retaliation, and the like. But these states are among the very factors that produced need for complete dependence in the first place. Examination of such a patient will show *at any one moment* most of these factors coexisting in continual flux and mutual reinforcement. While a genetic analysis may show priority of one feature over another in time, a dynamic analysis will never show this. All the factors will be equally causes and effects.

Or some individuals may attempt to maintain their security by adopting an overbearing and superior attitude. They would not have taken this attitude unless they felt rejected and disliked (insecure). But this very attitude makes people dislike them more, which in turn reinforces the necessity for overbearing attitudes, and so forth.

> In race prejudice we can see this type of circular determination very clearly. The haters will point to certain undesirable traits that excuse their hatred, but these very traits in the disliked group are almost all the product in part of the hatred and rejection.[9]

[9]We are describing in these examples only synchronous dynamics. The question of the origin or determination of the whole syndrome, of how the circular determination ever came to be in the first place, is a historical question. Even if such a genetic analysis shows one particular factor to have been first in the chain, this in no way guarantees that this same factor will have basic or prior importance in the dynamic analysis (Allport, 1961).

If we were to use the more familiar cause-effect vocabulary to describe this concept, we should say that A and B cause each other and are effects of each other. Or we could say that they were mutually dependent or mutually supportive or reinforcing variants.

Resistance to Change

No matter what the level of security may be, it is difficult either to raise or to lower it. This phenomenon is something like that described by Freud as resistance but has a much wider and more general application. Thus we find some tendency to hang on to the life style in the healthy as well as in the unhealthy person. The person who tends to believe that all people are essentially good will show the same resistance to change of this belief as will the person who believes all people are essentially bad. Operationally this resistance to change may be defined in terms of the difficulty experienced by the psychological experimenter when attempting to raise or lower an individual's security level.

Personality syndromes can sometimes maintain a relative constancy under the most surprising conditions of external change. There are many examples of the maintenance of security feelings in emigres who have undergone the most grueling and harrowing experiences. Studies of morale in bombed areas also give us proof of the surprising resistance that most healthy people have to external horrors. Statistics show that depressions and wars do not make for any large increase in the incidence of psychosis.[10] Changes in the syndrome of security are usually in great disproportion to changes in the environment, and sometimes there seems to be almost no personality change at all.

A German emigre, formally a man of great wealth, came to the United States completely stripped of all his goods. He was diagnosed, however, as a secure personality. Careful questioning showed that his underlying philosophy of human nature had not changed. He still felt that it was essentially sound and good if given a chance, and that the nastiness he had witnessed was explicable in various ways as an externally caused phenomenon. Interviews with people who had known him in Germany showed that he had been about the same kind of person before his financial downfall.

Many other examples are seen in the resistance of patients to psychotherapy. Sometimes there can be found in a patient, after a period of analysis, a surprising degree of insight into the false basis and the evil consequences of certain beliefs. Even so the patient may hang on to the beliefs with a determined tenacity.

[10]Such data are usually misinterpreted, since they are often used to refute any environmental or cultural theory of determination of psychopathy. Such a contention simply shows a misunderstanding of dynamic psychology. The real claim that can be made is that psychopathy is immediately the result of internal conflicts and threats rather than external calamities. Or at least that external calamities have dynamic influence on the personality only insofar as they relate to the main goals of the individual and to his or her defensive system.

Reestablishment After Disruption

If a syndrome level has been forced to change, it is often observed that such shift is only temporary. For instance, a traumatic experience very frequently has only a passing effect. There may then be a spontaneous readjustment back to the previous status quo. Or else the symptoms created by the trauma are nullified with especial ease (Levy, 1939). Sometimes also this tendency of the syndrome can be inferred as one of the processes in a larger system of changes in which other syndrome tendencies are also involved.

> The following case is typical. A sexually ignorant woman was badly shocked by her first experience after marriage to an equally ignorant man. There was in her a definite shift in the level of the whole security syndrome, namely, from average to low security. Investigation showed change, as a whole, in most aspects of the syndrome, in her external behavior, philosophy of life, dream life, attitude toward human nature, and so on. At this point she was supported and reassured, the situation was discussed in a nontechnical way, and she was given some simple advice over the course of four or five hours. Slowly she changed back, possibly because of these contacts, becoming steadily more secure, but she never quite attained her former level. There remained some slight but permanent effect of her experience, perhaps maintained in part by a rather selfish husband. What was more surprising than this permanent after effect was the strong tendency in spite of everything to think and believe as she had before she was married. A similar picture of sharp change with slow but complete recovery feelings was seen upon remarriage in a woman whose first husband became insane.

It is a tribute to the ubiquity of this tendency that our ordinary expectations in respect to friends who are regarded as normally healthy is that they can recover from any shock at all if only given enough time. The death of a spouse or child, financial ruin, and any other such basic traumatic experiences may throw individuals badly off balance for a while, but they usually recover almost wholly. It is only a chronically bad external or interpersonal situation that is able to create permanent changes in the healthy character structure.

Changing as a Whole

This tendency, already discussed above, is perhaps the easiest of all to see. If the syndrome changes at all in any part, the right kind of investigation will practically always show some other concomitant changes in the same direction in other parts of the syndrome. Often enough, such concomitant changes may be seen in almost *all* parts of the syndrome. The reason these changes are so often overlooked is simply that they are not expected and therefore not looked for.

It should be emphasized that this tendency to holistic change, like all the other tendencies we have spoken of, is just that—a tendency and not a certainty. There have been cases in which a particular stimulus seemed to have a specific and localized effect with no detectable generalized effect. These cases are rare, however, if we exclude the obviously superficial derangements.

In an unpublished experiment in 1935 on raising self-esteem by external means, a woman was instructed to *behave* in an aggressive fashion in about 20 specific and rather trivial situations. (For instance, she was to insist on a certain brand concerning which her grocer had always overruled her.) She followed instructions, and a wide investigation of personality changes was made three months later.[11] There was no doubt that there had been a generalized shift in her self-esteem. For instance, the character of her dreams had changed. She had bought form-fitting and revealing clothes for the first time. Her sexual behavior had become spontaneous enough for her husband to notice the change. She had gone swimming with other people for the first time, whereas she had always before been too bashful to appear in a swimming suit. And she felt very confident in a variety of other situations. These changes were not suggested, but were spontaneous changes of whose significance she was not at all aware. Change in *behavior* can produce personality change.

A very insecure woman, seen a few years after her very successful marriage, showed a general shift upward in security. When she was first seen (before her marriage) she had felt alone, unloved and unlovable. Her present husband had finally been able to convince her that he loved her—a difficult task in the case of an insecure woman—and they were married. Now she felt not only that her husband loved her, but also that she was *lovable*. She accepted friendships whereas she had not been able to before. Most of her generalized hatred against human beings had gone. She had developed a kindness and a sweetness of which there was little trace when I had first seen her. Certain specific symptoms had lessened or disappeared—among others a recurring nightmare, a fear of parties and other groupings of strangers, chronic slight anxiety, a specific fear of the dark, certain undesirable power and cruelty fantasies.

Internal Consistency

Even though a person is mostly insecure there may yet persist for various reasons a few specific behaviors, beliefs, or feelings that are characteristic of security. Thus, although a very insecure person more often than not has chronic nightmares, anxiety dreams, or other unpleasant dreams, still in a fair percentage of all such individuals the dream life is not usually unpleasant. In such individuals, however, relatively slight changes in the environment will induce such unpleasant dreams. There seems to be a special tension on these inconsistent elements always acting to pull them into line with the rest of the syndrome.

People with low self-esteem tend to be modest or bashful. Thus it is usual that many of them will either not appear in a swimming suit or will feel very self-conscious if they do. One girl, however, definitely low in self-esteem, was not only observed at the beach in a swimming suit, but in one that was definitely scanty and revealing. Later a series of interviews revealed that she was very proud of her body, which she considered perfect—an opinion which, for a woman of low self-esteem, is, like her behavior, very unusual. Through her

[11]Today this would be called a form of behavior therapy.

report it was evident, however, that this attitude toward bathing was inconsistent in that she invariably felt self-conscious, that she always had a robe nearby to cover herself with, and that anyone staring at her too openly could drive her from the beach altogether. She had been convinced by various external opinions that her body was attractive; she felt intellectually that she ought to behave a certain way about it, tried very hard to behave in this way, but found it difficult to do so because of her character structure.

Specific fears are often found in very secure persons who are not at all generally fearful. These fears can often be accounted for by specific conditioning experiences. It is very easy to get rid of these fears in such people, I have found. Simple reconditioning, the force of example, exhortation to be strong willed, intellectual explanation, and other such superficial psychotherapeutic measures are often quite sufficient. These simple behavioral techniques, however, should be less successful with fears in definitely insecure people. We might say that the fear that is inconsistent with the rest of the personality is easily removed; the fear that is consistent with the rest of the personality is more tenacious.

In other words, a person who is insecure *tends* to become more perfectly or consistently insecure; a person who is high in self-esteem *tends* to become more consistently high in self-esteem.

Tendency to Extremes

Side by side with the conserving tendencies we have already described, there is at least one opposing force deriving from the internal dynamics of the syndrome that favors change rather than constancy. It is the tendency for a fairly insecure person to become extremely insecure, for a fairly secure person to become extremely secure.[12]

In a fairly insecure person every external influence, every stimulus impinging on the organism is somewhat more apt to be interpreted insecurely rather than securely. For example, a grin is apt to be seen as a sneer, forgetfulness is apt to be interpreted as insult, indifference is apt to be seen as dislike, and mild affection as indifference. In such persons' worlds, then, there are more insecure influences than there are secure ones. We might say that the weight of evidence for them is on the side of insecurity. And so they are pulled steadily, even though slightly, in the direction of more and more extreme insecurity. This factor is of course reinforced by the fact that insecure people tend to behave insecurely, which encourages people to dislike and reject them, which makes them more insecure, which makes them behave still more insecurely—and so on in a vicious circle. Thus they tend, because of their inner dynamics, to bring about just what they fear most.

The most obvious example is jealous behavior. It springs from insecurity and practically always breeds further rejection and deeper insecurity. A man ex-

---

[12]This tendency is closely related to the previously described tendency toward greater internal consistency.

plained his jealousy as follows: "I love my wife so much that I am afraid that I would collapse if she left me or did not love me. Naturally I am disturbed by her friendliness with my brother." Therefore he took many measures to stop this friendliness, all of them foolish, so that he began to lose the love of both his wife and his brother. This of course made him even more frantic and jealous. The vicious circle was broken with the aid of a psychologist who instructed him first not to behave jealously even if he felt that way, and then started the more important task of relieving the general insecurity in various ways.

Change from External Pressures

It is very easy when preoccupied with inner dynamics of syndromes to forget temporarily that all syndromes are of course responsive to the external situation. This obvious fact is mentioned here only for the sake of completeness and as a reminder that the personality syndromes of the organism are not isolated systems.

Variables: Level and Quality

The most important and most obvious variable is that of *syndrome level*. A person is either high, middle, or low in security, and high, middle, or low in self-esteem. We do not necessarily imply that this variation is on a single continuum; we imply only variation from much to little, from high to low. *Syndrome quality* has been discussed chiefly with respect to the self-esteem or dominance syndrome. In the various species of infrahuman primates the phenomenon of dominance may be seen in all of them but it will have a different quality of expression in each. In the human being with high self-esteem we have been able to differentiate at least two qualities of high self-esteem that we have chosen to designate on the one hand as strength and on the other hand as power. A person with high self-esteem who is also secure shows this feeling of strength of self-confidence in a kind, cooperative, and friendly fashion. The person who is high in self-esteem and is also insecure is interested not so much in helping weaker people as in dominating them and hurting them. Both individuals have high self-esteem, but show it in different ways depending upon other characteristics of the organism. In extremely insecure people there are many ways in which this insecurity can express itself. For instance, it may have the quality of seclusiveness and withdrawal (if they are low in self-esteem), or it may have the quality of hostility, aggressiveness, and nastiness (if they are high in self-esteem).

Cultural Determinants

Certainly the relationships between culture and personality are too profound and too complex to treat briefly. More for the sake of completeness than for any other reason it must be pointed out that in general the paths by which the main goals in life are achieved are often determined by the nature of the particular culture. The ways in which self-esteem may be expressed and achieved are in large part, although not completely, culturally determined. The same is true for the love relations. We win the love of other people and express our affections for them through culturally approved channels. The fact that in a complex society status roles are also in part culturally determined will often shift the expression of personality syndromes. For instance, men with high self-esteem in our society are allowed to express this syndrome much more overtly and in many more ways than are allowed to women with high self-esteem. So also children are given very few opportunities for the direct expression of high self-esteem. It should also be pointed out that there is often a culturally approved syndrome level for each of the syndromes (e.g., security, self-esteem, sociality, activity). This fact can be seen most clearly in cross-cultural comparisons and in historical comparisons. For instance, the average Dobu citizen not only is, but also is expected to be, more hostile than the average Arapesh citizen. The average woman today is expected to be higher in self-esteem than the average woman 100 years ago.

STUDYING THE PERSONALITY SYNDROME

Standard Ways of Correlating

We have so far spoken as if the various parts of the syndrome are homogeneous, like the particles in a fog. Actually this is not the case. Within the syndrome organization we find hierarchies of importance, and clusterings. This fact has already been demonstrated in the simplest possible way for the self-esteem syndrome, namely, by the method of correlation. If the syndrome were undifferentiated, any part of it should correlate as closely with the whole as any other part. Actually, however, self-esteem (measured as a whole) correlates differently with various parts. For instance, the whole self-esteem syndrome as measured by the Social Personality Inventory (Maslow, 1940b) correlates with irritability $r = -0.39$, with the pagan sexual attitude $r = 0.85$, with a number of conscious inferiority feelings $r = -0.40$, with embarrassability in various situations $r = -0.60$, with a number of conscious fears $r = -0.29$ (Maslow, 1968a, 1968b).

Clinical examination of the data also shows this tendency toward a natural clustering of the parts into groups that seem intrinsically to belong close together. For instance, conventionality, morality, modesty, and regard for rules seem to fall together or belong together very naturally, as contrasted with another group of clustering qualities, such as self-confidence, poise, unembarrassability, lack of timidity, and shyness.

This tendency to cluster at once gives us the possibility of classifying within the syndrome, but when we actually attempt to do this we are presented with various difficulties. First of all we are confronted with the common problem of all classifications, that of the principle on which the classifying shall be based. Of course, if we knew all the data and their interrelationships, this would be easy. But when, as in our case, we proceed in partial ignorance, we find that we must be arbitrary at times, no matter how sensitive we try to be to the inner nature of the material. This inner hanging-togetherness gives us, in our case, an initial clue, an indication of general direction. But we can go only so far with such spontaneous groupings, and when we finally come to the point that we fail to perceive them, we must proceed on the basis of our own hypotheses.

Another apparent difficulty is that when we work with syndrome materials we soon find that we can classify any personality syndrome into a dozen main groupings, or a hundred, or a thousand, or ten thousand just as we please, depending on the degree of generality that we have in mind. We suspect that the usual attempt at classification is simply another reflection of the atomistic, connectionistic point of view. Certainly the use of an atomistic tool in dealing with interdepending data cannot get us very far. What is classification ordinarily if not the separation out of different parts, of discrete items? And how then shall we classify if our data are *not* esssentially different and separate from each other? Perhaps we shall have to reject atomistic classification and look for some holistic principle of classifying just as we found it necessary to reject reductive analysis in favor of holistic analysis. The following analogies are offered as indications of the direction in which we must probably look for such a holistic technique of classification.

Levels of Magnification

This phrase is a physical analogy derived from the way in which a microscope works. In studying a histological slide, one gets the whole character, the general structure, the formation, and interrelationships in their totality by holding the slide up to the light and looking at it with the naked eye, thereby encompassing the whole. With this whole picture held clearly in mind we then examine one portion of this whole at a low magnification, let us say 10 times. We are now studying a detail not for its own isolated sake, but with its relationship to the whole in mind. We can then go on to a closer study of this field within the whole by using another objective of still higher magnification, let us say 50 times. Further and finer analysis of the details within the whole are then made possible by using larger and larger magnifications to the practical limits of the instrument.

We might also think of the material as being classified, not in a straight-line series of separated and independent parts which can then be reshuffled in any order, but in terms of "being contained within," perhaps, like a nest of boxes. If we call the whole security syndrome a box, then the 14 subsyndromes are 14 boxes that are contained with it (Maslow, 1952). Within each of these 14 small boxes still other boxes are contained—perhaps 4 in one, 10 in another, 6 in another, and so forth.

Translating these examples into the terms of syndrome study, we may take the security syndrome and examine it as a whole, that is, at level of magnification No. 1. Specifically this means studying the psychological flavor or meaning or aim of the total syndrome as a unity. We may then take one of the 14 subsyndromes of the security syndrome and study it at what we might call level of magnification No. 2. This subsyndrome would then be studied in its particular wholeness, in its interdependence with the 13 other subsyndromes, but always understood as a holistic part of the total security syndrome. As an example we may take the power-submission subsyndrome in the insecure person. The generally insecure person needs power, but this shows itself in many ways and in many different forms, such as overambition, overaggression, possessiveness, hunger for money, overcompetitiveness, tendency to prejudice and hatred, and the like, or as their apparent opposites, such as bootlicking, submissiveness, or masochistic trends. But these characteristics themselves are obviously also general and may be further analyzed and classified. A study of any of these would be at level No. 3. Let us choose, perhaps, the need for or tendency toward prejudice, of which race prejudice is a good example. If we study this correctly, we study it not in itself or in isolation. We could phrase it more fully by saying that we are studying the tendency to prejudice, which is a subsyndrome of the need for power, which is a subsyndrome of the general insecurity syndrome. We need not point out that finer and finer studies would take us to level 4, level 5, and so on. We could take for instance one aspect of this particular complexity, let us say the tendency to seize upon differences (e.g., skin color, shape of nose, language spoken) as a means to bolster one's own need for security. This tendency to seize upon differences is organized as a syndrome and can be studied as a syndrome. To be more specific, in this case it would be classified as a sub-sub-sub-subsyndrome. It is the fifth box in the nest of boxes.

To sum up, such a method of classification, namely, one that is based on the fundamental concept of "being contained within" rather than of "being separate from," can give us the clue for which we have been seeking. It allows us to be sophisticated both about particulars and about wholes without falling into either meaningless particularism or vague and useless generality. It is simultaneously synthetic and analytic, and, finally, it allows us to study uniqueness and commonness simultaneously and effectively. It rejects dichotomies, the Aristotelian division into class A and class Not-A, and yet furnishes us with a theoretically satisfactory principle of classification and analysis.

Clustering According to Meaning

If we look for a heuristic criterion by which to differentiate between syndromes and subsyndromes, we can find it theoretically in the concept of concentration. What is the difference between the natural groupings in the self-esteem syndrome? Conventionality, morality, modesty, and regard for rules were found to cluster together into a group, which could be differentiated from another cluster formed by the characteristics of self-confidence, poise, unembarrassability, and boldness. These clusters or subsyndromes of course correlate with each other and with self-esteem as a whole. Furthermore, within each cluster the various elements correlate with one another. Probably our perception of clustering, the subjective feeling that various elements go together naturally, would be reflected in the correlations that would be obtained if we could get measures of these elements. Probably self-confidence and poise are more closely correlated than are poise and unconventionality. Perhaps a clustering could mean in statistical terms a high average of intercorrelation between all the members of the cluster. This average intercorrelation would presumably be higher than the average of correlation between members of two different clusters. Supposing we assume the intracluster average correlation to be $r = 0.7$ and the average correlation between members of different clusters to be $r = 0.5$, then the new syndrome formed by the merging of the clusters or subsyndromes will have an average correlation higher than $r = 0.5$ and lower than $r = 0.7$, probably closer to $r = 0.6$. As we move from sub-subsyndromes to subsyndromes to syndromes, we may expect that the average correlation will go down. This change we may call change in syndrome concentration, and we may reasonably stress the concept if only because it may furnish us with the working tool with which we may check our clinical findings.[13]

It follows from the basic assumption of a dynamic psychology that what can and should be correlated are *not* behaviors qua behaviors, but the meanings of behaviors, for example, not modest behavior, but the quality of modesty seen intact in its relations to the rest of the organism. Furthermore it must be recognized that even dynamic variables do not necessarily vary along a single continuum, but may at a certain point break sharply into something completely different. An example of this phenomenon may be found in the effects of hunger for affection. If we range young children in a series from fully accepted to fully rejected, we shall find that as we go down the scale, the children hunger more and more frantically for affection, but as we approach the extreme end of the scale—utter rejection from the earliest days of life—we find not a tremendous yearning for love, but a complete coldness and *lack* of desire for affection.

Finally we must of course use holistic data rater than atomistic data, that is, not the products of reductive analysis but of holistic analysis. In this way, single variables or parts may be correlated without doing violence to the unity of the organism. If we are properly cautious about the data that we correlate, and if we temper all statistics with clinical and experimental knowledge, there is no reason why correlation technique should not be highly useful in a holistic methodology.

Syndromes Interrelated Within the Organism

In his book on physical Gestalts, Köhler (1961) objects to the overgeneralization of interrelatedness, even to the extent of not being able to choose between a very general monism and a complete atomism. Accordingly, he stresses not only interrelatedness within a Gestalt, but also the fact of separateness of Gestalts. For him most of the Gestalts he works with are (relatively) closed systems. He carrries his analysis only to the point of analyzing within the Gestalt; he discusses less often the relations between Gestalts, either physical or psychological.

It must be apparent that when we deal with organismic data we have a different situation. Certainly there are almost no closed systems within the organism. Within the organism everything *does* actually relate with everything else, if only sometimes in the most tenuous and distant fashion. Furthermore, the organism taken as a whole has been shown to be related to and to be fundamentally interdependent with the culture, the immediate presence of other people, the par-

[13]It is the tendency of holistic psychologists to mistrust the correlation technique, but I feel that this is because the technique happens to have been used in an exclusively atomistic way rather than because its essential nature conflicts with holistic theory. Even though, for instance, self-correlations are mistrusted by the average statistician (as if anything else could be expected in the organism!), they *need* not be if certain holistic facts are taken into consideration.

ticular situation, physical and geographical factors, and so on. So far we may say at least that what Köhler should have done was to restrict his generalization to physical Gestalts and to psychological Gestalts in the phenomenal world, for his strictures certainly do not apply nearly so strongly within the organism.

It is possible to go beyond this minimum statement if we choose to argue about it. Actually a very good case can be made for saying that the whole world is theoretically interrelated. We can find relations of some sort between any part of the universe and any other part if we choose from any of the multitude of relation types that exist. It is only if we wish to be practical, or if we speak in a single realm of discourse rather than in a totality of realms of discourse, that we can assume that systems are relatively independent of one another. For instance, from the psychological point of view, universal interrelatedness breaks up because there are parts of the world that are not *psychologically* related to other parts of the universe, even though they may be related chemically, physically, or biologically. Furthermore the interrelatedness of the world might very well be broken up in a completely different fashion by the biologist or chemist or physicist. It seems to me that the best phrasing possible at the moment is that there are relatively closed systems, but that these closed systems are the product in part of the point of view. What is (or what seems to be) a closed system may not be so a year from now because scientific operations may improve enough next year to demonstrate that there is such relationship. If the reply were to be made that we should have to demonstrate actual physical processes obtaining rather than more theoretical relationships between all the part of the world, then it certainly must be said in reply that the monistic philosophers have never claimed such a universal *physical* interrelatedness but have spoken of many other kinds of interrelatedness. However, since this is not a main point in our exposition, it is not necessary to dwell upon it. It is quite sufficient to point out the phenomenon of (theoretical) universal interrelatedness within the organism.

LEVEL AND QUALITY OF THE PERSONALITY SYNDROMES

In this area of research we have at least one carefully studied example to offer. Whether this is a paradigm or a special case remains to be discovered by further research.

Quantitatively, that is to say in terms of simple linear correlations, there is a positive but small relationship between the security level and level of self-esteem, $r =$ about 0.2 or 0.3. In the area of individual diagnosis in normal people, it is quite clear that these two syndromes are practically independent variables. In certain groups there may be characteristic relations in the two syndromes: for example, in Jews there was (in the 1940s) a tendency to be simultaneously high in self-esteem and low in security, while in Catholic women we found often low self-esteem joined with high security. In neurotics both levels were and are apt to be low.

But more startling than this relationship (or lack of it) in level of the two syndromes is the very close relationship between *level* of security (or self-esteem) and the *quality* of self-esteem (or security). This relationship can be demonstrated most easily by contrasting two individuals both high in self-esteem but at opposite ends of the scale in security. Person A (high self-esteem and high security) tends to express self-esteem in a very different way from person B (high self-esteem and low security). Person A, who has both personal strength and love for humankind, will naturally use this strength in a fostering, kindly, or protecting fashion. But B, who has equal strength but has with it hate, contempt, or fear for humankind, will more likely use this strength to hurt, to dominate, or to assuage the insecurity. The strength must then be a threat to his or her fellows. Thus we may speak of an insecure quality of high self-esteem, and we may contrast it with a secure quality of high self-esteem. Similarly we may distinguish insecure and secure qualities of low self-esteem, that is, masochist or bootlicker on the one hand, the quiet, sweet, or serving, dependent person on the other hand. Similar differences in security quality correlate with differences in level of self-esteem. For instance, insecure people may be either retiring, withdrawing people or openly hostile and aggressive people accordingly as they are low or high in level of self-esteem. Secure people can be either humble or proud, followers or leaders as their self-esteem levels vary from low to high.

PERSONALITY SYNDROMES AND BEHAVIOR

In a broad fashion, preliminary to more specific analysis, we can say that the relations between the syndromes and overt behavior are about as follows. Each act *tends* to be an expression of the whole integrated personality. This means, more specifically, that each act tends to be determined by each and all of the personality syndromes (in addition to other determinants to be spoken of below). As John Doe laughs and responds to a joke, we can theoretically tease out from among the various determinants of this unitary act his security level, his self-esteem, his energy, his intelligence, and so on. Such a viewpoint is in clear contrast to that now obsolete brand of trait theory in which a single behavior act is determined wholly by a single trait. Our theoretical statement gets its best exemplification in certain tasks, like artistic creation. In producing a painting or a concerto, the artist clearly puts the self completely into the task, and accordingly it is an expression of the whole personality. But such an example, or, let us say, any creative response to an unstructured situation—as in the Rorschach test—is at the extreme of the continuum. At the other end is the isolated, specific act that has little or no relation to the character structure. Examples of such are immediate responses to the demands of a momentary situation (getting out of the way of a truck), purely habitual, cultural responses that have long since lost their psychological meaning for most people (the custom for men of standing when a woman enters the room), or, finally, reflex acts. Such behavior can tell us little or nothing about the character, for in these cases it is negligible as a determining factor. Between these extremes we find all sorts of gradations. There are, for example, acts that tend to be almost wholly determined by only one or two syndromes. A particular act of kindness is more closely related to the security syndrome than to any other. The feeling of modesty is largely determined by self-esteem, and so on.

These facts may raise the question of why, if all these types of behavior-syndrome relations exist, should it be said at the outset that behavior is generally determined by all the syndromes?

It is obvious that, by a kind of theoretical requiredness, a holistic theory would start with such a statement, while an atomistic approach would start with the selection of an isolated, discrete behavior, cut away from all its connection to the organism—a sensation or conditioned reflex, for instance. Here it is a problem of "centering" (from the point of view of which part is the whole to be organized). For atomistic theory the simplest fundamental datum would be a bit of behavior obtained by reductive analysis, that is, a behavior cut away from all its relationships to the rest of the organism.

Perhaps more to the point is the contention that the first type of syndrome-behavior relationship is more important. Isolated behaviors tend to be on the fringe of life's main concerns. They are isolated simply *because* they are unimportant, that is, have nothing to do with the main problems, the main answers, or the main goals of the organism. It is quite true that my leg kicks out when the patellar tendon is struck, or that I eat olives with my fingers, or that I cannot eat boiled onions because I was conditioned against them. It is certainly no truer that I have a certain life philosophy, that I love my family, or that I am drawn to do experiments of a certain kind—but the latter situations are far more important.

While it is true that the inner nature of the organism is a determinant of behavior, it is not the only determinant of behavior. The cultural setting in which the organism behaves, and which has already helped to determine the inner nature of the organism, is also a determinant of behavior. Finally, another set of determinants of behavior may be lumped under the head of "the immediate situation." While the goals and aims of the behavior are determined by the nature of the organism and the paths to the goals are determined by the culture, the immediate situation determines the realistic possibilities and impossibilities: which behavior is wise, which not; which partial goals are available and which not; what offers a threat and what offers a possible tool with which the goals may be achieved.

Conceived thus complexly, it becomes easy to understand why behavior is not always a good index of character structure. For if behavior is as much determined by the external situation and by culture as by character, if it is a compromise formation between three sets of forces, it cannot very well be a perfect indicator of any one of them. Again this is a theoretical statement. Practically there are certain techniques[14] whereby we may "control out" or nullify the influ-

---

[14]For instance, the situation may be controlled out as a determiner of behavior by making it sufficiently vague, as in the various projective tests. Or sometimes the demands of the organism are so overwhelming, as in insanity, that the external world is denied or disregarded and the culture defied. The prime technique for partially ruling out the culture is interview rapport or the psychoanalytic transference. In certain other situations the cultural compulsions may be weakened, as in drunkenness, rage, or other examples of uncontrolled behavior. Again there are many behaviors that culture neglects to regulate, such as various subtle, subliminally perceived variations of the culturally determined theme, the so-called expressive movements. Or we may study behavior in relatively uninhibited people, in children in whom cultural compulsions are as yet weak, in animals in which they are almost negligible, or in other societies so that we can rule out cultural influences by contrast. These few examples show that a sophisticated, theoretically sound study of behavior *can* tell us something about inner organization of personality.

ences of culture and situation so that in actual practice, behavior *may* sometimes be a good index of character.

A much higher correlation is found to obtain between character and impulse to behavior. Indeed, this correlation is so high that these impulses to behavior may themselves be considered part of the syndrome. These are far more free of external and cultural compulsions than are overt behavior acts. We may even go so far as to say that we study behavior only as an index of impulse to behavior. If it is a good index, it is worth studying; if it is not a good index, it is not worth studying, if the ultimate object of our studying is the understanding of character.

LOGICAL AND MATHEMATICAL EXPRESSION OF SYNDROME DATA

There is not now extant, so far as I know, any mathematics or logic that is suitable for the symbolic expression and manipulation of syndrome data. Such a symbolic system is by no means impossible, for we know that we can construct mathematics or logics to suit our needs. Currently, however, most of the various logics and mathematical systems that are available are based on and are expressions of the general-atomistic world view that we have already criticized. My own efforts in this direction are much too feeble to present here.

The sharp distinction between A and Not-A introduced by Aristotle as one of the bases of his logic has been carried on to modern logics even where other Aristotelian assumptions have been rejected. So, for instance, we find in Langer's *Symbolic Logic* that this notion, which she describes in terms of complementary classes, is for her one of the basic assumptions that need not be proven but can be taken for granted as common sense. "Every class has a complement; the class and its complement are mutually exclusive and exhaust the universe class between them" (1937, p. 193).

It must by now be obvious that with syndrome data there can be no such sharp cutting away of any part of the data from the whole, or any such sharp division between any single datum and the rest of the syndrome. When we cut A away from the whole, A is no longer A, Not-A is no longer what it was, and certainly simple addition of A and Not-A will not give us back the whole with which we started. Within a syndrome every part of the syndrome overlaps every other part. Cutting away a part is impossible unless we pay no heed to these overlappings. This neglect the psychologist cannot afford. Mutual exclusiveness is possible for data taken in isolation. If they are taken in context, as they must be in psychology, this dichotomizing is quite impossible. It is not, for instance, even conceivable that we could cut away self-esteem behavior from all other behavior, for the very simple reason that there is practically no behavior that is just self-esteem behavior and nothing else.

If we reject this notion of mutual exclusiveness, we call into doubt not only the whole logic that is partially based upon it, but also most of the systems of mathematics with which we are familiar. Most extant mathematics and logic deal with a world that is a collection of mutually exclusive entities, like a pile of apples. Separating one apple from the rest of the pile changes neither the essential nature of the apple nor the essential nature of the pile. With the organism it is quite different. Cutting away an organ changes the whole organism as well as the part that was cut away.

Another example may be found in the basic arithmetical procedures of addition, subtraction, multiplication, and division. These are all operations that clearly assume atomistic data. Adding an apple to another apple is possible because the nature of apples permits this. The case is different with personality. If we have two people who have high self-esteem and are insecure and we then make one of these people more secure ("add" security), we have one person who probably tends to be cooperative and another who tends to be a tyrant. The high self-esteem in one personality does not have the same quality as the high self-esteem in the other. In the person to whom security has been added there are two changes, not just one. Not only did that person acquire security, but the quality of the self-esteem changed, merely by being conjoined with high security. This is a labored example, but it is the closest that we can come to conceiving of anything like the additive processes in personality.

Apparently traditional mathematics and logic, in spite of their unlimited possiblities, seem actually to be handmaidens in the service of an atomistic, mechanical view of the world.

It seems even possible to say that mathematics is lagging behind modern physical sciences in its acceptance of dynamic, holistic theory. Essential changes in the nature of physical theory are made, not by changing the essential nature of mathematics, but by stretching its use, by doing tricks with it, by leaving its essentially static nature unchanged as much as possible. These changes can be made only by making various "as if" assumptions. A good example is found in calculus, which purports to deal with motion and change, but does this only by making the change into a succession of static states. The area under a curve is measured by splitting it into a series of oblongs. Curves themselves are treated "as if" they were polygonal figures with very small sides. That this has been a legitimate procedure with which we can have no ultimate quarrel is proven by the fact that the calculus works and is a highly useful instrument. But what is not legitimate is to forget that it works because of a series of assumptions, of dodges or tricks, of "as if" assumptions that clearly do not deal with the phenomenal world as psychological studies do.

The following quotation is an illustration of our contention that mathematics tends to be static and atomistic. So far as I know its purport has not been challenged by other mathematicians.

> But had we not previously declared quite fervently that we live in a motionless world? And had we not shown at great length, by employing the paradoxes of Zeno, that motion is impossible, that a flying arrow is actually at rest? To what shall we ascribe this apparent reversal of position?

> Moreover, if each new mathematical invention rests upon the old established foundations, how is it possible to extract from the theories of static algebra and static geometry a new mathematics capable of solving problems involving dynamic entities?

As to the first, there has been no reversal of viewpoint. We are still firmly entrenched in the belief that this is a world in which motion as well as change are special cases of the state of rest. There is no state of change, if change implies a state qualitatively different from rest; that which we distinguish as change is merely, as we once indicated, a succession of many different static images perceived in comparatively short intervals of time. . . .

Intuitively convinced that there is continuity in the behavior of a moving body, since we do not actually see the flying arrow pass through every point on its flight, there is an overwhelming instinct to abstract the idea of motion as something essentially different from rest. But this abstraction results from physiological and psychological limitations; it is in no way justified by logical analysis. Motion is a correlation of position with time. Chance is merely another name for *function,* another aspect of that same correlation.

For the rest, the calculus, as an offspring of geometry and algebra, belongs to a static family and has acquired no characteristics not already possessed by its parents. Mutations are not possible in mathematics. Thus, inevitably, the calculus has the same static properties as the multiplication table and the geometry of Euclid. The calculus is but another interpretation, although it must be admitted an ingenious one, of this unmoving world (Kasner & Newman, 1940, pp. 301–304).

Let us say again that there are two ways of looking at elements. For instance, blushing can be blushing per se (a reductive element) or it can be blushing in a context (a holistic element). The former involves a kind of "as if" assumption, "as if it were all alone in the world and had no relation to the rest of the world." This is a formal abstraction and in certain scientific areas may be quite useful. In any case certainly no harm can be done by the abstraction as long as it is remembered that it *is* a formal abstraction. Trouble arises only when mathematicians or logicians or scientists forget that they are doing something artificial when they talk about blushing per se, for certainly they would admit that there is in the real world no such thing as blushing without a human being to blush, something to blush about, and so on. This artificial habit of abstraction, or working with reductive elements, has worked so well and has become so ingrained a habit that the abstractors and the reducers are apt to be amazed at anyone who denies the empirical or phenomenal validity of these habits. By smooth stages they convince themselves that this is the way in which the world is actually constructed, and they find it easy to forget that even though it is useful it is still artificial, conventionalized, hypothetical—in a word, that it is an artifactual system that is imposed upon an interconnected world in flux. These peculiar hypotheses about the world have the right to fly in the face of common sense only for the sake of demonstrated convenience. When they are no longer convenient, or when they become hindrances, they must be dropped. It is dangerous to see in the world what we have put into it rather than what is actually there. Let us say this flatly. Atomistic mathematics or logic is, in a certain sense, a theory about the world, and any description of it in terms of this theory the psychologist may reject as unsuited to his purposes. It is clearly necessary for methodological thinkers to proceed to the creation of logical and mathematical systems that are more closely in accord with the nature of the world of modern science.

It is possible to extend these remarks to the English language itself. This too tends to reflect the atomistic world theory of our culture. It is not to be wondered that in describing syndrome data and syndrome laws we must resort to the most outlandish analogies, figures of speech, and various other twistings and turnings. We have the conjunction *and* to express the joining of two discrete entities, but we have no conjunction to express the joining of two entities that are not discrete and that when joined form a unit and not a duality. The only substitute that I can think of for this basic conjunction is the clumsy one *structured with*. There are other languages that are more sympathetic to a holistic, dynamic world view. In my opinion the agglutinate languages are more adequate to reflect the holistic world than is the English language. Another point is that our language organizes the world, as most logicians and mathematicians do, into elements and relationships, matter and things done to matter. Nouns are treated as if they were matter, and verbs as if they were actions done by matter to matter. Adjectives describe more accurately the kind of matter, and adverbs describe more accurately the kind of action. A holistic-dynamic view makes no such sharp dichotomy. In any case, words must be strung out in a straight line even when they are trying to describe syndrome data (Lee, 1961).

REFERENCES

Adler, A. (1939). *Social interest*. New York: Putnam's.

Adler, A. (1964). *Superiority and social interests: A collection of later writings* (H. L. Ansbacher and R. R. Ansbacher, eds.). Evanston: Northwestern University Press.

Alderfer, C. P. (1967). An organization syndrome. *Administrative Science Quarterly, 12,* 440–460.

Allport, G. (1955). *Becoming*. New Haven, CT: Yale University Press.

Allport, G. (1959). Normative compatibility in the light of social science. In A. H. Maslow (Ed.), *New knowledge in human values*. New York: Harper & Row.

Allport, G. (1960). *Personality and social encounter*. Boston: Beacon.

Allport, G. (1961). *Pattern and growth in personality*. New York: Holt, Rinehart & Winston.

Allport, G., & Vernon, P. E. (1933). *Studies in expressive movement*. New York: Macmillan.

Anderson, H. H. (Ed.). (1959). *Creativity and its cultivation*. New York: Harper & Row.

Angyal, A. (1965). *Neurosis and treatment: A holistic theory*. New York: Wiley.

Ansbacher, H., & Ansbacher, R. (1956). *The individual psychology of Alfred Adler*. New York: Basic Books.

Ardrey, R. (1966). *The territorial imperative*. New York: Atheneum.

Argyris, C. (1962). *Interpersonal competence and organizational effectiveness*. Homewood, IL: Irwin-Dorsey.

Argyris, C. (1965). *Organization and innovation*. Homewood, IL: Irwin.

Aronoff, J. (1962). Freud's conception of the origin of curiosity. *Journal of Psychology, 54,* 39–45.

Aronoff, J. (1967). *Psychological needs and cultural systems*. New York: Van Nostrand Reinhold.

Asch, S. E. (1956). Studies of independence and conformity. *Psychological Monographs, 70*(Whole No. 416).

Baker, R. S. (1945). *American chronicle*. New York: Scribner's.

Bartlett, F. C. (1932). *Remembering*. Cambridge: Cambridge University Press.

Benedict, R. (1970). Synergy in society. *American Anthropologist*.

Bennis, W. (1966). *Changing organizations*. New York: McGraw-Hill.

Bennis, W. (1967). Organizations of the future. *Personnel Administration, 30*, 6–24.

Bennis, W., & Slater, P. (1968). *The temporary society*. New York: Harper & Row.

Bergson, H. (1944). *Creative evolution*. New York: Modern Library.

Bernard, L. L. (1924). *Instinct: A study in social psychology*. New York: Holt, Rinehart & Winston.

Bonner, H. (1961). *Psychology of personality*. New York: Ronald Press.

Bronowski, J. (1956). *Science and human values*. New York: Harper & Row.

Bugental, J. (1965). *The search for authenticity*. New York: Holt, Rinehart & Winston.

Bühler, C., & Massarik, F. (Eds.). (1968). *The course of human life: A study of life goals in the humanistic perspective*. New York: Springer.

Cannon, W. G. (1932). *Wisdom of the body*. New York: Norton.

Cantril, H. (1950). An inquiry concerning the characteristics of man. *Journal of Abnormal and Social Psychology, 45*, 491–503.

Chenault, J. (1969). Syntony: A philosophical promise for theory and research. In A. Sutich and M. Vich (Eds.), *Readings in Humanistic Psychology*. New York: Free Press.

Chiang, H. (1968). An experiment in experiential approaches to personality. *Psychologia, 11*, 33–39.

D'Arcy, M. C. (1947). *The mind and heart of love*. New York: Holt, Rinehart & Winston.

Davies, J. C. (1963). *Human nature in politics*. New York: Wiley.

Deutsch, F., & Miller, W. (1967). *Clinical interview*, Vols. I & II. New York: International Universities Press.

Dewey, J. (1939). Theory of valuation. *International encyclopedia of unified science* (Vol. 2, No. 4). Chicago: University of Chicago Press.

Drucker, P. F. (1939). *The end of economic man*. New York: Day.

Eastman, M. (1928). *The enjoyment of poetry*. New York: Scribner's.

Einstein, A., & Infeld, L. (1938). *The evolution of physics*. New York: Simon & Schuster.

Erikson, E. (1959). *Identity and the life cycle*. New York: International Universities Press.

Farrow, E. P. (1942). *Psychoanalyze yourself*. New York: International Universities Press.

Frankl, V. (1969). *The will to meaning*. New York: World.

Frenkel-Brunswik, E. (1949). Intolerance of ambiguity as an emotional and perceptual personality variable. *Journal of Personality, 18*, 108–143.

Freud, S. (1920). *General introduction to psychoanalysis*. New York: Boni & Liveright.

Freud, S. (1924). *Collected papers*, Vol. II. London: Hogarth Press.

Freud, S. (1930). *Civilization and its discontents*. New York: Cape & Smith.

Freud, S. (1933). *New introductory lectures on psychoanalysis*. New York: Norton.

Fromm, E. (1941). *Escape from freedom*. New York: Farrar, Straus & Giroux.

Fromm, E. (1947). *Man for himself*. New York: Holt, Rinehart & Winston.

Goldstein, K. (1939). *The organism*. New York: American Book.

Goldstein, K. (1940). *Human nature*. Cambridge: Harvard University Press.

Grof, S. (1975). *Realms of the human unconscious*. New York: Viking Press.

Guiterman, A. (1939). *Lyric laughter*. New York: Dutton.

Harding, M. E. (1947). *Psychic energy*. New York: Pantheon.

Harlow, H. F. (1950). Learning motivated by a manipulation drive. *Journal of Experimental Psychology, 40*, 228–234.

Harlow, H. F. (1953). Motivation as a factor in the acquisition of new responses. In R. M. Jones (Ed.), *Current theory and research in motivation.* Lincoln: University of Nebraska Press.

Harper, R. (1966). *Human love: Existential and mystical.* Baltimore: Johns Hopkins Press.

Hayakawa, S. I. (1949). *Language and thought in action.* New York: Harcourt, Brace & World.

Herzberg, F. (1966). *Work and the nature of man.* New York: World.

Hoggart, R. (1961). *The uses of literacy.* Boston: Beacon.

Horney, K. (1937). *The neurotic personality of our time.* New York: Norton.

Horney, K. (1939). *New ways in psychoanalysis.* New York: Norton.

Horney, K. (1942). *Self-analysis.* New York: Norton.

Horney, K. (1950). *Neurosis and human growth.* New York: Norton.

Howells, T. H. (1945). The obsolete dogma of heredity. *Psychology Review, 52,* 23–34.

Howells, T. H., & Vine, D. O. (1940). The innate differential in social learning. *Journal of Abnormal and Social Psychology, 35,* 537–548.

Husband, R. W. (1929). A comparison of human adults and white rats in maze learning. *Journal of Comparative Psychology, 9,* 361–377.

Huxley, A. (1944).*The perennial philosophy.* New York: Harper & Row.

James, W. (1890). *The principles of psychology.* New York: Holt, Rinehart & Winston.

James, W. (1958). *The varieties of religious experience.* New York: Modern Library.

Johnson, W. (1946). *People in quandaries.* New York: Harper & Row.

Jourard, S. M. (1968). *Disclosing man to himself.* New York: Van Nostrand Reinhold.

Kasner, E., & Newman, J. (1940). *Mathematics and the imagination.* New York: Simon & Schuster.

Katona, G. (1940). *Organizing and memorizing.* New York: Columbia University Press.

Klee, J. B. (1951). *Problems of selective behavior.* (New Series No. 7). Lincoln: University of Nebraska Studies.

Koestler, A. (1945). *The yogi and the commissar.* New York: Macmillan.

Köhler, W. (1961). Gestalt psychology today. In M. Henle (Ed.), *Documents of gestalt psychology.* Berkeley: University of California Press.

Langer, S. (1937). *Symbolic logic.* Boston: Houghton Mifflin.

Lee, D. (1961). *Freedom and culture.* Englewood Cliffs, NJ: Prentice-Hall.

Levy, D. M. (1934a). Experiments on the sucking reflex and social behavior of dogs. *American Journal of Orthopsychiatry.*

Levy, D. M. (1934b). A note on pecking in chickens. *Psychoanalytic Quarterly, 4,* 612–613.

Levy, D. M. (1937). Primary affect hunger. *American Journal of Psychiatry, 94,* 643–652.

Levy, D. M. (1938). On instinct-satiations: An experiment on the pecking behavior of chickens. *Journal of General Psychology, 18,* 327–348.

Levy, D. M. (1939). Release therapy. *American Journal of Orthopsychiatry, 9,* 713–736.

Levy, D. M. (1943). *Maternal overprotection.* New York: Columbia University Press.

Levy, D. M. (1944). On the problem of movement restraint. *American Journal of Orthopsychiatry, 14,* 644–671.

Levy, D. M. (1951). The deprived and indulged forms of psychopathic personality. *American Journal of Orthopsychiatry, 21,* 250–254.

Lewin, K. (1935). *Dynamic theory of personality.* New York: McGraw-Hill.

Likert, R. (1961). *New patterns in management.* New York: McGraw-Hill.

Lynd, R. (1939). *Knowledge for what?* Princeton, NJ: Princeton University Press.

Maier, N. R. F. (1939). *Studies of abnormal behavior in the rat*. New York: Harper & Row.

Maier, N. R. F. (1949). *Frustration*. New York: McGraw-Hill.

Marmor, J. (1942). The role of instinct in human behavior. *Psychiatry, 5,* 509–516.

Maslow, A. H. (1935). Appetites and hunger in animal motivation. *Journal of Comparative Psychology, 20,* 75–83.

Maslow, A. H. (1936). The dominance drive as a determiner of the social and sexual behavior of infra-human primates, I-IV. *Journal of Genetic Psychology, 48,* 261–277, 278–309, 310–338; *49,* 161–190.

Maslow, A. H. (1937). The influence of familiarization on preference. *Journal of Experimental Psychology, 21,* 162–180.

Maslow, A. H. (1940a). Dominance-quality and social behavior in infra-human primates. Journal of Social Psychology, *11,* 313–324.

Maslow, A. H. (1940b). A test for dominance-feeling (self-esteem) in women. *Journal of Social Psychology, 12,* 255–270.

Maslow, A. H. (1943). The authoritarian character structure. *Journal of Social Psychology, 18,* 401–411.

Maslow, A. H. (1952). *The S–I Test: A measure of psychological security–insecurity.* Palo Alto, CA: Consulting Psychologists Press.

Maslow, A. H. (1957). Power relationships and patterns of personal development. In A. Kornhauser (Ed.), *Problems of power in American democracy.* Detroit: Wayne University Press.

Maslow, A. H. (1958). Emotional blocks to creativity. *Journal of Individual Psychology, 14,* 51–56.

Maslow, A. H. (1964a). *Religions, values and peak experiences.* Columbus: Ohio State University Press.

Maslow, A. H. (1964b). Synergy in the society and in the individual. *Journal of Individual Psychology, 20,* 153–164.

Maslow, A. H. (1965a). Criteria for judging needs to be instinctoid. In M. R. Jones (Ed.), *Human Motivation: A Symposium.* Lincoln: University of Nebraska Press.

Maslow, A. H. (1965b). *Eupsychian management: A journal.* Homewood, IL: Irwin-Dorsey.

Maslow, A. H. (1966). *The psychology of science: A reconnaissance.* New York: Harper & Row.

Maslow, A. H. (1967). A theory of metamotivation: The biological rooting of the value-life. *Journal of Humanistic Psychology, 7,* 93–127.

Maslow, A. H. (1968a). Some educational implications of the humanistic psychologies. *Harvard Educational Review, 38,* 685–686.

Maslow, A. H. (1968b). Some fundamental questions that face the normative social psychologist. *Journal of Humanistic Psychology, 8,* 143–153.

Maslow, A. H. (1968c). *Toward a Psychology of Being* (2nd ed.). New York: Van Nostrand Reinhold.

Maslow, A. H. (1969a). The farther reaches of human nature. *Journal of Transpersonal Psychology, 1,* 1–10.

Maslow, A. H. (1969b). Theory Z. *Journal of Transpersonal Psychology, 1,* 31–47.

Maslow, A. H. (1969c). Various meanings of transcendence. *Journal of Transpersonal Psychology, 1,* 56–66.

Maslow, A. H., & Mittelman, B. (1951). *Principles of abnormal psychology (rev. ed.).* New York: Harper & Row.

McClelland, D. (1961). *The achieving society*. New York: Van Nostrand Reinhold.

McClelland, D. (1964). *The roots of consciousness*. New York: Van Nostrand Reinhold.

McClelland, D., & Winter, D. G. (1969). *Motivating economic achievement*. New York: Free Press.

McGregor, D. (1960). *The human side of enterprise*. New York: McGraw-Hill.

Menninger, K. A. (1942). *Love against hate*. New York: Harcourt, Brace & World.

Milner, M. (1967). *On not being able to paint*. New York: International Universities Press.

Money-Kyrle, R. E. (1944). Towards a common aim—A psychoanalytical contribution to ethics. *British Journal of Medical Psychology, 20,* 105–117.

Mumford, L. (1951). *The conduct of life*. New York: Harcourt, Brace & World.

Murphy, G. (1947). *Personality*. New York: Harper & Row.

Murphy, L. (1937). *Social behavior and child personality*. New York: Columbia University Press.

Myerson, A. (1925). *When life loses its zest*. Boston: Little, Brown.

Northrop, F. S. C. (1947). *The logic of the sciences and the humanities*. New York: Macmillan.

Pieper, J. (1964). *Leisure, the basis of culture*. New York: Pantheon.

Polanyi, M. (1958). *Personal knowledge*. Chicago: University of Chicago Press.

Polanyi, M. (1964). *Science, faith and society*. Chicago: University of Chicago Press.

Rand, A. (1943). *The fountainhead*. Indianapolis: Bobbs-Merrill.

Reik, T. (1948). *Listening with the third ear*. New York: Farrar, Straus & Giroux.

Reik, T. (1957). *Of love and lust*. New York: Farrar, Straus & Giroux.

Ribot, T. H. (1896). *La psychologie des sentiments*. Paris: Alcan.

Riesman, D. (1950). *The lonely crowd*. New Haven, CT: Yale University Press.

Rogers, C. (1954). *Psychotherapy and personality changes*. Chicago: University of Chicago Press.

Rogers, C. (1961). *On becoming a person*. Boston: Houghton Mifflin.

Schachtel, E. (1959). *Metamorphosis*. New York: Basic Books.

Schilder, P. (1942). *Goals and desires of man*. New York: Columbia University Press.

Shostrom, E. (1963). *Personal Orientation Inventory (POI): A test of self-actualization*. San Diego, CA: Educational and Industrial Testing Service.

Shostrom, E. (1968). *Bibliography for the P.O.I.* San Diego, CA: Educational and Industrial Testing Service.

Suttie, I. (1935). *The origins of love and hate*. New York: Julian Press.

Taggard, G. (1934). *The life and mind of Emily Dickinson*. New York: Knopf.

Thorndike, E. L. (1940). *Human nature and the social order*. New York: Macmillan.

Van Doren, C. (1936). *Three worlds*. New York: Harper & Row.

Wertheimer, M. (1959). *Productive thinking* (2nd ed.). New York: Harper & Row.

Whitehead, A. N. (1938). *Modes of thought*. New York: Macmillan and Cambridge University Press.

Wilson, C. (1967). *Introduction to the new existentialism*. Boston: Houghton Mifflin.

Wilson, C. (1969). *Voyage to a beginning*. New York: Crown.

Wolff, W. (1943). *The expression of personality*. New York: Harper & Row.

Wootton, G., (1967). *Workers, unions and the state*. New York: Schocken.

Yeatman, R. J., & Sellar, W. C. (1931). *1066 and all that*. New York: Dutton.

Young, P. T. (1941). The experimental analysis of appetite. *Psychological Bulletin, 38,* 129–164.

Young, P. T. (1948). Appetite, palatability and feeding habit; A critical review. *Psychological Bulletin, 45,* 289–320.

afterword

THE RICH HARVEST OF ABRAHAM MASLOW

By Ruth Cox

I had thought that I'm at the peak of my powers and usefulness now, so whenever I die it will be like chopping down a tree, leaving a whole crop of apples yet to be harvested. That would be sad. And yet acceptable. Because if life has been so rich, then hanging on to it would be greedy and ungrateful (Maslow's journal, February 12, 1970, in Lowry, 1979, p. 997).

INTRODUCTION

Four months after writing these words in his journal, Abraham Maslow died at the age of 62. Today, Maslow's vision of the potential for individual well-being and a synergistic society is being applied in numerous areas of social and psychological thought. One measure of his philosophy can be found in the wide range of its applications.

This chapter examines some of the practical and theoretical ways in which Maslow's vision is reflected in our lives and society. He contributed immeasurably to a new view of human nature and was a founder of two branches of contemporary psychology, the humanistic and the transpersonal. Through the 1970s and into the 1980s there has been an ongoing harvest of Maslow's ideas in the areas of psychology, education, business and management, health, and social studies.

His speculations and theories touch our personal and social lives in so many ways that it is difficult, as Joyce Carol Oates wrote "to do justice to the challenge of Maslow's amazingly fertile mind; his combining of teacher, seer, physician, visionary, social planner, critic; his ambition in tying together all varieties of apparently unrelated phenomena; his unstoppable optimism" (in Leonard, 1983, p. 335).

By objective standards, Maslow's body of published work is impressive: 6 major books and over 140 journal articles, many reprinted in various collections of contemporary psychological thought. Yet more important than the sheer volume of Maslow's publications is the *impact* that his ideas have had on our lives and our society. His writing originated from a belief that human beings can never be understood unless their highest aspirations are taken into account. He articulated that as human beings we possess an innate thrust to cultivate these aspirations in ways that fulfill us and serve society.

A Sense of Wonder

Maslow's love for life and his unending belief in the positive nature of the human species grew as he devoted his life to a holistic understanding of human nature. Human beings are not merely a collection of neuroses, but a wealth of potential. Even in his early years, he was infused with wonder, openness, and honest perception. In 1928 he wrote in an undergraduate philosophy paper:

> Why not ascribe [the wonder of the mystical experience] to man himself? Instead of deducing from the mystic experience the essential helplessness and smallness of man . . . can we not round out a larger, more wonderful conception of the greatness of the human species? (in Lowry, 1973a, p. 77).

More than 40 years later, when Maslow had become one of the most distinguished psychologists of our time, his theme remained unaltered, as he discussed his book *The Farther Reaches of Human Nature* (1971, 144):[1]

> If I had to condense this whole book into a single sentence, I [would say] that it spells out the consequences of the discovery that man has a higher nature and that this is part of his essence—or more simply, that human beings can be wonderful out of their own human and biological nature (in Lowry, 1973a, p. 77).

His willing and curious intellect allowed a psychological approach beyond neurotic behavior and psychosis, toward a psychology of human growth and self-actualization. "What we can study are the unconscious and preconscious depths, rational and irrational, sick and healthy, poetic and mathematical, concrete and abstract. Freud put these medical spectacles on our nose. It's time to take them off," wrote Maslow in 1959 (in Lowry, 1979, p. 66).

The Unnoticed Revolution

In the preface to the revised second edition of *Motivation and Personality,* Maslow wrote that the humanistic philosophy "is still almost completely overlooked by

---

[1]All references to Maslow's work are listed in the "Bibliography of the Writings of Abraham Maslow"; the number following the year refers to the number of the work as listed in the bibliography.

much of the intellectual community. . . . For this reason, I have taken to calling it the Unnoticed Revolution" (1970, 142, p. x).

In March of 1985, participants in the 25th anniversary of the Association of Humanistic Psychology reviewed the impact of the "unnoticed revolution" and noted the infusion of humanistic ideas into everyday life. While mainstream graduate studies and texts in psychology often do not reflect the humanistic perspective, in other areas the humanistic philosophy has clearly not gone unnoticed. Trends in psychotherapy, education, medicine, and management reflect Maslow's emphasis on self-realization, values, choice, and responsibilities, and on a more holistic view of the individual within family, cultural, and work environments.

Richard J. Lowry of Vassar College, a friend and former student of Maslow's and editor of his journals, has played a principal role in examining Maslow's contributions. In his book *A. H. Maslow: An Intellectual Portrait* (1973a), Lowry examined the major themes of Maslow's ideas and their theoretical status in the history of psychology and Western thought.

Lowry described the span of Maslow's intellectual life as being of extraordinary coherence and consistency in pursuit of the "wonderful possibilities and inscrutable depths of human nature" (Lowry, 1973a, pp. 78–79).

In preparation for his book *New Pathways in Psychology: Maslow and the Post-Freudian Revolution* (1972), the English writer Colin Wilson received detailed cooperation from Maslow and his wife Bertha. This book and *The Third Force, The Psychology of Abraham Maslow* by Frank Goble (1970) chronicle Maslow's philosophy and his achievements within a larger historical perspective.

Wilson wrote, "Maslow's achievement is enormous. . . . Like all original thinkers, he has opened a new way of *seeing* the universe. His ideas developed slowly and organically, like a tree; there are no breaks, or sudden changes of direction. His instinct was remarkably sound" (1972, p. 198).

A Psychologist and Philosopher of Science

Maslow believed that the general approach of empirical science, "of objects, animals, things and part-processes is limited and inadequate when we attempt to know and understand whole and individual persons and cultures" (Maslow, 1966, 115, p. xiii).

In his search for appropriate means of study in the field of psychology, Maslow was also a philosopher of science. He found it impossible to isolate the pursuit of psychological truth from philosophical questions, and held that science has no right to exclude *any* relevant data or experience. In *The Psychology of Science: A Reconnaissance* he wrote: "Science should be capable of dealing with problems of value, individuality, consciousness, beauty, transcendence and ethics" (Maslow, 1966, 115, p. xiv).

Maslow was more interested in pioneering and originating theories than in applying or verifying them, but he constantly challenged and invited others to experiment with and prove or disprove his ideas.

I'm someone who likes plowing new ground then walking away from it. I get bored. I like discovery, not proving. For me the big thrill comes with the discovering (Maslow, in Lowry, 1979, p. 231).

He acknowledged in his book *The Farther Reaches of Human Nature* (1971, 144) that verification is the "backbone of science," yet felt that it was "a great mistake for scientists to consider themselves merely and only verifiers" (p. 4). He was preoccupied with discoveries that merged *both* experience and theory—and challenged science and its principles to seek new methods for acquiring knowledge of human behavior. His call for research extended from the laboratory to the field and included the study of factories, homes, hospitals, communities, and even nations.

HUMANISTIC PSYCHOLOGY

Humanistic psychology today is many things: a cultural movement, a social network, a series of experiences by people, a set of techniques, a value system, an organization, and a *theory.* Ideally, each of these interacts with and enriches the others (Maslow, in Greening, 1984, p. 3).

I am a Freudian, I am behavioristic, I am humanistic . . . (Maslow, 1971, 144, p. 4).

The Theory

Maslow's theories of human motivation and self-actualization are most commonly contrasted with Freudian and behavioristic models. Yet for Maslow personally, the hierarchy of needs was a logical extension of his earlier work with the behaviorist, Freudian, and Adlerian models. He thought of himself as a Freudian and a behaviorist, not as the father of the revolution against them. Maslow saw himself as a creative synthesizer, not a dissenter, and regarded his work as an extension of modern trends in psychology.

Why were the theories of Maslow and other humanistic thinkers so revolutionary? His work and that of other humanistic psychologists is scientific, in the sense of relying on empirical studies of human behavior, yet it differs from other psychological systems in emphasizing certain *philosophical* beliefs about human beings (Buhler & Allen, 1972).

Humanistic psychology is revolutionary in presenting a positive model of human experience. Humanistic psychologists present themselves as human beings first and scientists second. They do not claim to be objective. They are intent on the discovery of methods within the highly subjective interchange of a relationship that will reveal personal knowledge of another human being (Buhler & Allen, 1972; Polanyi, 1958).

The following basic themes are the distinctive characteristics of contemporary humanistic psychology.

- Dissatisfaction with pathology-centered theories
- Recognition of the human potential to grow, to be self-determining, and to exercise choice and responsibility

- A belief that people do not live by bread alone, but also by higher needs, such as learning, work, love, creativity, and the like
- A valuing of feelings, desires, and emotions instead of objectifying or explaining away these responses
- The belief that humans are capable of knowing right and wrong and behaving in accordance with a higher good; belief in ultimate values, such as truth, happiness, love, and beauty

The Humanistic Movement

This definition of the "third force" in psychology was written by Maslow in the summer of 1957 and was included in the introduction to the first issue of the *Journal of Humanistic Psychology* (Sutich, 1961, pp. viii–ix):

> The *Journal of Humanistic Psychology* is being founded by a group of psychologists and professional men and women from other fields who are interested in those human capacities and potentialities that have no systematic place either in positivistic or behavioristic theory or in classical psychoanalytic theory, e.g., creativity, love, self, growth, organism, basic need-gratification, self-actualization, higher values, ego-transcendence, objectivity, autonomy, identity, responsibility, psychological health, etc.

Two organizations shaped the identity of humanistic psychology as an intellectual movement during the early 1960s. The Esalen Institute of California, the prototype for other growth centers, was founded in 1962. Also in 1962, Abraham Maslow and his colleagues founded the Association of Humanistic Psychology (AHP).

The main purpose of both the journal and the Association of Humanistic Psychology was to explore the behavioral characteristics and emotional dynamics of *full and healthy human living*. The new association represented a revolt against mechanistic, deterministic, psychoanalytic, and behavioristic orthodoxy. In 1985, membership in the AHP numbered 5200 with members in all 50 states and many other foreign countries.

In the foreword to Frank Goble's book *The Third Force, The Psychology of Abraham Maslow* (1970, p. vii), Maslow himself wrote,

> I want to stress that any one of a dozen theorists would have been quite as useful as a representative of Third Force Psychology. As a movement it has no single leader, no one great name by which to characterize it. In contrast to most revolutions in world view which have been characterized by the name of a single person; for example the Freudians, the Darwinians, the Marxians, the Einsteinians etc., the Third Force is the work of *many* people. Not only this, but it is also paralleled by independent advances and discoveries in other fields as well. There is rapidly developing a new image of society and of all its institutions.

Humanistic psychologists explored ways in which self-actualization could be fostered and measured in individuals, groups, and organizations. In 1968, the

Personal Orientation Inventory (POI) was designed to measure degrees of self-actualization (Shostrom, 1968). This instrument has been widely applied in business, education, and psychology.

Humanistic Psychotherapy

The practice of contemporary psychotherapy has been radically influenced by theories articulated by Maslow and other early third force psychologists. Although Maslow himself was not a practicing clinician, his ideas have had a significant impact on the practice of psychotherapy. He did not develop a system of techniques, but rather an ethical approach to human relationships in general.

Maslow believed that satisfactory results could be obtained by all of the various clinical methods and that the successful therapist must help the individual to satisfy the basic needs, thus moving the individual up the path toward self-actualization, which Maslow defined as the "ultimate goal of all therapy" (*Motivation and Personality,* 1970, 142, pp. 241–264). "Implicit is a belief that truth heals much. Learning to break through one's repressions, to know one's self, to hear impulse voices, to uncover the triumphant nature, to reach knowledge, insight—these are the requirements," he wrote in the *Farther Reaches of Human Nature* (1971, 144, p. 52).

The humanistic ethic, which was described by Maslow (1970, 142) and articulated by Bugental (1971), has had specific implications in the therapeutic experience. Some major tenets of the ethic are

- Accepting responsibility for one's own actions and experiences;
- Mutuality in relationships: Recognizing the perspective of another;
- An existential or *here and now* perspective, emphasizing that one always lives only at the present moment;
- A recognition that emotions such as pain, conflict, grief, anger, and guilt are parts of the human experience to be understood and even valued rather than suppressed and hidden; the expression of emotion reveals an experienced meaning in the person's life;
- People who have embodied the humanistic ethic are united in seeking growth-facilitating experiences.

Carl Rogers (1942, 1961) must be credited with first introducing a new, humanistic concept of the therapist-patient relationship. While Maslow and Rogers exerted a mutual influence over each other's theories, Rogers applied the concepts in developing new patterns of procedures in treating clients. He termed his work the *client-centered approach.* Rogers spoke of the therapist as a facilitator, an active but nondirective therapeutic participator. Various humanistic psychotherapists have developed variations on this person-to-person relationship.

Humanistic therapists recognize and utilize their own experience, and believe that the impact and importance of the personality of the therapist in the process of counseling can not be underestimated. The therapist serves as a model, implicitly demonstrating the potential for creative and positive action to the client. Humanistic therapists also believe that final decisions and choices rest with the client. Although the therapist may play a supporting role, the client retains the basic responsibility for his or her life and will always be the most powerful figure in it (Buhler & Allen, 1972; Maslow, 1970, 142; Rogers, 1961).

> We must remember, that knowledge of one's own deep nature is also simultaneously knowledge of human nature in general (Maslow, 1971, 144, p. xvi).

TRANSPERSONAL PSYCHOLOGY

> I consider Humanistic, 3rd force to be transitional, a preparation for a still higher 4th psychology, transpersonal, transhuman, centered in the cosmos rather than in human needs and interest, going beyond humanness, identity, Self-Actualization and the like (Maslow, *Toward A Psychology of Being,* 1968, 128, pp. iii–iv).

Toward the end of his life, Maslow saw further possibilities of human development. As more studies became available on human performance at the farther reaches of well-being, the absence of relevant guidelines in traditional Western psychology became increasingly apparent. Indeed, the humanistic model by itself was inadequate. Maslow realized that certain states of consciousness (altered, mystical, ecstatic, or spiritual states) were experiences beyond self-actualization in which the individual transcended customary limits of identity and experience (Walsh & Vaughn, 1980).

In 1968, Maslow wrote to Anthony Sutich to discuss the name for this new "fourth force" in psychology. A journal with Sutich as editor was already being planned.

> The main reason I am writing is that in the course of our conversation [with Stan Grof] we thought of using the word "transpersonal" instead of the clumsier word "transhumanistic" or "transhuman." The more I think of it, the more this word says what we are all trying to say, that is, beyond individuality, beyond the development of the individual person into something which is more inclusive (Maslow, in Sutich, 1976, p. 16).

Maslow lived to see the first issue of the new *Journal of Transpersonal Psychology* published in 1969. The opening article was from a talk he had given entitled "The Farther Reaches of Human Nature."

Here is Sutich's original statement of purpose for the journal, which Maslow enthusiastically endorsed:

> The emerging Transpersonal Psychology ("fourth force") is concerned specifically with the *empirical,* scientific study of, and responsible implementation of the findings relevant to, becoming, individual and species-wide meta-needs, ultimate values, unitive consciousness, peak experiences, B-values, ecstasy, mystical experience, awe, being, self-actualization, essence, bliss, wonder, ultimate meaning, transcendence of the self, spirit, oneness, cosmic awareness, individual and species-wide synergy, maximal interpersonal encounter, sacralization of everyday life, transcendental phenomena, cosmic self humor and

playfulness, maximal sensory awareness, responsiveness and expression, and related concepts, experiences, and activities (Sutich, 1976, pp. 13–14).

In 1985, membership in the Association for Transpersonal Psychology numbered 1200. An International Transpersonal Association has also been formed and has sponsored conferences worldwide.

Emergence of the Transpersonal Perspective

During the late 1960s, emergence of transpersonal psychology was facilitated by cultural factors that indicated the need for a new model of human behavior and growth. The human potential movement and widespread use of psychedelics and consciousness-altering techniques such as meditation had a major impact on beliefs about consciousness, health, experience, and motivation.

As many individuals experienced a range of states of consciousness outside of the realm of daily living, there emerged an appreciation of the validity and importance of non-Western psychologies and religions. And as theoretical understanding of altered states of consciousness evolved, it was recognized that certain non-Western traditions represented techniques designed for the induction of higher states of consciousness.

"It became apparent," wrote Walsh and Vaughn (1980, p. 21), "that the capacity for transcendent states, which could be interpreted either religiously or psychologically as one chose, and the deep insights into self and one's relationship to the world that accompanied them, lay latent within us all."

Inquiry into the Nature of Being

Transpersonal psychology cannot strictly be called a model of personality because it considers personality as only one aspect of our psychological nature; rather, it is an inquiry into the essential nature of being.

Transpersonal psychology explores the following themes:

1. *Consciousness* is the essence of being human, especially self-reflective consciousness (Walsh & Vaughn, 1980).
2. *Conditioning* is the next dimension of the person. It is held that we are trapped much more in our conditioning than we imagine, but that freedom from conditioning is possible, at least experientially (Goleman, 1977).
3. *Personality* is given less importance than in other psychologies. Health is seen as a disidentification from personality, rather than a modification of it (Wilber, 1977).
4. *Internal, intrapsychic phenomena and process* are more important than external identification.

Therapies

"Transpersonal psychotherapy includes treatment of the full range of behavioral, emotional and intellectual disorders, as well as uncovering and supporting strivings for full self-actualization." wrote James Fadiman and Kathleen Speeth (1980, p. 684). "The end state of psychotherapy is not seen as successful adjustment to the prevailing culture but rather the daily experience of that state called liberation, enlightenment, individuation, certainty or gnosis according to various traditions."

The psychotherapeutic techniques of the transpersonal field are drawn from clinical work, mystical traditions, meditation, behavioral analysis, and physiological technologies. The focus is on developing and integrating the physical, mental, emotional, and spiritual dimensions of the person.

> The exploration of the highest reaches of human nature and of its ultimate possibilities, involved for me the continuous destruction of cherished axioms, the perpetual coping with seeming paradoxes, contradiction, and vaguenesses, and the occasional collapse around my ears of long-established, firmly believed in, and seemingly unassailable laws of psychology (Maslow, 1968, 128, p. ii).

"Are we all that we can be? Or are there greater heights and depths of psychological capacity within us, undreamed of by most, glimpsed and nurtured by some and brought to fruition by but a few? If such capacities exist, then what is their nature, how can they be recognized, how can we learn from them, and how can they best be cultivated?" (Walsh & Shapiro, 1983, p. 5).

These were questions that Abraham Maslow raised more than 30 years ago. Today, within the fields of humanistic and transpersonal psychology there is a search for a new context for self-understanding and a movement toward an integrative psychology of well-being.

EDUCATION: HUMANISTIC VALUES AND
NEW WAYS OF LEARNING

> All of life is education and everybody is a teacher and everybody is forever a pupil (Maslow, in Lowry, 1979, p. 816).

> If I think of the great educational experiences in my life, the ones that taught me the most, then it would be those that taught me what kind of a person I was. . . . my marriage and fatherhood; the experiences that drew me out, strengthened me, made me taller and stronger, more fully human ("Conversation with Abraham H. Maslow," *Psychology Today,* 1968, p. 57).

For Maslow, learning was in some way relevant to all of the human needs. Learning involves not merely the acquisition of data and facts, but the holistic reintegration of the individual, continually producing changes in self-image, feeling, behavior, and relationship to the environment. He viewed education as occurring during the entire span of life, and not as confined to the classroom.

Maslow thought that awakening and fulfilling "Being-values" in children could lead to a flowering of a new kind of civilization. Like other visionaries, he believed that a new society could be created by changing the education of the young. Humanistic values in education have been the banner of many reformers and educational pioneers. In *Summerhill* (1960), A. S. Neill described beliefs that parallel Maslow's. These include the freedom to work joyfully, find happiness, and develop personal interests. Awakening self-assurance, insight, spontaneity, and growth is at the heart of Maslow's approach.

Herbert Kohl (1969) and many other educational reformers have applied this philosophy to the public and private school settings. Advocating the *open classroom,* Kohl developed a classroom environment in which the teacher abrogates the authoritarian role, talks to students as equals, and is led by students' interests. Research has shown that children learn best from adults who are creative, spontaneous, and supportive, who convey meanings rather than just facts, who possess high self-esteem, and see their jobs as liberating rather than controlling.

The humanistic approach to education, a concept known as *affective education,* stresses the nonintellectual side of learning: the side having to do with emotions, feelings, interests, values, and character. *Confluent education,* originally introduced by George Brown, attempts to integrate the affective and cognitive elements in individual and group learning (Miller, 1976).

Basic themes in humanistic education have included:

- Responsibility for one's own learning and identity development;
- Support and acknowledgment of the need for love and a sense of self-worth;
- Teacher as structuring agent of an open classroom;
- The use of peer groups in the learning process, for example, team learning with student-led discussion, the enhancement of individual effort through group interaction and process.

Readiness is recognized as a critical factor in Maslow's hierarchy. Affective education stresses that no strategy should be employed before learner or teacher is ready. If the learners' needs and readiness can be more closely determined, wrote Morris (1981), then organizational guidelines, curriculum decisions, and even school environments can be improved. Using Maslow's hierarchy in a public school setting, individual needs and readiness concepts such as self-concept, self-insight, self-understanding, and self-actualization have been used to personalize curriculum and increase the likelihood of learning.

School districts have reviewed programs (Guest, 1985) for whether they meet *physiological* (e.g., free lunches, clothes, transportation), *safety* (e.g., fire drills, child abuse awareness, absence calls), and *love and belonging needs* (e.g., class meetings, friendship groups, counseling, genuine caring for children). For developing *esteem and self-actualization,* programs have included the display of student work, explanations along with graded report cards, reinforcement awards, and participation in productions and special activities.

Multiple Intelligences and Creativity

Maslow observed that all self-actualizers are creative—artistically, scientifically, or in a myriad of ways, but *always* creative. He believed that there could be many different ways to solve a problem and is often quoted as having warned his students, "when the only tool you have is a hammer, every problem begins to look like a nail" (Ostrander & Schroeder, 1979, p. 147).

Based on many years of research in cognitive psychology and neuropsychology, Howard Gardner (1983), through the Project on Human Potential, has published a theory of multiple intelligences. Gardner's work confirms Maslow's contention that there are many ways to solve problems and to actualize potential. Individuals can possess linguistic, musical, logical-mathematical, spatial, bodily kinesthetic, or personal intelligences. Insight, intuition, and kinesthetic awareness are valued as expressions of a fundamental characteristic of human nature—a potentiality natural to all human beings at birth.

Maslow believed that education should be learning about personal growth, what to grow toward, what to choose, and what to reject. In a chapter entitled "Education and Peak Experiences," (in *The Farther Reaches of Human Nature*, 1971, 144, pp. 168–179), he suggested that early education in art, music, and dance are essential to our psychological and biological identity.

In *Education and Ecstasy* (1968), George Leonard combined a look at Maslow's theory of human potential, innovative schools, brain-research laboratories, and experimental communities. He believed, like Maslow, that the ultimate creative capacity of the brain may be infinite. Leonard wrote about free learners and challenged students, parents, and educators to a new vision of learning with new technologies and environments capable of creating the delight of learning.

Humanistic Education and Beyond to Transpersonal Education

> Creative education *can* prepare people for the unknown (Maslow, in Lowry, 1979, p. 18).
>
> One of the goals of education should be to teach that life is precious (Maslow, 1971, 144, p. 187).

Movement toward a paradigm in education that meets our knowledge of human potential is still very new. Conventional education aimed to adjust the individual to society as it exists, whereas humanistic educators of the 1960s maintained that society should accept its members as autonomous and unique. Transpersonal experience aims for a new kind of learner and a new kind of society. Beyond self-acceptance, it promotes self-transcendence (Ferguson, 1980).

Transpersonal education means education of the whole person, a process of exposing people to the mysterious in themselves. The emphasis is on learning *how* to learn. Learning is a process, a journey reflecting the discoveries of personal transformation. Maslow advocated that schools should exist to help people to look *within themselves* and from this knowledge to develop a set of values.

Jonathan Kozol, an author and teacher, proposed that education must be concerned with ethical values such as truth, integrity, and compassion and must apply these to events outside the classroom. Maslow also firmly believed that individual health cannot be separated from collective health any more than personal growth can be separated from spiritual growth.

New Modes for Learning

Maslow's theories of human potential can also be tied to the development of learning techniques. There is a current generation of literature and methodology that speaks to new modes of learning. Techniques and new learning tools include relaxation techniques, visualizations, hypnosis, sense awareness, developing intuition and hunches, sleep learning, affirmations, memory development, and mind games. These learning tools are geared to help dissolve fear, self-blame, cramped self-images, and negative images about limited abilities.

Transpersonal techniques for learning are being used by teachers and counselors, as evidenced by books of games and techniques for classroom use (Castillo, 1974; Hendricks & Fadiman, 1976; Hendricks & Willis, 1975; J. B. Roberts & Clark, 1975).

A very significant area of study has been in states of consciousness. Research has shown that people have a variety of states of consciousness available to them. Not only do we have many states of consciousness, but we can also deliberately alter those states that inhibit learning and cultivate those states that enhance our capacities. Techniques include dreaming, psychic healing (LeShan, 1974), paranormal phenomena (Ullman, Krippner, & Vaughn, 1973), and control of the autonomic nervous system through biofeedback (Green & Green, 1977).

Superlearning techniques are also becoming more popular. In the mid-1960s, Dr. Georgi Lozanov, a Bulgarian doctor and psychiatrist, developed a rapid learning system. This technique, which he called suggestology, was created by drawing from mental yoga, music, sleep learning, physiology, hypnosis, autogenics, parapsychology, and drama. He applied altered states of consciousness for learning, healing, and intuitive development (Ostrander & Schroeder, 1979).

Learners are encouraged by concrete results and a glimpse into their true capacities. There is more emphasis on the organic nature of learning and the need for self reliance (Holt, 1970; Kohl, 1969; Maslow, 1971, 144). Perhaps as these techniques become more mainstream, we will find ourselves closer to Maslow's concepts of education and psychology.

Clearly the need for high expectation and more focus on the outer reaches of human educability is essential if we are to deepen our self-inquiry. Abe Maslow, standing in front of his college class, posed an important question to the students:

"Which of you expects to achieve greatness in your chosen field?"

The class looked at him blankly. After a long silence, Maslow said: "*If not you, who then*?" (Wilson, 1972, p. 15).

MASLOW'S IMPACT ON WORK AND MANAGEMENT

Human nature has been sold short. Man has a higher nature, just as "instinctoid" as his lower nature, and this human nature includes the need for meaningful work, for responsibility, for creativeness, for being fair and just, for doing what is worthwhile, and for *preferring to do it well* (Maslow, 1971, 144, p. 238).

In the summer of 1962, Maslow came to California as a visiting fellow at

Non-Linear Systems, a high-technology plant in Del Mar. That move proved to be a personal turning point. In reviewing his reasons for moving into management psychology, he wrote: "There was also a big shift over because of my interest in mass therapy. Individual therapy is useless for the masses. I had thought of education as the best bet for changing the society. But now the work situation seems even better" (Lowry, 1979, p. 191).

Through his observations at Non-Linear Systems, Maslow found that his theories could be applied to organizational management. He found that people achieve an optimal level of functioning when organizations develop practices that embrace the holistic nature of human beings. He believed that a humane, enlightened management policy focused on human potential would prove financially profitable as well.

Calling this concept of utopian leadership eupsychian management, he pointed out that while not everyone can afford psychotherapy, many individuals can experience a therapeutically oriented work situation. *Eupsychia* was a word that Maslow coined to describe those institutions that were moving toward his ultimate understanding of psychological health. Maslow was influenced by McGregor's (1960) Theory X and Theory Y, which showed how assumptions—whether authoritarian (X) or humanistic (Y)—affect management practices. But he went further by suggesting another set of assumptions, transpersonal in nature, which he named Theory Z.

Theory Z revolutionized the classic economic scarcity model by including the impulse to self-actualize, to love, and to reach for the highest of human values. Theory Z sees shared decision making, mutual trust, intimacy, caring, and co-operation as essential to organizational development.

Companies that use this theory are concerned with ongoing employee education, reinforcing the idea that *business* holds the potential for transforming and supporting self-actualizing people. It acknowledges the complex and changing relationships between people within all levels of a company. The needs of personal growth and esteem are as important as economic security. Work is seen as both a psychological experience and an economic pursuit.

Maslow's Theory Z predated by 20 years Ouchi's well-known book on Japanese business practices, aptly titled *Theory Z* (1981). Oddly enough, there is no reference made to Maslow in Ouchi's book.

Humanistic Developments in Business

Humanistic psychology suggested the existence and importance of psychological needs, such as the need to achieve, to be independent and autonomous, to feel good about oneself, and to grow and self-actualize (Argyris, 1964; Drucker, 1974; Maslow, 1965, 112; McGregor, 1960). Emerging through the 1960s and 1970s, a crosscurrent of ideas about people-oriented management and business practices has continued to flourish. Many organizations have introduced such techniques as sensitivity training (French & Bell, 1980), participative decision making (Hackman & Oldham, 1980), management by objectives (Drucker, 1974), and programs to improve the quality of working life (Carlson, 1980).

Maslow's book *Eupsychian Management,* a collection of notes published in 1965 in journal form, foreshadowed many ideas appearing in more recent popular writings on management such as Peters and Waterman's *In Search of Excellence* (1982), Pascale and Athos's *The Art of Japanese Management* (1981), and Ouchi's *Theory Z* (1981). American firms are looking at success at home and abroad with new eyes, and many of the innovations and conditions that are now being confirmed as paths to excellence in the workplace were described by Maslow in the early 1960s.

Maslow realized in 1965 what Peters and Waterman confirmed in 1982: namely, that successful leadership is focused on *human* values, is directed toward satisfying people's need for meaning, and creates organizational purpose. Maslow developed a set of 36 assumptions or preconditions for a fully functioning organization. These include (1) Assume in all your people the impulse to achieve, that they are for good workmanship and against wasting time, want to do a good job, and so on; (2) assume that people prefer to feel important, needed, useful, successful, proud and respected; (3) assume everyone is to be trusted; (4) everyone is to be informed as completely as possible of as many facts and truths as possible, everything relevant to the situation; and (5) ultimately, assume that there is a preference or tendency to identify with more and more of the world and a yearning for values such as truth, justice, perfection, and the like (Maslow, 1965, 112).

Major American companies such as Hewlett-Packard, Apple Computer, Texas Instruments, Eastman Kodak, and Levi Strauss all employ management styles that depend on individual responsibility, teamwork, and a concern for people. These large companies reflect the growing acknowledgment that industrial life requires high levels of human interdependence, mutual trust, and cooperation for sustained productivity to occur.

The VALS Project: A Direct Application of the Needs Hierarchy

One of the most direct and successful business applications of Maslow's theory has been developed at Stanford Research International (SRI) in Menlo Park, California. A project known as VALS (Values and Lifestyles) has been profiling Americans in a unique way. Building upon Maslow's needs hierarchy, the VALS system has devised elaborate portraits of nine types of people. Each type describes "a unique way of life defined by its distinctive array of values, drives, beliefs, needs, dreams and special points of view" (A. Mitchell, 1983, p. 4).

Referred to as *lifestyle information,* VALS is being used to determine how employees may be attracted and retained, how to match individuals to jobs so they will be both productive and happy, and how to build work groups. The VALS typology has also been used to determine market segmentation and size and to aid in product development, packaging, and design.

Advertising agencies such as Young & Rubicam, Ogilvy & Mather, and Leo Burnett are using VALS psychographics to determine consumers' preferences. In a persuasively powerful way, this application of the needs hierarchy is touching the lives of millions of Americans today.

HEALTH AND THE WHOLE PERSON

Maslow's influence has been felt in two major directions in health care. The first brought direct application of his theories to established medical institutions. The second has been the explosion of the holistic health perspective.

There are literally hundreds of studies using Maslow's models in the areas of nursing, medicine, hospital administration, education, and gerontology. Many of these studies introduced the concept of higher needs to medical institutions such as hospitals, clinics, psychiatric hospitals, and nursing homes. Physicians, nurses, and other health care professionals began to acknowledge and encourage more personal concern for a broader range of patient needs. Policy in many institutions reflected this shift. For example, physicians in a London clinic built their practice around the premise that "health is more powerful and infectious than disease" (Pioneer Health Center, 1971, cited in Duhl, L. J., "The social context of health," p. 42 in Hastings, Fadiman, & Gordon, 1980). (The many medical journals referencing Maslow in the citation index indicate his influence in these fields.)

Holistic Health

In recent years the word *holistic* has been most frequently connected with the area of health. "Reductionist thinking anywhere, medicine included, results in the compartmentalization of the human being and human experience into those aspects or parts that are amenable to detailed analysis or intervention," Rick Carlson (1980, p. 486)—writing on the future of health care in the United States—echoed Maslow's beliefs. "This is one of the basic premises that underlies the prevailing medical practice. Although it has its utility, it is a profoundly limited view of the human being. The shift toward holism is really irreversible, not because it is being forced upon medicine . . . but rather because the shift is part of a much larger change in perspective about who and what the human being is."

In the area of health, much evidence can be found of holistic approaches to improved well-being, as well as an attitude that lends itself to the physical, mental, and spiritual aspects of those who come for care. Holistic medicine emphasizes the patients's genetic, biological, and psychosocial uniqueness as well as the importance of tailoring treatment to meet each individual's needs (Gordon, 1980).

Healing Ourselves

Illness is potentially transformative because it can cause a sudden shift in values, an awakening. Many people have begun to take responsibility for their own wellness. Self-help books on diet, nutrition, exercise, and stress reduction have become best sellers. "If anything can solve the crisis of medical depersonalization and rising costs, it is this classically Maslovian shift: more and more people working against a pathogenic environment and society while taking personal responsibility for their own positive good health" (Leonard, 1983, p. 335).

Increasing awareness of the effects of mental and emotional states on health and illness and of the integral role of the patient as an active participant in the healing process has led to a variety of techniques to mobilize the individual's natural process of healing. These techniques include autogenic training (Lindemann, 1974), hypnosis (Crasilneck & Hall, 1975), meditation (Shapiro & Walsh, 1980), and clinical biofeedback (Pelletier, 1977).

Phil Nuernberger, in *Freedom from Stress—A Holistic Approach* (1981), declared that self-actualizers do not create the same degree of stress as others do. In addition, they suffer from fewer illnesses and show consistently higher levels of satisfaction with life. Yet self-actualizers are consistently high achievers, working in the same pressure cooker that exists for everyone in our society. Tension, worry, anxiety, and nerves are not necessary ingredients for their high achievement and performance. They have learned to manage stress.

Applications of a holistic perspective have affected all phases of our life cycle, from alternative approaches to childbirth, "healthy" aging, and new awareness of the stages of dying and death. Our belief about medicine is expanding to include the many personal, familial, environmental, and social factors that promote health, prevent illness, and encourage healing. As we assume more responsibility for our own health, we claim our capacity not only to grow and change but also truly to *heal* as well.

MOTIVATION AND SELF-ACTUALIZATION THEORY AND THE PSYCHOLOGY OF WOMEN

> Women are really kind of perpetual miracles. They are like flowers. Every person is a mystery to me, but women are more mysterious to me than men (Maslow, in Hall, 1968, p. 56).

While Maslow forged new territory in many areas, like many of his contemporaries, he assumed a common process of psychological development for both sexes, characterizing the height of human development in terms of individuation and achievement. This assumption has been used to encourage as well as to constrict a comprehensive psychology of women. Maslow thought about the differences between the sexes, but never fully developed his observations.

Betty Friedan, in *The Feminine Mystique* (1977), refers to Maslow extensively as she encourages women toward a vision of self-actualization beyond the roles of wife and mother. Yet when the needs hierarchy is applied to women they consistently cannot be characterized by some of Maslow's "higher" levels. Women's experiences and development are different from those of men, centering on attachment and intimacy rather than separation and autonomy (Norman, Murphy, & Gilligan, 1982).

Maslow puzzled over this difference while writing in his journal in 1962 (in Lowry, 1979, p. 251):

> Only the woman *needs* to be loved, first and foremost . . . (the more I think of this, the more impressed I get. And nothing has been written on it. No research has been done.)

His own questioning foreshadowed the study of these differences. Yet in emphasizing the qualities of detachment and independence, Maslow's hierarchy overlooks some essential differences between men and women.

In her well-known book *In a Different Voice,* Carol Gilligan wrote that "the psychology of women, that has consistently been described as distinctive in its greater orientation toward relationships and interdependence, implies a more contextual mode of judgement and a different moral understanding. Given the differences in women's conceptions of self and morality, women bring to the life cycle a different point of view and order human experience in terms of different priorities" (1982, p. 22). Women not only define themselves in a context of human relationship but also judge themselves in terms of their ability to care. Women's place in the life cycle has been that of nurturer, caretaker, and helpmate, the weaver of those networks of relationships on which she in turn relies (Gilligan, 1982, p. 17).

The distinctions between women's independence and the characteristics of personal dependence were not yet clear when Maslow wrote. Thus some of his work appears to describe women's values and priorities as "deficiency motivated."

> Deficiency-motivated people *must* have other people available, since most of their main need gratifications (love, safety, respect, prestige, belongingness) can come only from other human beings. But growth motivated people may actually be *hampered* by others (Maslow, 1970, 142, p. 162).

Although Maslow was attempting to define self-actualization in both sexes, his definition of psychological health does not fundamentally represent the psychology of women. When the focus on individuation and individual achievement extends into adulthood and maturity is equated with personal autonomy, concern with relationships appears as a weakness of women, rather than as a human strength (Miller, 1976).

THE SYNERGIC SOCIETY

> Self-actualizing people have to a large extent transcended the values of their culture. They are not so much merely Americans as they are world citizens, members of the human species first and foremost. They are able to regard their own society objectively, liking some aspects of it, disliking others (Maslow, 1971, 144, p. 184).

Social Implications

Maslow did not state what social or political theories might be derived from his work, but he did outline some ideas about his conceptualization of a healthy (he called it synergic or Eupsychian) society. His outline was a combination of his interest in full health and development in the individual and also an elaboration on the later anthropological work of Ruth Benedict. Benedict had distinguished between "low synergy" and "high synergy" societies, the latter being those that "have social orders in which the individual, by the same act and at the same time, serves one's own advantage and that of the group" (in Goble, 1970).

Applying her criteria to American society, Maslow found it to be of mixed synergy, capable in some areas of fulfilling needs and facilitating growth while in other areas tending to frustrate needs and stunt development, to pit people unnecessarily against each other or against society itself (Anderson, 1973).

During the last 20 years of his life, Maslow devoted much of his time to studying the social implications of his philosophy of the value hierarchy. This led him eventually to a position that might be described as "capitalist anarchism," using anarchism in its original sense of fruitful cooperation between equals (Wilson, 1972, p. 179).

He saw the third force as more of a world view than a school of psychology—he called it a *Zeitgeist,* a spirit of the age, a change of basic thinking along the entire range of human endeavors, a potential change in every social institution.

This section has examined some trends within the field of psychology, business, education, science, and health care. All indicate Maslow's pioneering work on the potential for personal growth is becoming better known within our society.

Arnold Mitchell of the VALS project at SRI wrote, "Choice based on value is coming to dominate over mere capacity. The time seems at last to be arriving when many people are able to employ the full range of their powers to choose what kind of lives they truly want to lead" (1983, p. viii).

However, along with this power of choice has come the "maladaptive features of people's self-fulfillment strategies." Daniel Yankelovich has conducted surveys of social trends and public attitudes that indicate a "me-first" attitude in people. Calling this the "psychology of affluence," he pointed to a majority of people who interpret self-fulfillment as a way to justify "more of everything" (Yankelovich, 1981, pp. 234–243).

This personal elitism at the cost of a larger ethic of social commitment was a constant source of debate for Maslow. And it seems deeply relevant today, in our world faced with finite resources, the nuclear dilemma, and population growth projected at 6.5 billion people by the end of the century.

> Unfortunately, physical and economic wealth do not inevitably get used for higher need gratification. Higher needs can be gratified under poverty, it's harder, but possible if we remember what we're dealing with—respect, love, self-actualization, *not* autos, money, bathtubs (Maslow, in Lowry, 1979, pp. 373–374).

Maslow believed that people could never find themselves solely by looking inward, because the search for self must, if one is truly attentive, immediately direct one outside again. George Leonard observes that the "counterculture of the 1960's has become a major and influential segment of the main-stream culture of the 1980's. It is also becoming clear that while the search for self-actualization does lead some people to a narrow preoccupation with the self, the 'me first' stage is generally temporary, a way station on the journey to social consciousness" (Leonard, 1983, p. 335).

The Problem of Evil

Some critics have argued that Maslow did not fully address issues of evil and the dark side of humanity, and that his positive outlook distorted his findings. After World War II, in the wake of genocide and atomic weaponry, Maslow knew that a comprehensive psychology had to take into account both good and evil. His view was that most evil in human life is due to ignorance—but he was not sentimental and could never ignore the need to understand the realities of weakness, failure, and cruelty. His last diaries are filled with inner questioning and debate about the universality of evil motivations:

> I read about the riots, the meanness and nastiness, the suspicion and cynicism. . . . I seem to be alone in the insistence on the reality of goodness, decency, generosity—everybody else keeps silent. There is good and evil in the world and they keep on struggling back and forth—it's an inconclusive battle. But if the good people give up, *then* the battle is lost (Maslow, in Lowry, 1979, p. 1235).

A psychology of evil might have been Maslow's next contribution. In an interview in *Psychology Today,* Maslow commented

> "It's a psychological puzzle I've been trying to solve for years. Why are people cruel and why are they nice? Evil people are rare, but you find evil behavior in the majority of people. The next thing I want to do with my life is to study evil by understanding it" (Maslow, in Hall, 1968, p. 35).

Future Directions

Maslow once said that he thought a society with 8 percent self-actualizing people would soon be a self-actualizing society. "The remarkable person will be the agent of change," wrote Mitchell (1983, p. 4). Mitchell's study predicts that by 1990, the "inner-directeds" (or self-actualizers) will constitute nearly a third of the population in the United States.

Whether the issue is energy, politics, community self-help, the consumer movement, or holistic health, the new creed is becoming one of self-reliance and local initiative. This newly evolving world will require new forms of social organization.

John Naisbitt, in his bestseller *Megatrends* (1982), delineated new trends in American society, such as the move away from centralized hierarchies to decentralized networks. For example, one network form, the quality control circle, has helped to revitalize worker participation and productivity in American businesses. Maslow predicted that we would need to abandon traditional structures that had served the development of centralized, industrial society. Maslow's ideas are congruent with Naisbitt's "network model of organization and communication, which has its roots in the natural and egalitarian formation of like-minded groups" (p. 251).

American society today holds many factors that could bring about collective transformation. In *The Aquarian Conspiracy: Personal and Social Transformation in the 1980's,* Marilyn Ferguson confirmed evidence of Maslow's perspective in many fields. Ferguson wrote, "To imagine a destiny, to transcend a past, we have begun to know ourselves, we sense the limits of our old science, the dangers of our top heavy hierarchies, and we see the context of our planet. We have awakened our power to learn and to change. We have begun to imagine the possible society" (1980, p. 142).

One future direction will possibly be a better understanding of cross-cultural motivational and self-actualization patterns. There have been world-wide applications of Maslow's work: Studies include the observation of work motivation in developing countries and comparison of Maslow's theories with those of Eastern philosophers. A synthesis of studies relating to Maslow's theories is needed. Global focus could add to an international synergy and lead to better understanding about cross-cultural norms and values.

THE PERENNIAL HARVEST

The movement toward psychological health is also the movement toward spiritual peace and social harmony (Maslow, 1971, 144, p. 195).

Abraham Maslow's theories have been applied in an amazing range of organizations and settings, from farms to banks, meditation groups to the military, nursing homes to preschools. They have been used to develop commercial television advertising as well as public health announcements.

In capturing the spirit of his age, Maslow's psychology has been woven into the very fabric of American life. His work, grounded in careful observation, has branched continuously into many dimensions of our culture. The powerful vision articulated in *Motivation and Personality* has had a penetrating impact on what we value, how we think and learn, *the very way we live.*

The harvest of Abraham Maslow's psychology continues to raise unique questions and guide us forward. He opened a new way of seeing the human universe and in so doing, lifted us up, highlighted the nature of our human potential, encouraged us to reach farther, and reminded us that *greatness is in each and every one of us.* Ultimately, the truth of Maslow's impact lives within each one of us, in the expression of our own search to become more fully human.

A CITATION REVIEW OF *MOTIVATION AND PERSONALITY*

Motivation and Personality is Maslow's most extensively referenced book. Maslow's other books were written for the general public, but academicians are more familiar with *Motivation and Personality* because it has been most widely used as a textbook.

The following findings were taken from the Social Sciences and Arts and Humanities Citation indexes. The numbers that follow include references to both the 1954 and 1970 editions of *Motivation and Personality* and cover a total of 20 years.

In the 5-year period from 1966 to 1970, there were 300 citations. In the 5 years from 1971 to 1976 . . . 489 citations. And 20 years after publication, from 1976 to 1980, the text was cited 791 times in various sources.

More recently, between 1981 and 1985, *Motivation and Personality* received 550 citations. Interest, referencing, and challenges drawn from *Motivation and Personality* have increased steadily. This trend appeared to be leveling off into 1985, but there is no indication that interest is dropping at this time.

The diversity of publications in which references to *Motivation and Personality* appear is remarkable. The wide range of interest in Maslow's theory is established within the first 5 years of this study (1966–1970), and a growing diversity can be seen in the next 10 years (1970–1980).

Most citings listed are in the general areas of psychology, followed closely by education, business, medicine and nursing, and social studies. Listings also appear in the areas of engineering, genetics, political science, philosophy, gerontology, social criticism, broadcasting, peace studies, and religion.

Most of the abstracts of articles in the following journals focus on Maslow's theory of motivation and hierarchy of needs as they relate to specific fields and studies. Many are empirical and applied studies of the validity of Maslow's theory.

Motivation and Personality has been most frequently cited in the following major journals, among others.

Psychology   *Journal of Applied Psychology, Psychological Review, Journal of Humanistic Psychology, Journal of Individual Psychology, Journal of Psychology and Theology, Psychology Today, Journal of Counseling Psychology, Journal of Consulting and Clinical Psychology, Personality and Individual Differences, Journal of Personality, Journal of Psychology, Psychology in the Schools, Journal of Transpersonal Psychology, Psychoanalytic Quarterly, Journal of Marriage and the Family*

The book appears to be cited in most journals relating to psychology covered by the Social Sciences Index.

Education   *Child Development, Harvard Educational Review, Education, Gifted Child Quarterly, American Educational Research Journal, Reading Teacher, Educational Review, Educational Administration Quarterly, Educational Leadership and Journal of Education for Teaching, Adolescence, Language Learning*

Business   *Administrative Science Quarterly, Vocational Guidance Quarterly, Training and Development Journal, Management Science, Harvard Business Review, Business Horizons, Journal of Management Studies, Personnel and Guidance Journal, Organizational Behavior and Human Performance, American Business Law, Journal of Business, Management Focus, Journal of Vocational Behavior*

Medicine, Nursing, and Aging   *Journal of the American Medical Association, Journal of Nervous and Mental Diseases, Hospital Administration, Nurse Research, Journal of Nursing Administration and Education, Gerontologist, Gerontology, Aging and Human Development, International Journal of Aging, Aging and Work*

Social Studies   *Public Health Research, Human Relations, Sociology Review, Journal of Social Issues, Journal of Leisure Research, Horizons, Journal of American Culture, Social Problems, Social Service Review, Social Policy, Social Work, Social Science Quarterly, Public Welfare, Public Opinion Quarterly, Social Science and Medicine, Health Policy and Education*

BIBLIOGRAPHY AND SELECTED READINGS

Humanistic and Transpersonal Psychology

Assagioli, R. (1972). *Psychosynthesis.* New York: Viking Press.
Boorstein, S. (Ed.). (1980). *Transpersonal psychotherapy.* Palo Alto, CA: Science and Behavior Books.
Bugental, J. F. T. (1967). *Challenges of humanistic psychology.* New York: McGraw-Hill.
Bugental, J. F. T. (1971). The humanistic ethic—The individual in psychotherapy as a societal change agent. *Journal of Humanistic Psychology, 11*(1), 11–25.
Buhler, C., & Allen, M. (1972). *Introduction to humanistic psychology.* Monterey, CA: Brooks/Cole.
Fadiman, J., & Frager, R. (1976). *Personality and personal growth.* New York: Harper & Row.
Fadiman, J., & Speeth, K. (1980). Transpersonal psychotherapy. In R. Herink (Ed.), *The psychotherapy handbook* (pp. 684–686). New York: New American Library.
Frick, W. B. (1971). *Humanistic psychology interviews with Maslow, Murphy and Rogers.* Columbus, OH: Merrill.
Frick, W. B. (1982). Conceptual foundations of self-actualization: A contribution to motivation theory. *Journal of Humanistic Psychology, 22*(4), 33–52.
Geller, L. (1982). The failure of self-actualization theory: A critique of Carl Rogers and Abraham Maslow. *Journal of Humanistic Psychology, 22*(4), 56–73.
Gendlin, E. (1978). *Focusing.* New York: Bantam.
Glasser, W. (1965). *Reality therapy.* New York: Harper & Row.
Goble, F. (1970). *The third force, the psychology of Abraham Maslow.* New York: Grossman.
Goleman, D. (1977). *The varieties of the meditative experience.* New York: Dutton.
Goleman, D., & Davidson. R. (Eds.). (1979). *Consciousness: Brain, states of awareness and mysticism.* New York: Harper & Row.
Greening, T. (1984, Fall). Commentary by the editor. *Journal of Humanistic Psychology,* pp. 3–6.
Grof, S. (1975). *Realms of the human unconscious.* New York: Viking.
Hall, M. H. (1968, July). A conversation with Abraham H. Maslow. *Psychology Today,* pp. 35–37, 54–57.

Leonard, G. (1978). *The silent pulse*. New York: Dutton.
LeShan, L. (1977). *Alternative realities: The search for the full human being*. New York: Ballantine.
Lowry, R. J. (1973a). *A. H. Maslow: An intellectual portrait*. Monterey, CA: Brooks/Cole.
Lowry, R. J. (Ed.). (1973b). *Dominance, self-esteem, self-actualization: Germinal papers of A. H. Maslow*. Monterey, CA: Brooks/Cole.
Lowry, R. J. (1979). *The journals of A. H. Maslow* (Vols. I & II). Monterey, CA: Brooks/Cole.
May, R. (1967). *Psychology and the human dilemma*. Princeton, NJ: Van Nostrand.
McCain, E. W., & Andrews, H. B. (1969). Some personality correlates of peak experiences—A study in self-actualization. *Journal of Clinical Psychology, 25*, 36–40.
Needleman, J. (1976). *On the way to self knowledge*. New York: Knopf.
Ornstein, R. (1972). *The psychology of consciousness*. San Francisco: Freeman.
Polanyi, M. (1958). *Personal knowledge*. Chicago: University of Chicago Press.
Roberts, T. (1972). *Maslow's human motivation needs hierarchy: A bibliography*. (Report No. SO 005 008). De Kalb: Northern Illinois University, Secondary Professional Education. (ERIC Document Reproduction Service No. ED 069 591).
Rogers, C. R. (1942). *Counseling and psychotherapy*. Boston: Houghton Mifflin.
Rogers, C. (1961). *On becoming a person*. Boston: Houghton Mifflin.
Rogers, C. R. (1963). The actualizing tendency. In M. R. Jones (Ed.), *Nebraska Symposium on Motivation* (Vol. 11). Lincoln: University of Nebraska Press.
Shostrom, E. (1965). A test for the measurement of self-actualization. *Educational and Psychological Measurement, 24*, 207–218.
Shostrom, E. (1968). *Bibliography for the P.O.I.* San Diego, CA: Educational and Industrial Testing Service.
Severin, F. (1965). *Humanistic viewpoints in psychology*. New York: McGraw-Hill.
Smith, M. B. (1973). On self-actualization: A transambivalent examination of a focal theme in Maslow's psychology. *Journal of Humanistic Psychology, 13*, 17–33.
Sutich, A. (1961, Spring). Introduction. *Journal of Humanistic Psychology, 1*(1), vii–ix.
Sutich, A. (1976). The emergence of the transpersonal orientation: A personal account. *Journal of Transpersonal Psychology, 1*, 5–19.
Tart, C. (1975a). *States of consciousness*. New York: Dutton.
Tart, C. (1975b). *Transpersonal psychologies*. New York: Harper & Row.
Walsh, R., & Shapiro, D. (Eds.). (1983). *Beyond health and normality: Explorations of exceptional psychological well being*. New York: Van Nostrand Reinhold.
Walsh, R., & Vaughn, F. (Eds.). (1980). *Beyond ego: Transpersonal dimensions in psychology*. Los Angeles: Tarcher.
White, J. (Ed.). (1974). *Frontiers of consciousness*. New York: Julian Press.
Wilber, K. (1977). *The spectrum of consciousness*. Wheaton, IL: Theosophical Publishing House.
Wilber, K. (1979). *No boundary*. Los Angeles: Center Publications.
Wilber, K. (1980). *The Atman project*. Wheaton, IL: Theosophical Publishing House.
Wilson, C. (1972). *New pathways in psychology: Maslow and the post-Freudian revolution*. London: Victor Gollancz.

Education

Arieti, S. (1976). *Creativity: The magic synthesis*. New York: Basic Books.
Brown, G. (1971). *Human teaching for human learning*. New York: Viking.

Canfield, J., & Phillips. M. (1975). A guide to resources in humanistic and transpersonal education. In T. Roberts (Ed.), *Four psychologies applied to education*. New York: Schenkman/Halsted.

Canfield, J., & Wells, H. C. (1976). *100 ways to enhance self-concept in the classroom: A handbook for teachers and parents*. Englewood Cliffs, NJ: Prentice-Hall.

Castillo, G. (1974). *Left-handed teaching*. New York: Praeger.

Fairfield, R. (1971). *Humanistic frontiers in American education*. Englewood Cliffs, NJ: Prentice-Hall.

Ferguson, M. (1973). *The brain revolution*. New York: Taplinger.

Ferguson, M. (1980). *The aquarian conspiracy*. Los Angeles: Tarcher.

Gardner, H. (1983). *Frames of mind: The theory of multiple intelligences*. New York: Basic Books.

Green, E., & Green, A. (1977). *Beyond biofeedback*. New York: Delacorte.

Guest, W. (1985). *Societal changes: Implications for education*. Unpublished report to Superintendent of Schools, Rio Linda Unified School District, Rio Linda, CA.

Hendricks, G., & Fadiman, J. (1976). *Transpersonal education: A curriculum for feeling and being*. Englewood Cliffs, NJ: Prentice-Hall.

Hendricks, G., & Willis, R. (1975). *The centering book*. Englewood Cliffs, NJ: Prentice-Hall.

Holt, J. (1970). *Freedom and beyond*. New York: Dutton.

Kohl, H. (1969). *The open classroom*. New York: New York Review Books.

Kozol, J. (1968). *Death at an early age*. New York: Houghton Mifflin.

Leonard. G. (1968). *Education and ecstasy*. New York: Delta.

LeShan, L. (1974). *How to meditate: A guide to self-discovery*. Boston: Little, Brown.

Montessori, M. (1967). *The absorbent mind*. New York: Dell.

Miller, J. (1976). *Humanizing the classroom: Models of teaching in affective education*. New York: Praeger.

Morris, R. (1981). An assessment of student perceptions of needs deficiencies. *Education, 102*, 2–18.

Naisbitt, J. (1982). *Megatrends: Ten new directions transforming our lives*. New York: Warner Books.

Neill, A. S. (1960). *Summerhill: A radical approach to child rearing*. New York: Hart.

Ostrander, S., & Schroeder, L. (1979). *Superlearning*. New York: Delta/Dell.

Pearce, J. C. (1977). *Magical child*. New York: Dutton.

Roberts, J. B., & Clark, F. V. (1976). Transpersonal psychology in education. In G. Hendricks & J. Fadiman (Eds.), *Transpersonal education*. Englewood Cliffs, NJ: Prentice-Hall.

Roberts, T. (Ed.). (1975). *Four psychologies applied to education*. New York: Halsted/Shenkman.

Ullman, M., Krippner, S., & Vaughn, F. (1973). Dream telepathy: *Experiments in nocturnal ESP*. New York: Macmillan.

Vaughan, F. (1979). *Awakening intuition*. New York: Anchor Press/Doubleday.

Weinstein, G., & Fantini, M. (1970). *Toward humanistic education: A curriculum of affect*. New York: Praeger.

Business and Management

Adams, J. (Ed.). (1984). *Transforming work*. Alexandria, VA: Miles River Press.

Alderfer, C. P. (1972). *Existence, relatedness and growth: Human needs in organizational settings*. New York: The Free Press.

Allen, R. F., & Kraft, C. (1982). *The organizational unconscious*. Englewood Cliffs, NJ: Prentice-Hall.

Argyris, C. (1964). *Integrating the individual and the organization*. New York: Wiley.

Argyris, C. (1978). *Participative management*. Reading, MA: Addison-Wesley.

Argyris, C., & Schon, D. (1978). *Organizational learning: A theory of action perspective*. Reading, MA: Addison-Wesley.

Atlas, J. (1984, October). Beyond demographics. *The Atlantic Monthly*, pp. 49–58.

Beauchamp, G. (1982). *Transpersonal management: Application of psychological principles in a business setting*. Unpublished doctoral dissertation, California Institute of Transpersonal Psychology.

Carlson, H. (1980). GM's quality of work life efforts: An interview. In F. Schuster (Ed.), *Contemporary issues in human resources management*. Reston, VA: Reston Publishers, Prentice-Hall.

Cleland, D., & King, I. (1979). *Managment: A systems approach*. New York: McGraw-Hill.

Dale, E. (1978). *Management: Theory and practice*. New York: McGraw-Hill.

Drucker, P. (1966). *The effective executive*. New York: Harper & Row.

Drucker, P. (1974). *Management tasks, responsibilities, practices*. New York: Harper & Row.

French, W., & Bell, J. (1980). Organizational development, objectives, assumptions and strategies. In F. Schuster (Ed.), *Contemporary issues in human resources management*. Reston, VA: Reston Publishers, Prentice-Hall.

Hackman, J., & Oldham, G. (1980). *Work redesign*. Reading, MA: Addison-Wesley.

Hamner, W. (1979). Motivation theories and work applications. In S. Kerr (Ed.), *Organizational behavior*. Columbus, OH: Grid Publishing.

McGregor, D. (1960). *The human side of enterprise*. New York: McGraw-Hill.

Mitchell, A. (1983). *The nine American lifestyles*. New York: Warner Books.

Mitchell, T. (1978). *People in organizations*. New York: McGraw-Hill.

Ouchi, N. (1981). *Theory Z*. Reading, MA: Addison-Wesley.

Pascale, R., & Athos, A. (1981). *The art of Japanese management*. New York: Simon & Schuster.

Peters, T., & Waterman, R., Jr. (1982). *In search of excellence*. New York: Harper & Row.

Sarmiento, F. (1984). *Bringing the spirit back to work: A transpersonal approach to organizational development*. Unpublished doctoral dissertation, California Institute of Transpersonal Psychology.

Schuster, F. (Ed.). (1980). *Contemporary issues in human resources management*. Reston, VA: Reston Publishers, Prentice-Hall.

Snyder, R., & Williams, R. (1982). Self-theory: An integrative theory of work motivation. *Journal of Occupational Psychology, 55*, 257–267.

Stanton, E. (1982). *Reality centered people management*. New York: Amacom.

Terkel, S. (1974). *Working*. New York: Random House.

Toffler, A. (1980). *The third wave*. New York: Bantam.

Vroom, V., & Deci, E. (Eds.). (1982). *Management and motivation*. New York: Penguin.

Wahba, S., & Bridwell, H. (1976). Maslow reconsidered: A review of research on the need hierarchy theory. *Organizational Behavior and Human Performance, 15*, 616–622.

Williams, A. (1978). *Participative management*. Reading, MA: Addison-Wesley.

Yankelovich, D. (1982). The new psychological contracts at work. In F. Schuster (Ed.),

Contemporary issues in human resources management. Reston, VA: Reston Publishers, Prentice-Hall.

Health

Carlson, R. (1980). The future of health care in the United States. In A. Hastings, J. Fadiman, & J. Gordon (Eds.), *Health for the whole person* (pp. 483–495). Boulder, CO: Westview Press.

Crasilneck, H., & Hall, J. (1975). *Clinical hypnosis: Principles and applications*. New York: Grune & Stratton.

Duhl, L. J. (1980). The social context of health. In A. Hastings, J. Fadiman, & J. Gordon (Eds.), *Health for the whole person* (pp. 39–52). New York: Grune & Stratton.

Dychtwald, K. (1977). *Bodymind*. New York: Pantheon.

Gordon, J. (1980). The paradigm of holistic medicine. In A. Hastings, J. Fadiman, & J. Gordon (Eds.), *Health for the whole person* (pp. 3–35). Boulder, CO: Westview Press.

Graettinger, J. (1978). The results of the NIRMP for 1978. *Journal of Medical Education, 53*, 500–502.

Illich, I. (1976). *Medical nemesis*. New York: Pantheon.

Hastings, A., Fadiman, J., & Gordon, J. (Eds.). (1980). *Health for the whole person*. Boulder, CO: Westview Press.

Leonard, G. (1983, December). Abraham Maslow and the new self. *Esquire Magazine*, pp. 326–336.

Lindemann, H. (1974). *Relieve tension the autogenic way*. New York: Wydon.

Nuernberger, P. (1981). *Freedom from stress—A holistic approach*. Honesdale, PA: Himalayan Publications.

Pelletier, K. R. (1977). *Mind as healer, mind as slayer: A holistic approach to preventing stress disorders*. New York: Delta.

Popenoe, C. (1977). *Wellness*. Washington, DC: Yes! Inc.

Samuels, M., & Bennett, H. (1973). *The well-body book*. New York: Random House.

Shapiro, D., & Walsh, R. (1980). *Meditation: Self regulation strategy and altered states of consciousness*. New York: Aldine.

Sobel, D. (Ed.). (1979). *Ways of health*. New York: Harcourt Brace Jovanovich.

The Psychology of Women

Friedan, B. (1977). *The feminine mystique*. New York: Dell.

Gilligan, C. (1979). Woman's place in man's life cycle. *Harvard Educational Review, 49*, 431–446.

Gilligan, C. (1982). *In a different voice: Psychological theory and women's development*. Cambridge, MA: Harvard University Press.

Hall, M. H. (1968, July). A conversation with Abraham Maslow. *Psychology Today*, pp. 35–37, 54–57.

Miller, J. (1976). *Toward a new psychology of women*. Boston: Beacon Press.

Norman, D., Murphy, M., & Gilligan, C. (1982). Sex differences and interpersonal relationships: A cross-sectional sample in the U.S. and India. *International Journal of Aging and Human Development, 14*(4), 291–305.

Roaldo M., & Lamphere L. (1974). *Women, culture and society*. Stanford, CA: Stanford University Press.

Synergic Society

Anderson, W. (1973). *Politics and the new humanism*. Pacific Palisades, CA: Goodyear.

Ferguson, M. (1980). *The aquarian conspiracy*. Los Angeles: Tarcher.

Goble, F. (1970). *The third force: The psychology of Abraham Maslow*. New York: Grossman.

Mitchell, A. (1983). *The nine American lifestyles*. New York: Warner Books.

Naisbitt, J. (1982). *Megatrends: Ten new directions transforming our lives*. New York: Warner Books.

Yankelovich, D. (1981). *New rules: Searching for self-fulfillment in a world turned upside down*. New York: Random House.

BIBLIOGRAPHY OF THE WRITINGS OF ABRAHAM MASLOW

If you write something, you just love it to be read. It's a great pleasure.

ABRAHAM H. MASLOW
Abraham H. Maslow: A Memorial Volume, 1972, p.115

1932

1. Delayed reaction tests on primates from the lemur to the orangoutan. (With Harry Harlow and Harold Uehling.) *Journal of Comparative Psychology, 13,* 313–343.
2. Delayed reaction tests on primates at Bronx Park Zoo. (With Harry Harlow.) *Journal of Comparative Psychology, 14,* 97–101.
3. The "emotion of disgust in dogs." *Journal of Comparative Psychology, 14,* 401–407.

1933

4 Food preferences of primates. *Journal of Comparative Psychology, 16,* 187–197.

1934

5. Influence of differential motivation on delayed reactions in monkeys. (With Elizabeth Groshong.) *Journal of Comparative Psychology, 18,* 75–83.
6. The effect of varying external conditions on learning, retention and reproduction. *Journal of Experimental Psychology, 17,* 36–47.

7. The effect of varying time intervals between acts of learning with a note on proactive inhibition. *Journal of Experimental Psychology, 17,* 141–144.

1935

8. Appetites and hungers in animal motivation. *Journal of Comparative Psychology, 20,* 75–83.
9. Individual psychology and the social behavior of monkeys and apes. *International Journal of Individual Psychology, 1,* 47–59. Reprinted in German translation in *Internationale Zeitschrift für Individual Psychologie,* 1936, *1,* 14–25.

1936

10. The role of dominance in the social and sexual behavior of infra-human primates: I. Observations at Vilas Park Zoo. *Journal of Genetic Psychology, 48,* 261–277.
11. II. An experimental determination of the dominance behavior syndrome. (With Sydney Flanzbaum.) *Journal of Genetic Psychology, 48,* 278–309. Reprinted in W. Dennis (Ed.), *Readings in general psychology,* Prentice-Hall, 1949.
12. III. A theory of sexual behavior of infra-human primates. *Journal of Genetic Psychology, 48,* 310–338.
13. IV. The determination of hierarchy in pairs and in groups. *Journal of Genetic Psychology, 49,* 161–198.

1937

14. The comparative approach to social behavior. *Social Forces, 15,* 487–490.
15. The influence of familiarization on preferences. *Journal of Experimental Psychology, 21,* 162–180.
16. Dominance-feeling, behavior and status. *Psychological Review, 44,* 404–429.
17. Personality and patterns of culture. In R. Stagner, *Psychology of personality,* McGraw-Hill. Reprinted in S. Britt (Ed.), *Selected readings in social psychology,* Rinehart, 1950.
18. An experimental study of insight in monkeys. (With Walter Grether.) *Journal of Comparative Psychology, 24,* 127–134.

1939

19. Dominance-feeling, personality and social behavior in women. *Journal of Social Psychology, 10,* 3–39.

1940

20. Dominance-quality and social behavior in infra-human primates. *Journal of Social Psychology, 11,* 313–324.

21. A test for dominance-feeling (self-esteem) in college women. *Journal of Social Psychology, 12,* 255–270.

1941

22. *Principles of abnormal psychology: The dynamics of psychic illness.* (With Bela Mittelmann), Harper. Recorded as Talking Book for the Blind.
23. Deprivation, threat and frustration. *Psychological Review, 48,* 364–366. (Included in No. 57.) Reprinted in T. Newcomb and E. Hartley (Eds.), *Readings in social psychology,* Holt, 1947; in M. Marx (Ed.), *Psychological theory: Contemporary readings,* Macmillan, 1951; C. Stacey and M. DeMartino (Eds.), *Understanding human motivation,* Howard Allen, 1958.

1942

24. Liberal leadership and personality. *Freedom, 2,* 27–30.
25. *The Social Personality Inventory: A test for self-esteem in women* (with manual), Consulting Psychologists Press.
26. The dynamics of psychological security-insecurity. *Character and Personality, 10,* 331–344.
27. A comparative approach to the problem of destructiveness. *Psychiatry, 5,* 517–522. (Included in No. 57.)
28. Self-esteem (dominance-feeling) and sexuality in women. *Journal of Social Psychology, 16,* 259–294. Reprinted in M. DeMartino (Ed.), *Sexual behavior and personality characteristics,* Citadel Press, 1963; H. M. Ruitenbeek (Ed.), *Psychoanalysis and female sexuality,* College and University Press, 1966.

1943

29. A preface to motivation theory. *Psychosomatic Medicine, 5,* 85–92. (Included in No. 57.)
30. A theory of human motivation. *Psychological Review, 50,* 370–396. (Included in No. 57.) Reprinted in P. Harriman (Ed.), *Twentieth century psychology,* Philosophical Library, 1946; H. Remmers, et al. (Eds.), *Growth, teaching and learning,* Harpers 1957; C. Stacey and M. DeMartino (Eds.), *Understanding Human Motivation,* Howard Allen, 1958; W. Lazer and E. Kelley (Eds.), *Managerial marketing,* Richard Irwin, 1958; W. Baller (Ed.), *Readings in psychology of human growth and development,* Holt, Rinehart & Winston, 1962; J. Seidman (Ed.), *The child,* Rinehart, 1958; L. Gorlow and W. Katkowsky (Eds.), *Readings in the psychology of adjustment,* McGraw-Hill, 1959; I. Heckman and S. Huneryager (Eds.), *Human relations in management,* South-Western, 1960; P. Hountras (Ed.), *Mental hygiene: A test of readings,* Merrill, 1961; J. A. Dyal (Ed.), *Readings in psychology: Understanding human behavior,* McGraw-Hill, 1962; T. Costello and S. Zalkind (Eds.), *Psychology in administration: A research orientation,* Prentice-Hall, 1963; R. Sutermeister (Ed.), *People and productivity,* McGraw-Hill, 1963; H. J. Leavitt and L. R. Pondy (Eds.), *Readings in managerial psychology,* University of Chicago Press, 1964; J. Reykowski (Ed.), *Prob-*

lemy osobowosci i motywacji w psychologii Amerykanskiej, Warsaw, Pan-stwowe Wydawnictwo Naokowe, 1964; D. E. Hamachek (Ed.), *The self in growth, teaching and learning,* Prentice-Hall, 1965; Bobbs-Merrill reprint series, 1966; Y. Ferreira Balcao and L. Leite Cordeiro (Eds.), *O comportamento humano na empresa,* Fundacao Getulio Vargas, Rio de Janeiro, 1967; M. S. Wadia (Ed.), *Management and the behavioral sciences,* Allyn & Bacon, 1968; H. Kassarjian and T. Robertson (Eds.), *Perspectives in consumer behavior,* Scott, Foresman, 1968; D. Hampton, C. Summer, and R. Weber (Eds.), *Organizational behavior and the practice of management,* Scott, Foresman, 1968; R. G. Brown, R. Newell, and H. G. Vonk (Eds.), *Behavioral implications for curriculum and teaching,* W. C. Brown, 1969; S. Frey and E. Haugen (Eds.), *Readings in learning,* American Book, 1969; L. D. Grebstein (Ed.), *Toward self-understanding: Studies in personality and adjustment,* Scott, Foresman, 1969.

31.   Conflict, frustration and the theory of threat. *Journal of Abnormal and Social Psychology, 38,* 81–86. (Included in No. 57.) Reprinted in S. Tomkins (Ed.), *Contemporary psychopathology: A sourcebook,* Harvard University Press, 1943.

32.   The dynamics of personality organization I & II. *Psychological Review, 50,* 514–539, 541–558. (Included in No. 57.)

33.   The authoritarian character structure. *Journal of Social Psychology, 18,* 401–411. Reprinted in P. Harriman (Ed.), *Twentieth century psychology: Recent developments in psychology,* Philosophical Library, 1946; R. S. Ross (Ed.), *Speech-communication,* Prentice-Hall.

1944

34.   What intelligence tests mean. *Journal of General Psychology, 31,* 85–93.

1945

35.   A clinically derived test for measuring psychological security-insecurity. (With E. Birsh, M. Stein, and I. Honigman.) *Journal of General Psychology, 33,* 21–41.

36.   A suggested improvement in semantic usage. *Psychological Review, 52,* 239–240. Reprinted in *Etc., A Journal of General Semantics,* 1947, *4,* 219–220.

37.   Experimentalizing the clinical method. *Journal of Clinical Psychology, 1,* 241–243.

1946

38.   Security and breast feeding. (With I. Szilagyi-Kessler.) *Journal of Abnormal and Social Psychology, 41,* 83–85.

39.   Problem-centering vs. means-centering in science. *Philosophy of Science, 13,* 326–331. (Included in No. 57.)

1947

40.   A symbol for holistic thinking. *Persona, 1,* 24–25.

1948

41. "Higher" and "lower" needs. *Journal of Psychology, 25*, 433–436. (Included in No. 57.) Reprinted in C. Stacey and M. DeMartino (Eds.), *Understanding human motivation*, Howard Allen, 1958. Reprinted in K. Schultz (Ed.), *Applied dynamic psychology*, University of California Press, 1958.
42. Cognition of the particular and of the generic. *Psychological Review, 55*, 22–40. (Included in No. 57.)
43. Some theoretical consequences of basic need-gratification. *Journal of Personality, 16*, 402–416. (Included in No. 57.)

1949

44. Our maligned animal nature. *Journal of Psychology, 28*, 273–278. (Included in No. 57.) Reprinted in S. Koenig et al. (Eds.), *Sociology: A book of readings*, Prentice-Hall, 1953.
45. The expressive component of behavior. *Psychological Review, 56*, 261–272. (Included in No. 57.) Condensed in *Digest of Neurology and Psychiatry*, Jan., 1950. Reprinted in H. Brand (Ed.), *The study of personality: A book of readings*, Wiley, 1954.

1950

46. Self-actualizing people: A study of psychological health. *Personality symposia: Symposium #1 on Values*, Grune & Stratton, pp. 11–34. (Included in No. 57.) Reprinted in C. Moustakas (Ed.), *The self*, Harpers, 1956; G. B. Levitas (Ed.), *The world of psychology*, George Braziller, 1963; C. G. Kemp (Ed.), *Perspectives on the group process*, Houghton Mifflin, 1964.

1951

47. Social Theory of Motivation. In M. Shore (Ed.), *Twentieth century mental hygiene*, New York: Social Science Publishers. Reprinted in K. Zerfoss (Ed.), *Readings in counseling*, Association Press, 1952.
48. Personality. (With D. MacKinnon.) In H. Helson (Ed.), *Theoretical foundations of psychology*, New York: Van Nostrand.
49. Higher needs and personality. *Dialectica* (Univ. of Liege) *5*, 257–265. (Included in No. 57.)
50. Resistance to acculturation. *Journal of Social Issues, 7*, 26–29. (Included in No. 57.)
51. *Principles of abnormal psychology* (rev. ed.). (With Bela Mittelmann), Harper & Bros. Recorded as Talking Book for the Blind. Chapter 16 reprinted in C. Thompson et al. (Eds.), *An outline of psychoanalysis*, Modern Library, 1955.
52. Volunteer-error in the Kinsey study. (With J. Sakoda.) *Journal of Abnormal and Social Psychology, 47*, 259–262. Reprinted in *Sexual behavior in American society*, J. Himelhock and S. Fava (Eds.), Norton, 1955.
53. *The S-I Test (A measure of psychological security-insecurity)*, Consulting Psychologists Press. Spanish translation, 1961, Instituto de Pedagogia, Universidad de Madrid. Polish translation, 1963.

1953

54. Love in healthy people. In A. Montagu (Ed.), *The meaning of love*, Julian Press. (Included in No. 57.) Reprinted in M. DeMartino (Ed.), *Sexual behavior and personality characteristics*, Citadel Press, 1963.

55. College teaching ability, scholarly activity and personality. (With W. Zimmerman.) *Journal of Educational Psychology, 47,* 185–189. Reprinted in U. S. Dept. Health, Education & Welfare, *Case book: Education beyond the high school,* 1958.

1954

56. The instinctoid nature of basic needs. *Journal of Personality, 22,* 326–347. (Included in No. 57.)

57. *Motivation and personality,* Harper & Bros. (Includes papers 23, 27, 29, 30, 31, 32, 39, 41, 42, 43, 44, 45, 46, 49, 50, 54, 56, 59.) Spanish translation, 1963, Sagitario, Barcelona. Selections reprinted in W. Sahakian (Ed.), *Psychology of personality: Readings in theory,* Rand-McNally, 1965. Japanese translation, 1967, Sangyo Noritsu Tanki Daigaku.

58. Abnormal psychology. *National Encyclopedia.*

59. Normality, health and values. *Main Currents, 10,* 75–81. (Included in No. 57.)

1955

60. Deficiency motivation and growth motivation. In M. R. Jones (Ed.), *Nebraska symposium on motivation: 1955,* University of Nebraska Press. (Included in No. 86.) Reprinted in *General Semantics Bulletin,* 1956, Nos. 18 and 19, 33–42; J. Coleman, *Personality Dynamics and Effective Behavior,* Scott, Foresman, 1960; J. A. Dyal (Ed.), *Readings in psychology: Understanding human behavior,* McGraw-Hill, 1962; R. C. Teevan and R. C. Birney (Eds.), *Theories of motivation in personal and social psychology,* Van Nostrand, 1964.

60a. Comments on Prof. McClelland's paper. In M. R. Jones (Ed.), *Nebraska symposium on motivation, 1955,* University of Nebraska Press, pp. 65–69.

60b. Comments on Prof. Old's paper. In M. R. Jones (Ed.), *Nebraska symposium on motivation, 1955,* University of Nebraska Press, pp. 143–147.

1956

61. Effects of esthetic surroundings: I. Initial effects of three esthetic conditions upon perceiving "energy" and "well-being" in faces. (With N. Mintz.) *Journal of Psychology, 41,* 247–254. Reprinted in D. C. Barnlund (Ed.), *Interpersonal communication,* Houghton Mifflin, 1968.

62. Personality problems and personality growth. In C. Moustakas (Ed.), *The self,* Harpers. Reprinted in J. Coleman, F. Libaw, and W. Martinson, *Success in college,* Scott, Foresman, 1961; F. Matson (Ed.), *Being, becoming and behavior,* Braziller, 1967; D. Hamachek (Ed.), *Human dynamics in psychology and education,* Allyn & Bacon, 1968.

63. Defense and growth. *Merrill-Palmer Quarterly, 3,* 36–47. (Included in No. 86.) Reprinted in T. Millon (Ed.), *Theories of psychopathology,* Saunders, 1967.

64. A philosophy of psychology. *Main Currents, 13,* 27–32. Reprinted in *Etc.,* 1957, *14,* 10–22; J. Fairchild (Ed.), *Personal problems and psychological frontiers,* Sheridan Press, 1957; *Manas,* 1958, *11,* 17 & 18; S. I. Hayakawa (Ed.), *Our language and our world,* Harpers, 1959; L. Hamalian and E. Volpe (Eds.), *Essays of our times: II,* McGraw-Hill, 1963; *Human growth institute buzz sheet,* 1964; F. T. Severin (Ed.), *Humanistic viewpoints in psychology,* McGraw-Hill, 1965; *Forum for correspondence & contact,* 1968, *1,* 12–23. Translated into Urdu in *Fikr-O-Nazar,* Muslim University of Alibarh, India, 1968.

1957

65. Power relationships and patterns of personal development. In A. Kornhauser (Ed.), *Problems of power in American democracy,* Wayne University Press.

66. Security of judges as a factor in impressions of warmth in others. (With J. Bossom.) *Journal of Abnormal and Social Psychology, 55,* 147–148.

67. Two kinds of cognition and their integration. *General Semantics Bulletin, 20 & 21,* 17–22. Reprinted in *New Era in Home and School,* 1958, *39,* 202–205.

1958

68. Emotional blocks to creativity. *Journal of Individual Psychology, 14,* 51–56. Reprinted in *Electro-Mechanical Design,* 1958, *2,* 66–72; *The Humanist,* 1958, *18,* 325–332; *Best Articles and Stories,* 1959, *3,* 23–35; S. Parnes and H. Harding (Eds.), *A source book for creative thinking,* Scribners, 1962; *Humanitas,* 1966, *3,* 289–294.

1959

69. Psychological data and human values. In A. H. Maslow (Ed.), *New knowledge in human values,* Harpers. (Included in No. 86.) Reprinted in B. J. Ard, Jr. (Ed.), *Counseling and psychotherapy: Classics on theories and issues,* Science & Behavior Books, 1966.

70. Editor, *New knowledge in human values,* Harpers. Hebrew translation, Daga Books, Tel-Aviv, Israel, 1968. Paperback edition, Regnery, 1970.

71. Creativity in self-actualizing people. In H. H. Anderson (Ed.), *Creativity and its cultivation,* Harpers. (Included in No. 86.) Reprinted in *Electro-Mechanical Design,* 1959 (Jan. & Aug.); *General Semantics Bulletin,* 1959, *24 & 25,* 45–50; L. Nelson and B. Psaltis (Eds.), *Fostering creativity,* S. A. R., 1967.

72. Cognition of being in the peak experiences. *Journal of Genetic Psychology, 94,* 43–66. (Included in No. 86.) Reprinted in *International Journal of Parapsychology,* 1960, 2, 23–54; B. Stoodley (Ed.), *Society and self: A reader in social psychology,* Free Press, 1962; W. Fullager, H. Lewis, and C. Cumbee (Eds.), *Readings in educational psychology* (2nd ed.), Crowell,

1964; D. E. Hamachek (Ed.), *The self in growth, teaching, and learning,* Prentice-Hall, 1965.

73. Mental health and religion. In *Religion, science and mental health,* Academy of Religion and Mental Health, New York University Press.

74. Critique of self-actualization. I. Some dangers of being-cognition. *Journal of Individual Psychology, 15,* 24–32. (Included in No. 86.)

1960

75. Juvenile delinquency as a value disturbance. (With R. Diaz-Guerrero.) In J. Peatman and E. Hartley (Eds.), *Festschrift for Gardner Murphy,* Harpers.

76. Remarks on existentialism and psychology. *Existentialist Inquiries, 1,* 1–5. (Included in No. 86.) Reprinted in *Religious Inquiry,* 1960, *28,* 4–7; R. May (Ed.), *Existential psychology,* Random House, 1961; D. E. Hamachek (Ed.), *The self in growth, teaching and learning,* Prentice-Hall, 1965. Japanese translation, 1965.

77. Resistance to being rubricized. In B. Kaplan and S. Wapner (Eds.), *Perspectives in psychological theory, essays in honor of Heinz Werner,* International Universities Press. (Included in No. 86.)

78. Some parallels between the dominance and sexual behavior of monkeys and the fantasies of patients in psychotherapy. (With H. Rand and S. Newman.) *Journal of Nervous and Mental Disease, 131,* 202–212. Reprinted in M. DeMartino (Ed.), *Sexual behavior and personality characteristics,* Citadel Press, 1963. Reprinted in W. Bennis et al., *Interpersonal dynamics* (2nd ed.), Dorsey, 1968.

1961

79. Health as transcendence of the environment. *Journal of Humanistic Psychology, 1,* 1–7. (Included in No. 86.) Reprinted in *Pastoral Psychology,* 1968, *19,* 45–49.

80. Peak-experiences as acute identity experiences. *American Journal of Psychoanalysis, 21,* 254–260. (Included in No. 86.) Reprinted in A. Combs (Ed.), *Personality theory and counseling practice,* University of Florida Press, 1961. Digested in *Digest of Neurology and Psychiatry,* 1961, *439.* Reprinted in C. Gordon and K. Gergen (Eds.), *The self in social interaction* (Vol. I), Wiley, 1968.

81. Eupsychia—The good society. *Journal of Humanistic Psychology, 1,* 1–11.

82. Are our publications and conventions suitable for the personal sciences? *American Psychologist, 16,* 318–319. (Included in No. 86.) Reprinted in *WBSI Report* No. 8, 1962; *General Semantics Bulletin,* 1962, *28 & 29,* 92–93; A. A. Hitchcock (Ed.), *Guidance and the utilization of new educational media: Report of 1962 conference,* American Personnel and Guidance Association, 1967.

83. Comments on Skinner's attitude to science. *Daedalus, 90,* 572–573.

84. Some frontier problems in mental health. In A. Combs (Ed.), *Personality theory and counseling practice,* University of Florida Press.

1962

85. Some basic propositions of a growth and self-actualization psychology. In A. Combs (Ed.), *Perceiving, behaving, becoming: A new focus for education. 1962 yearbook of Association for Supervision and Curriculum Development*, Washington, DC. (Included in No. 86.) Reprinted in C. Stacey and M. DeMartino (Eds.), *Understanding human motivation* (rev. ed.), Howard Allen, 1963; G. Lindzey and L. Hall (Eds.), *Theories of personality: Primary sources and research*, Wiley, 1965; B. J. Ard, Jr. (Ed.), *Counseling and psychotherapy: Classics on theories and issues*, Science & Behavior Books, 1966; W. Sahakian (Ed.), *History of psychology: A source book*, Peacock, 1968.

86. *Toward a Psychology of Being.* Van Nostrand. (Includes papers 60, 62, 63, 69, 71, 72, 74, 76, 77, 79, 80, 82, 85, 93.) Preface reprinted in *General Semantics Bulletin*, 1962, *28 & 29*, 117–118. Japanese translation, Tuttle, Tokyo, 1964 (Y. Ueda, Translator).

87. Book review: John Schaar, *Escape from authority. Humanist, 22*, 34–35.

88. Lessons from the peak-experiences. *Journal of Humanistic Psychology, 2*, 9–18. Reprinted as *WBSI Report*, No. 6, 1962. Digested in *Digest of Neurology and Psychiatry*, 1962, p. 340. Reprinted in *Turning On*, 1963, No. 2; R. Farson (Ed.), *Science and human affairs*, Science and Behavior Books, 1965.

89. Notes on being-psychology. *Journal of Humanistic Psychology, 2*, 47–71. Reprinted in *WBSI Report* No. 7, 1962; H. Ruitenbeek (Ed.), *Varieties of personality theory*, Dutton, 1964; A. Sutich and M. Vich (Eds.), *Readings in humanistic psychology*, Free Press, 1969.

90. Was Adler a disciple of Freud? A note. *Journal of Individual Psychology, 18*, 125.

91. Summary comments: Symposium on human values. L. Solomon (Ed.), *WBSI Report* No. 17, 41–44. Reprinted in *Journal of Humanistic Psychology*, 1962, *2*, 110–111.

92. *Summer notes on social psychology of industry and management*, Non-Linear Systems, Inc. (Includes papers Nos. 97, 100, 101, 104.) Edited and improved revision published as *Eupsychian management: A journal*, Irwin-Dorsey, 1965.

1963

93. The need to know and the fear of knowing, *Journal of General Psychology, 68*, 111–125. (Included in part in No. 86.) Reprinted in H. J. Peters and M. J. Bathroy (Eds.), *School counseling: Perspectives and procedures*, Peacock, 1968; D. Lester (Ed.), *Explorations in exploration*, Van Nostrand Reinhold, 1969.

94. The creative attitude. *The Structurist, 3*, 4–10. Reprinted as a separate monograph by *Psychosynthesis Foundation*, 1963. Reprinted in *The Ethical Forum*, 1966, No. 5; R. Mooney and T. Razik (Eds.), *Explorations in creativity*, Harper & Row, 1967.

95. Fusions of facts and values, *American Journal of Psychoanalysis, 23*, 117–131. Reprinted in *The Ethical Forum*, 1966, No. 5.

96.   Criteria for judging needs to be instinctoid. *Proceedings of 1963 International Congress of Psychology,* North-Holland, Amsterdam, pp. 86–87.
97.   Further notes on being-psychology. *Journal of Humanistic Psychology, 3,* 120–135.
98.   Notes on innocent cognition. In L. Schenk-Danzinger and H. Thomas (Eds.), *Gegenwartsprobleme der Entwicklungspsychologie: Festschrift für Charlotte Bühler,* Verlag für Psychologie, Gottingen. Reprinted in *Explorations,* 1964, *1,* 2–8.
99.   The scientific study of values. *Proceedings 7th Congress of Interamerican Society of Psychology,* Mexico, DF.
100. Notes on unstructured groups. *Human Relations Training News, 7,* 1–4. (Included in No. 112.)

1964

101. The superior person. *Trans-action, 1,* 10–13. (Included in No. 112.)
102. *Religions, values and peak-experiences.* Ohio State University Press. Chap. 3 reprinted in *The Buzz Sheet,* Dec. 1964. Paperback edition, The Viking Press, 1970.
103. Synergy in the society and in the individual. *Journal of Individual Psychology, 20,* 153–164. (With L. Gross.) Reprinted in *Humanitas,* 1964, *1,* 161–172; M. C. Katz, *Sciences of man and social ethics,* Branden Press, 1969.
104. Further notes on the psychology of being. *Journal of Humanistic Psychology, 4,* 45–58.
105. Preface to Japanese translation of *Toward a psychology of being,* Seishin-Shobo, Tokyo.

1965

106. Observing and reporting education experiments. *Humanist, 25,* 13.
107. Foreword to A. Angyal, *Neurosis and treatment: A holistic theory,* Wiley, pp. v–vii.
108. The need for creative people. *Personnel Administration, 28,* 3–5, 21–22.
109. Critique and discussion. In J. Money (Ed.), *Sex research: New developments.* Holt, Rinehart & Winston, pp. 135–143, 144–146.
110. Humanistic science and transcendent experiences. *Journal of Humanistic Psychology, 5,* 219–227. (Included in No. 115.) Reprinted in *Manas,* July 28, 1965, *18,* 1–8; *Challenge,* 1965, *21 & 22; American Journal of Psychoanalysis,* 1966, *26,* 149–155; E. P. Torrance and W. F. White (Eds.), *Issues and advances in educational psychology,* Peacock, 1969.
111. Criteria for judging needs to be instinctoid. In M. R. Jones (Ed.), *Human motivation: A symposium,* University of Nebraska Press, pp. 33–47.
112. *Eupsychian management: A journal.* Irwin-Dorsey. (Edited version of No. 92.) (Includes papers No. 100, 101.) Japanese translation, 1967, Tuttle, Tokyo.
113. Art judgment and the judgment of others: A preliminary study. (With R. Morant.) *Journal of Clinical Psychology,* 389–391.

1966

114. Isomorphic interrelationships between knower and known. In G. Kepes (Ed.), *Sign, image, symbol,* Braziller. Reprinted in F. W. Matson and A. Montagu (Eds.), *The human dialogue: Perspectives on communication.* Free Press, 1966.

115. *The psychology of science: A reconnaissance.* New York: Harper & Row. (Includes paper No. 110.) Paperback edition, Regnery, 1969.

116. Toward a psychology of religious awareness. *Explorations, 9,* 23–41.

117. Comments on Dr. Frankl's paper. *Journal of Humanistic Psychology, 6,* 107–112. Reprinted in A. Sutich and M. Vich (Eds.), *Readings in humanistic psychology,* Free Press, 1969.

1967

118. Neurosis as a failure of personal growth. *Humanitas, 3,* 153–169. Reprinted in *Religious Humanism,* 1968, *2,* 61–64; W. Bennis et al. (Eds.), *Interpersonal dynamics* (2nd ed.), Dorsey, 1968.

119. Synanon and eupsychia, *Journal of Humanistic Psychology, 7,* 28–35. Reprinted in H. Ruitenbeek (Ed.), *Group therapy today,* Atherton, 1969.

120. Preface to Japanese translation of *Eupsychian management.* (Included in No. 128.)

121. A theory of metamotivation: The biological rooting of the value-life. *Journal of Humanistic Psychology, 7,* 93–127. Reprinted in *The Humanist,* 1967, *27,* 83–84, 127–129; *Psychology Today,* 1968, *2,* 38–39, 58–61; P. Kurtz (Ed.), *Moral problems in contemporary society: Essays in humanistic ethics,* Prentice-Hall, 1969; A. Sutich and M. Vich (Eds.), *Readings in humanistic psychology,* Free Press, 1969; *Humanitas,* 1969, *4,* 301–343; H. M. Chiang and A. H. Maslow (Eds.), *The healthy personality: Readings,* Van Nostrand Reinhold, 1969; *Bobbs-Merrill Reprint Series in Psychology,* 1970.

122. Dialogue on communication. (With E. M. Drews.) In A. Hitchcock (Ed.), *Guidance and the utilization of new educational media: Report of the 1962 conference,* American Personnel and Guidance Association, 1–47, 63–68.

123. Foreword to Japanese translation of *Motivation and personality.*

124. Self-actualizing and beyond. In J. F. T. Bugental (Ed.), *Challenges of humanistic psychology,* McGraw-Hill. Reprinted in D. Hamachek (Ed.), *Human dynamics in psychology and education,* Allyn & Bacon, 1968.

1968

125. Music education and peak-experiences. *Music Educators Journal, 54,* 72–75, 163–171. Reprinted in *The arts and education: A new beginning in higher education,* Twentieth Century Fund, 1969.

126. The farther reaches of human nature. *Journal of Transpersonal Psychology, 1,* 1–9. Reprinted in *Psychological Scene* (South Africa), 1968, *2,* 14–16; *Philosophical Research and Analysis,* 1970, *3,* 2–5.

127. Human potentialities and the healthy society. In H. Otto (Ed.), *Human potentialities,* Warren H. Green.

127a. The new science of man. In papers on *The human potential* for the Twentieth Century Fund.

128. *Toward a psychology of being* (2nd ed.), Van Nostrand. Italian translation, Ubaldini Editore, Rome, 1970.

129. Conversation with Abraham H. Maslow. *Psychology Today, 2,* 35–37, 54–57.

130. Toward the study of violence. In L. Ng (Ed.), *Alternatives to violence,* Time-Life Books.

131. Some educational implications of the humanistic psychologies. *Harvard Educational Review, 38*(4), 685–696. Reprinted in *Forum for Correspondence and Contact,* 1969, *2,* 43–52; *California Elementary Administrator,* 1969, *32,* 23–29; *Reflections,* 1969, *4,* 1–13.

132. Goals of humanistic education. *Esalen Papers.*

133. *Maslow and self-actualization* (Film). Psychological Films, Santa Ana, CA.

134. Some fundamental questions that face the normative social psychologist. *Journal of Humanistic Psychology, 8.*

134a. Eupsychian network (mimeographed). (Included in No. 128.)

1969

135. Theory Z. *Journal of Transpersonal Psychology, 1,*(2), 31–47.

136. Various meanings of transcendence. *Journal of Transpersonal Psychology, 1,* 56–66.

137. A holistic approach to creativity. In C. W. Taylor (Ed.), *A climate for creativity: Reports of the Seventh National Research Conference on Creativity,* University of Utah.

138. *The healthy personality: Readings.* (With Hung-Min Chiang), Van Nostrand Reinhold.

139. Notice biographique et bibliographique. *Revue de Psychologie Appliquée, 18,* 167–173.

140. Toward a humanistic biology. *American Psychologist, 24,* 724–735.

141. Humanistic education vs. professional education. *New Directions in Teaching, 2,* 6–8.

1970

142. *Motivation and Personality* (rev. ed.), Harper & Row.

143. Humanistic education vs. professional education. *New Directions in Teaching, 2,* 3–10.

1971

144. *The farther reaches of human nature,* Viking Press (Esalen Series).

145. *Humanistic psychology: Interviews with Maslow, Murphy, and Rogers* (edited by W. B. Frick), Merrill.

1972

146. *Abraham H. Maslow: A memorial volume,* Brooks/Cole.

1973

147. *A. H. Maslow: An intellectual portrait* (by Richard J. Lowry), Brooks/Cole.
148. *Dominance, self-esteem, self-actualization: Germinal papers of A. H. Maslow* (edited by Richard J. Lowry), Brooks/Cole.

1977

149. Politics 3 (Maslow's notes edited by Robert E. Kantor). *Journal of Humanistic Psychology, 17*(4), 5–20.

1979

150. *The journals of A. H. Maslow* (Vols. I & II) (edited by Richard J. Lowry), Brooks/Cole.
151. Humanistic education. *Journal of Humanistic Psychology, 19*(3), 13–26.

NAME INDEX

Adler, A., 15, 21, 23, 34, 39, 108, 131
Allen, R., 248, 251
Allport, G., 29, 31, 36, 61, 63, 66, 222
Anderson, O., 143
Angyal, A., 8, 39, 153
Ansbacher, H., 34
Ardrey, R., 20, 83
Aristotle, 46, 115–116
Aronoff, J., 41, 174

Baker, R., 208
Bartlett, F., 196, 203
Benedict, R., 60, 86, 138, 261–262
Bergson, H., 39, 46, 131, 137, 202–203
Bernard, L., 48
Birsh, E., 211
Bonner, H., 127
Bronowski, J., 183
Brown, G., 254
Bucke, R., 163
Bugental, J., 127, 250
Buhler, C., 39, 47, 134, 248, 251

Cannon, W., 15, 46
Carlson, R., 259
Chenault, J., 149

D'Arcy, M., 153
Darwin, C., 50
Davies, J., 41
Deutsch, D., 165
Dewey, J., 12–13, 15, 59, 63
Drucker, P., 114–115

Eastman, M., 136
Ehrenfels, C. von, 220
Einstein, A., 130, 171
Erikson, E., 38

Ferguson, M., 255, 264
Flanzbaum, S., 211
Frankl, V., 134
Freedman, D., 126
Frenkel-Brunswik, E., 130, 200
Freud, S., 13, 15, 21, 23, 38, 47, 88,
   108, 155, 174, 196–197
Frieden, B., 260
Fromm, E., 15, 21, 39, 47, 58, 80, 88,
   112, 116, 131, 133, 189, 207

Gesell, A., 112
Ghiselin, E., 163
Gilligan, C., 261

SUBJECT INDEX